From Movements to Parties in Latin America
The Evolution of Ethnic Politics

From Movements to Parties in Latin America provides a detailed treatment of a fascinating and important topic that heretofore has received no scholarly attention: the surprising transformation of indigenous peoples' movements into viable political parties in the 1990s in four Latin American countries (Bolivia, Colombia, Ecuador, Venezuela) and their failure to succeed in two others (Argentina, Peru). The parties studied are crucial components of major trends in the region. By providing clear programs for governing to voters and reaching out in particular to underrepresented social groups, they have enhanced the quality of democracy and representative government. Based on extensive original research and detailed historical case studies, the book links historical institutional analysis and social movement theory to a study of the political systems in which the new ethnic cleavages emerged. The book concludes with a discussion of the implications for democracy of the emergence of this phenomenon in the context of declining public support for parties.

Donna Lee Van Cott is associate professor of political science and Latin American studies at Tulane University. She is author of *The Friendly Liquidation of the Past: The Politics of Diversity in Latin America* (2000), editor of *Indigenous Peoples and Democracy in Latin America* (1994), and has published more than a dozen articles on related topics. She has been awarded a Fulbright Fellowship as well as a residential fellowship from the Helen Kellogg Institute of International Studies at the University of Notre Dame. Dr. Van Cott is the founding chair of the section on Ethnicity, Race, and Indigenous Peoples of the Latin American Studies Association.

From Movements to Parties in Latin America

The Evolution of Ethnic Politics

DONNA LEE VAN COTT
Tulane University

CAMBRIDGE UNIVERSITY PRESS
Cambridge, New York, Melbourne, Madrid, Cape Town, Singapore, São Paulo

Cambridge University Press
32 Avenue of the Americas, New York, NY 10013-2473, USA

www.cambridge.org
Information on this title: www.cambridge.org/9780521855020

First published 2005
First paperback edition 2007

Printed in the United States of America

A catalog record for this publication is available from the British Library.

Library of Congress Cataloging in Publication Data
Van Cott, Donna Lee.
From movements to parties in Latin America : the evolution of ethnic politics /
Donna Lee Van Cott.
   p.   cm.
Includes bibliographical references (p.   ) and index.
ISBN-13:   978-0-521-85502-0 (hardback)
ISBN-10:   0-521-85502-0 (hardback)
1. Political parties – Latin America.   2. Indians of South America –
Politics and government.   3. Latin America – Ethnic relations – Political aspects.
4. Latin America – Politics and government – 1980–   I. Title.
JL969.A45V36   2005
324.2'089'98 – dc22   2005002285

ISBN   978-0-521-85502-0 hardback
ISBN   978-0-521-70703-9 paperback

Contents

Preface and Acknowledgments

It is a crisp, sunny, late-June day in La Paz. At 3,600 meters, the Andean sky is an implausible Soviet-postcard blue. In the Plaza de San Francisco, supporters of coca growers' leader Evo Morales are setting up for this evening's end-of-campaign rally and a few hundred supporters are congregating near the stage. As the sun begins to set, an impromptu parade winds past the Plaza, stopping rush-hour traffic on the Prado, the city's main drag. It is led by Esther Balboa, a Quechua intellectual who is the Aymara leader Felipe Quispe's vice presidential running mate in Sunday's presidential election (the scene is depicted on the jacket of this book). Less than one week before the election, Morales and Quispe, leaders of parties representing the country's indigenous majority, are expected to finish behind the pack. No one predicts the transformation that is about to occur. Quispe will merely win twice the vote of any previous indigenous presidential candidate. Morales will finish second, less than two percentage points behind the winner.

Almost exactly five years earlier, after the 1997 elections, I wrapped up doctoral dissertation research in La Paz. I had a hunch that the new indigenous peoples' parties that had formed in the 1990s might be the basis of a study of how small parties representing the marginalized indigenous population are having an impact on the quality of democracy in Latin America. As I concluded fieldwork for this book in 2002, indigenous peoples' parties entered the government in Ecuador and controlled almost one-third of the Bolivian congress. They controlled regional governments in Colombia, Ecuador, and Venezuela. In five short years, the interesting little parties had come of age.

Preliminary field research in Bolivia and Colombia in 1997 was funded by a Fulbright dissertation fellowship. Two University of Tennessee Professional Development Awards and a grant from the UT Department of Political Science's Cordell Hull Fund supported trips to Ecuador in 1999, Venezuela in 2000, Bolivia in 2001 and 2002, and Peru in 2002. I gratefully acknowledge this support. A six-country study required a great deal of collaboration from colleagues. Jóhanna Kristín Birnir, Michael Coppedge, Andrew Crain, Miguel García Sánchez, Thea Gelbspan, Kevin Healy, Dieter Heinen, Steven Levitsky, José Antonio Lucero, Raúl Madrid, Pilar Martínez, and José E. Molina V. generously helped me to acquire data and materials, and Robert Andolina, Jóhanna Kristín Birnir, Jo-Marie Burt, Michael Coppedge, Javier Corrales, Jean-Jacques Decoster, Rebecca Demar, Henry Dietz, María Elena García, Janet Kelly, Chris Krueger, José Antonio Lucero, Cynthia McClintock, Jennifer McCoy, David Myers, Joanne Rappaport, Kenneth M. Roberts, Martín Tanaka, Wendy Weiss, Coletta Youngers, and Raquel Yrigoyen shared their contacts in the Andes. Jo-Ann Hegre provided a luxury apartment, gourmet meals, handsome Frenchmen, and friendship during my stay in Venezuela. Rayda Márquez and Jesús Avirama gave me shelter and helped arrange interviews during two trips to Popayán, Colombia. In Lima, Jorge Agurto generously assembled and photocopied materials from his private files. More than seventy indigenous movement and party leaders, social scientists, and development professionals agreed to be interviewed for this project. Their collaboration was vital to its successful completion and I thank them for their patience and generosity.

Portions of this book appeared in different form in "Institutional Change and Ethnic Parties in Latin America," *Latin American Politics in Society* 45, 2 (Summer 2003): 1–39, and in "From Exclusion to Inclusion: Bolivia's 2002 Elections," *Journal of Latin American Studies* 35, 4 (November 2003): 751–75, published by Cambridge University Press.

During the writing process Lisa Báldez, Robert Barr, Raúl Barrios, Scott Beck, Jóhanna Kristín Birnir, Claudia Briones, Michael Coppedge, Brian Crisp, Jonathan Hartlyn, Kevin Healy, Miguel Hilario, Silvia María Hirsch, Mala Htun, Mark Jones, Raúl Madrid, Ken Mijeski, Kathleen O'Neill, Eduardo Pizarro Leongómez, Benjamin Reilly, and Kenneth M. Roberts generously commented on drafts of various chapters and provided missing data. Their contributions improved the manuscript immensely. I am also indebted to two anonymous readers for their useful suggestions for reorganizing and clarifying my argument, and to Lewis Bateman for his skillful supervision of the editorial process. For their encouragement and solidarity during the long period of research and writing, I am deeply indebted to Willem Assies, Jóhanna Kristín Birnir, Mala Htun, Jean Jackson, Shannan Mattiace, and Kathleen O'Neill. This book is dedicated to these friends for their generosity and the spirit of collaboration that they inspire.

Donna Lee Van Cott
New Orleans

Abbreviations and Acronyms

AD	Acción Democrática (Democratic Action)
ADM-19	Alianza Democrática M-19 (Democratic Alliance M-19)
ADN	Acción Democrática Nacional (National Democratic Action)
AGAAI	Asociación Guatemalteca de Alcaldes y Autoridades Indígenas (Guatemalan Association of Indigenous Mayors and Authorities)
AICO	Autoridades Indígenas de Colombia (Indigenous Authorities of Colombia)
AIDESEP	Asociación Inter-étnica para el Desarrollo de la Selva Peruana (Interethnic Association for the Development of the Peruvian Jungle)
AIECH	Asociación de Iglesias Evangélicos de Chimborazo (Association of Evangelical Churches of Chimborazo)
AIRA	Asociación Indígena de la República de Argentina (Indigenous Association of the Republic of Argentina)
ANC	Asamblea Nacional Constituyente (National Constituent Assembly)
ANUC	Asociación Nacional de Usuarios Campesinos (National Association of Campesino Users)
APCOB	Apoyo Para las Comunidades Indígenas del Oriente Boliviano (Assistance for the Indigenous Communities of Eastern Bolivia)

APG	Asamblea del Pueblo Guaraní (Assembly of the Guaraní People)
APRA	Alianza Popular Revolucionaria Americano (American Popular Revolutionary Alliance)
APRE	Acción Popular Revolucionario del Ecuador (Revolutionary Popular Action of Ecuador)
ASI	Alianza Social Indígena (Indigenous Social Alliance)
ASP	Asamblea de la Soberanía de los Pueblos (Assembly for the Sovereignty of the Peoples)
CAAAP	Centro Amazónico de Antropología y Aplicación Práctica (Amazonian Center for Anthropology and Applied Practice)
CCIIRA	Comisión Coordinadora de Institutiones Indígenas de la Argentina (Coordinating Commission of Indigenous Institutions of Argentina)
CCP	Confederación Campesina del Perú (Peasant Confederation of Peru)
CDCQ	Confederación Departmental Campesina de Qosqo
CEDOC	Confederación Ecuatoriana de Organizaciones Clasistas (Ecuadorian Confederation of Classist Organizations)
CEJIS	Centro de Estudios Jurídicos e Investigación Social (Center for Legal Studies and Social Research)
CESC	Coordinadora Etnica de Santa Cruz (Ethnic Coordinator of Santa Cruz)
CFP	Concentración de Fuerzas Populares (Concentration of Popular Forces)
CFR	Concentración de Fuerzas Revolucionarios (Concentration of Revolutionary Forces)
CGTP	Confederación General de Trabajadores del Perú (General Confederation of Workers of Peru)
CIDOB	Confederación Indígena del Oriente Boliviano, later Confederación Indígena del Oriente y Amazonía de Bolivia (Indigenous Confederation of Eastern Bolivia, later Indigenous Confederation of the East and Amazon of Bolivia)
CINA	Consejo Indígena Nacional de la Amazonía (Amazon National Indigenous Council)

CIPA   Centro de Investigación y Promoción Amazónica
              (Center for Amazon Research and
              Promotion)
CIRABO   Central Indígena de la Región Amazónica Boliviana
              (Indigenous Central of the Amazon Region of
              Bolivia)
CISA   Consejo Indio de Sud América (Indian Council of
              South America)
CMS   Coordinadora de Movimientos Sociales
              (Coordinator of Social Movements)
CNA   Confederación Nacional Agraria (National
              Agrarian Confederation)
CNCTK   Confederación Nacional de Campesinos Tupak
              Katari (Tupak Katari National Confederation
              of Campesions)
CNE   Corte Nacional Electoral (National Electoral Court)
CNTCB   Confederación Nacional de Trabajadores
              Campesinos de Bolivia (National
              Confederation of Peasant Workers of Bolivia)
COB   Central Obrero Boliviano (Bolivian Workers
              Central)
CODENPE   Consejo de Desarrollo de las Nacionalidades y
              Pueblos del Ecuador (Council for the
              Development of the Nationalities and Peoples
              of Ecuador)
COICA   Coordinadora de Organizaciones Indígenas de la
              Cuenca Amazónica (Coordinator of
              Indigenous Organizations of the Amazon
              Basin)
COICE   Coordinadora de Organizaciones Indígenas de la
              Costa del Ecuador (Coordinator of the
              Indigenous Organizations of the Ecuadorian
              Coast)
CONACAMI   Coordinadora Nacional de Comunidades Afectados
              por la Minería (National Coordinator of
              Communities Affected by Mining)
CONACCIP   Coordinadora Nacional de Comunidades
              Campesinos e Indígenas del Perú (National
              Coordinator of Peasant and Indigenous
              Communities of Peru)

CONACNIE   Consejo Nacional Coordinador de los
                Nacionalidades Indígenas del Ecuador
                (National Coordinating Council of the
                Indigenous Nationalities of Ecuador)
CONAICE   Coordinadora Nacional de los Indígenas de la
                Costa del Ecuador (National Coordinator of
                the Indigenous of the Ecuadorian Coast)
CONAIE   Confederación de Nacionalidades Indígenas del
                Ecuador (Confederation of Indigenous
                Nationalities of Ecuador)
CONAMAQ   Consejo de Ayllus y Markas del Qullasuyu (Council
                of Ayllus and Markas of Qullasuyu)
CONAP   Confederación de Nacionalidades Amazónicas del
                Perú (Confederation of Amazonian
                Nationalities of Peru)
CONAPAA   Comisón Nacional de Pueblos Andinos,
                Amazónicos y Afroperuanos (National
                Commission of Andean, Amazonian, and
                Afro-Peruvian Peoples)
CONDEPA   Conciencia de Patria (Conscience of the Fatherland)
CONFENIAE   Confederación de Nacionalidades Indígenas de la
                Amazonía Ecuatoriana (Confederation of
                Indigenous Nationalities of the Ecuadorian
                Amazon)
CONFEUNASSC   Confederación de Afiliados al Seguro Social
                Campesino (Confederation of Affiliates of
                Peasant Social Security)
CONIVE   Consejo Nacional Indio de Venezuela (National
                Indian Council of Venezuela)
COPEI   Comité de Organización Política Electoral
                Independiente (also known as Partido
                Socialcristiano) (Independent Committee of
                Electoral Political Organization, Social
                Christian Party)
COPPIP   Conferencia Permanente de los Pueblos Indígenas
                del Perú, Coordinadora Permanente de los
                Pueblos Indígenas del Perú (Permanent
                Conference of the Indigenous Peoples of Peru,
                Permanent Coordinator of the Indigenous
                Peoples of Peru)

CORACA	Corporación Agropecuaria Campesina (Peasant Agricultural Corporation)
CPESC	Coordinadora de Pueblos Etnicas de Santa Cruz (Coordinator of Ethnic Peoples of Santa Cruz)
CPIB	Central de Pueblos Indígenas del Beni (Indigenous Peoples Central of the Beni)
CRIC	Consejo Regional Indígena del Cauca (Regional Indigenous Council of Cauca)
CRIT	Consejo Regional Indígena del Tolima (Regional Indigenous Council of Tolima)
CRIVA	Consejo Regional Indígena del Vaupés (Regional Indigenous Council of Vaupés)
CSCB	Confederación Sindical de Colonos Bolivianos (Syndical Confederation of Bolivian Colonists)
CSUTCB	Confederación Sindical Unica de Trabajadores Campesinos de Bolivia (Unitary Syndical Confederation of Peasant Workers of Bolivia)
CTE	Central de Trabajadores Ecuatorianos (Ecuadorian Workers Central)
DINEIB	Dirección Nacional de Educación Intercultural y Bilingue (National Director of Intercultural and Bilingual Education)
DM	district magnitude
DP	Democracia Popular (Popular Democracy)
ECUARUNARI	Ecuador Runacunapac Riccharimui (The Awakening of the Ecuadorian Indian)
EGTK	Ejército Guerrillero Tupak Katari (Tupak Katari Guerrilla Army)
ELN	Ejército de Liberación Nacional (Army of National Liberation)
EMIDINHO	Encuesta de Medición de Indicadores de la Niñez y los Hogares (Survey of Measurement of Indicators of Children and Homes)
ENPS	effective number of parties for seats
EPL	Ejército Popular de Liberación; Esperanza, Paz y Libertad (Popular Liberation Army; Hope, Peace, and Liberty)

FADI	Frente Amplio de la Izquierda (Broad Front of the Left)
FARC	Fuerzas Armadas Revolucionarios de Colombia (Revolutionary Armed Forces of Colombia)
FARTAC	Federación Agraria Revolucionaria Túpac Amaru (Túpac Amaru Revolutionary Agrarian Federation)
FDCC/FDCQ	Federación Departamental del Campesinos de Cuzco/Qosqo (Cuzco/Qosqo Departmental Peasant Federation)
FECONAYA	Federación de Comunidades Yanesha (Federation of Yanesha Communities)
FEDEPICNE	Frente de Defensa de los Pueblos Indígenas, Campesinos y Negros del Ecuador (Front for the Defense of the Indigenous, Peasant, and Black Peoples of Ecuador)
FENCAP	Federación General de Yanaconas y Campesinos del Peru (General Federation of Yanaconas and Peasants of Peru)
FEI	Federación Ecuatoriana de Indios (Ecuadorian Federation of Indians)
FEINE	Federación Ecuatoriana de Iglesias Evangélicas (Ecuadorian Federation of Evangelical Churches)
FENACLE	Federación Nacional de Campesinos Libres del Ecuador (National Federation of Free Peasants of Ecuador)
FENAMAD	Federación de Nacionalidades Amazonicas del Rio Madre de Dios y Afluentes (Federation of Amazonian Nationalities of the Madre de Dios River and Effluents)
FENOC	Federación Nacional de Organizaciones Campesinas (National Federation of Peasant Organizations)
FENOCIN	Federación Nacional de Organizaciones Campesinas, Indígenas, y Negras (National Federation of Peasant, Indigenous, and Black Organizations)
FIB	Federación Indígena del Estado de Bolívar (Indigenous Federation of the State of Bolivar)

FICI	Federación Indígena y Campesina de Imbabura (Indigenous and Peasant Federation of Imbabura)
FIJO	Fuerza de Integración Juntos con Orgullo (Force of Integration Together with Pride)
FOCEP	Frente Obrero, Campesino, Estudiantil y Popular (Worker, Peasant, Student, and Popular Front)
FOIN	Federación de Organizaciones Indígenas de Napo (Federation of Indigenous Organizations of Napo)
FREPASO	Frente Para un País en Solidaridad (Front for a Country in Solidarity)
FTC	Federación de Trabajadores de Cuzco (Federation of Workers of Cuzco)
FULKA	Frente de Unidad de Liberación Katarista (United Front for Katarista Liberation)
FUT	Frente Unitario de los Trabajadores (Unitary Front of the Workers)
GAP	Guyana Action Party
ICCI	Instituto Científico de Culturas Indígenas (Scientific Institute of Indigenous Cultures)
ID	Izquierda Democrática (Democratic Left)
ILO	International Labour Organization
IMF	International Monetary Fund
INAI	Instituto Nacional de Asuntos Indígenas (National Institute of Indigenous Affairs)
IPSP	Instrumento Político para la Soberanía de los Pueblos (Political Instrument for the Sovereignty of the Peoples)
IU	Izquierda Unida (United Left)
JNE	Jurado Nacional Electoral (National Electoral Juror)
KND	Katarismo Nacional Democrática (National Democratic Katarism)
LCR	La Causa R (Radical Cause)

LN	Liberación Nacional (National Liberation)
LPP	Ley de Participación Popular (Law of Popular Participation)
MACPIO	Ministerio de Asuntos Campesinos, Pueblos Indígenas y Originarios (Ministry of Peasant, Indigenous, and Original Peoples Affairs)
MARQA	Movimiento por la Autonomía Regional Quechua y Aymara (Movement for Quechua and Aymara Regional Autonomy)
MAS	Movimiento al Socialismo (Movement Toward Socialism)
MBL	Movimiento Bolivia Libre (Free Bolivia Movement)
MCC	Movimiento Ciudadano para el Cambio (Citizens for Change Movement)
MCI	Movimiento Cívico Independiente (Independent Civic Movement)
MIAP	Movimiento Indígena de la Amazonía Peruana (Indigenous Movement of the Peruvian Amazon)
MIC	Movimiento Indígena Colombiano (Colombian Indigenous Movement)
MICNP	Movimiento Independiente de Ciudadanos Nuevo Pais (New Country Independent Movement of Citizens)
MIIAA	Movimiento Independiente Integracionista del Alto Amazonas (Independent Integrationist Movement of Upper Amazonas)
MIP	Movimiento Indígena Pachakuti (Pachakuti Indigenous Movement)
MIR	Movimiento de Izquierda Revolucionario (Movement of the Revolutionary Left)
MITKA	Movimiento Indio Tupak Katari (Tupak Katari Indian Movement)
MKN	Movimiento Katarista Nacional (National Katarista Movement)
MNCL	Movimiento Nacional de Cristianos por la Liberación (National Movement of Christians for Liberation)

MNR	Movimiento Nacional Revolucionario (National Revolutionary Movement)
MPD	Movimiento Popular Democrático (Popular Democratic Movement)
MPN	Movimiento Popular Nacional (National Popular Movement)
MRIC	Movimiento Revolucionario de la Izquierda Cristiana (Revolutionary Movement of the Christian Left)
MRTA	Movimiento Revolucionario Túpac Amaru (Túpac Amaru Revolutionary Movement)
MRTK	Movimiento Revolucionario Tupak Katari (Tupak Katari Revolutionary Movement)
MRTKL	Movimiento Revolucionario Tupak Katari de Liberación (Tupak Katari Revolutionary Movement of Liberation)
MSN	Movimiento de Salvación Nacional (National Salvation Movement)
MUPP-NP	Movimiento de Unidad Plurinacional Pachakutik-Nuevo País (Pachakutik Movement of Plurinational Unity–New Country)
MVR	Movimiento Quinto República (Fifth Republic Movement)
NFR	Nueva Fuerza Republicana (New Republican Force)
NGO	nongovernmental organization
OBA	Organización de Bases Aymaras (Organization of Aymara Bases)
OBAAQ	Organización de Bases Amazónicos, Aymaras, y Quechuas (Organization of Amazonian, Aymara, and Quechua Bases)
ONIC	Organización Nacional Indígena de Colombia (National Indigenous Organization of Colombia)
ONPE	Oficina Nacional de Procesos Electorales (National Office of Electoral Processes)

OPIAC   Organización de Pueblos Indígenas de la Amazonía
             Colombiana (Organization of Indigenous
             Peoples of the Colombian Amazon)
OPIP   Organización de Pueblos Indígenas de Pastaza
             (Organization of Indigenous Peoples of
             Pastaza)
ORPIA   Organización Regional de Pueblos Indígenas de
             Amazonas (Regional Organization of
             Indigenous Peoples of Amazonas)
ORPIZ   Organización Regional de Pueblos Indígenas de
             Zulia (Regional Organization of Indigenous
             Peoples of Zulia)

PCB   Partido Comunista de Bolivia (Communist Party of
             Bolivia)
PCV   Partido Comunista Venezolano (Venezuelan
             Communist Party)
PIAK   Partido Indio Aymara Kechua (Aymara Kechua
             Indian Party)
PIB   Partido Indio de Bolivia (Indian Party of Bolivia)
PJ   Partido Justicialista (Justicialist Party)
PMDB   Partido de Movimiento Democrático Brasileiro
             (Brazilian Democratic Movement Party)
POS   political opportunity structure
PPC   Partido Popular Cristiano (Popular Christian
             Party)
PPT   Patria Para Todos (Fatherland for All)
PR   proportional representation
PRD   Partido de la Revolución Democrática (Party of the
             Democratic Revolution)
PRE   Partido Roldosista Ecuatoriano (Ecuadorian
             Roldosist Party)
PRIN   Partido Revolucionario de la Izquierda Nacionalista
             (Revolutionary Party of the Nationalist
             Left)
PRODEPINE   Programa Nacional para el Desarrollo de los
             Pueblos Indígenas y Negros (National
             Program for the Development of the
             Indigenous and Black Peoples)
PS   Partido Socialista (Socialist Party)

PSC	Partido Social Conservador (Social Conservative Party) (Colombia), Partido Social Cristiano (Social Christian Party) (Ecuador)
PSE	Partido Socialista Ecuatoriano (Ecuadorian Socialist Party)
PS-FA	Partido Socialista-Frente Amplio (Socialist Party–Broad Front)
PSP	Partido Sociedad Patriótica (Patriotic Society Party)
PT(B)	Partido Trabalhista (Brasiliera) ([Brazilian] Workers Party)
PUAMA	Pueblo Unido Multiétnico de Amazonas (United Multiethnic People of Amazonas)
PUM	Partido Unido Mariateguista (United Mariateguist Party)
RENIEC	Registro Nacional de Identificación y Estado Civil (National Registry of Identification and Civil Status)
RGAF	Revolutionary Government of the Armed Forces
SETAI	Secretaría Técnica de Asuntos Indígenas (Technical Secretariat of Indigenous Affairs)
SIISE	Sistema Integrado de Indicadores Sociales del Ecuador (Ecuadorian Integrated System of Social Indicators)
SINAMOS	Sistema Nacional en Apoyo de la Mobilización Social (National System in Support of Social Mobilization)
SMD	single member district
THOA	Taller de Historia Oral Andina (Andean Oral History Workshop)
TSE	Tribunal Supremo Electoral (Supreme Electoral Tribunal)
UCAPO	Unión de Campesinos Pobres (Union of Poor Peasants)
UCR	Unión Cívica Radical (Radical Civic Union)
UCS	Unión Cívica de Solidaridad (Civic Union of Solidarity)

UDP	Unidad Democrática Popular (Popular Democratic Unity)
UMOPAR	Unidad Móvil de Patrullaje Rural (Mobile Rural Patrol Unit)
UNCA	Unión de Comunidades Aymaras (Union of Aymara Communities)
UNDICH	Unión Departamental Indígena del Chocó (Indigenous Departmental Union of the Chocó)
UNORCAC	Unión de Organizaciones Campesino e Indígenas de Cotacachi (Union of Peasant and Indigenous Organizations of Cotacachi)
UP	Unión Patriótica (Patriotic Union)
UPP	Unión por el Perú (Union for Peru)
VAIPO	Viceministerio Asuntos Indígenas y Pueblos Originarios (Vice Ministry of Indigenous and Original Peoples Affairs)
VR	Vanguardia Revolucionaria

From Movements to Parties in Latin America

The Evolution of Ethnic Politics

1

Introduction

Toward a Comprehensive Theory of Ethnic Party Formation and Performance

Political parties are the primary link between state and society in modern democracies. The quality of representation secured through parties and the responsiveness of party systems to the interests and demands of organized groups has a significant impact on the quality and the stability of democratic institutions. For that reason, one of the most enduring questions in political science is how social cleavages and collective interests are translated into party systems. In multiethnic societies, ethnic cleavages are likely to generate political parties and to organize political competition (Harmel and Robertson 1985: 503; Horowitz 1985: 291–3). Yet prior to the 1990s, there were few political parties in Latin America organized around ethnic identity, despite the ethnic diversity of the region. In the rare cases these existed they did not achieve enduring electoral success and had little impact on the political party system or the representation of their constituency in formal politics (Stavenhagen 1992: 434).[1]

In the 1990s, at the same time that many Latin American party systems began to exhibit severe stress and decomposition, indigenous social movement organizations increased their level of political mobilization and, in

---

[1] For example, in Chile as early as the 1940s, the Mapuche participated in elections as the Araucanian Corporation, winning several congressional and municipal council seats in 1945 and 1953. It was defeated in the 1957 elections and thereafter joined forces with leftist parties (Albó 1996: 819). In 1989 Chile's Aymara Indians formed the Party for Land and Identity, but it quickly disappeared after little success at the polls (Albó 1996: 850). In Bolivia several indigenous parties formed in the late 1970s and participated throughout the 1980s, but they individually never earned more than two percent of the vote until the 1990s. There have been even fewer parties organized around black identity. In Brazil the Frente Negra Brasileira (Brazilian Black Front) emerged in the 1930s, but was abolished after the 1937 military coup (Htun 2004a: 64–5)

some cases, formed political parties. Indigenous peoples are the descendants of the peoples and cultures existing in the Americas prior to the arrival of Europeans, who seek to preserve contemporary forms of these cultures within particular territories, while exercising considerable powers of self-government.[2] Some of the new parties that indigenous peoples' organizations formed in the 1990s achieved impressive results in a short period of time. In Ecuador, the Confederation of Indigenous Nationalities of Ecuador (CONAIE) formed a party that was part of the coalition that won the 2002 presidential elections and two of its long-time leaders were appointed to the cabinet. In Bolivia, Quechua and Aymara coca growers formed a party that came within two percentage points of first place in the 2002 presidential elections. Although both parties formed in 1995, only seven years later they were contesting control of the government. What is more intriguing, this success is not limited to countries with large indigenous populations. In Colombia and Venezuela, where the indigenous proportion of the population does not exceed 3 percent, ethnic parties elected governors in several states and achieved representation in the national legislature in competition with more established and better-financed parties. Indigenous peoples also have formed parties in Argentina, Guyana, Mexico, Nicaragua, and Peru, with less impressive results. The convergence in time of these events suggests that there may be a relationship between the decomposition of established political party systems, the decline of class identities and cleavages, and the emergence of new parties organized around ethnicity, a newly politicized cleavage. And it raises questions: Why, after decades of dormancy, are ethnic cleavages becoming politically salient at a time when class cleavages appear to be eroding? Why, amidst a general deterioration of parties and their links to society, are indigenous peoples forming viable parties that are firmly rooted in vibrant social movements? Why are these parties successful in some countries and not in others?

---

[2] I use the U.N. Subcommission on the Prevention of Discrimination and Protection of Minorities to define *indigenous peoples*: "Indigenous communities, peoples and nations are those which, having a historical continuity with pre-invasion and pre-colonial societies that developed on their territories, considered themselves distinct from other sectors of the societies now prevailing in those territories, or parts of them. They form at present nondominant sectors of society and are determined to preserve, develop and transmit to future generations their ancestral territories, and their ethnic identity, as the basis of their continued existence as peoples, in accordance with their own cultural patterns, social institutions and legal systems" (United Nations 1986: para. 379). The term *Indian* is sometimes used to refer to indigenous individuals, in the absence of a noun form for indigenous.

I define an "ethnic party" as an organization authorized to compete in elections, the majority of whose leaders and members identify themselves as belonging to a nondominant ethnic group, and whose electoral platform includes among its central demands programs of an ethnic or cultural nature. While using the broader term "ethnic party" in order to relate my research to the literature on ethnic parties, this study focuses on parties based on an ethnic identity as "indigenous," as that term is defined in the preceding text. My definition of ethnic party includes entities that call themselves "political movements" in order to distance themselves from the negative connotations associated with political parties, but that otherwise meet the definition. I also include parties that incorporate nonindigenous candidates and form electoral alliances with nonindigenous parties and social movements, provided that ethnic rights and recognition are central to the party's platform and that Indians constitute at least half of the party's leadership. The ethnic homogeneity of members and the emphasis on ethnic demands within the party's platform may vary at different levels of the political system and across regions. For example, an ethnic party in Ecuador might be almost exclusively indigenous in an Amazonian province but incorporate more nonindigenous candidates in a semiurban highland province, and it might focus more on the issue of territorial autonomy in the former rather than the latter. I exclude from this category parties that are dependent clients of other parties.

Conventional explanations for the formation and performance of the new ethnic parties are not helpful. The proportional size of the ethnic population is not a determining factor because successful ethnic parties formed in countries with minuscule indigenous populations (Colombia, Venezuela) and performed poorly or failed to form at all in several countries with large populations (Peru and Guatemala). Ethnic parties are not a natural result of democratization in the 1980s and 1990s since this occurred almost everywhere, but successful ethnic parties were formed in a minority of countries. And their formation is not attributable solely to the collapse or decline of party systems, since one of the most spectacular collapses occurred in Peru, where ethnic parties have had little success.

As the performance of parties as channels for the expression of collective interests has declined, other forms of political representation have become more important (Roberts 2002a: 25). Social movements not only offer an equally effective means of expression, they often achieve substantive programmatic goals that parties are unable to deliver through deadlocked, fragmented, or corrupt legislatures. In some countries, indigenous organizations can participate in elections without forming parties.[3] Why, then, did effective indigenous peoples' social movements form parties? This choice is particularly puzzling because indigenous movements' *raison d'etre* is the defense of indigenous cultural institutions and forms of self-government and the construction of new political institutions that strengthen traditional culture and authority while linking indigenous cultures to the state. Why, then, adopt a Western form of political struggle, subject to foreign logics and structures that indigenous movements claim to abhor? At least in countries where they comprise a substantial proportion of the electorate, why did indigenous organizations not instead choose to form alliances with existing parties and use their votes to demand programmatic benefits?

This book seeks to answer these questions. The broader theoretical questions the research illuminates are: Under what conditions do ethnic parties form and endure? Under what conditions will an ethnic cleavage emerge in a party system? Under what conditions do social movements generate electoral vehicles? These questions cut to the heart of contemporary theoretical and policy debates about democratization in Latin America. Although parties remain crucial to the quality of democracy in Latin America, particularly with respect to stability and representation (Levitsky and Cameron 2001: 1), parties and party systems in the region have suffered a marked deterioration in the last two decades.[4] Roberts notes the "severe erosion" of linkages between parties and voters and the resulting dampening of participation in parties, which he attributes to the dislocations and hardships caused by socioeconomic, political, and technological changes (2001: 17; 2002a). The 1990s saw the emergence of numerous "outsider" candidates that took advantage of declining public support for parties.[5] The personalist linkages they form

---

[3] For example, Guatemala since 1987, Colombia since 1991, Ecuador since 1995, and Venezuela since 1999.

[4] A chorus of recent studies bemoans the crisis of parties in Latin America, for example, Alcántara and Freidenberg (2001); Canton (1995); Coppedge (1998); Domínguez (1995); Levitsky (2001); Mainwaring (1999); Mainwaring and Scully (1995); and Roberts and Wibbels (1999).

[5] Latinobarometro's 2003 survey of public attitudes toward political institutions ranked parties last, with only 10–15 percent of respondents expressing "some" or "a lot" of confidence (FOCAL 2004: 3). This represents a considerable drop since 1998, when only 21 percent of the public reported "much" or "some" confidence in parties. Of the seventeen countries surveyed, those countries eliciting the largest number of "no confidence" responses were Venezuela, Ecuador, Argentina, Panama, Nicaragua, Peru, Colombia, and Bolivia, in that order (Alcántara and Freidenberg 2001: Cuadro IV). All six countries in

have replaced organic links between parties and voters and are even less able to ensure that politicians are held accountable to voters (Roberts 2001: 22). The fragmentation of party systems and the lack of cohesion within parties have prevented the construction of durable legislative majorities, resulting in deadlocks and institutional crises (Levitsky and Cameron 2001: 3). Understanding how Latin American societies' most disadvantaged group achieved autonomous representation in political office at a time when most analysts are speaking of a crisis of representation or a crisis of parties will help us to identify conditions under which other social groups may gain effective representation.

Many of the region's most militant and influential indigenous peoples' movements, and its earliest and most successful ethnic parties, are located in the Andean region, the most multiethnic and ethnically divided in Latin America. In Andean countries (Bolivia, Colombia, Ecuador, Peru, and Venezuela) a deep divide separates the subordinate indigenous population from the ruling white–mestizo population. Scholarly and policy interest in the region increased in the 1990s owing to its extraordinary political instability, stagnant or reversed economic development and social indicators, and increased rates of crime and violence (Arnson 2001; Mauceri and Burt 2004). Political scientists note the region's low levels of political party system institutionalization and high level of institutional deadlock, the recent collapse of party systems in Peru and Venezuela, and the severe fragmentation of party systems in Bolivia and Ecuador (Dietz and Myers 2001; *Journal of Democracy* 2001; Kornblith 1998; Levitzky 1999; Levitsky and Cameron 2001; Mainwaring and Scully 1995; McCoy et al. 1994; Roberts 2001; Romero 1994; Rospigliosi 1995; Tanaka 1998; Whitehead 2001). Yet, despite the importance of ethnic politics in the Andes, and the great scholarly and policy interest in the poor performance of parties, there has been little comparative research connecting these two phenomena.[6] Most consists of monographic studies of individual parties or countries. Political scientists have paid the most attention to Ecuador, which has

---

our study (all of the above except for Panama and Nicaragua) fall in the bottom half in terms of public support.

[6] Van Cott (2000a) and (2003b) are exceptions. Among the most interesting and truly comparative works are those by Jóhanna Kristín Birnir (2000, 2003). A 2001 edited volume surveyed the relationship between indigenous peoples and political parties more globally (Wessendorf 2001). It focuses mainly on indigenous peoples' alliances with existing parties and extraelectoral political strategies, while almost ignoring the new ethnic parties, apart from a brief paragraph on Ecuador's Pachakutik (Ruiz Hernández and Burguete Cal y Mayor 2001).

the ethnic party with the most stunning electoral success (Andolina 1999; Beck and Mijeski 2001; Collins 2000a, 2001; Pallares 2002; Selverston-Scher 2001). Scholarly research on the new ethnic parties in Bolivia produced by anthropologists and Bolivian political analysts is predominantly descriptive and interpretative (Albó 1994a; Ticona, Rojas, and Albó 1995; Various Authors 1997). To my knowledge, no other political scientist has investigated the equally interesting cases of Colombia and Venezuela, demonstrating a theoretically unjustified bias in favor of studying countries with proportionally large indigenous populations (Van Cott 2000b; 2003a).

The new ethnic parties in Latin America are not just interesting as ethnic parties. They also constitute examples of social movements or interest groups that launched electoral vehicles. Since the dawn of modern parties in the nineteenth century it has been commonplace for parties to develop from social movements or in close association with them, particularly in settings where parties have lost public support (Glenn 2003: 149). Their activities do not replace or stand in for party activity; rather, both types of activity tend to rise and decline together (Goldstone, ed. 2003: 4; Gunther and Montero 2002: 6). Yet there have been few studies of the relationship between social movements/interest groups and political parties, which usually are analyzed in separate literatures, or of why, and with what consequences, social movements might form political parties (Goldstone, ed. 2003; Thomas 2001b; Yishai 1994: 184). This is a research program that deserves further attention and "much more systematic analysis" (Tilly 2003: 255).

The new ethnic parties also are significant because in many cases they pose a fresh model of democratic representation, one that is more inclusive, deliberative, and participatory. The successful ones are programmatic parties with clear policy goals and ideologies. They have deep roots in society. Their leaders have been champions of transparency and have been at the forefront of the fight against corruption. Thus, the majority of the new ethnic parties exemplify the practices and values that political scientists find most beneficial for democracies, and which have been rare in Latin America since the return to elected civilian rule.

INSTITUTIONS, PARTY SYSTEMS, AND SOCIAL MOVEMENTS

The decision to form a political party and the factors that determine electoral success are complex. A comprehensive approach must combine an analysis of the permissiveness of the institutional environment, an understanding of long-standing patterns and recent changes in the party system, as well as factors related to the opportunity structure in which social movements operate and the resources they are able to mobilize.

My approach diverges from traditional approaches, which assume that ethnic parties form automatically wherever ethnic identities are important sources of collective meaning because ethnic groups perceive their own shared interests and their shared sense of competition with other ethnic groups. Ethnic parties form to represent the internal dynamics of ethnic groups as distinct communities and in reaction to other groups in society. In addition, ethnic elites organize coethnics into parties in order to secure their particular interests. Because ethnic identity is ascriptive, ethnic elites understand that once they have captured their ethnic constituency they will be able to count on its support (Horowitz 1985: 293–5). Voters support ethnic parties in order to improve their access to material goods, mainly through improved access to the state, as well as to enhance their self-esteem by enhancing the status of their ethnic group (Horowitz 1985: 143).

This view complements the abundant literature on how social cleavages naturally give rise to political parties. It is based mainly on the work of Lipset and Rokkan, who observed that Western European party systems reflected underlying social cleavages, such as rural–urban, religious, and class cleavages (1967: 72–144). The social-cleavage approach is based on three assumptions: (1) that social identities determine voters' political interests; (2) that voters are aware of these interests and will vote accordingly; and (3) that they will do so consistently, which facilitates the institutionalization of political parties organized to represent these cleavage-dependent interests (Mainwaring 1999: 52). Similarly, scholars of the "materialist" school assume that those sharing an ethnic identity naturally have common material and psychic interests that they pursue through the formation of ethnic parties, which maximize their likelihood of attaining them. Where access to such jobs is influenced by ethnicity, as is common in Africa and Asia, ethnic elites form parties in order to secure them (Chandra 2004: 8).

The social-cleavage approach currently is out of favor because many cases have arisen to dispute its simplistic claims. As Chhibber observes, only under certain conditions can political parties activate social cleavages (1999: 6–8). An ethnic party's emergence requires the existence of an ethnic cleavage and the *politicization* of that cleavage, which most often occurs where access to public and private goods is determined by ethnicity. Ethnic cleavages became politicized in Latin America when indigenous

social movement organizations mobilized independently of nonindigenous political actors in favor of collective rights for indigenous peoples
in massive mobilizations above the local level – a process underway in
most countries by the 1980s. If ethnic parties form automatically in the
presence of politicized ethnic cleavages, why did indigenous peoples not
form ethnic parties as soon as ethnicity became politicized and they had
received the right to vote?[7] In the rare cases where parties were formed,
why were they not more successful?

I argue that political institutions and configurations of power within
a party system help to determine the likelihood that ethnic parties will
form and become successful. An open institutional environment, or a
shift to more permissive constitutional provisions, laws, and rules that
structure electoral competition, facilitates the formation of ethnic parties. Three changes are particularly important: decentralization, improved
access to the ballot for aspiring parties, and the reservation of seats for
ethnic minorities. Decentralization opens new playing fields for relatively
weak political actors at local and regional levels, where indigenous peoples are often concentrated demographically and where fewer financial
resources are necessary to compete. New laws that allow social movements to compete in elections without formally registering as political
parties, or that made registration easier to achieve and maintain, enabled
new ethnic parties to compete for the first time. Reserved seats for indigenous peoples provide a guaranteed foothold in the political system that
indigenous movements can use to energize indigenous voters and to launch
successful parties in nonindigenous districts.

A "frozen" political party system, one in which existing parties are
entrenched and the axis of competition revolves around existing cleavages, may impede the formation of a new ethnic cleavage. But a relatively
open system, one in which many voters lack loyalty to existing parties,
or a change that significantly opens the system to new entrants, may lead
to the emergence of ethnic parties. The electoral decline of established
parties in the 1990s and the resulting increase in party system fragmentation helped to erode existing party loyalties. The increased number of
parties gaining votes in the system lowered the threshold of votes needed
to secure representation and increased the leverage of small parties in legislative bodies. Another type of party system change – the decline of the
left – contributed significantly to the success of ethnic parties. It opened

---

[7] Literacy requirements prevented many Indians from voting in Ecuador until 1979, Peru
until 1980, and Brazil until 1985.

space on the left of the political spectrum for ethnic parties to make class-based appeals to the poor, adjusted the balance of power between the traditional left and indigenous movements in favor of the latter, and made experienced political operatives and resources available to fledgling ethnic parties.

A permissive institutional environment and/or open party system constitute necessary conditions. They are not sufficient to explain the formation and performance of ethnic parties. Party formation requires political actors to make a conscious, strategic decision, which occurs under particular conditions. Electoral performance is determined by a variety of factors related to the qualities and resources of the new vehicle, its leaders, and its constituency. The resources available to movements include the inspirational example of successful ethnic parties in neighboring countries, which emboldened social movement leaders to take the electoral plunge, even under adverse circumstances. Viable ethnic parties studied here were spawned by well-institutionalized indigenous social-movement organizations. In contrast, ethnic elites lacking the support of a well-rooted and institutionalized organization failed in their attempts to form ethnic parties.

Indigenous community-level organizations with their own leadership structures, kinship ties, and customary law have existed since the invasion of Europeans destroyed political organizations of larger geographical scope. In some areas, supra-community organizations persisted or were newly formed to facilitate economic production, the reproduction of indigenous cultures, and the defense of collectively held territory. Between the 1920s and 1950s political parties and leftist movements formed dependent peasant organizations in order to co-opt and control indigenous voters and rural workers. These organizations struggled for access to land and for improved wages and employment conditions for agricultural workers. In the 1960s and 1970s, the nature and scope of such organizations changed. Many that had been subordinated to political parties, labor unions, and the Church asserted their autonomy. Independent indigenous organizations also formed and espoused a more diverse set of cultural, economic, and political demands. Although these often adopted Western forms of political organization and relied upon external support, they struggled to maintain independence and were explicitly oriented toward defending cultural and ethnic rights and to advancing long-standing territorial claims, as opposed to the limited set of socio-economic demands that the left promoted. The authoritarian context in which they emerged restricted the achievements and geographic reach of indigenous organizations. Throughout Latin America independent indigenous organizations endured violent repression. In nominally democratic Colombia and Venezuela, Indians organized mainly in defense of land rights, which pitted them against armed groups defending the claims of landowners.

The regionwide transition to democracy gradually opened up space for existing organizations to mobilize more effectively and for new organizations to form. Domestic and international nongovernmental organizations became interested in the concerns of indigenous peoples, particularly with respect to their human rights and the protection of their natural habitat. Their financial support and advocacy helped fledgling organizations to expand (Brysk 2000; Keck and Sikkink 1998). Neoliberal reforms imposed in the 1980s threatened collective property rights, reduced access to markets, and cut state subsidies to small farmers (Brysk and Wise 1997; Yashar 1998), although many indigenous peoples never benefited from such programs. In response to these threats to their economic survival, and in order to press more effectively their cultural and territorial rights claims, the number of indigenous organizations grew rapidly throughout Latin America during this period and existing local organizations united to form larger regional and national organizations.[8] Their emphasis on opposition to neoliberal reforms helped the movements to attract numerous nonindigenous supporters and to form interethnic popular alliances.

By the time states in the region embarked on a series of far-reaching constitutional changes in the 1990s, indigenous organizations had become consolidated in most Latin American countries, with hierarchical leadership structures and a multi-tiered network of affiliates. Although some countries had reformed their constitutions at the time of the transition to democracy, by the mid-1990s it was clear that institutional problems prevented the consolidation of legitimate, governable democratic regimes. To address these problems, political elites undertook a second wave of reforms. Elsewhere, significant constitutional reforms had not occurred for decades and elites and civil society organizations pressed for radical reforms to modernize the state and legitimize ailing democratic regimes. Indigenous social movement organizations were among the civil society

---

[8] On the rise of indigenous movements in the 1970s and 1980s, see Albó (1994b); Gros (1997); Stavenhagen (1992; 1996); Van Cott (1994; 2000b); Wade (1997); and Yashar (1998, 2005).

actors that took advantage of these opportunities for radical institutional change to frame their rights agendas as national issues and to achieve the codification of unprecedented indigenous rights (Assies, van der Haar, and Hoekema 2001; Dandler 1999; Sánchez 1996; Van Cott 2000b, 2002).

Active participation in a major constitutional reform process is a motivating factor for the formation of ethnic parties by indigenous social movements, which seek to ensure their new constitutional rights are realized, while providing an excellent mobilizational tool for future electoral competition. Mature and unified social movements are most likely to gain access to such processes and to spawn viable or successful parties. Their dense networks of affiliates can be mobilized for elections and can offset the lack of financial resources that challenge new ethnic parties. Where indigenous movements are divided by region, ideology, or ethnicity, or where sponsoring social movement organizations were less than four years old, successful ethnic parties did not emerge. Where examples of successful ethnic parties were known to social movement leaders, they were more likely to try to form an ethnic party, notwithstanding unfavorable conditions. With respect to party performance, the geographic concentration or dispersion of indigenous populations interacts with institutional rules to influence electoral outcomes. Where the settlement patterns of indigenous populations converge with institutions that tend to promote new party success, ethnic parties are more likely to form and succeed.

ETHNIC POLITICS, SOCIAL MOVEMENTS, AND POLITICAL PARTIES

My approach improves upon existing work on ethnic parties. This literature focuses mainly on Europe and has ignored Latin America, with the exception of Guyana (e.g., Horowitz 1985: 311–18; Premdas 1995). Parties in Latin America differ appreciably from their European progenitors, and "third wave democracies" differ from the established systems of Europe and North America (Mainwaring 1999: 3). Latin American party systems tend to be less institutionalized, to have more shallow roots in society, and weaker, less formal party organizations. Latin American party systems are more characterized by associations based on personal connections, corruption, and clientelism, which facilitate their monopoly over state power (Mainwaring 1999: 332). The economic and social conditions in which they operate are marked by persistent economic crisis and high levels of inequality and poverty that are not seen in Western

Europe, and which do not figure into theories explaining the emergence of new parties in that region (e.g., Hug 2001; Kitschelt 1989; Mayer and Ely 1998; Thomas 2001). Thus, we cannot directly apply theories derived from European parties to Latin America.

Lessons from other developing areas offer some insights but also are difficult to apply to Latin America because ethnic identity is experienced and expressed in different ways in Asia and Africa. In Latin America, three main ethno-racial groups – European, indigenous, and African – constitute important economic, social, and (in some cases) political cleavages. In addition, the presence of significant mixed-race groups and the possibility of "whitening" oneself through education, economic advancement, and acculturation, makes ethnic identity more mutable, situational, and voluntary (Wade 1997). Although there are hundreds of distinct groups within the indigenous category – there are more than eighty in Colombia alone – since the 1970s they have increasingly worked together and share a common identity by virtue of their common ethnic oppression and socioeconomic exploitation.

In India, in contrast, the principal ethno-political cleavage lies *within* the dominant ethno-religious grouping, between upper- and lower-caste Hindus. In her work on this country, Chandra (2004) develops an instrumental theory of ethnic voting in "patronage democracies," arguing that ethnic parties succeed when they are better able than competing parties to incorporate new upwardly mobile elites from their ethnic group and members of that group have the numbers to elect one of their own to an influential position. This model may help explain the behavior of some ethnic parties in Latin America,[9] but it is less applicable to those formed by indigenous peoples because these parties have tended to be crusaders against corruption and clientelism and have campaigned against long-standing patronage practices. Although some have been seduced by access to power, many have refused to betray their principles. For example, Evo Morales, who finished second in Bolivia's 2002 presidential election representing the Movement Toward Socialism (MAS),[10] refused to make a deal with any other party that would bring him the presidency in exchange for a share of government jobs and resources for MAS militants.

---

[9] For example, Afro-Colombian parties in Colombia's northwest promote an agenda of equitable access to state power and resources (Van Cott 2000b: 97, 110, 229, 287n13; Wade 1993).

[10] This party, calling itself the Instrumento Político para la Soberanía de los Pueblos borrowed the legal registration of the tiny leftist party MAS when the National Electoral Court denied its own registration. See Chapter 5.

In fact, indigenous movement militants in Bolivia and Ecuador have attacked and ostracized leaders that obtained positions within the state and seemed to benefit from enhanced access to resources. Thus, ethnic relations are distinct in India compared to Latin America and a patronage-based model of ethnic party formation is unlikely to explain our cases.

Studies of ethnic parties in Africa also are difficult to transfer to Latin America. Mozaffar, Scarritt, and Galaich attribute the region's relative scarcity of ethnic parties to the interaction of political institutions with the number and relative size of the region's ethnic groups (2003). In most African countries there are numerous groups, none of which constitutes a numerical majority, and within most large groups there are numerous subgroups that "weaken group loyalty and unity" (Mozaffar, Scarritt, and Galaich 2003: 6). In most African countries no single politically salient ethnic cleavage can be identified. In only twelve countries can a national dichotomous cleavage – a clear divide between the dominant national group and the rest of the population – be identified. Mozaffar and Scarritt argue that certain institutions – particularly electoral institutions – play a large role in determining how many and which ethnic cleavages will generate ethnic parties (Mozaffar et al. 2003). Their model is less applicable to Latin America, where ethnic relations are organized around racial divides and complicated by the existence of a numerically dominant mixed-race group in most countries.

My approach contributes to the literature linking social movements and political parties. This mainly focuses on Europe. Thomas's 2001 edited volume constructs a typology of various relationships between interest groups/social movements and political parties. In the "integration/strong partisan" model, a political party and its associated interest group are organizationally connected, since one usually creates the other. In the electoral arena the two operate jointly, with a single ideology and purpose (Thomas 2001b: 20).[11] The classic example of this model is the labor union–social democratic party relationship, which can be observed in Britain, Germany, and Sweden, but Thomas notes other examples as well: the German Greens, the Pensioners' Party in the Czech Republic, and anti-immigrant and neofascist groups in Austria, France, and Germany (2001c: 281). Maguire calls such entities "parties of movement" and argues that they are more likely to be formed by social movements with

---

[11] This ideal type approximates the "organic" model in Roberts's (1998: 75) threefold typology of leftist party–social movement relations.

strong organizational, cultural, constituency, and policy resources in electoral systems with low barriers to entry (Maguire 1995: 201–5).[12] Most
of the new ethnic movement–parties in South America approximate this
model.

Despite the distinct political and economic context, Kitschelt's work on
the emergence of left–libertarian parties in Western Europe in the 1970s
and 1980s is theoretically relevant to the present study. Like ethnic parties in South America, left–libertarian parties were spawned by diverse
coalitions of social movements seeking not only to change particular
policies, but also to change the form and substance of politics and to
construct a more participatory, decentralized, egalitarian political model
(Kitschelt 1989: 3). Indigenous organizations and their social movement
allies had the same goal when they formed electoral vehicles in the 1990s.
Kitschelt identifies a combination of necessary (i.e., favorable institutional
structures) and sufficient conditions (i.e., political opportunities and the
capacity of social-movement actors to mobilize human and organizational
resources) for the emergence and success of left–libertarian parties that
are similar to those found in this study (1989: 14–15). Left–libertarian
parties emerge where existing parties fail to respond to the claims of new
groups at the same time that the political conjuncture is favorable to the
creation of new parties (Kitschelt 1989: 19).

The best Latin American example of this phenomenon is the Brazilian
Workers Party (PT), which a coalition of labor movement leaders, intellectuals, and an assortment of grassroots organizations and social movements created in 1978–9. Like the new ethnic parties, the PT was the
organic creation of disenfranchised groups wishing to push an agenda
not represented in the political system and to invent a more participatory, democratic way of doing politics (Keck 1992: 3–15). Keck explains
the emergence and rise of this movement by focusing on two factors: the
perceived political opportunities present in the conjuncture of democratic
transition in the late 1970s and 1980s, and organizational factors, such as
the availability of leadership and mass membership. She also illuminates
the critical role of the left, which increased its public visibility and support in the 1990s, opening space in the party system for the PT to occupy
(Keck 1992: 73). In addition, a sector of the left felt marginalized within

---

[12] See also Mayer and Ely's (1998) study of the German Green Party and Yael Yishai's study
of "interest parties," political institutions that straddle the border between interest group
and political parties (1994: 204).

the main opposition party Brazilian Democratic Movement Party (PMDB) and left to join the PT, bringing with it an organizational structure and logistical resources that proved to be crucial in the birth of the party (Keck 1992: 73). In a similar way the incorporation of leftist party cadre and intellectuals would be critical to the development of the most successful ethnic parties in South America.

Roberts's work on the modern left in Chile and Peru also focuses on the political party–social movement relationship and also emphasizes the importance of relations with the left for social movements seeking formal political representation. Roberts argues that the left in Chile and Peru offered the idea of "deepening democracy" as a means to reach out to unrepresented popular groups (1998: 3). Although both Roberts and I focus on electoral alliances between the left and social movements, in Roberts's study it is the left that seeks to organize popular groups behind an electoral project. Indeed, leftist parties have organized and mobilized indigenous and peasant movements since the 1930s. But in the 1990s, with the left reeling in most countries from a number of ideological, structural, and strategic defeats, indigenous social movement organizations struck out on their own and rejected the domination and manipulation that characterized prior relations with leftist parties, while incorporating sympathetic fragments of a diminished and dependent left.

RESEARCH DESIGN

My research design is a structured, focused comparison of cases drawn from six South American countries (George 1979). Similar data was collected systematically across carefully selected cases in order to test propositions derived from the political party and social movement literatures (King, Keohane, and Verbn 1994: 45). While seeking to connect outcomes with their causes, I do not assume that the political world is imbued with a causal structure, in which particular causes always result in the same outcomes, causes have no effect on each other, and in which distinct political systems can be considered independent from each other. Instead, I assume that outcomes are produced by complex interactions among diverse variables through processes and sequences that vary among cases. Rather than trying to concentrate on simpler relationships, or to reject explanations that only work under certain conditions, I employ Peter Hall's method of "systematic process analysis," in which the process that causes a class of outcomes receives as much attention as the "causal variables" involved

(Hall 2003: 391). This is a deductive method in which predictions are made about the impact of particular variables and their validity is assessed based on a comparative study of the outcomes in particular cases and the processes leading thereto. Process analysts predict the outcomes, contours, and sequencing of political processes, while probing for the motivations and likely behaviors of key actors involved in the process under study (ibid.: 393–4). I ruled out multivariate statistical analysis because of the small number of cases, the high degree of multicollinearity among the variables, the nonnormal distribution of dependent variable data, and the interdependence among the cases caused by cross-national diffusion effects. Nevertheless, intensive historical analysis based on detailed case studies, combined with the systematic comparison of cases with different outcomes on the dependent variable, provided a framework for scientific inference about causal processes more rigorous than that afforded by large-N statistical analysis (Hall 2003: 397).

Although six countries are studied in detail, numerous cases of potential party formation are encountered within them because distinct indigenous leaders and organizations considered forming parties at various times during the period under study, 1980 through 2002. For example, in Bolivia more than twenty ethnic parties were formed in the late 1970s and early 1980s; some had modest success but most did not. In the 1990s a new set of ethnic parties formed and enjoyed varying levels of success, while in some cases indigenous organizations intensively discussed the possibility of forming a party and decided not to do so. Thus, in the Bolivian case alone there are actually more than a dozen "cases" to examine, since each instance in which parties formed or did not form constitutes a country-case, while each election – six national elections and two municipal ones – constitutes an opportunity to assess performance.

My definition of ethnic party differs from Donald Horowitz's widely used definition. For Horowitz, ethnic parties must serve the interests of a particular ethnic group, from whom the party overwhelmingly derives its support (Horowitz 1985: 291–2). The distribution of the party's support, thus, is the defining property of the ethnic party. In Latin America, however, because indigenous peoples are often a minority of registered voters, a significant portion of an ethnic party's support may come from non-Indians who view indigenous candidates as an "outsider" alternative to corrupt, unresponsive traditional politicians. My definition of ethnic party also differs from that of Chandra, who emphasizes the inclusion or exclusion of members and followers on the basis of ethnicity (2004: 3). Most Latin American indigenous organizations eschew exclusionary rhetoric

Introduction

TABLE 1.1. *Typology of ethnic parties*

Mono-ethnic	Indigenous Only	Indigenous-based
Autoridades Indígenas de Colombia (AICO). Mainly Guambiano	Movimiento Indio Tupak Katari (MITKA), Bolivia	Alianza Social Indígena (ASI), Colombia
Movimiento Indígena Pachakuti (MIP), Bolivia. Mainly Aymara	Movimiento Revolucionario Tupaj Katari de Liberación (MRTKL), Bolivia	Movimiento Unido Pluricultural Pachakutik (Pachakutik), Ecuador
	Asamblea de la Soberanía del Pueblo (ASP), Bolivia	Movimiento al Socialismo (MAS)/Instrumento Político para la Soberanía de los Pueblos (IPSP), Bolivia
	Eje Pachakuti, Bolivia	
	Movimiento Indígena Colombiano (MIC)	
	Partido Unido Multiétnico de Amazonas (PUAMA), Venezuela	
	Movimiento Indígena de la Amazonía Peruana (MIAP)	

in order to avoid the common rebuke that their territorial and cultural claims seek to dismember and disunify the country.[13]

The ethnic parties studied here may differ from those elsewhere in the world because they usually do not represent a single ethnic group. Most organize around an aggregate identity as indigenous peoples, an identity composed from numerous distinct indigenous cultures. The typology of ethnic parties in Table 1.1 distinguishes among parties that are essentially mono-ethnic, those that represent several or many indigenous groups, and those that are predominantly indigenous, but which incorporate non-indigenous sympathizers. As Chandra (2004: 4) observes, however, it is difficult to distinguish clearly between "mono-ethnic" and "multiethnic" parties because many ethnic categories are aggregates of several component identities. For example, India's Hindu political parties represent an ethnic group that is divided by caste, language, and region. In Sub-Saharan Africa, most ethnopolitical groups may be divided into subgroups

[13] A clear exception is Felipe Quispe, a Bolivian indigenous leader who has proposed the creation of a separate Aymara Indian state and who appeals mainly to Aymara voters in western Bolivia. See Chapter 3.

(Mozaffar 2000). Nonetheless we can reserve the category "ethnic party" for those parties that explicitly represent one set of ethnic identities as opposed to implicitly specified others. The defining characteristic is the identity of the party's leaders and the message offered to voters (Chandra 2004: 3).[14] Following Chandra and Horowitz, I reserve the term "multiethnic parties" for those spanning the major ethnic groups and cleavages in society (Chandra 2004: 3; Horowitz 1985: 299).

My primary research questions are: (1) Why did Latin American indigenous peoples' organizations form ethnic parties in the 1990s? and (2) Why were some of these parties relatively more successful than others? These are distinct questions because we cannot assume that the conditions necessary for party formation and success are the same. Parties unlikely to win elections may form in order to gain attention for a political issue or to provide a platform for a particular personality (Harmel and Robertson 1985: 507; Herzog 1987: 321). Nevertheless, there is some relationship between formation and success, inasmuch as the decision to expend the resources necessary to form a party will incorporate a calculation as to the likely electoral result. As Hug observes, the investigation of these distinct questions typically requires two distinct research designs (2001: 65). Usually party formation is treated as a dichotomous variable, while party performance is treated as continuous or relative. I too treat formation as a dichotomous variable, while coding party performance as an ordinal variable with three possible values: not electorally viable, electorally viable, and successful. I define "party formation" as the legal registration of a political party or movement and its participation in an election. "Electoral viability" denotes the achievement of a sufficient level of consolidation and voter support to continue as a competitor in elections. Such parties may win local or regional elections but rarely can compete at the national level. A "successful" party meets the criteria of electoral viability and regularly elects its candidates to national office.

I limited the countries under study because a comprehensive understanding of the emergence of ethnic parties required intensive fieldwork in order to properly code the dependent variable,[15] to obtain electoral data at the subnational level, and to observe the complex interactions of numerous variables. As noted previously, I maximize my leverage by

---

[14] According to Chandra (2004: 3–4), it is common in India for ethnic parties to change their message in order to broaden or narrow the audience of its appeal. They may even completely submerge ethnicity in favor of more "nonethnic" appeals.

[15] Some ethnic parties use nonethnic sounding names (e.g., Movimiento al Socialismo, Guyana Action Party), while parties whose platforms contain no ethnic content may use indigenous-sounding names to attract indigenous voters.

studying multiple points of decision over time during the period under study, and by comparing within the countries among indigenous movement organizations and geographic regions (King, et al. 1994: 30). I limited the study to South America in order to hold a number of factors constant. Within this region the six countries chosen demonstrate wide variation on the dependent variable. The first four (Bolivia, Colombia, Ecuador, and Venezuela) were chosen because I knew that ethnic parties had had some success in these countries. I selected Peru in order to include a case with a proportionally significant indigenous population in which ethnic parties had not formed, to act as a control case for an examination of party formation and performance in Bolivia and Ecuador. During the course of research I discovered that an ethnic party had formed in the Peruvian Amazon, but had enjoyed only local success. All three countries have unitary political systems and significant indigenous populations, which allowed me to hold certain institutional and demographic factors constant. I selected Argentina to compare with Colombia and Venezuela because it shares a lot of demographic, institutional, and party system features with the other two countries but, to my knowledge, had no ethnic parties. Again, in the course of research I discovered that indigenous peoples in Argentina had formed some local ethnic parties, although these had had limited success. All three countries have minuscule indigenous populations; a federal system (in the case of Colombia a quasi-federal system), which allowed me to observe the operation of decentralizing measures in promoting the emergence of new parties; and a comprehensive constitutional reform in the 1990s in which reforms affecting indigenous peoples were included. The sample also includes a wide variety of party systems – two cases in which traditional party systems collapsed in the 1990s (Peru, Venezuela), two noted for their extreme fragmentation (Bolivia, Ecuador), and two with two-party-dominant systems (Argentina, Colombia) – which facilitates a comparison of the effects of different party-system configurations.

Finally, the countries in the sample may be divided into two subsets to hold constant the potentially important variable of indigenous population size, which might have endogenous affects on some of the independent variables studied, as well as influence the potential outcomes. Three cases (Bolivia, Ecuador, Peru)[16] constitute a subset of significantly sized indigenous populations in unitary political systems with fragmented, volatile

[16] The indigenous proportion of these countries is 60.25 percent, 24.85 percent, and 38.39 percent, respectively. The Bolivian figure is from the 2001 census; the other two figures are from the Inter-American Indigenist Institute (Deruyttere 1997: 1).

party systems. Argentina, Colombia, and Venezuela, in contrast, have minuscule indigenous populations,[17] and, thus constitute unlikely cases for the emergence of ethnic parties. These cases may reveal more about the responsiveness of party systems to representational needs and the mobilizational potential of well-organized, albeit small, social movements than studies of cases with large ethnic minorities, since in the latter ethnic parties are more likely to form, given their larger potential vote pool. All cases in this sub-set also are federal (or quasi-federal) and have traditionally had a two-party-dominant party system. Indigenous movements in such states can be important political actors, notwithstanding their minuscule proportion of the national population, because they are usually concentrated in particular states, departments, or provinces, where they can have an impact on local or regional politics. Moreover, because most indigenous-majority subnational districts are in sparsely populated regions, electoral rules that favor rural districts can bring indigenous politicians to national office. Guillermo O'Donnell (1994: 163) has noted the tendency of such rules to overrepresent at the national level rural "brown areas," which are typically dominated by conservative and authoritarian politicians. The same electoral rules enable indigenous peoples to penetrate national political institutions.[18]

The time period under study encompasses multiple elections in all six cases. Colombia and Venezuela held competitive elections throughout this period; Argentina and Bolivia resumed elections in 1983 and 1980–2, respectively, following brutal, conservative military regimes. Ecuador and Peru resumed elections following progressive military regimes in 1979 and 1980. The resumption of elections is a particularly important starting point for those two countries because it coincided with the elimination of literacy requirements that had disenfranchised the majority of indigenous voters.

Approximately seventy interviews were conducted in five countries (all except Argentina) with members and leaders of ethnic parties and

[17] The indigenous proportion of these countries is 1.1 percent, 2.7 percent, and 1.48 percent, respectively. The Colombian figure is from the 1993 census. The other two figures are from the Interamerican Indigenist Institute (Deruyttere 1997: 1).

[18] Indigenous population size correlates neatly with Mainwaring and Scully's (1995) ranking of Latin American party systems in terms of their institutionalization. Venezuela (11.5), Colombia (10.5), and Argentina (9.0) are clustered together near the top of the rankings as institutionalized party systems, while Bolivia (5), Ecuador (5), and Peru (4.5) are clustered together at the bottom of the rankings as "inchoate" party systems. As I have argued elsewhere (Van Cott 2000a), the correlation between ethnic heterogeneity and low party-system institutionalization in South America is not accidental.

indigenous social movement organizations, nonindigenous political elites, and social scientists. In addition, documents produced by ethnic parties and social movement organizations, such as newsletters, press releases, and manifestos, were examined. I also consulted official archives, the local media, and scholarly writing on each country. Field research took place in Bolivia in April–July 1997, December 1998, July 2001, and June–July 2002; in Colombia in January–March 1997; in Ecuador in July 1999; in Peru in July–August 2002; and in Venezuela in June 2000. I was not able to travel to Argentina. Instead I gathered information available in the United States and through the Internet and contacted social scientists familiar with the country in order to obtain data and to discuss my tentative ideas.

ORGANIZATION OF THE BOOK

The book begins with a chapter presenting theoretical explanations for choosing the independent variables selected for this study. The remainder of the book consists of four chapters that contain analytically organized narratives of each case. Chapters 3–5 present lengthy, detailed treatments of the three cases with significant indigenous populations. Chapter 6 presents more abbreviated, schematic narratives of the three cases with minuscule indigenous populations. In the conclusion I aggregate the findings of the individual chapters into a comprehensive model of ethnic party formation and performance in South America. I also discuss the implications of the emergence of these new parties for democracy in the region and for the indigenous peoples they represent.

2

Institutions, Party Systems, and Social Movements

I became interested in the topic of ethnic parties during research on constitutional change and ethnic rights in Bolivia, Colombia, Ecuador, and Venezuela. Indigenous peoples' organizations mobilized intensely around these constitutional reforms in order to obtain rights that they had been seeking for years through other means. The process of mobilizing around constitutional reform helped to consolidate indigenous organizations in all four countries and to increase public knowledge of and sympathy for indigenous peoples. Having secured new political rights and exceeded previous levels of mobilization, indigenous organizations in all four countries entered the electoral arena with newly formed political parties. Thus, the first area of exploration for this study was the connection between constitutional rights secured in the 1990s and the formation and performance of the new ethnic parties. The second stage of research focused on a closely related topic, party system change, which resulted from or caused the institutional changes of the 1990s. Latin American party systems underwent radical change in the 1990s, altering the context in which indigenous movements made strategic decisions.

The insights of social movement theory guided the final phase of research. While difficult to use as causal theory, social movement theorists point us to a set of variables associated with the emergence and performance of social movements. Since social movements sponsored all of the viable and successful ethnic parties, I suspected that these variables might help explain the decision to embark on a new mode of social-movement struggle – electoral politics – as well as the likelihood of success in this arena. My study of the literatures on institutions, party systems, and social movements yielded a large set of variables for analysis. The factors that proved to have explanatory power were used to structure the case studies that follow. The remainder were discarded, but are discussed in this chapter as potential alternative explanations.

ETHNIC PARTIES AND THE PERMISSIVE
INSTITUTIONAL ENVIRONMENT

The literature on the formation and performance of parties has paid the greatest attention to the effects of institutions, particularly electoral institutions, which create an underlying structure that constrains the development of party systems (Coppedge 1997).[1] However, there are many examples of cases where institutional openness should have encouraged new parties to form but they did not, as well as cases where new parties formed despite the existence of high institutional barriers.[2] As Coppedge argues, the institutional structure is a critical variable but alone cannot explain party formation (Coppedge 1997: 184). The difficulty is that institutions interact with party systems and their impact on minority group representation is heavily contingent upon the dispersion or concentration of the minority population. For example, geographically concentrated minority populations benefit from single-member district systems (SMD) where districts coincide with ethnic boundaries, but dispersed minorities benefit more from proportional representation.

Latin American political elites have tinkered with institutional rules repeatedly. These rules are the outcomes of political struggles and compromises that, in turn, shape future outcomes of political competition. Representatives of indigenous movements are well aware of the impact of these institutions on the political representation of their constituents. Foremost in the minds of indigenous representatives participating in constituent assemblies was the goal of securing greater rights to self-government, that is, the right to make administrative and political decisions within a particular territory, as well as the right to select their own representatives to the larger political system. For that reason, indigenous representatives and social-movement organizations campaigned vigorously for

---

[1] On party systems and institutions in Latin America, see Birnir (2000, unpublished manuscript); Coppedge (1997, 1998); Jones (1995, 1997); Roberts (2001); and Roberts and Wibbels (1999). On institutional impacts on party systems more generally, see Grofman and Lijphart (1986); Harmel and Robertson (1985); Lipset and Rokkan (1967); Mair (1997); Ordeshook and Shvetsova (1994), and Taagepera and Shugart (1989).
[2] Hug (2001: 4) and Kitschelt (1989), for example, note that institutional and political conditions were favorable for the emergence of an ecology party in Holland in the 1970s and early 1980s, but one did not form until much later.

decentralization, which would serve as the basis for local and regional self-government. They also advocated guaranteed representation of indigenous peoples in national legislatures through the allocation of seats by ethnicity.

Elites' selection of new institutions affecting indigenous peoples' political representation depended to a great extent on the proportional size of the target population as well as the nature of other unrelated goals. In Colombia and Venezuela, not only were indigenous groups relatively small and, thus, did not threaten existing power relations, a key goal of a significant number of political elites in those countries was the opening of a traditionally closed two-party system to more diverse political, social, and economic interests. Colombian elites hoped to reinvigorate a party system that had lost meaning for most citizens and to provide peaceful alternatives for armed actors to achieve their goals. In Venezuela, President Hugo Chávez used the constituent assembly to further dismember a gravely weakened two-party system and to shore up his own political movement. In both countries, indigenous political parties benefited from the new, more permissive institutional environment. Conversely, in Ecuador and Bolivia, political elites designed institutional rules with the intention of containing persistent party system fragmentation and to defend their space in the political system against challenger parties that emerged in the 1990s. Both countries had a long history of political elites designing rules to disenfranchise independent indigenous electoral vehicles: in Ecuador through literacy requirements that were not dropped until the 1980s, and difficult party-registration rules that were not relaxed until the mid-1990s and in Bolivia through high barriers to ballot access and the centralization of the political system. In sum, the institutional changes discussed in the following text were the result of intense intraelite struggles, as well as the persistence of indigenous peoples and their allies (Van Cott 2000b, 2002).

The permissiveness of the institutional environment for party formation and success is determined by the interaction of many individual institutional structures and rules. Scholars have identified five institutions as tending to permit the emergence of new political parties and party system cleavages: (1) decentralization; (2) low barriers for parties to register on the ballot; (3) reserved seats or list quotas for minorities; (4) a proportional representation electoral system; and (5) a relatively low "threshold of representation" (composed of a more proportional electoral formula, a low threshold for earning seats, and a relatively large district magnitude).[3]

---

[3] I thank Mark P. Jones for his suggestion to combine these elements.

Decentralization

New parties are likely to be more successful in countries that are decentralized rather than centralized because new parties have the opportunity to develop at geographical levels where the cost of party formation is lower, that is, transportation and advertising costs are smaller, a smaller organization is needed to mount a campaign, and fewer signatures are required to appear on the ballot. As Dalton, Flanagan, and Beck observe, political parties that win subnational elections in areas of constituency strength can use these as the basis of support for elections in other districts and at higher levels (1984: 467). This is precisely what occurred in Belgium and West Germany, where ecology parties competed first in local and regional elections, reasoning that voters would be more likely to "waste" votes on them in secondary elections as opposed to important national contests. They proved their electoral viability in these elections before entering the national arena (Kitschelt 1989: 75). Moreover, territorial decentralization aids new parties by multiplying access points to the state (Kriesi 1995: 171).

Ethnic groups are particularly disposed to benefit from local and regional elections because they usually are concentrated geographically, provided that the borders of electoral districts do not fragment concentrated populations. Ethnic minorities tend to be concentrated geographically because sufficient numbers must exist in one place to constitute a self-reproducing cultural community and because minorities that are surrounded by people different from themselves, and who are victims of discrimination or violence, prefer to settle in areas where their numbers are greatest and bonds of solidarity can protect them. Indigenous peoples, like many ethnic minorities, feel a particular attachment to specific territories and prefer to settle in their vicinity to protect long-standing territorial claims. States may even create laws and norms that require or encourage indigenous peoples to live in certain places and not others.[4] Once ethnic parties become established at the local or regional level by competing where they have the votes to win, they are better equipped to compete at the national level where more resources are required.

Levels of decentralization for most South American countries are contained in Table 2.1. Direct municipal and regional elections were instituted in Colombia (municipal 1988, departmental 1991), Bolivia (municipal

---

[4] For example, Colombia's Law 48 of 1993 exempts Indians from military service provided that they live in constitutionally recognized *resguardos*.

TABLE 2.1. *Decentralization and federalism in South America*

Country	Level of Decentralization	Federal?
Argentina	49.3%	yes
Brazil	45.6%	yes
Colombia	39%	no
Bolivia	26.7%	no
Venezuela	19.5%	yes
Uruguay	14.2%	no
Chile	13.6%	no
Peru	10.5%	no
Ecuador	7.5%	no
Paraguay	6.2%	no

Source: Inter-American Development Bank, cited in Moreno (2000: 5).

1995), and Venezuela (municipal 1989). In Colombia and Bolivia, ethnic parties competed immediately in newly established subnational elections to considerable success. In Venezuela, as part of a nationwide decentralization process in the 1990s, the federal territories of Amazonas and Delta Amacuro, which have large indigenous populations, became states. Whereas prior to the reform governors had been appointed from Caracas, afterward they were elected. In Colombia, similarly, in 1994, following a recent decentralization, several new departments (regional governments that directly elect governors and departmental assemblies) were created, several of which had indigenous majorities or significant minorities. In all three cases, both decentralization and the creation of new departments with significant indigenous populations constituted significant improvements in the permissiveness of the institutional environment. In Bolivia, notwithstanding obstacles to ballot access, the municipal decentralization of 1995 alone was significant enough to encourage indigenous social-movement organizations to form ethnic parties that performed well from the very first election. Ethnic parties were particularly successful in departments or states where Indians comprise a significant minority or a majority, even in countries where they are a minuscule minority nationwide.

Ecuador underwent decentralization in 1980, at the beginning of the period under study, and made no significant changes. Similarly, Argentina was a decentralized, federal system, and remained so throughout the period. Thus, we cannot observe the "before" and "after" effects of decentralization. Only Peru reversed the regionwide trend toward greater decentralization. Following a brief experiment with regional government (1989–93), President Fujimori recentralized the country in the 1993 Constitution. Regional governments were reestablished in 2002.

Increased Ballot Access

Given the meager financial resources of Latin American indigenous populations, laws that place a high financial or logistical burden on party registration tend to inhibit their formation. Conversely, low requirements for registration and the absence of penalties for poor electoral performance should encourage new party formation. Barriers to party registration are highest in the three Andean countries with the greatest party system fragmentation (Bolivia, Ecuador, and Peru) and traditionally have been employed to limit the number of personalist and populist electoral vehicles. Only in Ecuador did ballot access improve significantly (in 1994). This set of institutional changes, which made it much easier for new parties, movements, and electoral alliances to compete in elections, was decisive in the decision of leaders of the indigenous movement finally to support their own electoral vehicle. In Colombia and Venezuela ballot access also improved. Both countries' new constitutions allow indigenous social movement organizations to participate in elections without forming a political party. (Bolivia allowed indigenous movements and civil society groups to contest elections for the first time in December 2004).[5]

Reserved Seats and Quotas

Lijphart argues that the creation of electoral districts along ethnic rather than geographic criteria is the simplest way to guarantee ethnic representation. This usually involves creating ethnic voting rolls, which have been used in Cyprus, New Zealand, and Zimbabwe (Lijphart 1986b: 116). Reserved seats guarantee access to the political process. This access provides experience to fledgling ethnic minority politicians and their party organizations, and also may bring with it free access to the media and campaign financing. The creation of reserved seats may also increase interest in and enthusiasm for the political process among marginalized groups that had heretofore chosen not to participate. Another route to achieving greater representation of ethnic minorities is to require that political parties include them on their lists – just as many European and Latin

[5] Pursuant to the February 20, 2004, constitutional reform.

American countries have done to increase the representation of women. However, this is more likely to discourage the formation of ethnic parties, because some of their potential candidates will be included in the lists of nonethnic parties and ethnic voters may prefer to support prominent coethnics running with traditional parties, which have a better chance of winning than new ethnic parties. In fact, this is what occurred in 2002, when Peru became the first country in Latin America to require quotas on political party lists for ethnic minorities.[6] A 15 percent quota was applied to Amazonian districts for the 2002 regional elections. As expected, many prominent indigenous leaders ran with nonethnic parties and the fledgling ethnic party Indigenous Movement of the Peruvian Amazon (MIAP) obtained disappointing results.

Special districts for indigenous candidates were created in Colombia and Venezuela during constitutional reforms in 1991 and 1999, respectively. Rather than using ethnic voting rolls, candidates must fulfill a variety of requirements indicating their "indigenousness," but all voters may vote in the district. Once achieved, the special districts not only guaranteed a legal minimum of representation, they provided resources to expand representation above this minimum level. Although the districts significantly improved the prospects for electoral performance of indigenous candidates and parties, in both cases they were created *after* indigenous social movements already had demonstrated their ability to elect candidates to constituent assemblies against enormous odds and in competition with nonindigenous candidates.

Proportional Representation

The literature on parties concurs that proportional representation (PR) electoral systems are more likely than majoritarian systems to encourage the formation of and ensure the success of new parties. PR systems lower barriers to party system entry by creating a more proportional vote-to-seat calculation and by giving voters more choices (Sartori 1986: 58). Majoritarian systems, in contrast, tend to produce a two-party system and to make it difficult for new parties to form (Lijphart 1986b: 113; Riker 1986). Proportionality is particularly important for minorities because other types of electoral systems tend to underrepresent or even

---

[6] Between 2000 and 2001, Brazil instituted a variety of quota policies to improve employment opportunities for blacks in the public sector. These did not affect elected offices (Htun 2004a).

exclude them (Lijphart 1986b: 113; Mozaffar 1997: 149). As noted previously, this is not true for geographically concentrated minorities, which may benefit more from SMD systems. All six countries studied began with PR systems. Colombia and Peru retained them. Bolivia and Venezuela shifted, in 1994 and 1993, respectively, to a mixed system in which half the lower chamber of a bicameral legislature is elected by SMD. The 1999 Venezuelan Constitution shifted to a unicameral National Assembly that retained the mixed system used for the lower chamber. The 1998 Ecuadorian Constitution shifted from PR to a multiseat candidate-based majoritarian system in which only 20 of 121 seats are elected on national party lists. In Argentina, the 1994 constitutional reform shifted the election of the lower chamber of congress to SMD from multimember PR, which had prevailed since the return to democracy in 1983 (the country's twenty-three electoral districts are the twenty-two provinces plus Buenos Aires). No correlation was found between this variable and the formation and performance of ethnic parties. Majoritarian and mixed systems did not impede the formation and success of ethnic parties, and PR systems did not help them in the absence of other permissive conditions.

Threshold of Representation

Seat allocation formulas work with seat thresholds – the number of votes necessary to earn a seat – to determine the ratio of votes to seats for each party. Formulas that award seats to parties winning small proportions of the vote should promote the formation and improve the electoral performance of new parties. Formulas favoring larger parties should inhibit new party formation and electoral viability. The lower the minimum vote requirement for the allocation of seats, the more likely it is that new parties, which tend to win few votes, will gain seats (Taagepera and Shugart 1989: 133). Thus, lower thresholds will enable new parties to gain access to political power and the resources it brings, which can be used to enhance the new party's vote share in the next election. The d'Hondt formula, which tends to favor larger parties, is the most common seat allocation formula in Latin America and has been used throughout the period under study in Argentina and Peru for the lower chamber. Venezuela used d'Hondt until 1993, when half the lower house was elected by SMD, while the remaining half continues to be elected by d'Hondt. Venezuela during the period under study also has allocated compensatory seats to underrepresented parties winning at least one quota (Jones 1997: 14). In general, seat allocation formulas and thresholds were unfavorable to new parties in the six countries during the period under study. In fact, the tendency during that period of institutional change was to make them more restrictive, in part a response to the high party-system fragmentation of the period, as well as the desire of the larger parties to maintain their level of representation. Seat thresholds never were lowered.

The number of seats in a district (district magnitude, DM) mediates the impact of seat allocation formulas and thresholds. Political scientists expect DM to have a significant impact on the number of parties in a political system owing to both mechanical and psychological effects (Coppedge 1997: 157; Taagepera and Shugart 1989: 112). The mechanical effect is that the larger the magnitude of the district, the more proportional will be the translation of votes into seats. Larger DMs help challenger parties because they don't have to win a plurality to gain seats, even in plurality districts, provided there is more than one seat (Taagepera and Shugart 1989: 115). Psychologically, small DMs discourage voters from "wasting" their votes on smaller parties that are unlikely to win seats (Taagepera and Shugart 1989: 119). The extent to which smaller parties are helped by a given seat allocation formula depends on DM and the size of divisors and remainders used in the allocation formula (Taagepera and Shugart 1989: 29–35). The impact of DM depends on whether the system is PR or plurality. Under PR, the larger the DM the closer to proportionality the allocation of votes will be and, thus, the more favorable the system is to new party success. Under plurality, increasing DM decreases proportionality (Sartori 1986: 53; Taagepera and Shugart 1989: 19, 112).

Constituent assembly elections are particularly important when observing the link between institutional and party system changes. Constituent assemblies often are elected from single national districts with more than seventy members. Thus, smaller parties, and even civil society organizations in some cases, are able to secure representation in constituent assemblies. The reciprocal effect, of course, is lower than usual representation for the system's most dominant parties. Five of our six cases experienced constituent assemblies between 1980 and 2002. In four cases (Colombia, Ecuador, Peru, and Venezuela), for different reasons, the representation of the major parties was unusually reduced, allowing potential party system entrants and challengers the opportunity to change electoral laws that had favored the major parties and to open the system to new parties.

The impact of DM may be particularly important in explaining the formation and electoral viability of ethnic parties. Based on data from Western industrialized democracies, Ordeshook and Shvetsova concluded that the impact of DM increases as societies become more ethnically fragmented (1994: 122). However, it is difficult to observe the impact of DM in our cases because it varies, sometimes significantly, within countries and can have different effects in different districts throughout the country. DM often reflects the density of the population in a district rather than a conscious effort to affect party formation (Taagepera and Shugart 1989: 125). Moreover, variations in DM interact with variations in the geographic dispersion and concentration of ethnic minorities. Where minorities are proportionally small and highly dispersed they are more likely to win seats in districts with a high number of seats. Where minorities are concentrated geographically they are more likely to win seats in districts that correspond to the boundaries of their settlement patterns, where they may be a numerical majority. Variations in DM and in the geographic concentration of ethnic minorities may generate distinct probabilities of formation and electoral viability within the same country.

An increase in DM was followed by the formation and electoral success of ethnic parties only in Colombia, where ethnic parties have won a Senate seat twice – outside their two reserved seats – since the shift to a single 100-member legislative body. Prior to this change, few minorities of any kind had gained representation in Colombia's legislature. In Ecuador, the already-formed Movimiento Unido Plurinacional Pachakutik (Pachakutik) won the same number of seats as it had won before, following an increase in DM in 1998. This translated to a smaller proportion of seats because of the increased size of the legislature. Thus, like the other representation threshold variables discussed in the preceding text, DM rarely had an impact on its own, but was one element of the institutional environment.

Given the multiplicity and diversity of institutional changes in the six cases studied, it is difficult to discern a systematic causal effect attributable to any one particular law or regulation. Moreover, the full impact of these changes may not yet be visible, since it should take several electoral cycles for actors to adapt to the changes, most of which are quite recent. We also must keep in mind that ethnic parties may form and become viable even in institutional environments that are unfavorable. As Mayer observes, when minority interests are intensely felt they may create such stress in the political system that it will have to change to accommodate them (1972: 221). The impact of institutions can only be fully appreciated if we observe how they interact with party systems and with the dispersion/concentration of ethnic minorities. These interactions are emphasized in the chapters that follow.

With these qualifications, three tendencies may be identified. First, regulations intended to reduce the number of parties – particularly vote thresholds and fines affecting party registration – make it difficult for ethnic minorities to form and sustain political parties. Such thresholds are highest in the three countries with significant indigenous populations. Highly fragmented, weakly institutionalized party systems are likely to emerge in Latin American countries with deep ethnic cleavages (Van Cott 2000a). Thresholds are likely to be instituted in such polities in order to reduce fragmentation and to exclude independent indigenous political movements. Second, decentralized political systems provide an opportunity for ethnic parties to form and succeed. Decentralization occurred or already existed in all four countries where viable or successful ethnic parties formed. Finally, reserving seats for indigenous candidates stimulates political mobilization among indigenous populations. Not surprisingly, reserved seats are only found in the systems with the smallest proportional indigenous population, where they pose less of a threat to established parties.

A final institutional change that may encourage the formation of ethnic parties is the creation of new electoral districts. In several countries, indigenous peoples first formed political parties in districts that had been created quite recently from other larger districts or from former federal territories. New states tended to be created in the 1990s in remote rural areas, which often have a relatively large indigenous population. Although there was not enough data to look at this variable systematically, it stands to reason that new parties are more likely to form and perform well in new electoral districts, where existing parties have not had a chance to become entrenched or to benefit from incumbency. Where new districts combine with significant ethnic minority populations that already are organized politically as social movements, we can expect conditions to be highly favorable.

ETHNIC PARTIES AND PARTY SYSTEMS

The literature on new party formation and success has focused relatively little attention on party systems as an independent variable. An exception is Simon Hug (2001), whose general theory of new party formation is based on strategic interactions between existing and potential parties. In an attempt to make his theory as general as possible, however, Hug does not theorize the variation in opportunities for new party formation presented by distinct configurations of parties. In contrast, I argue that the

configuration of power in the party system will influence social movements' decisions to make the leap from informal to formal politics and
affect the electoral performance of new parties. The opening of space in
the party system provides a permissive environment for the formation of
new ethnic parties in Latin America.

I examine three qualities of party systems that should open a party system to ethnic parties in Latin America: party system dealignment, party
system fragmentation, and electorally weak leftist parties. Change in any
of these three variables facilitates the detachment of a portion of the electorate from existing party identities. As Bruhn observes, detachment is
necessary to make available a sufficient number of voters to support new
parties and, thus, to create incentives for leaders to form them (1997: 14).
All three variables help us to measure the amount of space in the party
system for new parties or cleavages to emerge. Put another way, they measure the mobility of individual voters. Although they are distinct concepts
and measures, dealignment, fragmentation, and leftist party weakness are
interrelated variables because changes in one measure may cause changes
in the others.

Party system change will not encourage only ethnic parties to form, as
opposed to other types of parties. In fact, other parties did emerge in most
of the countries studied. None, however, constituted a new dimension of
competition, because in South America ethnicity was the only major social
cleavage that had not yet been activated politically by the 1980s. As will
be explained in the following text, the decline of the left has particular
relevance for indigenous peoples in South America.

Dealignment

Party system dealignment denotes a relatively short time period in which
the combined votes for the dominant parties in the system decline (Dalton,
Flanagan, and Beck 1984: 14). I categorize as "dominant" those parties
that consistently win more than 10 percent of the vote in national elections
and that competed in at least three elections between 1980 and 2002. The
greater the dealignment, the more detached voters there are and, thus,
the stronger is the incentive for new parties to form and the greater are
the prospects for the electoral success of new parties. Ordinarily, dominant parties, which design electoral rules to maintain their dominance,
present high barriers to prospective entrants to the party system. They
have the advantage of an established identity, their candidates may be
incumbents, and they may benefit from established clientelist networks.

As Mair observes, it is particularly unusual for new political cleavages to emerge once party systems have established a set of parties and cleavages. These become "frozen" and tend to crowd out new cleavages that do not conform to the existing patterns of competition (1997: 13–14; see also Lipset and Rokkan 1967: 50). Party system dealignment provides an opening for ethno-nationalist movements to establish a new dimension of competition (Máiz n.d.: 19–20).

Despite the strong theoretical relationship between dealignment and new party system cleavages, no systematic correlation was found in the six countries studied. Significant party system dealignment occurred in Peru and Venezuela, but only in Venezuela did it appear to encourage the formation of an ethnic party. More moderate dealignment occurred in Colombia and did indeed appear to open space for new parties. But dealignment was less important than institutional changes, which significantly increased the permissiveness of the institutional environment and were the main cause of the dealignment in the first place.

Party System Fragmentation

Party system fragmentation is a complicated variable that can have both static and dynamic effects. Persistently fragmented party systems are more open to the emergence of new parties because they are more likely to convert votes won into seats and, thus, into legislative and material benefits for their constituents, which in turn facilitate continued or increased electoral success. Although it is true that aspiring parties may face competition from throughout the political spectrum, in highly fragmented systems existing parties typically win less than 25 percent of the vote and, thus, do not constitute formidable competitors. Persistent fragmentation also is likely to encourage electoral and postelectoral alliances among parties because single parties need allies to form a governing majority, even in presidential systems. This gives smaller parties more clout and the opportunity to endure and grow through access to government resources. Smaller parties able to win seats also have enhanced leverage in bipolar systems where the two parties are fairly evenly matched in terms of votes and seats because they can function as swing votes.

Increases in party system fragmentation open more space for new parties to compete by lowering the number of votes necessary to win seats. Based on their study of the emergence of postmaterial value cleavages in Europe, Dalton et al. argue that fragmentation is the variable most likely to permit the establishment of new cleavages because fragmentation provides more parties through which new interests may seek representation, while lowering barriers to the emergence of new and small parties, which tend to represent minority interests (1984: 466). Fragmentation may be an indicator of dealignment, since an increasing number of parties may reflect declining support for existing ones. Moreover, fragmentation is not just a cause of new party formation, it is a measure of it, since we may assume that as new parties are formed the number of parties in the system will increase. Thus, party system fragmentation may influence the decision to form a party and its electoral performance in two ways. First, the long-standing fragmentation of a system may combine with changes in other variables to give prospective entrants the perception that they will face relatively weak competition. Once the decision has been made to compete, the more fragmented the party system is the more likely are votes won to result in representation. Second, an increase in fragmentation may encourage new parties to form and improve their electoral chances by creating relatively more space in the party system.

Party system fragmentation typically is measured using Laakso and Taagepera's (1979) formula for calculating the effective number of parties for seats (ENPS).[7] Based on calculations by other scholars, as well as my own calculations, I found no systematic correlation between fragmentation and the formation and performance of new ethnic parties (see Table 2.2). It is likely that this variable interacted with other more powerful ones to open the party system somewhat, but we cannot say that fragmentation alone was decisive. Moreover, almost every country I studied had experienced significant fragmentation by the end of the 1990s, a phenomenon witnessed throughout the region.

The Weakness or Decline of Leftist Parties

By far the most important party system variable is the decline of leftist parties in the 1990s, just as indigenous movements were consolidating themselves as regional and national collective political actors. Since Indians are overwhelmingly poor (Psacharopoulos and Patrinos 1994), leftist parties, which appeal to lower-class voters, should attract indigenous votes. In fact, there is a long history of leftist parties incorporating indigenous communities and fighting along side them for agrarian reform. But relations were always difficult because Marxist party leaders believed

---

[7] The measure is calculated by squaring the proportion of seats won by each party, adding up all of the squares, and dividing one by that number.

TABLE 2.2. *Effective number of parties for seats*

Year[a]	Argentina	Bolivia	Colombia	Ecuador	Peru	Venezuela
Average ENPS	2.7	4	2.1	5.8	3.8	3
	(1983–93)	(1979–93)	(1970–90)	(1978–92)	(1978–90)	(1973–93)
Early 1980s	2.94 (83)	4.12 (80)	1.98 (82)	3.94 (79)	2.46 (80)	2.65 (78)
Mid-1980s	2.37 (85)	4.32 (85)	2.45 (86)	6.10 (84)	2.32 (85)	2.42 (83)
Late 1980s	2.58 (87)	3.92 (89)	–	5.63 (88)	–	2.83 (88)
Average 1980s	2.63	4.12	2.22	5.22	2.39	3.95
Early 1990s	2.82 (93)	4.17 (93)	2.18 (90)	6.61 (92)	5.84 (90)	4.50 (93)
Mid-1990s	2.73 (95)	–	2.53 (94)	5.71 (94)	2.89 (95)	–
Late 1990s	2.74 (97)[a]	5.07 (97)[b]	2.74 (98)[c]	5 (98)	–	6.31 (98)
Average 1990s	2.76	4.62	3.73	5.77	4.37	5.41
Latest	2.84 (01)[a]	4.82 (02)[b]	7.01 (02)[a]	6.45 (02)	4.15 (01)	3.77 (00)

Note: All ENPS are for lower or single chamber legislatures, except where noted.

[a] Chamber of Deputies only.

[b] Senate plus Chamber of Deputies.

[c] Calculation by Boudon (2000).

Source: First row from Mainwaring and Scully (1995: 30). ENPS for 1980s, early 1990s, and mid-1990s from Michael Coppedge, Latin American party systems data set, www.nd.edu/~mcoppedg/crd/datalaps.htm. ENPS for late 1990s and latest calculated by author, except where noted, based on these sources: www.georgetown.edu/pdba, except Bolivia 1997, *La Razón*, June 12, 1997; Bolivia 2002, *La Razón*, July 9, 2002, online; Colombia 2002, www.registraduria.gov.co; Venezuela 1998, 2000, Molina (2002).

that the peasantry must disappear in order for socialism to prevail, that cultural claims were anachronistic and counterrevolutionary, and because the racism of the left prevented indigenous and peasant movements from becoming equal partners. Nevertheless, indigenous peoples first gained access to the political arena through relations with the left. Moreover, as Mexican indigenous rights activists Margarito Ruiz Hernández and Araceli Burguete Cal y Mayor put it,

This experience was fundamental in fuelling a broad segment of the contemporary *indianista/autonomista* movement. The political biographies of a significant number of *indianista/autonomista* indigenous leaders over the age of 40 today highlight the roots of their training in the worker/peasant movements and/or in the communist or socialist parties – or even the guerrilla movements, in Guatemala, Nicaragua and Chile – of their respective countries.   (2001: 25)

Relationships with leftist parties and movements had a profound ideological and organizational influence on contemporary indigenous leaders. The decline of the left opened space in the political system for indigenous movements accustomed to participating in politics through leftist parties. Tarrow observes that leftist parties are important allies for subaltern groups that seek greater representation in the political system because they tend to be more open than center or conservative parties to new ideas expressed by challengers (1998: 80). Indigenous movements in South America demand redistribution and challenge the neoliberal economic model. They also promote a new set of values connected to a vision of a multicultural state. Thus, their agenda is compatible with both "new" left parties, which are concerned with lifestyle and values issues and "old" left parties, which are more oriented toward redistributive agendas (ibid.; see also Kreisi 1995: 181; Maguire 1995: 2001).

Although cross-national data on the preferences of indigenous voters is not available, interviews in the five Andean countries, anecdotal surveys,[8] and the secondary literature on each country revealed a marked tendency of indigenous organizations to form alliances with leftist parties. Thus, where leftist parties have weakened, we might expect ethnic parties to emerge as an alternative. Moreover, where leftist parties are not

---

[8] In a survey of highland indigenous voters in Ecuador, Chiriboga and Rivera found that 70 percent voted for center-left parties, compared to 11.5 percent for populist, and 9.01 percent for right-wing parties (1989: 195). Interviews in Lima, Peru, with Wilder Sánchez, Eduardo Cáceres, Eliana Rivera Alarcón, July 2002; La Paz, Bolivia, with María Eugenia Choque, Hugo Salvatierra, June–July 2002; Venezuela with Dieter Heinen, May 2000; Quito, Ecuador with Jorge Leon, Luis Macas, July 1999; Pasto, Popayán, Colombia with Antonio Navarro Wolff, Claudia Piñeros, February–March 1997.

competitive, cadres from defunct or diminished leftist parties, organized labor, and leftist intellectuals searching for a viable alternative political project, may be absorbed by ethnic parties launched by dynamic indigenous social movements. These cadres bring ideological coherence, organizational skills, and experienced candidates to the often less-experienced indigenous organizations seeking to enter formal politics. These alliances between indigenous and nonindigenous politicians are qualitatively different than alliances of the past because the relative power balance weighs in favor of the former rather than the latter. In two cases (Argentina and Colombia) the left traditionally has been weak, leaving room on the left of the political spectrum for indigenous movements. In those two countries, indigenous movements had relatively less experience with electoral politics except as passive parts of traditional clientelist networks, and they were not able to benefit from the availability of experienced leftist cadres. Thus, the decline of a once-strong electoral left is a greater boon to ethnic parties than long-standing electoral weakness on the left.

Part of the explanation for leftist party decline in four of our cases lies in global or regional factors, such as the decline of socialism after the fall of the Berlin Wall in 1989, the breakup of the Soviet Union in 1991, and harsh structural adjustment policies that devastated organized labor movements throughout the region beginning in the mid-1980s. The global decline of socialism made it difficult for Latin American leftist parties to put forward socialist platforms as a viable alternative (Alcántara and Freidenberg 2001; Roberts 1998: 20–2). At the same time, the neoliberal reforms of the 1980s reduced the size of the organized working classes and debilitated the union and peasant organizations that had previously served as the base of support and as key organizational mechanisms for the leftist parties (Levitsky and Cameron 2001: 26). These blows affecting the entire Latin American left, combined with *sui generis* challenges, resulted in varying levels of electoral decline, notwithstanding their convergence with institutional openings.

In sum, leftist party decline appears to encourage the formation and improve the electoral performance of ethnic parties, whose base has tended to support leftist candidates. The most successful new ethnic parties are those that are alliances between a mature, consolidated indigenous organization and leftist militants, labor activists, and intellectuals who previously supported now defunct or disarticulated leftist movements. This leftist flotsam brings vital logistical, ideological, and financial resources to the fledgling ethnic parties, enabling them to gain early success despite their inexperience with elections – as Brazil's PT benefited from the incorporation of leftists defecting from the main opposition party during its early years (Keck 1992: 73).

Roberts constructs a typology of relations between leftist parties and social movements. His "vanguard model" has a hierarchical, top-down, disciplined structure in which the party controls social movements, typically unions, students, and peasant organizations. In the "electoralist model," leftist party leaders seek to mobilize unorganized sectors of society during election campaigns, but do not seek to build a permanent civil society–based movement. In Roberts's third model, the "organic model,"

> distinctions between the party and its constituent social organizations are deliberately blurred; indeed, the party may appear to be more of a movement than an apparatus for electoral contestation, as it is directly engaged in social struggles outside the sphere of institutional politics, and party members and leaders are drawn directly from social movements rather than from the ranks of a separate, professional political caste. (Roberts 1998: 75)

In contrast to the vanguard parties, where electoral success is the priority, in the organic model when tensions emerge between the social movement and the electoral vehicle, they are resolved in favor of furthering social movement goals. Whereas vanguard parties maintain hierarchical, disciplined structures, organic parties are typically more open to grassroots participation and a diversity of viewpoints and strategies (Roberts 1998: 75).

In the 1970s, relations between Latin American indigenous organizations and leftist parties more closely approximated the vanguard and electoralist models. However, as the left declined, indigenous organizations were more able to dictate the terms of the relationship and, thus alter the model. The new ethnic parties emerged along the lines of Roberts's organic model, absorbing the detritus of the left and exploiting its ideological, financial, and logistical resources. In addition, in the 1990s we see more temporary, strategic alliances between autonomous indigenous movement–based parties and leftist parties.

A significant amount of party system change occurred in all of the cases where viable or successful ethnic parties were formed. In every positive case, at least two types of change occurred – dealignment and fragmentation in Colombia and Venezuela; the decline of the left and fragmentation in Bolivia, Ecuador, and Colombia. Since the main impact on ethnic parties of the first two variables (dealignment and fragmentation) was expected to be the same – the opening of a previously closed system to allow the introduction of a new cleavage – it makes sense that the presence of moderate levels of either would have the same effect. Similarly, leftist party decline opens space in a part of the political spectrum that is likely to attract indigenous voters, which may be enough to encourage ethnic party formation and ensure success. This variable, however, has another effect that may be equally important: the availability of professional political cadre to provide ideology, organizational skills, and experienced candidates for fledgling ethnic parties. Since all three kinds of party system change occurred in Peru, but no viable ethnic parties emerged, party system change may be a necessary but not a sufficient condition for the success of new ethnic parties.

ETHNIC PARTIES AND SOCIAL MOVEMENTS

With one possible exception (Bolivia's Pachakuti Indigenous Movement [MIP]) an established social movement organization created all of the new viable ethnic parties. In Latin America, historically, it has been more common to see the opposite: political parties forming social movement organizations. But since the return to democracy in the 1980s, social movement organizations have formed political parties, often to achieve autonomy from the very parties that formed them. This phenomenon is not confined to indigenous peoples' movements: it includes Brazil's Workers' Party (PT), Colombia's Democratic Alliance M-19 (ADM-19), and Mexico's Party of the Democratic Revolution (PRD) (Foweraker 1995: 87–8). With the exception of the PT and PRD, few of these movement-sponsored parties have had enduring electoral success, until the emergence of indigenous-movement–based parties.

Social movement theorists have identified a set of variables that create conditions for social movement formation and mobilization. The political opportunity structure (POS) approach emphasizes the constraints on and incentives for collective action that the state and political system present to social movements in order to explain the timing and/or the outcome of social movement mobilization (Foweraker 1995: 19; McAdam 1996: 29). The variables associated with this approach are the availability of elite allies; splits within and fragmentation of the ruling elite and the stability of its internal alignments; changes in the state and its institutions that may open access to politics; the influence of international actors and forces; and the state's use of repression (Foweraker 1995: 71–3; McAdam 1996: 34; McAdam, McCarthy, and Zald 1996b: 10; Tarrow 1996: 54; 1998: 19–20, 80). In contrast, the resource mobilization approach assumes that collective political action is difficult and that social movements require financial, organizational, cultural, and human resources to form, endure, and achieve political effectiveness (Foweraker 1995: 15–16). I used insights from both approaches to identify factors that might explain the strategic decision of social movements to form political parties, as well as factors that might contribute to the successful performance of social movement–sponsored parties. In the course of field research I gathered as much information as possible on all of the variables identified in the preceding text.

Some of the variables associated with the POS approach already have been discussed (institutional changes and the openness of the political system). Two others proved significant: the unusual opportunity structure created by radical constitutional reform, particularly when constituent assemblies were convened, and a "diffusion effect" caused when the success of ethnic political parties in one country influenced an indigenous peoples' organization in another to form a party.

Access to the Constitutional Reform Process

In all four cases where viable or successful ethnic parties formed, this occurred immediately after successful social movement mobilizations that secured constitutional rights. As Foweraker and Landman observe, seeking and securing rights can serve as a strong incentive for political mobilization, a framework for a group's discourse, and a tool for continued political action. The discourse of rights is particularly attractive for excluded groups seeking to justify their inclusion (Foweraker and Landman 1997: 228). The discourse around rights that permeated the constitutional reform conjuncture in Latin America helped to stimulate demands for greater political inclusion. Thus, the formation of ethnic parties can be viewed as part of the "protest cycle" (McAdam et al., 1996b: 13) or "cycle of contention" (Tarrow 1998: 10) surrounding constitutional reform conjunctures. It occurred during the descending arc of nationwide mobilizations in which indigenous peoples' organizations played a major role. This is where the literatures on social movements and political parties meet: at the moment when the heightened state of mobilization and the euphoria created by the achievement of long-standing demands causes social movement leaders to see themselves not as outsiders trying to push into the political system, but as viable actors within a system whose institutions they have just helped to shape. These moments constitute strategic decision-making scenarios and are analyzed in detail in Chapters 3–6. Tarrow refers to this moment when he describes the choice of social movements in democracies to transform themselves into

political parties once they have tasted success in "finding legitimate channels" to express their opinions and have accumulated sufficient numbers
within the movement to make electoral competition appear to be a viable
option for pursuing its agenda within the state (1998: 84).

In all six countries indigenous peoples' organizations participated to
varying degrees in the "cycle of contention" surrounding major constitutional reforms. Participation was relatively more intensive and effective in
Colombia, Ecuador, and Venezuela, followed by Bolivia, with Argentine
and Peruvian Indians experiencing fair and poor levels of participation,
respectively. The greater the level of participation and success, the greater
the sense of confidence and euphoria generated by this experience and,
thus, the greater the probability that indigenous movements would seek to
move their informal political strategy to the formal sphere. Where indigenous candidates had won election to national constituent assemblies they
had the opportunity to prove their electoral strength and to forge alliances
with sympathetic delegates during the reform process. Where rights were
achieved, indigenous movements sought to gain congressional representation in order to influence the drafting of legislation implementing those
rights. Thus, the constitutional reform conjuncture had an impact on the
propensity of indigenous social movements to form political parties separate from the mechanical effect of the institutional changes that they
produced.

The Diffusion Effect

Indigenous movements and aspiring parties are influenced by the cross-
border diffusion of experiences in neighboring countries. This is particularly important for weaker indigenous movements with poor access to
resources because weaker movements pattern their activities on those
of more successful movements (Tarrow 1998: 189). Similarly, Kitschelt
expects that the success of left-libertarian parties in countries where conditions are favorable will inspire the formation of similar parties in countries
where they are less favorable (1989: 38). The stunning success of parties
in four South American countries, then, is likely to inspire indigenous
movements in neighboring countries to follow their example, despite the
existence of less favorable conditions.

The resource mobilization approach helped me to identify four
resources that appeared to make an impact on the decision to form a political party, as well as the electoral performance of indigenous movement–
sponsored parties: (1) the density and extension of organizational

networks for the highest-level indigenous organization in each country; (2) organizational unity within the indigenous peoples' movement in the country, or region of the country, where the party formed; (3) the maturity (in years) of the social movement organization that spawned the party; and (4) the percentage of subnational units with at least 25 percent indigenous population.

Dense Organizational Network of Affiliates

Dense networks of affiliates are likely to promote mobilization and to make those mobilizations successful (Foweraker 1995: 16). In the absence of financial resources, these solidary networks are the primary resource on which ethnic parties can draw during campaigns and organizations with strong ties to numerous organizations rooted in civil society will have an advantage in mobilizing their target constituency during elections. According to the social cleavage model of party system development, social cleavages must generate organizations with a firm institutional base in order for a new social cleavage to be represented in a party system so that this base can provide the organizational and human resources necessary for political campaigns, particularly in the absence of significant financial resources (Dalton et al. 1984: 458). The creation of an extensive, hierarchical network of social movement organizations also helps to promote political cohesion, which Dalton et al. find to be essential to the emergence of durable new political cleavages (1984: 473). These social movement networks are embedded in larger "movement webs" that link the movement's core members to sympathizers and that widen the pool of potential voters (Alvarez, Dagnino, and Escobar 1998: 16; Yishai 1994: 220). A dense network of affiliates, however, does not guarantee political party success, as Roberts discovered in his study of social movements in Chile and Peru (1998: 71–8).

Organizational Maturity of Indigenous Movements

The organizational maturity of an indigenous movement is measured by the years in existence of its highest-tier social movement organization – usually the national level, although in cases where a national organization was not formed regional organizations were examined. The longer a social movement organization has been in existence and the more political experience its leaders and members have, the more its members will feel a sense of loyalty to and collective identification with the organization. In addition, established social movement organizations have had the time

TABLE 2.3. *Maturity of indigenous social movement organizations prior to party formation*

Argentine Indigenous Organizations/Year Formed	Argentine Ethnic Parties/Year Formed	Time Elapsed
Asociación Indígena de la República Argentina (AIRA) (1975)		

Bolivian Indigenous Organizations/Year Formed	Bolivian Ethnic Parties/Year Formed	Time Elapsed
Confederación Sindical Unica de Trabajadores Campesinos de Bolivia (CSUTCB) (1979)	ASP/IPSP/MAS (1995) MIP (2000)	16 years 21 years
Comité Coordinador (1988) (coca growers)	ASP/IPSP/MAS (1995)	7 years
Confederación Indígena del Oriente Boliviano (CIDOB) (1982)		
Coordinadora de Pueblos Etnicas de Santa Cruz (CPESC) (1992)		

Colombian Indigenous Organizations/Year Formed	Colombian Ethnic Parties/Year Formed	Time Elapsed
Consejo Regional Indígena del Cauca (CRIC) (1972)	ASI (1991)	19 years
Autoridades Indígenas de Colombia (AICO) (1977)	AICO (1990)	13 years
Organización Nacional Indígena de Colombia (ONIC) (1982)	ONIC (1990)	8 years

Ecuadorian Indigenous Organizations/Year Formed	Ecuadorian Ethnic Parties/Year Formed	Time Elapsed
Federación Ecuatoriana de Indios (FEI) (1944)		
Federación Nacional de Organizaciones Campesinas, Indígenas y Negras (FENOCIN) (1968)		
Ecuador Runacunapac Riccharimui (ECUARUNARI) (1972)		
Confederación de Nacionalidades Indígenas de la Amazonía Ecuatoriana (CONFENIAE) (1979)	MUPP (1996)	17 years
Fed. Ecuatoriana de Indígenas Evangélicas (FEINE) (1980)	Amauta Jatari (mid-1990s)	15 years[a]
Confederación de Nacionalidades Indígenas del Ecuador (CONAIE) (1986)	MUPP (1996)	10 years

TABLE 2.3 *(continued)*

Peruvian Indigenous Organizations/Year Formed	Peruvian Ethnic Parties/Year Formed	Time Elapsed
Confederación Campesina del Peru (CCP) (1947)		
Confederación Nacional Agraria (CNA) (1971)		
Asociación Interétnica de la Selva Peruana (AIDESEP) (1979)	MIAP (1998)	19 years
Confederación de Nacionalidades Amazónicas del Perú (CONAP) (1987)		
Conferencia Permanente de los Pueblos Indígenas del Perú (COPPIP) (1998)		
Coordinadora Nacional de Comunidades Afectados por la Minería (CONACAMI) (1999)		
Venezuelan Indigenous Organizations/Year Formed	Venezuelan Ethnic Parties/Year Formed	Time Elapsed
Federación Indígena del Estado de Bolivar (FIB) (1973)	MOPEINDIGENA (2000)	27 years
Consejo Nacional Indio de Venezuela (CONIVE) (1989)	CONIVE (2000)	11 years
Organización Regional de Pueblos Indígenas de Amazonas (ORPIA) (1993)	PUAMA (1997)	4 years

a I was not able to ascertain the year that Amauta Jatari was formed. This figure is an estimate based on its mention in journalistic and academic accounts.

to attract domestic and international allies, to train and professionalize permanent staff, and to articulate a coherent program.

Table 2.3 presents the time elapsed between the establishment of a national, regional, or subnational indigenous organization and the formation by that organization of an ethnic party. The average time elapsed between movement formation and party formation for the nine parties listed is 14.33 years. It ranges from only four years (United Multiethnic People of Amazonas [PUAMA] in Venezuela), to nineteen years (Indigenous Social Alliance [ASI] in Colombia and MIAP in Peru). Thus, we may predict that it takes at least four years for a social movement organization to attain sufficient maturity to form a political party, and it is likely to take ten years longer.

Another component of organizational maturity is the unity of the indigenous movement within a country or region. Where indigenous movements form rival organizations it is likely that, should such organizations form ethnic parties, they will compete against each other and split the indigenous vote. All indigenous organizations and movements studied contain internal tensions and divisions. These are based on (1) regional differences, since indigenous groups from the coast, highlands, and rainforest have different developmental needs and histories of relations with the state; (2) interethnic rivalries, particularly when some groups have a history of dominating other, smaller groups; (3) ideological differences, which typically emerge between those preferring to forge class alliances with other popular sectors and those preferring to emphasize the ethnic basis of indigenous exploitation; and (4) personal conflicts concerning access to resources and leadership positions. Sometimes these conflicts are negotiated within existing indigenous organizations. Elsewhere, differences are too severe to maintain organizational unity and rival, parallel organizational structures develop.

Proportional Size, Dispersion, and Concentration of Indigenous Population

Most of the successful ethnic parties originated in an electoral district where the indigenous proportion of the population was high and then used this base to expand to other areas. The logic is compelling: in districts where the indigenous population is proportionally significant – once this population is politically incorporated and mobilized – if nonethnic parties do not address their demands or incorporate their leaders, ethnic parties are likely to form and win seats. I was only able to obtain complete demographic information by department, state, or province for five of the six countries because there is no reliable data for Argentina. In Table 2.4 data is presented on the percentage of departments with an indigenous majority, the percentage of departments that are at least one-quarter indigenous, the percentage having indigenous populations between 10 and 25 percent, and the percentage of departments with less than 10 percent indigenous population.

More than half of Bolivia's departments, one-fifth of Peru's departments, and 14 percent of Ecuador's provinces have indigenous majorities. In Colombia, three Amazonian departments have indigenous majorities (9 percent). In Venezuela one state (Amazonas) is quite close to a majority (49.7 percent of the population). We can expect that if ethnic

TABLE 2.4. *Dispersion and concentration of indigenous population*

Case	% of Subnational Units with Indigenous Majority	% of Subnational Units 25–50% Indigenous	% of Subnational Units 10–25% Indigenous	% of Subnational Units Less Than 10% Indigenous
Argentina	0% (0/23)	0% (0/23)	13% (3/23)	87% (20/23)
Bolivia	56.5% (5/9)	22.2% (2/9)	11.1% (1/9)	0% (0/9)
Colombia	9% (3/33)	6.1% (2/33)	3% (1/33)	81.8% (27/33)
Ecuador	14.3% (3/21)	28.6% (6/21)	4.8% (1/21)	52.4% (11/21)
Peru	20% (5/25)	8% (2/25)	32% (8/25)	40% (10/25)
Venezuela	0% (0/23)	0.04% (1/23)	0.04% (1/23)	91.3% (21/23)

Source: Bolivia, 2001 Censo Nacional de Población y Vivienda. Ecuadorian figures for highland provinces are based on Zamosc (1995). Other figures in Ecuador are based on Grijalva (1998). Peru, based on 1993 census. Colombia, based on 1990 municipal census taken by DANE. 1992 Venezuela, Censo Indígena Venezolana.

parties are able to compete, they eventually will do well in these districts. Significant indigenous minorities (25–50 percent of the population) are found in 22 percent of Bolivia's departments, 28 percent of Ecuador's provinces, 8 percent of Peru's departments, and 6.1 percent of Colombia's departments. It is likely that indigenous candidates and parties will gain office in these districts if nonindigenous parties number more than two or three, the number of seats available in the district exceeds two, or ethnic parties can form alliances with popular movements or existing parties. If we add these departments to those that are majority-indigenous, we get 78.7 percent in Bolivia, 42.9 percent in Ecuador, 28.0 percent in Peru, 15.1 percent in Colombia, and 0.04 percent in Venezuela. In the given proportion of electoral districts, indigenous parties have a good chance of winning representation. The fact that Venezuela's and Colombia's majority-indigenous districts are in sparsely populated lowland areas enhances their potential to achieve indigenous representation at the national level because fewer votes are needed to gain office in sparsely populated districts.

I did not explore a number of resources that may help explain why some indigenous organizations and movements form viable ethnic parties while others do not, such as variations in culture, identity, and geography. Indigenous peoples' diverse cultures and identities are experienced, practiced, and expressed in a myriad of ways. As Smith observes, in the precolonial period, core areas developed differently than areas on the periphery of Aztec, Maya, or Inca rule (2002: 11). These variations may affect the propensity of indigenous organizations to form political parties and the nature of the parties that are formed, as may the proximity of an indigenous group to centers of colonial domination and the economic model imposed during the colonial and postcolonial periods. But I leave these complex issues to anthropologists and historians. I also do not fully explore the importance of geography, apart from its interaction with electoral rules. For example, it is easier to organize indigenous peoples where land or river travel is relatively easy year round and where the climate and ecology support a relatively dense population. But I leave an analysis of the implications of variations in climate, altitude, and ecology to geographers.

CONCLUSION

Institutional changes, party system changes, and social movement factors were important in encouraging or discouraging the formation of ethnic parties, and in influencing their relative success, in all six countries. However, different variables within each of the three categories were relatively more salient in some countries compared to others, and the interactions among these variables differed in particular cases. These differences, as well as similarities among the cases, are emphasized in the chapters that follow.

3

"A Reflection of Our Motley Reality"

Bolivian Indians' Slow Path to Political Representation

> We are entering here – in the Congress – in order to sit ourselves down and
> see ourselves face to face with our oppressors; this is going to be a struggle
> of the mind, of the indigenous mind against the *q'ara* [white] mind, and
> there we are going to fight.
>
> Felipe Quispe, at closing ceremony of presidential campaign[1]

On the surface, Bolivia would appear to be a most-likely case of ethnic
party formation and success. The indigenous proportion of the population
constitutes more than 65 percent of the total and significant indigenous
populations are found in a majority of electoral districts. Indigenous social
movements have a long history of militant protest activity and exclusion
from political representation. The highland indigenous population is organized into dense networks of *campesino* (indigenous peasant) unions that
date back to the 1950s and earlier. Ethnic identities are strong and experienced a revival in the 1980s, when lowland indigenous groups formed
contemporary social movement organizations for the first time. Because
illiterates have had the vote since 1952, one would expect to see the emergence of successful ethnic parties after the transition to democracy in
1978–82. Indeed, ethnic parties were formed much earlier in Bolivia than
in any other country in South America. Two distinct waves of party formation and competition occurred. The first began with the transition to
democracy in 1978 and ended in the late 1980s. The second began in
1995 and ended in 2002. Multiple parties were formed in both waves.
However, although numerous tiny ethnic parties formed during the first

[1] Cited in *La Prensa* (La Paz) (2002g: 8).

wave, no ethnic party achieved viability until after 1995. Why did it take
so long?

Despite the auspicious conditions noted in the preceding text, indigenous leaders attempting to form independent electoral vehicles faced challenging obstacles. Most daunting have been institutional structures and
rules that elites designed to restrict access to the ballot and to centralize
political competition. These barriers did not begin to tumble until the mid-
1990s, when President Gonzalo Sánchez de Lozada led a constitutional
reform that included municipal decentralization and granted a modest
array of rights to indigenous peoples. Equally important in explaining
the delay is the relationship between indigenous social movements and
political parties, particularly those on the left. Since the 1930s, political parties have permeated and tried to manipulate indigenous peoples'
organizations. In a context of centralized politics, where considerable
financial resources are necessary to launch electoral campaigns, fledgling
indigenous parties repeatedly became dependent upon external sponsors,
particularly leftist parties. The internal fragmentation of the left and the
propensity of leftist parties to compete for the loyalty of particular indigenous leaders and organizations exacerbated the already fractious nature
of Bolivia's indigenous movement. Partisan alignments further fragmented a population already divided by ethnic, regional, and ideological
differences.

Given these obstacles, observers were stunned when viable ethnic parties emerged in 1995 and went on in 2002 to challenge the traditional
parties' grip on national power. Permissive institutional changes, the electoral failure of leftist parties after 1989, and the ability of charismatic
indigenous leaders to mobilize dense networks of organizational affiliates, finally enabled indigenous peoples to become major players in formal
politics.

INDIGENOUS SOCIAL MOVEMENTS IN BOLIVIA

Bolivia is the most indigenous country in South America, with Indians
constituting approximately 62.05 percent of the population of 8,274,325
(Rivero 2003: 10). Indians are a majority of the population in the highland
provinces of La Paz, Oruro, and Potosí, as well as in the valleys and lowlands of the departments of Cochabamba and Chuquisaca (see Table 3.1).
Once a primarily rural population, most Indians now live in urban areas,
particularly migrant neighborhoods formed around the cities of La
Paz, El Alto, and Cochabamba. The indigenous population is internally

TABLE 3.1. *Bolivian indigenous population by department, 1992/2001*

Department	1992			2001			
	Total	Indigenous	% Indigenous	Total	Total Aged 15+	Total Indigenous 15+	% Indigenous
Beni	276,174	80,582	29.18	362,521	202,169	66,217	32.75
Chiquisaca	453,756	336,354	74.13	531,522	308,386	202,204	65.57
Cochabamba	1,110,205	822,394	74.08	1,455,711	900,020	669,261	74.36
La Paz	1,900,786	1,242,786	65.38	2,350,466	1,501,970	1,163,418	77.46
Oruro	340,114	217,624	63.99	391,870	250,983	185,474	73.90
Pando	38,072	13,985	36.73	52,525	30,418	4,939	16.24
Potosí	645,889	538,313	83.34	709,013	414,838	347,847	83.85
Santa Cruz	1,364,389	621,122	45.52	2,029,471	1,216,658	456,102	37.49
Tarija	291,407	107,369	36.85	391,226	239,550	47,175	19.69
Total/average	6,420,792	3,980,529	61.99	8,274,325	5,064,992	3,142,637	62.05

Note: Indigenous population in 2001 census is only for population above age 15.

Sources: 1992 Censo Nacional de Población y Vivienda, cited in Prada Alcoreza (2002: 2). 2001 Censo Nacional de Población y Vivienda, online at www.ine.gov.bo/beyond/esn/Report Folders/Review/explorerp.asp.

diverse, with 37 distinct ethnic groups, including a 30,000-member Afro-Bolivian group the government classifies as "indigenous."[2] By far the largest groups are the Aymara (1,549,320) and Quechua (2,298,980), who are concentrated in the western highlands. The remaining 286,726 Indians live mainly in the eastern lowland departments of Santa Cruz and Beni. The largest groups there are the Guaraní (75,500), Chiquitano (61,520), and Moxeño (38,500) (VAIPO 1998: 35).

Internal fragmentation and conflict permeates the history of indigenous peoples' organizations and parties. The political rivalry between the Aymara and Quechua groups is particularly pronounced. The Aymara have led the campesino movement, sometimes espousing an exclusionary Aymara ethnonationalism, while the Quechua are more numerous but less politically organized and ethno-nationalistic. In the lowlands, leaders of smaller groups chafe against the dominance of the Guaraní and Chiquitano. But the most significant internal division, one also found in Colombia, Ecuador, and Peru, is between highland and lowland Indians, who have markedly different modes of economic and social organization and distinct histories of relations with political parties and the state. With few exceptions, until the late 1990s political activity for both indigenous populations evolved on separate tracks, meeting only under extraordinary circumstances.

In this section, I trace the development of the indigenous social movement organizations from which ethnic parties would emerge, paying particular attention to their organizational unity and maturity and the density of their networks of affiliates. In addition, I look at the evolution of relations between indigenous social movements and political parties. I also describe tensions within the indigenous movement because these have tended to retard the development of a unified movement.

The First Wave of Highland Indigenous Organizations

Relations between indigenous peoples and political parties began in the period following the Chaco War (1932–35) when ex-soldiers, frustrated with their leaders and the oligarchic state, became politically active. New revolutionary parties formed, such as the Partido Obrero Revolucionario and the National Revolutionary Movement (MNR), which gained the support of the emerging labor and campesino movements (Ticona

---

[2] Brought to Bolivia to work in the mines, the Afro-Bolivian population has assimilated into the Aymara group.

Alejo 2000: 30–1). After the 1952 Revolution the leadership of the campesino organizations was associated with political parties, particularly with the MNR, which had used the campesinos to win the revolution and assume power. In order to control them, the MNR incorporated campesinos into a state-sponsored sindicato structure. Grateful for the agrarian reform and for the right to vote, campesinos voted mainly for the MNR. In many cases they had no choice because opposition party ballots – which parties are responsible for distributing – didn't arrive in many rural locations (Ticona et al. 1995: 167). After the 1964 Barrientos coup peasant leaders exchanged their support for the military dictatorship for agrarian rights (Albó 1994a: 58; Ticona Alejo 2000: 36–8).

In 1968, General Barrientos announced a new tax plan. For the first time, indigenous campesinos publicly criticized him and formed independent campesino organizations and radical political movements. The most important of the new movements was the Katarista movement, which emerged in the Aymara highlands of the Department of La Paz in the late 1960s. It takes its name from the late eighteenth century Aymara leader Julián Apaza who led a rebellion against colonial rule under the *nom de guerre* Tupak Katari. The Spanish executed him in 1781 (Ticona Alejo 2000: 41–4). The dozens of organizations that emerged bearing the name of Tupak Katari can be divided into two camps with distinct ideologies: Indianism and Katarism.

Indianism emphasizes the ethnic basis of the subordination of the indigenous population and is overtly anti–Western and antiwhite. Indianists typically call for the return of the majority of Bolivia's land directly to ethnic authorities, the reconstruction of precolonial forms of authority, and the expulsion of Europeans. Indianists reject the labor-union model of organization as a Western imposition and reject, at least publicly, alliances with nonindigenous groups. In contrast, *Katarism* blends class consciousness with ethnic rights claims and calls for the reconstruction of the Bolivian state along ethnic criteria. The state envisioned is tolerant of ethnic diversity and incorporates both indigenous and Western forms of government. Kataristas sought alliances with nonindigenous social movements and leftist and populist political parties. Their less-ethnicist, more liberal-democratic and classist orientation gained them many nonindigenous adherents and, thus, greater access to political and financial resources than the Indianists. Not all Indians followed these two tendencies. A sector of the independent campesino movement strengthened relations with leftist parties and offered socialism as a solution to economic exploitation (Albó 1994a: 59).

Indianism's most famous proponent was Fausto Reynaga, who tried to form an indigenous political party, the Partido Indio de Bolivia, in the 1960s.[3] Like many politicians to follow, he chose the ruin of the ancient city of Tiwanaku (also spelled *Tiahuanacu*), in the spot that Indian rebel leader Tupak Katari had been executed, for the foundation ceremony, which was held November 15, on the anniversary of Katari's execution. The Partido Indio never had a real organization and was mainly symbolic (Ticona Alejo 2000: 44). Its ideology was too radical for most campesinos and at the time of its emergence most were still committed to patronage relations with the military and the MNR, which had led the 1952 social revolution, enfranchised the indigenous, and instituted agrarian reform (Canessa 2000). But Reynaga inspired a generation of leaders and cultivated symbols and discourses of rage and injustice that indigenous leaders would brandish thirty years later (Pacheco 1992: 35).

Katarists and Indianists gradually took over the government-sponsored peasant confederation, the National Confederation of Peasant Workers of Bolivia (CNTCB) in the early 1970s by winning adherents among the base–level organizations. But the Banzer coup later that month and the repression that followed cut short independent indigenous political activity. Many Indianists and Katarists fled into exile, together with many leftist militants. Despite threats against his life, Katarista Genaro Flores returned from exile in Chile in 1972 to form a clandestine campesino organization to resist the dictatorship. In 1973, he circulated a "Manifesto of Tiahuanacu," which presented the philosophy of the Katarista movement. Under the section entitled "The Political Parties and the Campesinos," Flores declared that political parties had never represented their true interests – not the MNR, nor the leftist parties, nor the party of General Barrientos. The manifesto declares:

If the peasants have voted for them, it was because they had no other electoral choices. We had no party we could call our own. . . . For a balance of interests and representation to exist, the peasants must have their own party that will reflect their social, cultural and economic interests. This is the only way we can truly and positively take part in the political process, and the only way to facilitate an authentic and integral rural development.   (Manifesto of Tiahuanacu 1980: 25)

Similarly, after he returned from exile, Indianist Luciano Tapia established an organization to liberate the Aymara people, the Tupak Katari Indian Movement (MITKA). Its early years were difficult because it lacked

---

[3] The party was originally founded as the Aymara Kechua Indian Party (PIAK). The name was changed to Indian Party of Bolivia (PIB) in July 1966 (Rocha 1992: 249–51).

resources and suffered repression (Tapia 1995: 330–2, 363). In the absence of free elections, its prospects were limited.

The government's 1973 massacre of at least thirteen Quechua campesinos in Tolata, Cochabamba, gave an additional boost to the incipient Katarist and Indianist movements in the Aymara highlands. The shooting of unarmed campesinos protesting agricultural policies outraged the Aymara and radicalized their nascent political movement (Albó 1994a: 58; Rivera Cusicanqui 1987: 144–6, 1991: 18–19). Independent campesino activities surged in 1978, when the first of a series of elections were held during Bolivia's tumultuous transition to democracy. In 1979, Bolivia's umbrella labor organization, the Bolivian Workers Central (COB), convened a congress in order to form a unified campesino organization. At that 1979 congress, the most important contemporary campesino organization, the Unitary Syndical Confederation of Peasant Workers of Bolivia (CSUTCB) was born. Despite calls for unity, Katarists and Indianists remained divided between those leaning toward the MNR and those supporting the leftist coalition Popular Democratic Unity (UDP) (Ticona Alejo 2000: 43).

In December 1979, a CSUTCB roadblock paralyzed transportation throughout the country for more than a week, effectively preventing the flow of food to the cities.[4] The immense mobilization, the largest since the 1952 Revolution, signaled the return of the peasantry as an independent national political actor (Healy n.d.: 3). Notwithstanding the more open climate after the return to elected, civilian rule, the CSUTCB encountered numerous difficulties as a political organization. Now independent from the state, it was no longer subsidized and its leaders lost access to government employment. Because it required living in La Paz, leadership became a financial hardship. Many leaders succumbed to the seduction of political parties, which offered financial resources in exchange for political loyalty; others took salaried government jobs.

When individual leaders within the Indianist and Katarist tendencies began to form political parties, existing parties, particularly from the left, attempted to infiltrate them. As the campesino movement gained in importance it became a field of battle for political parties seeking to control indigenous voters. In the mid-1980s, the CSUTCB began allowing some nondelegates – academics and representatives of political parties and nongovernmental organizations (NGOs) – to attend its congresses. These

---

[4] Campesinos were protesting an International Monetary Fund–mandated plan to maintain low agricultural prices while increasing consumer prices (Healy n.d.: 3).

outsiders attempted to influence the proceedings by funding congressional activities and the travel, lodging, and food expenses of the delegates. Because the most important decisions are made at the end of the multiday congresses, parties that can fund the continued presence of their adherents are more likely to prevail in the selection of the leadership and the design of the organization's political program. After 1985, with the labor movement suffering a severe decline in the face of economic austerity policies and massive layoffs in the mining sector, political parties more aggressively tried to influence the campesino movement and the CSUTCB leadership. Elections for leadership became struggles among different political parties and exacerbated the existing tendency toward fragmentation caused by personal rivalries and ideological differences (Ticona Alejo 2000: 96–118). Partisan interference exploded into open conflict during the 1989 CSUTCB IV Extraordinary Congress, when two rival sets of leftist coalitions struggled openly for control of the organization.

Manipulation by political parties exacerbated the problem of leadership formation and retention. The tradition in indigenous communities is to rotate leadership because it is a burden that takes leaders away from their families and economic activities. As a result, leaders are typically inexperienced and must rely on advisors from NGOs or political parties to help them to operate in the national political environment. Often they find themselves used or manipulated by these advisors. Because most of the advising is done clandestinely in order to maintain an appearance of independence, gossip circulates regarding which leader is with which party. If leaders deviate from the tradition of rotation and remain in office for an extended period, they are subject to accusations of corruption and co-optation from their base, from whom they tend to grow more distant, given the absence of resources to facilitate regular communication with campesino communities (Ticona Alejo 2000: 96–113). Leaders that emerged with a strong following were co-opted by political parties, which often resulted in the loss of support. Leaders attracted by the financial resources that political parties could provide lacked an incentive to create independent electoral vehicles.

Ticona divides relations between the CSUTCB and political parties into two stages. In the first stage, the CSUTCB was allied openly with parties that had been generated by the same Katarist/Indianist movement from which the CSUTCB emerged. At the same time, the organization's leaders enjoyed more covert relations with leftist parties, particularly the UDP coalition (Ticona Alejo 2000: 116–17). In the second stage, beginning in the mid-1980s, rivalries among political parties became more salient as campesino leaders struggled for control of the organization and parties struggled to control campesino leaders who could deliver electoral support (Ticona et al. 1995: 169). In the 1990s, the politicization of the campesino movement increased as CSUTCB leaders participated in elections as candidates of political parties – often without the required permission of the organization (statement of Paulino Guarachi, published in Ticona Alejo 2000: 209). But indigenous militants were forced to work in a subordinate position toward mestizos (Rivera Cusicanqui 1993: 107). This subordination was manifested in the lower placement of indigenous candidates on party lists and the ideological predominance of classist analysis and economic themes, while cultural identities and the problem of racism were submerged (Guarachi 1994: 228). On balance, the involvement of political parties had a mainly negative impact on the campesino movement. Relations continued to be vertical – from the political parties down to the campesinos – as they had been during the period of MNR tutelage. Kataristas complained that the parties refused to engage them in a dialogue of equals and openly discriminated against their indigenous "allies" (Ticona Alejo 2000: 136–7; Ticona et al. 1995: 194).

In the late 1980s, the mostly Quechua-speaking coca growers seized control of the CSUTCB from the Aymara Katarists (Healy 1991: 98; Ticona et al. 1995: 68). The coca growers' movement coalesced in the lowland coca-growing regions of Cochabamba, particularly the Chapare. Many of the growers were migrants from higher elevations who began moving to this area looking for agricultural land in the 1960s. With the assistance of the COB, intellectuals, and opposition parties, the colonists of central Cochabamba formed a confederation of colonists in 1971 – the same year that Katarists and Indianists in La Paz reached the height of their mobilization prior to the Banzer coup (Ticona et al. 1995: 64). The influx of migrants to Cochabamba increased dramatically in the mid-1980s as the Paz Estenssoro government's economic austerity policies caused massive unemployment, particularly among miners. After being expelled from the mining zones, thousands of unemployed miners and their families moved to the Chapare and the Yungas of La Paz and cultivated coca leaf for export (Patzi Paco 1999: 49).

Political mobilization began shortly after the democratic transition in 1983 with road blockades. By 1984, coca growers began forming their own federations to present their agricultural demands and to protest increased government eradication efforts (Healy 1988). Under U.S. pressure, in 1986, and again in 1988, the Bolivian government intensified its anticoca efforts in an attempt to forcibly eradicate all coca leaf destined for export.[5] Battles raged between the drug eradication agency UMOPAR (Mobile Rural Patrol Unit) and the growers' self-defense committees. The prevalence of ex-miners among the coca growers infused the movement with the militancy characteristic of that sector – traditionally the labor movement's most militant. The common experience of government repression helped to unify the movement and to strengthen ties between leaders and their base (Patzi Paco 1999: 85; Ticona et al. 1995: 67–8).[6]

In 1988, the five Cochabamba coca growers federations formed a Comité Coordinador. By 1990, there were approximately 50,000 coca growers in the Chapare (Healy n.d.: 17), organized into 160 local sindicatos and thirty subfederations (*centrales*), which are affiliated with five federations (Healy 1991: 88–9). Another five federations united the coca growers in the Yungas of La Paz (CSUTCB n.d.). In the absence of local government in this part of Bolivia – the country would not achieve complete municipal government coverage until 1995 – the sindicatos acted as local governments, adjudicating property limits and setting transport fares. They even collected "taxes" on coca leaf markets in the Chapare and used them to fund local public works programs (Healy 1991: 89). By the late 1990s, there were approximately 300,000 indigenous migrants in the Chapare–Chimoré region (Albó 1999a: 476).

The coca growers defend a traditional cultural practice that has come to symbolize indigenous resistance to the Bolivian state and Bolivian resistance to U.S. imperialism. Andean peoples have used coca leaf, a mild stimulant, for centuries for ceremonial and cultural purposes, to promote social cohesion, and to reduce hunger and fatigue (Zurita Vargas 2003: 50). As coca growers' leader Evo Morales declared, "coca constitutes the flag of unity and struggle of the Aymara and Quechua peoples" (my translation, cited in Rivero Pinto 2003: 13). Félix Santos, who represents the coca growers–based party MAS in the congress (2002–7), echoes this sentiment: "[C]oca is part of our philosophy and culture, is for us the essence of our identity. It is nourishment, medicine. . . . Thus, when they say that they must eradicate coca, they are saying that they must kill the

---

[5] Law 1008 of 1988 equated coca leaf with cocaine and presumed coca growers to be guilty, requiring them to prove their innocence (Albó 1999a: 476). The cultivation of coca leaf for traditional purposes and its consumption in tea or other products is legal in Bolivia.

[6] According to Bolivia's Defensor del Pueblo (human rights ombudsperson), since 1987 the conflict between coca growers and the Bolivian state has left fifty-seven dead and 500 wounded by gunshots in the Cochabamba tropics, while another 4,000 coca growers have been detained without due process in jail (*La Prensa* 2002d: 15).

Aymaras and Quechuas" (my translation, cited in Rivero Pinto 2003: 13).
As a cultural struggle, the defense of coca resonates with the majority of
indigenous Bolivians who don't grow coca leaf (Gustafson 2003: 49). The
coca growers' discourse of a struggle for cultural and religious freedom,
combined with a nationalist discourse that defends coca consumption as
a Bolivian tradition, earned them the support of nonindigenous social
sectors (Patzi Paco 1999: 86; see also Healy 1991: 93–4). During the
1980s, the Chapare movement gained support from influential actors in
Cochabamba, such as the department's Civic Committee, human rights
organizations, anthropologists, lawyers, and a sector of the media.[7] The
September 1994 March for Sovereignty and Dignity helped to consolidate
the coca growers' movement and attract public support. More than ten
thousand marchers participated in that event. Additional marches were
organized in 1995, 1996, and 1998 (Patzi Paco 1999: 89; Ticona et al.
1995: 69). The 1994 march made Evo Morales, an Oruro migrant with
both Aymara and Quechua parents, a national political figure. A 1994
media poll named Morales, who had been imprisoned at the beginning of
the 1994 march, "Man of the Year" (my translation, Ticona et al. 1995:
69n16; *Latin American Weekly Report* 2002a: 53).

Despite its problems, the CSUTCB is the largest indigenous organization in the country, with affiliates in every department. Campesinos
are organized into local subcentrals, which are organized into approximately 200 centrals corresponding to the provincial level. Federations in
each of the country's nine departments unite the centrals. There are also
twenty-six regional or special federations affiliated with CSUTCB, as well
as lowland indigenous and colonists organizations (CSUTCB n.d.).[8]

[7] Despite the movement's cultural content, its main goal is economic, since tens of thousands
of growers and their families depend on the crop for their livelihood and have no economic
alternatives. Although there is a legal domestic market for coca leaf, most coca leaf grown
in the Chapare is destined for cocaine production (Albó 1999a: 476; Patzi Paco 1999:
49–50).

[8] In the late 1980s, a movement emerged to reconstitute the traditional highland *ayllu*, a
pre-Conquest form of social and territorial organization that consists of a kinship network
governed by a system of authorities headed by a *mallku*. Until the 1952 Revolution, ayllu
authorities acted as intermediaries between the state and indigenous populations. Afterward, the MNR-imposed peasant-union structure replaced them. The ayllu reconstruction
movement seeks to displace that structure, now seen as politicized, co-opted, and decultur-
alized by the state and political parties, and to reject "foreign" and "imposed" authority
structures. Beginning in the late 1980s, indigenous communities in the departments of La
Paz, Oruro, and Potosí began reconstituting their ayllu authority structures and forming
regional federations of ayllus. In 1997, an umbrella organization, the Consejo de Ayllus y

Indigenous Movements in the Lowlands

Lowland indigenous peoples comprise a substantial portion of the rural population of the departments of Beni, Santa Cruz, and Pando. No organizations worked specifically on indigenous rights in the eastern lowlands until 1976, and no outside popular organizations sought to organize lowland Indians, who they considered to be relics of the past (Riester 1985: 55). Independent local and regional organizations were formed after 1978, and this activity intensified in the 1980s. The Indigenous Confederation of Eastern Bolivia, later Indigenous Confederation of the East and Amazon of Bolivia (CIDOB) emerged from a series of meetings organized mainly at the initiative of the Guaraní between 1978–82, with assistance from the anthropological NGO Assistance for the Indigenous Communities of Eastern Bolivia (APCOB) (CIDOB 1995: 27; Riester 1985: 60–5). Once the Guaraní had been organized, their leaders reached out to the Ayoreo and authorities from both groups sought relations with the Chiquitanos and Guarayos. The four peoples formed CIDOB in 1982 at a congress in Santa Cruz attended by eighty indigenous leaders representing communities inhabited by roughly 80,000 Indians. They invited the CSUTCB to this founding congress (CIDOB 1995: 43; Pessoa 1998: 175; Riester 1985: 61).

CIDOB helped individual language groups and regional movements to establish their own allied organizations. In addition to federations and centrals, which join indigenous communities in a given territorial space in a manner similar to the *sindicato* structure of the highlands, CIDOB affiliates include the umbrella organizations of particular ethnic groups, as well as multiethnic department-level confederations (Gustafson 2002). During the 1980s, lowland organizations received financial and technical assistance from private development institutions, NGOs, churches, as well as international financial institutions (Patzi Paco 1999: 50–1). This enabled them to develop permanent offices and full-time leaders. In 1989, CIDOB kept the familiar acronym, but changed its name to Confederación Indígena del Oriente y Amazonía de Bolivia in order recognize the group's geographic expansion (CIDOB 1995: 28).[9]

In 1990, CIDOB affiliate Indigenous Peoples Central of the Beni (CPIB) organized a March for Territory and Dignity. On August 15, more than

---

Markas del Qullasuyu (CONAMAQ) was established, with an office in La Paz (Choque and Mamani 2001: 218–19). This organization was just beginning to become a coherent collective actor as this manuscript went to press.

[9] According to Gustafson (2002), in the late 1990s CIDOB dropped the "oriente" from the name of the organization in order to present itself as a national organization.

700 marchers left the Benian capital of Trinidad for a thirty-five-day walk to La Paz. CIDOB leaders accompanied the marchers, who were joined along the way by hundreds of supporters, including highland Indians (Rivera Cusicanqui 1991: 23). Ultimately CPIB secured its main goal: collective title to more than two million hectares of land, which grew to nine million after subsequent presidential decrees. The march dramatically raised awareness of the existence and contemporary demands of Bolivia's indigenous peoples in a way that gained more sympathy and support from white and *mestizo* (mixed race) Bolivians than had the more violent, radical actions of the highland movement. It also made a national figure of CPIB leader Marcial Fabricano, who would later lead CIDOB and run for vice president with the small leftist party Free Bolivia Movement (MBL).

By 1994, CIDOB had experienced twelve years of institutional development, had weathered internal disputes, expanded its geographic reach, and obtained external funding and key allies (CIDOB 1995: 32). It had created a six-tiered organizational structure that encompassed four regional organizations – CPIB, the Indigenous Central of the Amazon Region of Bolivia (CIRABO), which unites indigenous communities in Pando and northern Beni, the Consejo Yuqui, and the Ethnic Coordinator of Santa Cruz (CESC). CESC was formed between 1992 and 1994 to represent Indians in the department of Santa Cruz so that Santa Cruz–based CIDOB could focus on the role of representing the group nationally and internationally (CIDOB 1995: 44–6). It later added the word *Pueblos* (Peoples) to its name, becoming CPESC. As CIDOB deteriorated as an organization between 1997 and 2002, owing to internal rivalries as well as a rift between its more moderate and more radical factions, CPESC became the more dynamic organization. Below the four regional organizations are twenty-four subregional ones, some uniting single ethnic groups and others that are multiethnic in nature (CIDOB 1995: 49). The fourth tier consists of thirty-nine "microregional" organizations, mainly representing a single people, organized into ethnic federations or *capitanías*. For example, the Guaraní organization, Asamblea del Pueblo Guaraní, unites twelve Guaraní *capitanías* and seven zonal organizations (CIDOB 1995: 50). At this level, indigenous authority systems prevail. The fifth level comprises zonal organizations of single ethnic groups that are affiliated with the organizations in level four. The lowest level consists of multifamily communities, which number between 883 and 969, depending on the source (CIDOB 1995: 43). By 2000, CIDOB had included four additional regional organizations representing the Amazonian regions of Cochabamba and La Paz, as well as a new Pando organization. It must be

emphasized that at the lower tiers, particularly in remote areas, there may
be little or no knowledge of CIDOB's existence among Indians outside the
leadership structure.

Notwithstanding this extensive organizational structure, a 1995 audit
of the organization instigated by external funders revealed a number of
organizational problems. The auditors observed:

> The rapid growth of CIDOB generated a series of maladjustments and internal
> problems. In general, we can say that these are due to the asymmetrical advance of
> the organization that, on the one hand, grew in importance and saw itself obligated
> to assume new roles and, on the other, did not generate new internal organiza-
> tional structures that permitted it to confront successfully the new challenges.
> (my translation; CIDOB 1995: 80)

Among the problems mentioned are the lack of a budgeting process to
ensure the proper allocation of funds; the ideological and organizational
dependence of many of its member organizations on evangelical missions;
the co-optation of its leaders by the state; and a pronounced distancing
from its bases, as the organization spent more time dealing with national
and international actors (CIDOB 1995: 82). Nevertheless, in 1996 CIDOB
assumed its most confrontational posture yet toward the Bolivian state in
response to the Sánchez de Lozada government's efforts to enact an agrarian reform law contrary to their dearest interest: the collective titling of
indigenous territories. With the CSUTCB and the colonists' organization
Syndical Confederation of Bolivian Colonists (CSCB), CIDOB organized
a march to protest the proposed law. CIDOB abandoned the march mid-
way after signing an agreement with the government that recognized its
key demands, leaving the CSUTCB and the colonists to continue alone.
The decision added tension to the already difficult relations between the
lowland and highland movements. In addition, within CIDOB a gulf
was growing between more conciliatory leaders like CPIB leader Marcial
Fabricano, who were willing to negotiate with the government, and a more
radical element, which accused the former of selling out the movement in
exchange for government jobs and resources.

UNDERSTANDING ETHNIC PARTY FORMATION

The five decision-making scenarios presented in the following text share
some similarities. First, indigenous leaders tried to form parties even under
extremely adverse institutional conditions. An institutional environment
that restricted the formation of new parties prevailed from the beginning

of the period under study until the 1995 municipal decentralization. For example, various laws have instituted a de facto 3 percent threshold to maintain party registration since 1979, when an electoral law was enacted that required parties not receiving 50,000 votes to share the costs of printing ballots (Birnir 2000: 21). Fines and the loss of a party's registration also have been imposed on parties receiving less than 3 percent of the vote. Many indigenous political parties unable to pay the fines lost their registration in the 1980s and 1990s. In addition, the National Electoral Court has disqualified the registration of many indigenous parties for small infractions, often without merit, according to their leaders. A related problem is the fact that only formally registered political parties may compete in elections (until December 2004). This requirement existed in all of the Andean countries after the transition to democracy, but was dropped in the others in the 1990s. Finally, until 1995 virtually all Bolivian elections were national elections and all political parties had highly centralized structures. National legislative seats were elected from large districts through PR using the d'Hondt seat-allocation method, which favors large parties.[10] Few municipal districts existed and fewer still elected their own government officials.

Second, indigenous leaders sought to form parties notwithstanding strong competition from existing parties, particularly on the left. The electoral left surged at the dawn of the democratic transition in 1978. Most of the left – including the new Aymara indigenous parties formed in the 1970s – united behind Hernan Siles Zuazo and the leftist UDP coalition. In 1980, the UDP won the elections with 38.7 percent of the vote. Outside the UDP, the Socialist Party (SP–1) gained an additional 8.7 percent, bringing the combined share of the left to 47.4 percent (see Table 3.2). The disastrous economic performance of the Siles government led to early elections in 1985 and the enduring decline of leftist parties (Domingo 2001: 143; McDonald and Ruhl 1989: 414). The collapse of the UDP generated divisions within one of its larger constituent parties, the Movement of the Revolutionary Left (MIR), which ran three lists in 1985. That year the combined total for the left fell to 29.3 percent. The rump MIR gradually moved toward the center and can no longer be

---

[10] The exception to this was the 1993 national elections, when this system shifted to the Sainte-Lague formula, which favors smaller parties. This resulted in an increase in the representation of small parties. The system was changed back to d'Hondt in 1997 and a 3 percent threshold was established for representation in half of the Chamber of Deputies.

TABLE 3.2. *Bolivia: Vote share for dominant and leftist parties*

Election	Combined Votes Dominant Parties MNR + ADN + MIR	+ Condepa + UCS	Combined Votes Leftist Parties	ENPS
1980(P/L)	37%		47.4%	4.12
1985(P/L)	63.9%		14.3%	4.32
1989(P/L)	65.3%	76.3%	29.3%	3.92
1993(P/L)	54.1%	80.8%	6%	4.17
1995(M)	42%	75%	16.3%	
1997(P/L)	56.7%	88.4%	6.2%	5.07
1999(M)	61%	66.9%	7.3%	
2002(P/L)	42.17%	48.1%	21.6%	4.82

Notes: Dominant parties are MNR, ADN, MIR, Condepa, UCS. Leftist parties are UDP, MIR until 1989, MBL, IU, PS-1, PCB, MAS, Partido Socialista (PS). (P/L) joint presidential and legislative. Figures do not include uni-nominal ballot results for half chamber of deputies, after 1997.
Sources: Gamarra and Malloy (1995: 399–433); www.georgetown.edu/pdba, Romero Ballivian (1998). Previously published in Van Cott (2003c: 757).

categorized as a leftist party after 1989. That year the left consisted of the MBL[11] and a handful of Marxist parties. Thereafter the left's vote share in national elections would not exceed 6.2 percent until 2002. The left's poor showing in 1997's national elections left most leftist parties on the brink of extinction (*La Prensa* [online], June 4, 2001).

After decades of working with leftist parties, indigenous movement leaders had grown frustrated with the interference, manipulation, deceit, and racism that permeated these alliances. The electoral decline of the left after 1989, just as indigenous organizations were gaining mobilizational strength and public support, gave indigenous leaders more leverage vis-à-vis leftist party militants and intellectuals. Ethnic parties formed after 1995 greatly benefited from the availability of leftist parties that were legally registered but politically stagnant, as well as experienced leftist militants, who were needed to fill the required slots on party registration lists, and who had no other viable option.

The 1995 municipal decentralization and other reforms of the era inspired experienced indigenous leaders to reconsider the possibility of forming an independent electoral vehicle after many had rejected the

---

[11] The MBL became the most significant leftist party of the late 1980s and 1990s (Arauco and Belmont 1997: 125–9). Like the MIR, the MBL drifted toward the center in order to participate in government with the MNR in 1993–7 and 2002–7.

option following a decade of frustration and poor results. Indigenous movements in the highlands and in the lowland coca-growing regions were savvy enough about politics to understand the enormous advantage the new rules would give them, since their constituents are geographically concentrated within the new municipal districts. Conversely, in the low-lands, where urban voters decided district elections, indigenous leaders expected that an indigenous electoral vehicle could not win, even if it captured the entire indigenous vote. They pursued other strategies.

Strategic Decision-Making Scenario I

Leaders of both the Katarist and Indianist movements formed political parties in 1978. The two tendencies originally were more or less organizationally coherent – the Katarists affiliated with the Movimiento Revolucionario Tupak Katari, and the Indianists with the Movimiento Indio Tupak Katari – but both parties later fractured repeatedly. Luciano Tapia began forming the MITKA in the early 1970s. According to Tapia's account, he had heard that forming a political party did not require a great number of people; parties had won legislative seats with only two or three collaborators. He sought out intellectual Fausto Reynaga and made contacts in the various colonist organizations. In 1973, the Banzer government arrested Tapia and sent him to a jail full of political prisoners, including many from the leftist MIR. While in prison, Tapia learned about Marxism and met another important MITKA leader, Constantino Lima (1996: 331–44). Although MITKA was born through Tapia's efforts in 1971, the Banzer military coup and the repression that followed delayed its formal establishment and registration with the National Electoral Court (CNE) until April 1978 (Rocha 1992: 258; Tapia 1995: 373).

The Katarista party Tupak Katari Revolutionary Movement (MRTK) was formed in April 1978 as the political arm of the Tupak Katari National Confederation of Campesinos (CNCTK). Thus, from the beginning it had a wider social base in the Aymara community and a more solid organizational structure than the MITKA. But MRTK leaders were more urbanized and educated in Western ideas than the average campesino; their emphasis on ethnic identity resonated less with the larger base of campesinos, who were more focused on economic issues (Rocha 1992: 254). Founders Genaro Flores, Macabeo Chila, and Víctor Hugo Cárdenas aimed to attract the support of students, intellectuals, and the disaffected classes, and to appeal to a broad sector of popular organizations and working-class parties, while cultivating campesino organizations as its base (Rocha 1992: 254). The party's raison d'etre was presented by Macabeo Chila in a 1978 interview:

In Bolivia there have existed dozens of political parties. . . . None of them represent the interests and aspirations of the campesino family. Neither the liberals nor the conservatives; neither do the nationalists of diverse nuances that parade in turn through the Burnt Palace [the presidential residence] embody the very own essence of the campesinos. The state in their hands has always been an apparatus of oppression. . . . This is, in synthesis, the reason that accompanied the founding of the MRTK as a political instrument of liberation of the people, sustained fundamentally by the campesino class of Bolivia, constituted by aymaras, quechuas, cambas, chapacos, guaraníes, in addition to other ethnic groups catalogued as rural workers.   (my translation; cited in Rocha 1992: 254)

Chila's evaluation of relations between political parties and campesinos is strikingly similar in language and tone to statements made by indigenous political leaders throughout South America.

The final significant effort to form an ethnic party in the 1980s was the Eje de Convergencia Patriótica. It was intended to be an alliance between whites and Indians, but indigenous members claim that the whites never understood the Indians' demands. Indians left the alliance to form their own, more autonomous party, Eje Comunero, which was among the first parties to take up the struggle of the coca growers (Eje Comunero 1989: 13). After a number of leaders left to join the leftist parties MBL and MIR, the remainder formed a party that was to have a more "indigenous face," Eje Pachacuti[12] (Ticona Alejo 2000: 137; interview, Hugo Salvatierra, July 3, 2002). This officially was formed at a November 1992 meeting convened for another purpose by a proindigenous NGO.[13] The party (also known as Movimiento Pachacuti) was formed with the intention of participating in the 1993 elections. After several more meetings, it became more institutionalized and a meeting was arranged with Víctor Hugo Cárdenas, leader of the Tupak Katari Revolutionary Movement of Liberation (MRTKL), the most successful fragment of the Katarista

---

[12] *Pachacuti* is a Quechua/Quichua word with complex, multiple meanings. Rivera Cusicanqui; (1991: 19) says it means "disruption of the universe," which could mean *catastrophe* or *renovation* (1991: 23). The CSUTCB translates *Pachakuti* as "the return to independent life, the recuperation of our own political and religious forms in order to undertake the road to the future" (CSUTCB 1996: 66). Canessa translates *Pachakuti* as "the turning of the earth – literally, a revolution." Because *kuti* also may be translated as *return* it may evoke the fabled return of Tupaj Katari (Canessa 2000: 126).

[13] The purpose was to discuss the reasons for the failure of the Assembly of Original Nations and Peoples, which had been planned for Columbus Day, the previous month.

tendency, who agreed to form an alliance with the Eje Pachakuti for the 1993 elections.

However, Cárdenas already had begun talks with the MNR (Albó 1994a; Patzi Paco 1999: 76). After the MNR-MRTKL alliance was announced, Eje Pachakuti denounced Cárdenas as a traitor (Patzi Paco 1999: 76). The Eje was betrayed again when its vice presidential candidate, mestizo Ramiro Barrenechea, won the only seat in the Chamber of Deputies for the party. Barrenechea, head of the mestizo leftist party Eje de Convergencia Patriótica, which loaned its registration to the Eje Pachakuti in exchange for the vice presidential spot, was responsible for submitting the party's list of candidates to the CNE. At the last minute he erased the name of the indigenous candidate that was supposed to head the list, replacing it with his own (Patzi Paco 1999: 77). CSUTCB General-Secretary Paulino Guarachi commented on the problem of deceitful behavior by non-Indians in his November 1993 report to the organization: "The Bolivian campesinos affirm that the electoral promises must be complied with and we do not want to continue being tricked by those parties" (my translation; cited in Ticona Alejo 2000: 191).[14]

In sum, a highly politicized group of mostly Aymara intellectuals, frustrated with their experience with existing parties, formed their own organizations in the late 1970s and 1980s in order to provide professional opportunities for themselves and to fill the vacuum of representation for indigenous people.

Strategic Decision-Making Scenario II

By 1992, the CSUTCB had become devoted mainly to the defense of the coca growers, notwithstanding the fact that they made up approximately 10 percent of the national campesino population (Healy 1991: 114n2). In the early 1990s, coca growers began to discuss in earnest the possibility of forming a "political instrument" that would increase their influence within the government and enable them to overturn its coca eradication policies. Alejo Véliz, who would be the party's 1997 presidential candidate, maintains that forming a party was the next logical step in the maturation of the campesino movement. By 1994, the Quechua coca

[14] The Eje Pachakutik participated in elections throughout the 1990s. By 2002, the bulk of its nonindigenous leaders ended up in the government, the NFR, or center-right parties, while the majority of the campesino leaders, such as Juan de la Cruz Willka, joined the MAS. Interview, Hugo Salvatierra, July 3, 2002.

growers movement had achieved a certain level of political consensus and mobilization. Movement leaders decided that the purely social movement form of struggle would not be sufficient to achieve their demands and that for the "final conquest" it would be necessary to gain access to democratic political space (interview, Alejo Véliz, July 2001). As another leader put it: "We saw that being organized only at the level of a peasant union was insufficient. We had to move into the political arena" (Zurita Vargas 2003: 50–1).

The idea of forming an electoral vehicle had been discussed at many previous CSUTCB conferences since the early 1990s. The need for a new, independent campesino political instrument was ratified at CSUTCB congresses held in 1994, 1995, and 1996. The decision reflected a growing disenchantment with leftist parties, which had sought to control the movement. Weakened by the 1985 defeat of the UDP coalition, leftist parties had sought to increase their electoral strength by taking up the coca growers' cause (Healy 1991: 104). For example, MBL and Partido Socialista legislators opposed coca eradication legislation. In 1989, the leftist coalition United Left (IU) (organized in 1988 to unite the MBL, Partido Comunista, and an MIR splinter group) formally declared support for the coca-leaf producers as the vanguard of antiimperialism and the guardians of Andean culture. Support for the coca growers enabled the IU to increase its vote share in Cochabamba's coca-growing zones from 1.76 percent in 1985, to 10.17 percent in 1987 and 33.16 percent in 1989 (Healy 1991: 106). But the coca growers were not satisfied with the results of these alliances because leftist parties had little influence in the national government.

The 1994–5 constitutional reform opened up considerably the institutional environment for new political parties. No constituent assembly was held in Bolivia during the period studied. Instead, between 1993–7 President Sánchez de Lozada reformed the constitution in secrecy and pushed the reform through a congress where the government held a majority. The indigenous organization CIDOB and some affiliates of the peasant organization CSUTCB privately lobbied the Sánchez de Lozada administration and national legislators for a constitutional regime more favorable to indigenous peoples. Although leaders of these organizations were intensely involved in the discussions, there were no major mobilizations in favor of the reforms. In fact, when I interviewed indigenous leaders and their advisers in 1997, many told me that they had opposed any reform of the constitution because they feared losing corporate rights gained during the 1952 Revolution. Following the promulgation of the new constitution in 1995 – together with important restructuring laws, such as the 1994 Law of Popular Participation, the 1995 Law of Administrative Decentralization, as well as laws affecting indigenous rights in education, agriculture, and land holding – many indigenous leaders, particularly the national leadership of the CSUTCB, denounced the new laws as *"leyes malditas"* (damned laws) (Van Cott 2000b). The positive political implications of the reforms were not yet clear.

Because there was no constituent assembly, and because many indigenous leaders opposed the reforms, we do not find the intense political mobilization of the indigenous population around constituent assembly elections and in favor of indigenous constitutional rights that occurred in Colombia, Ecuador, and Venezuela. In Bolivia, there was no sense of euphoria among the indigenous population resulting from a great achievement. Indigenous representatives did not have the opportunity to forge alliances with representatives of political parties and civil society, as they did in other countries. However, a number of key leaders of the indigenous movement saw an opportunity to take advantage of the new reforms and to ensure that rights won were implemented faithfully.[15] The most important component of the reform was the 1994 Law of Popular Participation, which created municipal districts throughout the country, much of which had no civil authority. The law instituted the country's first–ever nationwide direct municipal elections, held in 1995. Each of 314 municipalities now directly elects its municipal councilors, who choose a mayor from among themselves. In addition, 20 percent of government revenues are distributed to municipal governments.

CSUTCB leaders meeting in December 1994 considered the subject of forming a party at a Congress of the Political Instrument, Land and Territory, convened in Santa Cruz, on March 25–7, 1995. At that 1995 meeting, for the first time all three major national federations – CSUTCB, the lowland organization CIDOB, and the colonists organization CSCB – were present (CSUTCB 1996: 15–16; Patzi Paco 1999: 116–19). Participants decided to form an indigenous political party – the Assembly for the Sovereignty of the Peoples (ASP) – in order to participate in the December 1995 municipal elections. The decision was made notwithstanding conflicting views on the best course of action. One group

---

[15] A national constituent assembly is scheduled for 2005. A massive march of indigenous peoples in favor of a constituent assembly in June 2002 and protests in October 2003 demanding the convocation of a constituent assembly ultimately forced President Sánchez de Lozada to flee the country (*Latin American Weekly Reports* 2004a: 8).

preferred to form an indigenous alternative to the Bolivian state, such as the failed Assembly of Peoples (CSUTCB 1996: 16, 45). But the coca growers wished to form a party. The following language is from the resolutions documenting the consensus at the CSUTCB's VII Congress in 1995. It echoes themes that indigenous leaders raised in previously cited interviews and manifestoes:

In March of 1995, in an historic congress, the campesinos and *originarios* of the country have said ENOUGH! to the manipulation of the parties of the oligarchy and of colonialism, and we have begun the path of the construction of our own political instrument. . . .

Until now the traditional parties only have spoken in our name in the Parliament and the mayors' offices, but they haven't done anything to resolve our problems.

The moment has arrived in which we represent ourselves, the moment has arrived in which the original peoples, the working class, and the exploited of the cities begin to forge our own destiny with our own hands, with our own ideas and our own representatives.

Nevertheless, this will not be possible if the Political Instrument only organizes the campesinos and *originarios*. The Indianist deviations are a form of favoring our enemies, so we must take a second step: INCORPORATE THE EXPLOITED AND OPPRESSED OF THE CITIES IN THE CONSTRUCTION AND CONSOLIDATION OF THE POLITICAL INSTRUMENT.

(my translation; CSUTCB 1996: 68–9)

Continued criticism within the campesino movement with respect to the legitimacy of the new party – particularly among the Aymara, the traditional rivals of the mostly Quechua coca growers – led to the convocation of a Second Congress of the Political Instrument and Territory in January 1997, where additional party structures were constituted (Patzi Paco 1999: 118).

The ASP was the first political party formed from within the indigenous and campesino movements. Leaders and advisors associated with the movements had sponsored parties, but these lacked roots in the communities and were not the result of a consensualized decision (interview, Hugo Salvatierra, July 3, 2002). In addition to this firmer organizational base, the ASP benefited from a recent institutional reform. ASP national deputy (1997–2002) Roman Loayza gives the municipal decentralization credit for the ability of the national campesino union to form its first-ever successful political party (interview, La Paz, 1997). Most analysts concur that municipal decentralization made an indigenous party a viable option (Patzi Paco 1999: 118; see also Albó 1997: 14). Moreover, at the same time that these institutional reforms made political participation easier, the collapse of the Indianist and Katarist parties and the electoral left opened the field for a new contender to represent the indigenous majority. Other possible electoral allies were unavailable: the MIR and MNR had moved to the center-right, leftist parties like MBL and IU had proved incapable of winning more than 10 percent at the national level, and the populist party Condepa appealed mainly to urban voters.

The campesinos' determination to form a viable national party increased after the 1995 municipal elections. The CSUTCB and the colonist confederation CSCB were disappointed by the ineffectiveness of their 1996 march to protest the government's proposed agrarian reform law. At the conclusion of a lengthy published account of the march the two organizations reaffirmed the necessity of a Political Instrument that would enable the campesinos and colonists to enter public decision-making spaces at the national level so that laws in favor of their interests could be approved (Condo 1998: 133).

But competing at the national level was difficult under the closed list, single-national district PR system, which had prevailed during democratic periods since 1956. The 1995 constitutional reform converted that system to a mixed PR/SMD formula for the Chamber of Deputies, in which uninominal seats are used to elect one-half of the 130 seats (there also are twenty-seven senators, three for each department, chosen in departmental districts). The change favored the ASP because the coca growers are geographically concentrated. The SMD formula helps small, regionally based parties, which would be less competitive against the centrally organized national parties in nationwide PR contests. This change inspired the party to run in the 1997 national elections.

Strategic Decision-Making Scenario III

Political parties traditionally have ignored geographically isolated lowland Indians, who have largely returned the favor, because parties have never offered them any benefits. Thus, when indigenous parties began to emerge in the mid-1990s, lowland Indians had no strong ties to existing parties. CIDOB decided as an organization to begin participating in electoral politics with the 1995 municipal elections. Having achieved a variety of institutional reforms to their benefit during the Sánchez de Lozada administration, CIDOB leaders sought access to elected and appointed office in order to ensure that these reforms were implemented properly

(Pessoa 1998: 179–80). This sentiment is expressed in a CIDOB document from 1996:

The municipalities and the emergence of new laws change the political scenario. The lines of action are coherent but they must be implemented. . . . The communities want social participation to be guaranteed and, thus, demand to participate in the national and regional elections.   (my translation; CIDOB 1996: 8)

The main obstacle to participation was the legal necessity of forming or joining political parties. While fighting to change this requirement, CIDOB forged alliances with political parties willing to respect the independence of the organizations, to incorporate their proposals in their political platforms, and to place their candidates in attractive spots on the ballot (Pessoa 1998: 180–1).

For the 1995 municipal elections, rather than choose a single party, local organizations formed a variety of alliances with locally strong parties. For example, the Chiquitanos formed a commission to study the alliance issue and to initiate conversations with the MNR, the right-wing National Democratic Action (ADN), the center-right MIR, the populist party Civic Union of Solidarity (UCS), and the tiny leftist party MBL. The first three had the greatest strength in their municipality of Concepción, but all three refused to include more than one Chiquitano candidate in their lists, to respect the candidate's status as a representative of the Chiquitano organization, or to place a Chiquitano at the top of the list. The Chiquitanos chose to ally with the MBL because they had programmatic affinities with the leftist party and because, having little presence in the area, the MBL did not put many demands on their allies. The Chiquitano-MBL alliance garnered CIDOB vice president Vicente Pessoa a municipal council seat (Pessoa 1998: 184–6). The MBL was the party of choice for indigenous organizations in the 1995 municipal elections, representing 23.7 percent of the campesino-indigenous councilors elected in the entire country (Albó 1997: 12). The MBL achieved its greatest electoral results ever in those elections, winning 13.3 percent of the national vote.

In a March 1997 interview, CIDOB leader Marcial Fabricano recalled a September 1996 meeting with campesino leaders Román Loayza and Modesto Condori in La Paz during the agrarian reform march to discuss the possibility of forming a joint political instrument. The creation of a campesino–CIDOB political pact was rejected at that time, due partly to the disunity among the three major movements – campesinos, colonists, and lowland Indians – engendered by their different strategies in negotiating with the government on the agrarian law (*La Razón*, June 11, 1997: A14). In addition, the pragmatic, conciliatory nature of the lowland movement at the time clashed with the militancy of the more radical highland organizations (Arias cited in Archondo 1997: 2; Guarachi 1994: 228). According to Fabricano, sufficient support did not exist in 1996 within CIDOB for the formation of a new party:

> We don't want to be a party, because to be one more would not help democracy. We want to be a different option for the Bolivian people. An option in which a party and a social movement – the civil society itself – unite in order to seek the common cause of the integrated rural and urban country.
>
> (my translation; *La Razón*, June 11, 1997: A14)

According to anthropologist Iván Arias (interviewed in Archondo 1997), CIDOB leaders decided to increase their participation in formal politics following the 1995 municipal elections, after they learned that of the 465 new campesino or indigenous municipal councilors elected, only 25 represented lowland indigenous communities affiliated with CIDOB. Whereas the coca growers had gained a majority in their areas of demographic predominance, lowland indigenous organizations had failed to take advantage of the opportunity. CIDOB militants also became frustrated with the level of participation and authority offered by the 1994 Law of Popular Participation through the creation of "vigilance committees," on which all indigenous organizations had representation but no actual power (CIDOB 1996: 8). The lack of formal representation also hit home in September 1996 during the agrarian reform march, when CIDOB did not have a conciliatory president with which to negotiate. As Arias observes, it was left to lobby a congress without a single CIDOB representative, while indigenous deputies in congress "did not fulfill even the function of messengers between the social movement and the Congress" (my translation; Arias cited in Archondo 1997: 2–3). Arias recalls Fabricano declaring in frustration from the parliamentary balcony: "Someone of us must be there below" (my translation; ibid.: 3).

At a 1996 CIDOB assembly, participants debated four alternatives for the 1997 national elections: (1) borrowing the registered name of an existing party and running their own candidates; (2) allying with an existing party and presenting candidates representing both CIDOB and that party with a jointly decided platform; (3) supporting an existing party and its indigenous candidates; and (4) allying with a nonindigenous candidate who supported CIDOB's program. The organization elaborated a detailed comparison of the pros and cons of all three courses of action

Alternative	Advantage	Disadvantage	Suggestion
Uni-nominal Deputies			
1) Borrow registration of existing party.	Own candidates, not of a party.	The party doesn't help with resources.	Train "table delegates" to control the electoral process.
2) Alliance with a party and presentation of candidates of both parties.	The party contributes resources, votes increase.	The alternate is not able to gain office easily.	Only convenient if the candidates are titular.
3) Alliance with the program of another indigenous candidate.	The party contributes resources, votes increase.	Annuls programmatic independence.	If it goes against the program, it is unacceptable.
4) Alliance of indigenous program with an outside candidate.	The candidate (or his/her party) provides resources.	Compliance with the indigenous program is not guaranteed.	Is only convenient if the candidate is proven to be indentified with the indigenous movement.
Pluri-nominal Deputies			
1) Alliance with a party or a candidate likely to win (*dentro de la franja de seguridad*).	Resources are shared.	They lose the indigenous platform.	Is only convenient if each one goes with its own program, and they maintain partisan independence.
2) Alliance with a consensualized program.	Joint elaboration of the program.	The other party is strengthened.	Is only convenient if each one goes with its own program, and they maintain partisan independence.

FIGURE 3.1. Alternatives for Achieving Spaces of Power. *Source*: From author's notes based on CIDOB (1996: 17, graphic 5).

before deciding on the second (see Figure 3.1). The CIDOB leaders rejected the first option because of the organization's lack of economic resources, which led to a consensus that "it is not convenient at this time to present our own party" (CIDOB 1996: 18). The third and fourth options were rejected because the chance was great that the party or candidate supported would not fulfill promises after it won election. These options were feasible only if a party or candidate with a strong, proven commitment to the indigenous movement could be found, which was not the case in 1996. The second option – an alliance with an existing party – was preferred, provided that CIDOB could gain a sufficient number of titular candidacies, as opposed to alternates, or positions too far down on lists to gain a seat (CIDOB 1996: 17).

Based on the success of the 1996 march, CIDOB leaders aspired to secure the vice presidential slot, four SMD candidacies, five alternates, two party-list candidacies, and positions in the executive to be determined later: "No more no less" (my translation; Archondo 1997: 3). The main three parties in contention – the MNR, MIR, and MBL – all had close relations with indigenous organizations. Although the consensus within the organization was that CIDOB only should ally with a party that had a possibility of being in the next government, MBL was included because it had been part of the MNR-based government in 1993–7 and might form a preelectoral alliance. The assembly proclaimed Fabricano to be the organization's vice presidential candidate and authorized an eleven-member National Commission on Political Participation to seek an alliance with the MNR, MIR, or MBL. Commission members also met with representatives of ADN and UCS (CIDOB 1997: 4).

Between January and May of 1997 the main issue in contention was whether CIDOB should choose a single party with which to ally or continue to form diverse pragmatic local alliances. An alliance between CIDOB and the MBL – the only party to approve the ambitious number of candidates CIDOB had sought – was announced on February 15 (CIDOB 1997: 4).[16] The decision provoked protests from within CIDOB, mainly due to the widespread belief that the MBL could not win. Although Fabricano denied the dissent, others pointed to profound discord on the issue (Archondo 1997: 3; *La Razón*, June 11, 1997: A14).[17] In order to address the swell of internal discontent, Fabricano's faction published a rare "open letter" from a faction of the National Political Commission

---

[16] According to Arias, the MNR offered two uni-nominal and two pluri-nominal deputy candidacies, while the MIR offered two uni-nominals and three pluri-nominals. Cited in Archando (1997: 3).

[17] The interviewer pressed Fabricano on this issue, asking whether the decision to support an alliance with the MBL that placed him as a vice-presidential candidate was a democratic one. He replied that, although no vote was taken, the decision was made in the usual way, by expressing contrary views and making decision "by consensus."

explaining the decision to CIDOB members (CIDOB 1997). In the end, the organization participated in the June contests using multiple strategies. CPESC, for example, supported the Eje Pachakuti. Chiquitano mayor Vicente Pessoa later commented on the decision, explaining that part of the National Commission had prioritized securing the vice presidency, and the MBL was the only party willing to offer that position. At the local level the Chiquitanos and Guarayos failed to secure a joint proposal, so an agreement was made with the MNR for Pessoa, then serving as mayor of Concepción, to be a candidate for uninominal deputy. In the same district the Guarayos made an alliance with the MIR. Thus, in one district inhabited by Guarayos and Chiquitanos, three indigenous candidates competed in alliances with three different parties (Pessoa 1998: 201).

In the end, the majority of CIDOB militants were right: MBL earned only 2.8 percent of the vote (Romero Ballivian 1998: 172). An analysis of its chances three months prior to the elections had predicted as much, since neither CIDOB nor the MBL had enough potential votes in more populous urban areas, whose choice would be decisive (Archondo 1997: 4). In the uni-nominal districts for the Chamber of Deputies, Indians only elected Vicente Pessoa as an alternate deputy through the Chiquitano alliance with the MNR (Pessoa 1998: 201). More Indians voted for nonindigenous candidates of traditional parties than for their own people because the traditional parties had spent money in the communities that the tiny MBL lacked (*Presencia* 1997b: 4, 1997c: 7).[18] In addition, high abstention among rural Indians was to blame, and partially attributable to the lack of documents: 81.2 percent of lowland Indians had no "carnet" of identity (required for voting), while 40 percent did not have a birth certificate (*La Razón*, June 11, 1997: A14). Following the defeat there was more discussion within CIDOB about the possibility of forming its own political party, according to statements made by the defeated Fabricano (*Presencia* 1997a: 6).

Strategic Decision-Making Scenario IV

Discussions within CIDOB concerning the desirability of forming their own political party resumed prior to the 2002 national elections. They

---

[18] According to the auxiliary bishop of the Beni, "Lamentably, the Indian within his misery lives for today. If someone offers him money, he votes for him. That is what happened with the bases in the elections" (*Presencia* 1997b: 4).

began in earnest during a series of meetings held in April–June 2000 with each of the eight regional confederations comprising CIDOB at that time. Participants called for constitutional changes to allow CIDOB and its affiliates to run their own candidates without having to form or ally with registered political parties and for the redrawing of electoral districts around indigenous populations, in order to avoid the problem experienced in 1997, when the urban bias of lowland circumscriptions made it numerically impossible for the MBL–CIDOB alliance to win (Alejandro Almaraz, cited in Orduna and Guzmán 2002: 17; CIDOB 2000). None of their proposals was approved in time for the 2002 contests, but in February 2004 congress approved constitutional changes that allowed social movements and indigenous organizations to participate in elections. For the 2002 elections CIDOB affiliates made multiple alliances, as they had in 1997.

Strategic Decision-Making Scenario V

The subject of the final decision-making scenario was an individual, rather than an organization. Former MITKA leader Felipe Quispe capitalized on his rise in stature during massive demonstrations that he led in 2000 by forming his own political party – the MIP. Unlike the consensualized, organizational decision to form the ASP, this was a personal decision and the MIP was Quispe's party. More than 10,000 Aymara Indians attended the formation ceremony in 2000 at the site of the execution of Tupaj Katari. Quispe announced that the party's main goal would be to improve working conditions for the indigenous majority and that it was time to "reclaim the Aymara nation, oppressed for 500 years by white people" (Reuters, November 15, 2000). He also promised to seek the reconstruction of precolonial forms of Andean government. Quispe had come full circle: from political party leader, to armed guerrilla, to social movement leader, and back to party leader.

In the year prior to the June 30, 2002 elections, Quispe orchestrated a nearly constant state of campesino mobilization in the Aymara highlands, with ebbs and flows as individual organizations abandoned the mobilization out of frustration, fatigue, or support for Quispe's rivals. Quispe's Aymara nationalism prevented the creation of an Aymara–Quechua alliance and exacerbated the feud among Quispe, the Quechua leader Alejo Véliz, and Evo Morales, who has mixed parentage, but leads a mostly Quechua population of coca growers. A "war of insults" between the three leaders drained public support for the indigenous movement (Cáceres 2001: 9).

As late as March 2002 Quispe declared that he would not run for president but would seek an alliance between his party and Morales's, now competing under the name Movimiento al Socialismo (MAS) (*Los Tiempos* [Cochabamba], March 20, 2002a, Internet). When that alliance failed to materialize, both parties registered their leaders as presidential candidates. As the two candidates joined a field of ten presidential hopefuls, a long-standing campaign of vicious attacks between the two rivals escalated. Thus, the main reason for the formation of this party was the inability of its leader to find a place in an existing, relatively successful ethnic party.

Despite the more permissive institutional conditions after 1995, ethnic parties continued to have difficulty registering. The ASP and its offshoot, the Political Instrument for the Sovereignty of the Peoples (IPSP), were unable to register under their own names and forced to run under the names of a series of legally registered but moribund leftist parties. As in the prior period, the National Electoral Court exacerbated their difficulties. The MIP almost did not appear on the ballot in 2002 and, by law, should not have. Even though the MIP fell ten thousand signatures short of those required for registration, the party was allowed to register, leaving MAS leaders complaining that the traditional parties ordered that Quispe's name be included. According to MAS spokesperson Marcelo Quezada, this was done to split the indigenous vote and to prevent a possible MAS–MIP electoral alliance, which might have occurred had Quispe been blocked from the presidential race. In fact, Quezada and other MIP leaders had met with MAS leaders and discussed an alliance five days before the registration deadline. According to Quezada, the MIP representatives favored an alliance because they knew they could not submit enough signatures and because the base communities were pushing for it (CEDIB, October 2001: 90). MAS militants were incensed by the court's decision because their registration had been rejected four times for minor infractions (*Pulso Semanario* [La Paz] 2002b: 13).

UNDERSTANDING NEW ETHNIC PARTY PERFORMANCE

I break the analysis of ethnic party performance into two time periods in order to account for the dramatic change in the permissiveness of the institutional environment following the 1994–5 constitutional reforms and changes in the party system after 1993.

The Pre–Reform Era (1978–1993)

During this period newly formed ethnic parties repeatedly failed to attract sufficient votes to maintain registration or to capture more than a handful of ineffectual seats in legislative office. The main obstacles were low levels of voter registration among Indians; the dominant parties' manipulation of the National Electoral Court; burdensome electoral regulations – for example, the necessity of winning 3 percent of the vote to maintain registration and to avoid fines, the requirement that parties distribute their own ballots to polling places – and the lack of financial resources for campaigning. MITKA, for example, lacked the resources to distribute its ballots and to position militants at voting tables to prevent fraud (Tapia 1995: 390). Because these earlier parties were the projects of intellectuals, who lacked strong links to grassroots indigenous organizations, they could not mobilize the organizational resources required in order to contest elections under extremely restrictive rules against better-funded competitors.

Although the military annulled the 1978 elections, the MITKA won 0.6 percent of the vote – an impressive result, given their lack of resources and weak organizational structure (see Table 3.3). According to MITKA leader Pedro Portugal, this "relative victory" for a party clearly defining itself as indigenous demonstrates the vacuum of authentic political representation for indigenous peoples (1989: 109). MITKA ran again in

TABLE 3.3. *Electoral results of Indianista and Katarista parties as a percentage of total vote*

Year	MITKA	MRTK	MRTKL	FULKA	MKN/KND	Eje Pachakutik
1978	0.6	[a]				
1979	1.6	[a]				
1980	2.1[b]	[a]				
1985		0.9	1.8			
1989			1.5	1.04		
1993			[c]		0.7	1.1
1995			1.2		0.23	
1997					[d]	0.84
1999			0.07		0.41	
2002						

[a] Ran in alliance with other parties.
[b] MITKA and MITKA-I combined.
[c] Ran with MNR.
[d] Ran with ADN.

1979, this time with more resources, which enabled the party to purchase a mimeo machine and to pay salaries to full-time office workers. MITKA leaders were invited to meet with other parties and movements in Cochabamba, Oruro, and Santa Cruz. Near the end of the campaign the Electoral Court disqualified the MITKA and the Socialist Party (PS-1) for failing to obtain sufficient votes in the previous election to allow their participation in 1979. In response, Tapia and PS-1 leaders Marcelo Quiroga Santa Cruz and Filemón Escóbar began a hunger strike (Tapia 1995: 402–5). In the end the parties were allowed to participate after depositing money with the court. The MITKA increased its vote share to 1.6 percent, earning a seat in congress (Romero Ballivian 1998: 204). The elections were annulled after the Natusch coup in November 1979. Also in 1979, a group left the MITKA to found the Partido Indio, which has been confused with Fausto Reynaga's earlier effort (Quispe 1999: 51).[19]

In 1980, the deep personal rivalry between Tapia and Lima divided the MITKA. Both leaders competed in the 1980 elections, each winning one seat (Lima's MITKA-1 won 1.1 percent of the vote; Tapia's MITKA won 1 percent) (Quispe 1999: 54; Romero Ballivian 1998: 204). These seats were lost after the Garcia Meza coup later that year. Many indigenous and leftist activists were tortured and imprisoned during this period. MITKA's 1980 vice presidential candidate, Eufronio Véliz, weakened the party's image by publicly supporting Garcia Meza and sending police to arrest Tapia. At this time Felipe Quispe was able to accumulate sufficient support to replace Jaime Apaza as leader of the MITKA (Tapia 1995: 423). Both indigenous deputies entered congress in 1982 and were assigned to the Agrarian Commission, where none of their proposals prospered.[20]

---

[19] Other tiny Indianist splinter groups using a similar name appeared in the 1980s: the Partido Indio del Kollasuyu in 1985, the Partido Indio de Liberación in 1988. None of them won an election.

[20] Tapia proposed bills to provide transportation to poor people in La Paz, to promote the cultivation of wheat, and to make Aymara and Quechua official Bolivian languages. Tapia attributes his failure to achieve substantive legislative gains to his lack of experience as a legislator and the racism of the other deputies – and even of the chamber's staff, which demanded extra payments to provide services to him offered "servilely" to nonindigenous legislators. He also blames the party's decision not to ally with nonindigenous parties. In contrast, Lima (MITKA-1) was part of the UDP legislative coalition. As a result, the press never covered Tapia's statements and he was isolated (Tapia 1995: 429–32). Felipe Quispe, who was Tapia's alternate, provides a less generous analysis of Tapia's ineffectiveness: "He remained mute as if his tongue had been mutilated; it is obvious that there were many militants and sympathizers who had hopes for him, because they thought that such an Indian Deputy could demand the return of political power. . . . [B]ut

Thereafter, tensions intensified between Tapia, the MITKA congressional deputy, and Felipe Quispe, the head of the party. After the Electoral Court determined that Tapia was the legal representative of the party, Quispe left with two other MITKA leaders. In 1986, he formed the Ofensiva Roja de Ayllus Tupakataristas, the political arm of the Ejército Guerrillero Tupak Katari, an armed movement (Quispe 1999: 2; Tapia 1995: 436).

As the MITKA disintegrated in the mid-1980s the Katarista tendency became dominant and would remain so through the first Gonzalo Sánchez de Lozada administration (1993–7).[21] The MRTK ran with the UDP coalition in 1978–80. In the 1985 elections, the MRTK won 0.9 percent and subsequently disappeared. A splinter of the MRTK led by Genaro Flores, the MRTKL, won 1.8 percent of the vote and became the most successful of the Katarista or Indianista parties, winning two deputies' seats in the national legislature (Patzi Paco 1999: 40; Romero Ballivian 1998: 204). Two MRTK offshoots – the MRTKL and the United Front of Katarista Liberation (FULKA) – competed in the 1989 elections: FULKA won 1.3 percent and MRTKL, now led by Víctor Hugo Cárdenas, won 1.45 percent (Calla 1993: 76). Although Cárdenas earned sufficient votes to retake the seat he had won in 1985, he lost it when the National Electoral Court, at the behest of the winning ADN–MIR coalition, manipulated the postelection seat-allocation rules to steal seats from the MRTKL and other parties (Mayorga 1995: 136n64; Rivera Cusicanqui 1993: 110; Romero Ballivian 1998: 204).

Thanks to an alliance with Cárdenas's MRTKL, in 1993 the MNR won the presidency with a significant plurality of the vote – the largest victory margin (14 percent) of any presidential candidate since the military annulled the 1980 elections. As partners in the winning coalition, three of the MRTKL's seven candidates for the Chamber of Deputies won seats. Many indigenous Bolivians were thrilled to see an indigenous leader obtain the vice presidency and Cárdenas's popularity with nonindigenous Bolivians and the international community soared as he developed a moderate reputation. But the CSUTCB declared Cárdenas "an enemy

---

Tapia didn't say anything. That high leader of the MITKA was not in the parliamentary debates, he preferred, rather, to stay silent and downcast. He was full of complexes and never opened his mouth to express the truth about the innumerable problems of the Indian-comunario" (my translation; Quispe 1999: 55).

[21] Tapia says that in the 1970s the MITKA tried to establish an alliance with Flores's organization, then called simply *Tupak Katari*, but the effort failed, due to the "campesinista" or classist, rather than "indianista," orientation of Flores's followers (Tapia 1995: 364). Flores's followers accused the MITKA of being "racist" and "retrograde."

and a traitor" during its 1994 VI Congress (Patzi Paco 1999: 116). His decision to run with the MNR left the movement divided.[22] Moreover, the MRTKL did not grow as an institution because Cárdenas marginalized its militants from the government, for example, by appointing non-indigenous, non-MRTKL advisors to important government positions, by excluding MRTKL congressional representatives from policy meetings, and by prohibiting the party from competing in the 1997 elections, when state campaign funds were available based on the party's strong showing in 1993, because Cárdenas himself was barred from seeking the presidency (Patzi Paco 1999: 42; Van Cott 2000b: 292n12; interviews, La Paz, 1997, 2001, 2002).[23] Rejected by the independent indigenous movement, Cárdenas's MRTKL never regained its prior support. In the 1995 municipal elections, the party won 1.2 percent of the national vote, which earned it only five mayors (1.6 percent of the national total) and twenty-two municipal councilors (2 percent of the national total) (Various Authors 1997: 17). In the summer of 2001, Cárdenas unsuccessfully sought alliances to enable the MRTKL to compete in the 2002 national elections. In order to participate, he would have had to pay fines imposed on the party for its poor showing in the 1999 municipal elections, when it gained only 0.07 percent of the national vote and only two municipal council seats in the department of Oruro (interviews, Víctor Hugo Cárdenas, July 14, 2001; Esteban Ticona, July 18, 2001). The MRTKL did not participate and its future as an electoral vehicle is in doubt.

The indigenous parties described in the preceding text collectively averaged a total of barely 2 percent of the vote between 1979 and 1993, never rising above a high of 2.77 percent, which the MRTKL earned in 1985. By 2000, the Katarista and Indianista parties had virtually disappeared.

---

[22] Three Katarista factions participated independently in the 1993 elections: Eje Pachakuti, won one seat in the Chamber of Deputies; Genaro Flores, head of FULKA, ran as vice presidential candidate for the IU; and the Movimento Katarista Nacional (MKN), "an ephemeral and artificial formation" of retired General Hugo Banzer's center-right ADN, led by Fernando Untoja, won 0.9 percent (Mayorga 1995: 140n71). Neither FULKA nor MKN won a seat (Canessa 2000: 124n41).

[23] In Bolivia, Article 252 of Ley 1779 (March 1997) provides for public financing of electoral campaigns. Fifty percent of the total budget appropriated is distributed sixty days prior to the election "in a form proportional to the number of votes that each party, front, or alliance, had obtained in the latest general or municipal elections, provided that they obtained the minimum three percent of the total valid votes at the national level and gained at least one seat in the Chamber of Deputies in the general elections. The other 50 percent will be distributed in the same manner, based on results in the corresponding general or municipal election, an amount to be disbursed in the same period of 60 days from the date of the election" (my translation).

Yet, despite the contemporary institutional and political weakness of Katarism, it would be a mistake to disregard the symbolic importance of the movement and its accomplishments. Cárdenas's vice presidency changed the perception of Indians and their capabilities (Canessa 2000: 128). Katarism infused mainstream Bolivian politics with ethno-cultural themes and constituted the only coherent alternative to neoliberal reform until the formation of the ASP in 1995 (Mayorga 1995: 135; Sanjinés 2001: 6). It also led to the emergence of Aymara nationalism, which Felipe Quispe would exploit after 1998 (Canessa 2000: 126).

In sum, institutional barriers prevented parties that were able to register for elections from maintaining their registration and attracting votes. Indianista and Katarista parties repeatedly lost their registration when they were unable to pay fines for poor performance. The tendency of the dominant political parties to manipulate politicized electoral authorities in ways that further disadvantaged struggling new parties exacerbated the impact of high barriers to ballot access. For example, before the 1985 elections, Luciano Tapia consulted the National Electoral Court about the fines the party still owed for failing to win 3 percent of the vote in 1980. He was assured that the party did not have to pay the fines. However, at the last minute the court changed its position and insisted that the MITKA pay the fine or be disqualified. At this time Constantino Lima, whose party was declining in support, suggested reuniting the MITKA-1 and the original MITKA. Tapia agreed, but the court refused to accept their registration because they were unable to pay the fines (Tapia 1995: 438–40). They never competed again.

Disunity also was a problem. The extreme fragmentation of the indigenous parties of the 1980s split the potential indigenous vote into fragments that failed to win seats or maintain registration. By 1989, the Indianista tendency had spawned more than half a dozen parties, each representing the aspirations of one or two activists (Portugal 1989: 112). Fragmentation also plagued the Katarista tendency, which launched a total of ten parties. After the 1978 elections, the MRTK broke with the UDP and personal rivalries divided it into three factions. For the 1979 elections, the fraction that retained the name MRTK, led by Macabeo Chila, allied with the MNR; a second fraction joined the UDP coalition; the third and largest was led by Genaro Flores, who declined to compete and "instructed [the party's] adherents to vote for the 'left'" (my translation; Calla 1993: 68; see also Rocha 1992: 257). Chila's MRTK competed in 1985 but subsequently disappeared. Flores added "de Liberación" to the old name and registered the MRTKL (Rocha 1992: 258). Within a year of its formation, divisions emerged within the MRTKL between Flores, on the one hand, and Víctor Hugo Cárdenas and Walter Reynaga, the party's two congressional deputies, on the other. In a 1988 party congress, Flores walked out with some of his supporters and formed the FULKA. Both parties lost support after the internal bickering became public (Patzi Paco 1999: 41). Flores's exit still did not achieve unity in the MRTKL: neither Cárdenas nor Reynaga would accept the second position in the new party hierarchy. Cárdenas eventually edged out his rival.

Although the indigenous candidates attracted large crowds, they found that many campesinos already were committed to the MNR, the MIR, or other parties that had a better chance of winning (Tapia 1995: 380–4). During the 1980s, the major parties enjoyed strong links with peasant leaders based on classist ideology and the promise of patronage. Indigenous voters proved too pragmatic to break ties with parties that offered material benefits (Canessa 2000: 127; Van Cott 2000a: 167, 2000b: 128). Another challenge was the larger parties' co-optation of indigenous leaders and their creation of electoral vehicles with Katarist names in order to confuse indigenous voters and disperse the indigenous vote.[24] As Katarist organizations declined in institutional strength and political influence in the late 1980s, leftist intellectuals and NGOs appropriated the Katarist themes and discourse to attract indigenous support, as well as support from international donors who favored "culturally appropriate" development projects (Albó 1999a: 477; Calla 1993: 78; Mayorga 1995: 10; Patzi Paco 1999: 45; Rivera Cusicanqui 1991: 22). Populist parties also appropriated Katarista symbols. In 1989, the populist party Conscience of the Fatherland (CONDEPA) borrowed the Aymara flag (*wiphala*) and the myth of Pachakuti,[25] and portrayed its leader, the Aymara-speaking media personality Carlos Palenque, as the *mestizo* incarnation of the indigenous hero (Mayorga 1995: 139). Max Fernández, leader of the populist UCS, often spoke Quechua on the campaign trail and used his ownership of a beer distributor to associate himself with indigenous rituals. Electoral pressure from the populist parties after 1989 convinced the traditional

---

[24] The MNR did this in 1978–9; the ADN did so in 1993 by creating the MKN (the current name is Katarismo Nacional Democrático [KND]) (interviews, Víctor Hugo Cárdenas, July 14, 2001, and Esteban Ticona, July 18, 2001).

[25] Bolivians and Peruvians honor Pachakuti, a mythic ruler who governed Tawantinsuyu during its era of greatest expansion (De la Cadena 2000: 165). The myth predicts the return of the executed Aymara leader Tupaj Katari. Canessa compares the belief in the return of Tupaj Katari – who vowed to return before being executed – to the Christian belief in Christ's second coming (Canessa 2000: 126).

parties to follow suit. After the MNR began incorporating Katarist themes and candidates in 1993, other large parties did likewise, particularly the MIR, which has enjoyed a long association with the Katarists and Indianists, beginning with contacts in the early 1970s among militants jailed by the Banzer dictatorship. Thus, as Calla observed, between 1985 and 1992, the number of white and *mestizo* political actors willing to espouse ethnicist or proindigenous views "expanded significantly," reducing the appeal of tiny ethnic parties without patronage resources (1993: 79).

Finally, Katarist and Indianist parties had to contend with the low level of voter registration in the rural highlands, which is attributable mainly to the lack of necessary documents. Until the registration drive of 2001–2, there weren't sufficient offices in the *altiplano* to provide documents to those lacking them and to register eligible voters. In 1992, in rural areas throughout the country, only 52.8 percent of men and 37.8 percent of women over the age of fifteen had identity documents (Ticona et al. 1995: 183–4).

The Post–Reform Era (1995–2002)

During this period institutional changes dramatically enhanced the ability of ethnic parties to attract sufficient votes to maintain registration and to win seats in office. In addition, an ethnic party finally formed that was the true organic expression of a well-rooted, highly mobilized social movement organization: the coca growers movement and, more generally, the campesino union (CSUTCB) to which it belongs. That party also benefited from the decline of the populist party CONDEPA, which formerly had attracted a significant segment of the urban indigenous vote, and the absence of an electorally viable leftist alternative to the neoliberal parties.

The 1995 municipal decentralization dramatically improved the performance of ethnic parties. Practically overnight indigenous candidates flooded elected offices, while the coca growers' new political vehicle instantly dominated the coca-growing districts. In its first outing, listed on the ballot under the name of the nearly defunct IU[26] because of problems with its own registration, the ASP swept municipal elections in the Chapare and won ten mayors, forty-nine municipal council seats, and six

---

[26] The IU's best showing was in 1989, when it won 7.2 percent of the vote in national elections, which corresponded to fifth place. That year the IU incorporated the indigenous movement's demand for the creation of a "plurinational state" into its campaign platform (Calla 1993: 75–8).

departmental-level *consejeros*, as well as five councilors in other highland
departments (Patzi Paco 1999: 119; Van Cott 2000b: 189). The mayoral
count would have been higher, had not the traditional parties prevented
the ASP from gaining control of five municipalities where it had won a
majority (Albó 1997: 21). Institutional reforms again benefited the geographically concentrated coca growers in 1997, when SMDs were first
created for the national legislature. In 1997, the ASP won four of the new
uni-nominal congressional seats, representing its base in the Chapare.
In fact, coca growers leader Evo Morales won a larger percentage of the
vote in his district than any other candidate in the country (approximately
60 percent). In addition, the ASP won 17.5 percent of the vote for party
lists in Cochabamba, 3.7 percent nationwide (Yaksic Feraudy and Tapia
Mealla, 1997: 196) (see Table 3.4).

Prior to the 1999 municipal elections, the ASP split in two over personal rivalries. The rump ASP led by Alejo Véliz and the splinter IPSP,
led by Evo Morales, earned a combined 4.4 percent share of the vote, a
marginal improvement from the ASP's 1995 showing (www.cne.org.bo).
The ASP, in alliance with other parties and using the valid registration of
the Communist Party of Bolivia (PCB), earned 1.12 percent of the vote,

TABLE 3.4. *Electoral results for ASP, IPSP/MAS, and MIP*

Election	ASP/IU	IPSP/MAS	MIP

1995 Municipal	3% of vote
	10 mayors
	54 municipal
	  councilors
	6 departmental
	  consejeros
		–	–

1997 National	3.7% of vote 4 national deputies	–	–

1999 Municipal	1.12% of vote
	4 mayors
	23 municipal
	  councilors
		3.27% of vote
		10 mayors
		79 municipal
		  councilors
			–

2002 National	–	20.94% of vote
		8 senators
		
		27 national
		  deputies
			6.09% of vote
			6 national
			  deputies

securing twenty-three municipal councilors and four mayors, all within Cochabamba (Ministerio de Desarrollo Sostenible y Planificación 2000: 25–6). The IU registration could not be used again because the National Electoral Court had invalidated it. The IPSP, using the valid registration of the moribund MAS, won 3.27 percent of the vote nationwide, which earned it seventy-nine municipal council seats in six departments. The largest number of seats was won in La Paz (eighteen) and Cochabamba (forty), where IPSP–MAS picked up ten mayors and a majority of councilors in five municipalities (www.cne.org.bo and Ministerio de Desarrollo Sostenible y Planificación 2000: 11, 13, 25–6).

The new ethnic parties also benefited from a massive government sponsored voter registration campaign in rural areas between 1993 and 2002. Voter registration enlarged the pool of potential voters for ethnic parties.[27] Nevertheless, the lack of identification papers continued in 1999 to be the main reason for the lack of indigenous voting, particularly among women, who are not required to obtain identity cards because they do not perform military service (Ministerio de Desarrollo Sostenible y Planificación 2000: 3). Voter registration is particularly low in the lowlands, where indigenous communities are more isolated and it is more expensive to deliver documents. By the 1997 elections, documents had only arrived in half the communities (Patzi Paco 1999: 124).

The increase in permissiveness of the institutional environment in the mid-1990s coincided with the opening up of space on the left of the political spectrum and the beginning of a dealignment away from the dominant elite parties, as well as the populist parties that had competed so well for indigenous votes in the first half of the decade. Since the end of military rule in 1982, Bolivia has had a highly fragmented party system with an axis of competition among three dominant parties: the center-right MNR, the rightist ADN, and the center-left MIR. These three parties dominated national elections until 1989. That year the populist party CONDEPA joined the system, winning 11 percent of the vote. The party's base was

---

[27] A massive government voter registration effort occurred between February 2001 and April 2002. During that period, the National Electoral Court registered 1,124,723 new voters, although this number declined somewhat after duplicates were purged. New voters include more than 100,000 Indians from rural areas of the department of La Paz, who voted massively for the new ethnic parties in 2002 (Corte Nacional Electoral 2002: 20). Although it is likely that more indigenous voters participated in the 2002 elections than in previous contests, the overall level of participation, as a percentage of registered voters, remained stable: 70.74 percent in 2002, 70.7 percent in 1997, 71.7 percent in 1993, and 70.4 percent in 1989 (*La Razón*, July 1, 2002: A20).

the majority-indigenous highland departments, particularly the millions of Aymara migrants who settled in the outskirts and poorer neighborhoods of La Paz. In 1993, the populist UCS first competed in national elections. From 1993 until 1997, the five parties mentioned shared – roughly equally – approximately 85 percent of the vote.

After 1997, however, the dominance of these five parties declined. As a result, the MAS and the MIP had more detached voters to attract than had the Katarist and Indianist parties of the 1980s and early 1990s. Moreover, leftist leaders were now relatively weaker than indigenous leaders and they offered their services to the fledgling ethnic parties. After 1989, the only dynamic sector of the left was the coca growers movement, whose new party competed in elections after 1995 borrowing the registered name of the nearly extinct IU from 1995 to 1997 and the MAS from 1999 to the present for reasons described in the preceding text. Thus, the first contribution that leftist parties made to the new ethnic parties was lending their own legal registrations. The left resurged in 2000, buoyed by popular discontent with the neoliberal economic model and the failure of traditional parties to do anything to ameliorate extreme poverty and inequality. This discontent overflowed in massive protest demonstrations in 2000 and 2001. But by this time most of the left was allied with the new ethnic parties. The only traditionally leftist party running in 2002, the Partido Socialista, earned 0.65 percent of the vote (*La Razón* [online] July 9, 2002). That year the MAS recruited numerous candidates from the traditional left to fill the required candidate slots on their lists (*La Razón*, June 25, 2002: B6).[28] As a leader of the Cochabamba-based populist party Nueva Fuerza Republicana (NFR) observed, "Evo is capturing the vote of the old left that has not abdicated its ideas and that until now has been dispersed" (my translation; *Pulso Semanario* 2002a: 12). In addition, many analysts observed that Morales and Quispe captured the old CONDEPA vote after that party collapsed after 1997, following the death of its leader (interviews, María Eugenia Choque, June 20, 2002; René Antonio Mayorga, June 25, 2002).

The new parties also benefited from persistently high party system fragmentation, which lowers the barrier to entry of new parties because fewer votes are needed to win office. Bolivia demonstrates consistently high party-system fragmentation since the democratic transition, with an

---

[28] Only ten MAS legislators identified themselves as indigenous or campesino; twelve were leftist intellectuals or labor leaders (*La Razón* 2002a).

increase in the 1990s. The effective number of parties for seats (ENPS) increased from an average of 4 between 1979 and 1993 to a high of 5.07 in 1997. With between three and five parties dominating the vote, winning presidential candidates since 1985 have had to form coalitions with other parties in order to obtain sufficient seats (an absolute majority) in the congress to assume the presidency. Even the most successful party during this period – the MNR, which won 33.8 percent of the vote in 1993 through an alliance with the Katarist party MRTKL – had to invite the UCS and the tiny leftist MBL to join it in order to form a government. In all other elections during the 1990s, the proportion of votes won by the winning presidential candidate never exceeded 23 percent.

Even the promising results of the 1999 municipal elections and preelection polling did not prepare Bolivians for the astounding performance of ethnic parties in the July 2002 national elections (see Table 3.5). The week prior to the election, Morales was estimated to be in third or fourth place. Upon his expulsion from congress in January 2002 (see the following text), Morales had threatened to return with ten legislators in 2002. Instead, he returned with thirty-five (*El Diario* 2002b). The MAS won 20.94 percent of the vote, finishing less than two percentage points behind the winning

TABLE 3.5. *Results of June 30, 2002 elections*

Party	% of Votes	Seats in Senate	Seats in Deputies	2002 Seats	1997 Seats
Movimiento Nacional Revolucionario	22.46	11	36	47	30
Movimiento Al Socialismo	20.94	8	27	35	4
Nueva Fuerza Republicana	20.92	2	25	27	0
Movimiento de la Izquierda Revolucionaria	16.31	5	26	31	30
Movimiento Indígena Pachakuti	6.09		6	6	0
Unidad Cívica de Solidaridad	5.51		5	5	23
Acción Democrática Nacional	3.40	1	4	5	43
Libertad y Justicia	2.72		0	0	0
Partido Socialista	0.65		1	1	0
Movimiento Ciudadano para el Cambio	0.63			0	0
CONDEPA	0.37			0	0
Total		27	130	157	152

Source: La Razón 2002k; Web site of the Bolivian Congress (www.congreso.gov.bo). Previously published in Van Cott (2003b: 753).

MNR (22.46 percent). The MAS finished first in the departments of La Paz, Cochabamba, Oruro, and Potosí, earning the party eight senators. Although he lost the presidency, Morales won his uni-nominal district and, thus, returned to congress.

Most analysts credit inflammatory remarks by U.S. Ambassador Manuel Rocha on June 26 for giving Morales the extra votes to pull ahead of third-place Manfred Reyes of the NFR, who trailed Morales in the final tally by only 0.02 percent (*La Prensa* 2002k: 3; *La Razón* 2002l; *Tiempo de Opinión* 2002). The ambassador had warned that the United States would cut off aid and trade if Morales were to win the elections. At a Morales campaign rally outside La Paz two days before the elections the crowd burned a U.S. flag (Scrutton 2002: 280), and MAS senate candidate Filemón Escóbar fired up voters, promising that "each vote that you give to the MAS is a kick in the behind of the Ambassador" (my translation, *La Prensa* 2002k: 3). More generally, Morales's anti-U.S. rhetoric appealed to many Bolivians who attribute their persistent poverty to U.S.-imposed neoliberal economic and coca eradication policies. Moreover, Morales gained support from middle- and upper-class Bolivians drawn to his nationalistic discourse and defense of Bolivian sovereignty. This support grew after Morales was expelled from congress on January 24, 2002, without proof of wrongdoing, while dozens of legislators implicated in criminal activities remained untouched (Cárdenas 2002: A28; Iturri 2002: A28; Orduna 2002a: 6).[29] As Iturri observes, Bolivians interpreted Morales's expulsion as an "act of submission before the [U.S.] Embassy" (my translation, 2002: A26) and expressed their disagreement with U.S. drug policy by voting for Morales.

The MAS phenomenon overshadowed the MIP's results, but they were impressive, given the fact that Quispe's party was formed less than a year prior to the elections and that MIP advisors did not meet to design the campaign until March 1, 2002. Quispe's 6.09 percent of votes was almost twice the highest total for indigenous parties in previous elections, exceeding the 4 percent predicted by polls in mid-June, and placing the new party ahead of established parties like UCS, ADN, and CONDEPA. The results netted the MIP six seats in the lower chamber, including one for Quispe. MIP's support mainly was limited to the department of La Paz, where it earned approximately 15 percent of the vote, dominating the four districts

---

[29] Morales was accused of being the "intellectual author" of the murder of four police officers during separate protest actions in mid-January. Morales was expelled by a 104 to 14 vote, with one blank vote (*La Razón* 2002i: 17; *La Prensa* 2002i: 15).

in El Alto and seven in the rural *altiplano* where Aymaras predominate (Guzmán and Orduna 2002: 120). The total for both indigenous parties together – 27.03 percent – is truly a revolutionary milestone in the representation of indigenous peoples and far exceeds the amount earned by the winning MNR.

Crucial to the success of the two ethnic parties after 1995 was the ability of their charismatic leaders to mobilize the dense network of indigenous organizations in their respective bases. As presidential candidates, both Quispe and Morales continued as leaders of their respective social movement organizations. They drew on resources of social movement organizations with decades of experience and vast networks of free campaign labor, which compensated for their lack of campaign funds. Only MAS was eligible for a small share in the approximately U.S. $10.3 million of state funding provided, based on votes won in 1997.[30] Morales also spent a U.S. $50,000 international prize that he won for defending human rights. The total figure spent is incalculable because regional and local organizations made unquantifiable contributions in labor and materials, while professors at public universities in La Paz and Cochabamba offered free media expertise (*La Prensa* 2002j: 9; *La Razón*, June 25, 2002: B5).

The MAS mobilized the coca growers' federations as well as CSUTCB affiliates throughout the country. In the lowlands, the party forged ties with the Santa Cruz indigenous organization CPESC. Although CPESC leaders had promoted the idea of having their own party, its base community organizations decided to put forward a candidate to run with an existing party. After a consensual process that selected CPESC president José Bailaba, the organization decided to make a deal with the MAS – the only party, they believed, that would give them a decent placement on their list. In addition to a popular candidate, CPESC contributed its organizational resources, since MAS had no organization in Santa Cruz. The strategy worked – Bailaba was elected a pluri-nominal deputy. Given MAS's weak base in Santa Cruz, all of its candidates were chosen by CPESC communities or affiliates – a strategy that suited MAS, which had to scramble to fill more than fifty places necessary to register a complete electoral list. For the required (since 1997) 30 percent female candidates, MAS recruited from the Bartolina de Sisa Women's Federation,

---

[30] The MAS received the portion corresponding to the IU/PCB/MAS alliance because the other two parties did not participate (*Los Tiempos* 2002h). Financing of parties is provided by Article 50 of the Ley de Partidos Políticos (Corte Nacional Electoral 2002: 8).

a national female campesino organization (interview, Hugo Salvatierra, July 3, 2002).[31]

Instead of the media, Quispe and other MIP candidates spread their messages at incessant visits to indigenous communities and appearances at union and campesino meetings in the departments of La Paz and Oruro (Espinoza 2002: 21). One MIP collaborator estimated the amount of money spent to be U.S. $15,000 (Guzmán and Orduna 2002: 12). While Morales allowed supporters throughout the country to organize their own campaigns for their local MAS candidate, Quispe maintained control over the entire, less-geographically broad MIP campaign, acting as campaign director and writing his own speeches, in keeping with the more personalist nature of his party.

The electoral results for ethnic parties might have been even better had not the indigenous movement continued to suffer from internal divisions. The breach between Quechua coca growers leader Alejo Véliz and Evo Morales was complicated by the reemergence on the national scene of Quispe, who had attended the 1998 CSUTCB congress in order to build support for his defense against further criminal charges stemming from his involvement in the guerrilla organization Tupak Katari Guerrilla Army (EGTK) (Patzi Paco 1999: 77–83). When the CSUTCB could not decide between Morales and Véliz, it elected Quispe as secretary-general (Patzi Paco 1999: 121–2). But Quispe's election did not unite the campesino organization. At a CSUTCB congress held in mid-January 2001 in Oruro, 1,500 delegates of twenty regional and departmental federations voted Quispe out of office. Quispe claimed that those interested in dividing the campesino movement had illegally convoked the congress (*La Razón* January 17, 2001). Observers called the congress the most violent and intolerant in the history of the CSUTCB. Although neither Quispe nor Morales were present, confrontations between Quispe's and Morales's supporters left one of the latter's allies dead. Humberto Choque, a Morales ally, was elected secretary-general of the CSUTCB. The following year, on May 1, 2002, a CSUTCB congress in La Paz confirmed Quispe as executive president and Alejo Véliz as secretary-general (Aruquipa 2001).

Disunity also hobbled the lowland movement. According to a CIDOB advisor, Marcial Fabricano's faction forged close ties to the Sánchez de Lozada and Banzer-Quiroga governments, leading to charges of co-optation and a steep decline in legitimacy for the organization. The

---

[31] Parties needed twenty-two titular deputies, three senatorial candidates, and twenty-five alternates.

decision of several CIDOB leaders in 2002 to be candidates of traditional parties, whose leaders are the landowners who prevent the realization of indigenous territorial rights, intensified these tensions (interview, Carlos Romero, June 23, 2002). Conflict between the moderate CIDOB and the more confrontational CPESC grew during a 2002 march in favor of a constituent assembly after CIDOB leader Fabricano signed an agreement with the government that CPESC rejected (it later signed an almost identical agreement). Accusations of co-optation were renewed when Fabricano accepted a position as vice minister in the second Sánchez de Lozada government (2002–3). At a CIDOB-sponsored congress on October 29, 2002, CPESC withdrew from its parent organization, in part over accusations that CIDOB's new president is controlled by the MIR. CIDOB leaders countered with accusations that the MAS controls CPESC. The organizational disarray gained national attention after a violent altercation between militants of both groups at CIDOB headquarters the same month. Conflict also emerged in the Beni over accusations that MIR militants control the regional organization CPIB (Rodríguez P. 2002).

Although the disunity among and within indigenous organizations and parties in the 1990s restricted their electoral performance – a Morales and Quispe alliance could have finished first in 2002 – the new ethnic parties MAS and MIP made substantial gains during this period. In fact, the indigenous movements in this study with the highest levels of internal fragmentation and disunity (those in Bolivia and Ecuador) produced the most successful indigenous parties. Similarly, the most successful social movement–spawned party in Latin America, Brazil's Workers' Party, always has had difficulty moderating internal conflicts among its diverse component movements and organizations (Keck 1992: 15, 87), yet it elected its leader to the presidency in 2002. Thus, internal disunity presents a challenge but is not an insurmountable obstacle for a fledgling social movement–based party.

The major parties attempted to counter the electoral threat of the MAS and MIP and to capitalize on the popularity of indigenous themes by incorporating prominent indigenous leaders as never before. Indigenous leaders were found in all political party lists in 2002, replacing the artists and journalists that had been the most prominent "outsiders" in previous elections (Los Tiempos 2002a). Although indigenous leaders had been incorporated in the past, this time they were given more prominent positions, such as uni-nominal and senatorial candidacies and the top of pluri-nominal lists. As MNR leader Jorge Lema observed, "We gained a majority in the 1999 municipal elections in rural areas. We have the

greatest presence in the municipalities, so we are obligated to, and it is
convenient for us, to have more campesino candidates, especially among
the uni-nominals. It is a good strategy for us because they have support
in rural areas" (my translation, interview, June 20, 2002).

CSUTCB leader Hipólito Choque and CIDOB leader Marcelino
Apurani ran with the MNR, as did Alejo Véliz's "right-hand" man, Celso
Carrillo, leader of the CSUTCB's Cochabamba affiliate, who left the ASP
to be an MNR senate candidate. The MNR also included indigenous candidates on its lists in rural Pando and Beni (interview, Marcial Humerez
Yapachura, MNR, June 25, 2002). The MIR, which had made significant
inroads in rural areas as head of the campesino and indigenous ministry during the Banzer-Quiroga government, also incorporated many
indigenous candidates, including campesino leaders Elsa Guevara and
Mateo Laura, CIDOB's Nicolás Montero, and a female Guaraní teacher
from rural Santa Cruz. MIR's traditional party cadre did not univer-
sally welcome the incorporation of indigenous and campesino candidates.
The MIR old guard, composed mainly of middle-level party professionals, resisted giving Elsa Guevara the prime spot as first senator from
Chuquisaca, but lost the internal battle that erupted within the party
on this issue (Cárdenas 2002: A28; confidential interviews, June 2002).
Although, when interviewed in July 2001, ASP leader Alejo Véliz had
expected to run for president (author interview), but he was unable to
pull together sufficient support. Véliz's more conciliatory, inclusive style
and his decision to seek support outside his base had led some to accuse
him of selling out. Véliz ran with the NFR, a Cochabamba-based party,
after failed efforts by the MIR to recruit the campesino leader. So anxious
was the NFR to land Véliz they offered him the choice of a uni-nominal
deputy or senatorial candidacy, or the leadership of the pluri-nominal
list (interview, Ivan Arias, La Paz, June 19, 2002; *Los Tiempos* 2002g).
Prominent Katarista leader Juan de la Cruz Villca, previously with Eje
Pachakuti, also ran with the NFR.

Another reason for the traditional parties' unprecedented recruitment
of indigenous candidates was the greater supply of qualified indigenous
aspirants, attributable to their own individual efforts to acquire education and experience, as well as training programs sponsored by NGOs,
international organizations, and private foundations. According to MNR
leader José María Centellas, today there are 50,000 new Aymara and
Quechua professionals with university educations, whose families have a
solid economic base. "So their professional children naturally desire to
take power, to be part of the government. This is natural. So this is a

process of socio-political change that the MNR generated with the 1952 revolution" (interview, June 25, 2002). Quispe's running mate Esther Balboa is an example of the growing number of female indigenous candidates, a response to demands from women in the traditional parties as well as a 1997 quota law that requires the allocation of 30 percent of places on party lists to women (interviews, Bertha Beatriz Acarapi, June 19, 2002; Elena Argirakis, June 19, 2002; José María Centellas, June 25, 2002; Jorge Lema, June 20, 2002).

Thus, in addition to the Indians that entered congress with the MAS or MIP, according to *La Razón*, eight Indians or campesinos gained office representing the MNR, NFR, MIR, or ADN (*La Razón* 2002a). Former Minister of Peasant, Indigenous, and Original Peoples Affairs (MACPIO) Wigberto Rivero, using different criteria, counts fifty-three indigenous legislators, including most of the MAS and MIP delegations, as well as seventeen entering congress with the MIR, NFR, and MNR (2003: 21). At the inauguration of the new congress, indigenous deputies wore traditional costumes and spoke in native languages, leaving nonindigenous members to search for translators (*El Diario* 2002a; *Los Tiempos* 2002b, 2002c). In his inaugural speech as president of the Chamber of Deputies, Guido Añez applauded the diversity of the new legislature: "The Congress is, finally, the reflection of our motley national reality; the expression of a Bolivia that is diverse, contradictory and, thus, fecund and possible" (*La Razón* 2002h). A campesino deputy put it more pungently, observing that the Congress "smells of coca and wears a poncho and sandals" (cited in Rivero 2003: 23).

CONCLUSION

In Bolivia, indigenous intellectuals sought to represent an indigenous majority that previously had been incorporated in a subordinate manner through patron-client relations. High barriers for party registration and a lack of resources for campaigning and distributing ballots continually thwarted these efforts. When parties did appear on the ballot the intrusion of clientelist and leftist parties into campesino politics and the multiple electoral projects launched by individual Indians fragmented the indigenous vote. These aspiring party leaders were affiliated with the major campesino organizations, but the parties they formed were not established by a collective, organizational decision and, thus, they could not count on organizational support. Unable to win 3 percent of the vote or to pay the resulting fines, many lost their registration.

After 1995, municipal decentralization enabled ethnic parties to compete below the more expensive and risky national level. Two ascendant sectors of the indigenous movement – the coca growers and the lowland organization CIDOB – sought to gain access to office in order to better pressure the state to fulfill their demands for legislative change and to achieve self-government. The coca growers were more united and more mobilized after a decade of combat with the state. They creatively surmounted continued ballot obstacles and a lack of financing and increased their share of the vote in each election. A more fragmented, less politically experienced lowland movement decided not to form a party because, given their small numbers, the lower level of political interest and registration among lowland Indians, and the urban bias of electoral districts, they were unlikely to win. After 2000, the persistent fragmentation of the party system and the sudden decline of dominant parties like CONDEPA, UCS, and ADN, opened unprecedented space for challenger parties. The dismal performance of ADN (3.4 percent), CONDEPA (0.37 percent), and UCS (5.5 percent) in 2002 – all three suffered the death of their charismatic founders – brought the share of the top three parties to 42.2 percent, and of the five once-dominant parties to 48 percent. The MAS and MIP filled the space they vacated. ENPS declined to 4.8 in 2002, reflecting the new ethnic parties' absorption of smaller leftist and populist parties (see Table 3.2).

Although it was unable to form a governing coalition – mainly due to Morales's refusal to ally with any other party – MAS gained control of eight of twenty-seven senate seats and 27 of 130 seats in the lower chamber, where it also gained the second vice presidency. This enabled the party to obtain the leadership of key committees. In the senate, MAS gained the presidency of the commissions on social development and cooperatives; labor, gender, and generational affairs; and agriculture, campesinos, and original communities. MAS also gained control of the committees on narcotrafficking and illicit drugs, interparliamentary affairs, sustainable development and environment, and local government (*Los Tiempos* 2002d). The refusal of both MAS and MIP to form a coalition with any other party probably boosted their future appeal among voters tired of politicians disavowing past promises and selling them out for a government job. Morales explained his position this way:

I want to reaffirm that the MAS, as a political movement that represents the Bolivian people, the marginalized, discriminated against and indigenous people, that the MAS is no prostitute party, it will not get mixed up with anyone and, well,

if [other political parties] seek alliances, they can seek them with those parties that
live from politics, those who negotiate politics.

(my translation; quoted in La Razón 2002g: A10)

This position was an abrupt change from that of parties like MRTKL
and CONDEPA, which had promised to defend the rights of the poor,
indigenous majority but then allied with neoliberal, center-right governments. Moreover, Morales promised to combine massive social mobilizations with legislative pressure if the party's political agenda did not move
forward. Quispe also declared his intention to maintain his struggle in
the legislature and in the streets. As he put it in a June 28, 2002, interview, with one hand he will play the game of democracy, with the other
he will hide a stone under his poncho (*La Prensa* Ud. Elige, June 28,
2002: 8; *Los Tiempos* 2002d; *La Razón* 2002g: A10; see also *La Razón*
2002c: A26).

CODA

The Bolivian political system received another jolt in October 2003 when
massive nationwide protests, led by Morales, Quispe, and others, forced
President Sánchez de Lozada to flee the country. They were preceded
by violent protests against proposed tax hikes in February of that year,
which left thirty-two dead. The original trigger for the October protests
was a skirmish in a town near Lake Titicaca in late September between
the police and Quispe's followers, who had killed two suspected cattle
rustlers. After police arrested one of those involved, Quispe organized
roadblocks in protest. The violence escalated after several protesters and
police were killed when the government tried to rescue tourists and others
being held hostage. Quispe added the president's proposal to sell natural
gas to multinational corporations through a port in Chile to the reasons for the roadblocks, which included seventy-two issues that had been
agreed upon by the government following protests in 2001, but which the
government had not fulfilled.

Evo Morales and other civil society leaders also picked up the gas issue.
In the weeks that followed, thousands of nonindigenous Bolivians joined
protests against the sale of natural gas at rates far below market value,
which seemed to symbolize the president's neglect of the poor majority
and his preference for policies that favored foreign and domestic elites.
The Sánchez de Lozada government ratcheted up its use of force over
the weekend of October 11–12 in an attempt to break up a blockade of

La Paz. The result was more than fifty-nine dead, most of whom died in battles between the army and protestors in the Aymara city of El Alto on Columbus Day, a day that symbolizes for indigenous peoples in the Americas the conquest by Europeans. After a week of massive protests, on October 17 the president fled the country. Morales and Quispe gave his successor, vice president Carlos Mesa, ninety days to fulfill his promises, which included a referendum on the gas issue and steps to legalize and convene a constituent assembly that would address indigenous organizations' long-standing demands (Mamani 2003; Schultz 2003; *The Economist* 2004). In February 2004, President Mesa secured congressional approval for constitutional changes that improved ballot access by breaking the monopoly of representation formerly held by parties. Article 61 permits "associations of citizens or indigenous peoples" to postulate candidates for elections. The February reforms also allow for the convocation of a constituent assembly. Indigenous organizations had been demanding these changes since 1995 (*Latin American Weekly Report* 2004b: 8).

As Bolivia prepared for municipal elections in December 2004, the leaders of the two new ethnic parties, while maintaining their identity as outsiders, were firmly established as central political figures. In a conjuncture where political parties had been rendered almost meaningless – Mesa is an independent and he appointed independents to his cabinet – all eyes were on Morales and Quispe. While Morales positioned himself as the statesman of the opposition, and an indispensable ally of President Mesa, Quispe projected a more radical profile. In May 2004, he resigned his seat in congress in order to pursue "the revolutionary struggle until Q'ullasuyo [the Aymara name for their territory] is liberated" (*Latin American Weekly Report* 2004b: 5).

4

"We Are the Government"

Pachakutik's Rapid Ascent to National Power

> The PSP–Pachakutik alliance will permit an era of transition, of changes that the indigenous movement plans to make. We are going to establish the bases of our project. The perspective is to construct a Plurinational State, which permits the exercise of the rights of everyone.
>
> Luis Macas, Pachakutik, Minister of Agriculture, 2003[1]

The Ecuadorian case has received considerable scholarly attention because of the meteoric rise of the indigenous-movement–based party Movimiento de Unidad Plurinacional Pachakutik (Pachakutik or MUPP). The party has been an important national actor since its first election in 1996. It helped elect President Lucio Gutiérrez in November 2002 in an alliance that garnered five Pachakutik militants seats in the cabinet. Pachakutik was formed by one of Latin America's most effective and internationally renowned indigenous peoples' organizations, CONAIE.

The Ecuadorian case emphasizes the importance of organizational unity and the existence of a dense network of affiliates to compensate for the absence of material resources. Despite the existence of numerous internal conflicts, based in regional, ethnic, religious, and personal rivalries, Ecuador's indigenous movement as a whole mobilized as a coherent collective actor during moments of crisis and opportunity. Both CONAIE and Pachakutik fended off challenges from rival organizations and harnessed the support of at least 80 percent of the indigenous population, while forging ties to sympathetic social organizations and political elites. But it wasn't easy. Significant attention is paid in this chapter to the fragile

---

[1] Quoted in *El Comercio* (Quito), January 1, 2003, cited in Hidalgo Flor (2003).

relationship between movement and party, which has reduced the electoral potential of the latter.

This chapter also highlights the importance of decentralization and rules offering easy access to the ballot, both in the decision to form a new ethnic party and in the ability of new parties to perform electorally. Ecuador decentralized at the beginning of the period under study, enabling indigenous organizations to gain experience as candidates and local government officials through alliances with sympathetic leftist parties. The limitations of these alliances, in which indigenous peoples were the junior partner, convinced an influential sector of the indigenous movement that an independent electoral vehicle was necessary. This did not become a viable option until 1996, when institutional reforms made it much easier for the indigenous movement to gather the necessary signatures to register its own party and to form alliances that would enable it to compete in a sufficient number of districts to make an electoral project worthwhile. By that time, the indigenous movement had consolidated itself as the most dynamic social movement and as the core of the political opposition. The electoral left, in contrast, had experienced a moderate decline and many of its militants were seeking a more dynamic political opportunity. Many chose to support and accompany the new indigenous electoral vehicle, Pachakutik, as members, or through numerous electoral alliances between Pachakutik and the four main leftist parties.

INDIGENOUS SOCIAL MOVEMENTS IN ECUADOR

The exact proportion of the 12,879,000 Ecuadorians that are indigenous is a hotly debated issue. The government did not include ethnicity in the census until 2001. That census, carried out jointly by the government indigenous affairs, Council for Development of the Nationalities and Peoples of Ecuador (CODENPE), and statistical, Ecuadorian Integrated System of Social Indicators (SIISE), offices estimated a total indigenous population of 6.6 percent, which combines the 6.1 percent of Ecuadorians over the age of fifteen self-identifying as indigenous with the 4.6 percent over fifteen who speak an indigenous language (Guzman 2003). These figures are substantially similar to those produced by a government survey of children and homes undertaken in 2000 (Survey of Measurement of Indicators of Children and Homes, EMIDINHO), and coincide with estimates by nonindigenous elites, such as former president Osvaldo Hurtado, who insist the number is 15 percent or less (interview, August 2, 1999). But the government figures are dramatically lower than those estimated by anthropologists, which typically range between

TABLE 4.1. *Ecuadorian indigenous population by province*

Province	% of Population Indigenous (1998)
Amazon	22.3 on average
Morona	25.5
Napo	24.5
Pastaza	46.9
Sucumbios	11.7
Zamora	2.7
Sierra	20.95 on average
Azuay	5.9
Bolivar	28.4
Cañar	18
Carchi	0
Chimborazo	49.3
Cotopaxi	27.9
Imbabura	39.6
Loja	5.2
Pichincha	9.4
Tungurahua	25.8
Coast	1.85 on average
El Oro	0
Esmeraldas	1.2
Galapagos	0
Guayas	5.2
Los Rios	0
Manabi	4.7

Source: Grijalva Jimenez (1998).

25 percent – the figure given by the Inter-American Indigenous Institute and listed on the Ecuadorian government's Web site (www.ecuador.org) – and 43 percent, the figure given by the International Labor Organization. The national indigenous organization CONAIE and its supporters claim 45 percent.

Indians are located throughout the country but are concentrated in the highland region. A large number have migrated to urban areas, particularly around Quito, the capital. As a proportion of the population, the indigenous population is largest in the Amazonian provinces of Pastaza, Morona Santiago, and Napo, and in the sierra provinces of Chimborazo, Imbabura, Cotopaxi, Tungurahua, Bolivar, and Cañar. A small number of Indians are settled in the coastal provinces, where they are on average 1.85 percent of the population (Grijalva Jiménez 1998; Pallares 2002: 6) (see Table 4.1).

The largest indigenous nationality is the Quichua, who are related to the Quechua peoples of Bolivia and Peru. The Quichua are found throughout the highlands and in the Amazon, where many have migrated. The highland Quichua population is estimated at approximately 1.3 million, although this figure is likely to undercount those living in urban areas (Pallares 2002: 6). While recognizing the Quichua as a "nationality," the government recognizes seventeen distinct "pueblos" or cultural subgroupings within the Quichua group. The government also recognizes twelve Amazonian "nationalities."[2] Quichua migrants to the Amazon comprise the largest ethnic group in that region, numbering approximately 90,000. The second-most-numerous nationality is the Shuar, with approximately 40,000 members. The remaining groups are tiny: for example, there are approximately 2,000 Huaorani and 600 Achuar (Pallares 2002: 6). In the Amazon, distinct language groups are more unified and unmixed with non-group members compared to the sierra, where ethnic identities are more blurred and indigenous forms of organization are more permeated by nonindigenous government and administrative structures. In sum, the dispersion and relative size of indigenous peoples in Ecuador affords the Quichua the dominant role, while the larger Amazonian groups defend their hegemony in particular lowland departments. Ecuador's population of African descent is located mainly on the coast and numbers approximately 2.2 percent of the total (Guzman 2003: 2). As in Bolivia, the government incorporates it into programs affecting indigenous peoples because Afro-Ecuadorians suffer from some similar conditions, such as economic underdevelopment, racial discrimination, and political underrepresentation (van Nieuwkoop and Uquillas 2000: 57). Unlike Bolivia, Afro-Ecuadorians mobilize politically as such, often in partnership with indigenous organizations.

As in Bolivia, indigenous social movements developed separately in the highland and Amazon regions. However, unlike Bolivia, the two movements merged in the 1980s into a coherent national movement and organization. The movements, and their distinct relations with political parties, are treated separately until the formation of the national organizations.

Indigenous Organizations in the Sierra

The rise of indigenous organizations in the sierra is closely tied to the activities of leftist parties. The first organized indigenous land protest occurred

---

[2] These are the Shuar, Huaorani, Siona, Secoya, Cofán, Huancavilcas, Manteños, Punaes, Chachi, Epera Tsáchilas, and Awa.

in February 1926, with the occupation of a hacienda in Cayambe. This protest gave rise to the Ecuadorian Socialist Party (PSE), which would become a frequent partner for indigenous organizations throughout the twentieth century. Middle-class radicals, workers, and intellectuals who founded the PSE saw the protest as an opportunity to build a broad-based revolutionary movement to transform economic and social relations in the highlands. They traveled throughout the region in the 1930s organizing indigenous and peasant communities into unions and leading strikes (Pallares 2002: 12). Indigenous communities mobilized around the government's 1936 proposed *Ley de Comunas*, which formally recognized indigenous and peasant community organizations in communities outside *hacienda* control. The law gave legal personality to communities with at least fifty persons, allowing for some degree of economic and political autonomy, since the communities were allowed to form their own local government (*cabildos*) and to own property collectively. Based on indigenous forms of organization, the comunas were linked institutionally to the state through local parishes (*parroquias*) (Becker 1999; Lucero 2002: 61–3; Macas 2002: 4).

In the 1940s, the Communist Party organized highland Indians as rural workers in a network of unions. It formed the Ecuadorian Federation of Indians (FEI) in 1944. Although it was nominally Ecuador's first national indigenous organization, the FEI was led and organized by non-Indians seeking to exploit the tensions between the state's promise of modern rural relations and the reality of feudalistic relations between haciendas and indigenous workers. Nevertheless, its formation was an important organizational milestone because it was the first effort to link indigenous sierra communities above the local level and, thus, served as a basis for future autonomous organizing in the 1960s and 1970s (Lucero 2002: 70–1). In the late 1950s, Indians formed local-level agricultural cooperatives and artisan workshops that were more autonomous and less class-centered than the political party–sponsored unions that leftist parties formed in the 1930s and 1940s (León 2001: 2). After the 1964 agrarian reform law ended the feudal relationship between Indians and haciendas, Indians organized to demand communal lands, control over natural resources, and access to agricultural assistance programs (Macas 2002: 4).

Two factors explain the boom in indigenous political organizing in the 1960s and 1970s: (1) the formation of a new indigenous leadership class, attributable to advances in access to education; and (2) the efforts of the Catholic Church and, to a lesser extent, evangelical Protestant churches, to train indigenous catechists and to form provincial and regional-level organizations (León 2001: 3). In the 1960s, the conservative Partido Democrático Cristiano helped organize the National Federation of Peasant Organizations (FENOC), which was founded in 1968, originally under a different name, and affiliated with the Catholic labor union Ecuadorian Confederation of Classist Organizations (CEDOC). The church gained indigenous support by promoting indigenous culture, rather than stressing class identity (León 2001: 3; Pallares 2002: 14–15). In 1971, priests and religious activists sponsored a series of meetings with indigenous community leaders and catechists in Cañar, Chimborazo, Loja, and Tunguruahua. These culminated in a 1972 conference of sierra organizations that formed the highland confederation ECUARUNARI (Ecuador Runacunapac Riccharimui), which means "The Awakening of the Ecuadorian Indian" in Quichua. ECUARUNARI's innovation was to link the indigenous population through its cabildo governments, rather than through economic associations, cooperatives, and unions. The number of indigenous comunas expanded dramatically as Indians took advantage of the 1937 *Ley de Comunas* and the redistribution of hacienda lands to establish autonomous community organizations. Their legally recognized governments formed the basis of the social movement networks that expanded in the 1970s and 1980s. ECUARUNARI helped establish strong local federations for virtually every distinct cultural group, some of which became powerful actors in their own right. ECUARUNARI distinguished itself from other campesino organizations by stressing the need to combat racial and cultural discrimination and by allowing indigenous leaders to serve in top leadership positions (Pallares 2002: 152). While putting relatively greater emphasis on the ethnic basis of Indians' oppression, ECUARUNARI leaders retained the class-based analysis they had learned through previous rural struggles as affiliates of FENOC or FEI (Lucero 2002: 74; Pallares 2002: 42).

In the early 1980s, some indigenous leaders ran as candidates with leftist and center-left political parties, while various local and provincial-level indigenous organizations formed alliances with political parties to run indigenous candidates or to support particular parties deemed sympathetic to the indigenous agenda. The parties with whom indigenous organizations most often allied were the center-right Democracia Popular and the leftist parties Broad Leftist Front (FADI), PSE, Democratic Left (ID), Concentration of Revolutionary Forces (CFR), and Popular Democratic Movement (MPD) (Andolina 1999: 217; Pallares 2002: 73). ECUARUNARI participated in the FADI alliance in the 1970s and until 1984 (Pallares 2002: 168). FENOC formed a national alliance with FADI until 1986, when it switched to the PSE. The organization traditionally has been allied with the PSE; during the 1998–2003 legislative session, its president, Pedro de la Cruz, was an alternate deputy for the party (interviews, Pedro de la Cruz, July 21, 1999; Luis Macas, July 28, 1999).

The sierra organization ECUARUNARI struggled in the 1970s and 1980s to protect its autonomy from political parties. For example, two church-based leftist parties (National Movement of Christians for Liberation, MNCL, and Revolutionary Movement of the Christian Left, MRIC) were active in the early years of the organization. These parties rejected cultural and racial claims as "racist and folkloric." In the mid-1970s, fighting between moderate and leftist Catholic forces within the organization threatened to divide the movement and to undermine its autonomy. ECUARUNARI expelled non-Indians from its 1976 congress in Riobamba and henceforth tightly controlled non-Indians' access to the organization (Pallares 2002: 152–3).

In the late 1970s–early 1980s, FADI and PSE did not explicitly address indigenous or ethnic rights in their platforms but they promoted economic and social policies that appealed to Indians, such as land reform, rural health insurance, and credit programs (Pallares 2002: 88). Until 1996, the ID was the only major party to include indigenous autonomy demands in its platform, one reason that the party gained most of its votes in the heavily indigenous sierra (Birnir 2000: 10). These appeals were effective because indigenous voters tended to favor leftist parties.[3] But indigenous organizations participating in alliances with leftist parties generally found them to be unsatisfactory for the same reasons that Bolivian indigenous leaders ultimately rejected them: (1) indigenous organizations were subordinated to the *mestizo* leadership of the parties, which refused to give them a decision-making role or as many opportunities for candidacies as leaders believed they deserved; (2) indigenous politicians were pressured to be loyal to the party, rather than the organization they represented; (3) indigenous organizations felt used and manipulated by parties who promised to press indigenous demands, but forgot them after the election; and (4) some indigenous militants who attained public office became co-opted or corrupted by the political parties, or at least there were many accusations of this happening (Andolina 1999: 218–19). In the mid-1980s,

---

[3] See Chapter 2, note 8, concerning Chiriboga and Rivera's (1989) survey of indigenous voters. The authors conclude that modern indigenous voters were influenced by programmatic appeals and institutional affiliations with the left, rather than the clientelist relations of the past (1989: 193).

a current within ECUARUNARI argued that it was time to break from class-based, *mestizo*-run organizations and to seek an autonomous route to political power. The organization's leaders began to reach out to lowland organizations (Pallares 2002: 169).

Indigenous Organizations in the Amazon

As in the sierra, in the Amazon the Catholic Church helped to form many of the first local-level indigenous organizations. Ecuador's Federation of Shuar Centers, formed in 1961, was among the earliest to form of South America's contemporary Amazonian organizations. The Catholic Church helped them to create a network of radio-based schools to promote bilingual education in 1972, and this enabled the organization rapidly to gain popularity. The Shuar gradually became more independent from the missionaries and developed good relations with the Ecuadorian military by helping to guard the contested border with Peru. Other Amazonian groups responded to the influx of colonists that followed the 1964 agrarian reform. After the discovery of oil in the 1970s, colonization intensified and Indians, often with assistance from environmental organizations, organized against the intrusion of oil companies and the environmental damage and cultural chaos they brought. In 1979, the Shuar, the Quichua Organization of Indigenous Peoples of Pastaza (OPIP), and other Amazonian organizations formed the Confederation of Indigenous Nationalities of the Ecuadorian Amazon (CONFENIAE). CONFENIAE then organized the Secoya, Cofán, Achuar, and Huaorani into ethnic federations and linked them to the confederation (León 2001: 3; Lucero 2002: 77–9).

The geographic isolation of Amazon Indians was a boon to political organizing. It allowed less interference and manipulation by leftist parties, apart from some brief alliances with CEDOC and FENOC. As a result, most Amazon organizations have no experience with classist organizations or parties (Pallares 2002: 170). In addition, whereas state-run schools in the highlands imposed the Spanish language, missionary-run schools in the Amazon provided bilingual education. This facilitated the construction of a strong cultural identity and cohesive language-group level organizations (Selverston 1994: 135).

National Indigenous Organizations

The highland federation ECUARUNARI, the Amazon confederation CONFENAIE, and Coordinator of the Indigenous Organizations of the Ecuadorian Coast (COICE), a weaker organization uniting coastal indigenous communities, formed a national coordinating body in 1979 called National Coordinating Council of the Indigenous Nationalities of Ecuador (CONACNIE). The Jaime Roldós regime (1979–81) launched a massive literacy campaign that increased indigenous literacy from 30 to 55 percent between 1974 and 1982. The increased availability of educated, Spanish-speaking leaders assisted the growth of the national movement. Many early movement leaders were bilingual teachers and bilingual education was the most important focus of early organizational efforts (Pallares 2002: 197).

The desire to have a more institutionalized national organization led in 1986 to the creation of CONAIE, which today can boast the affiliation of approximately 80 percent of the country's community-level indigenous organizations (PRODEPINE 1998). Despite their unification within CONAIE, CONFENIAE and ECUARUNARI continue to operate independently and to have significant political importance in their own right. Their interests often are opposed because, whereas sierra Indians seek to recuperate lands lost to haciendas and to demand access to more land, Amazonian Indians seek to defend territories they already inhabit from incursions by outsiders. In addition to extractive businesses, Amazonian Indians must contend with numerous colonists, including highland Indians, because the government's easiest answer to the land distribution question in the sierra has been to encourage landless Indians to resettle in the Amazon. As a result, the Amazonian population increased 135 percent during the agrarian reform (1962–74) (Lucero 2002: 84). In order to manage the regional rift, CONAIE rotates leadership between sierra and Amazonian leaders and balances the composition of their executive council by region. CONAIE maintains a permanent office in Quito and convenes delegates to national conferences every two to three years. By the late 1990s, it encompassed 220 organizations and had created a highly differentiated leadership structure consisting of a president, vice president, and leaders in charge of various programmatic and organizational priorities, such as land and territory, international relations, and education and research (Sánchez López and Freidenberg 1998: 70).

Because of problems encountered by the sierra organization described in the preceding text, following its formation in 1986, CONAIE officially frowned on indigenous organizations and militants participating in elections with political parties and urged them to focus on building the movement outside the formal political system. Between 1989 and 1992, CONAIE directed the organizations and individual indigenous militants to end these activities and to officially promote boycotts of elections, arguing that they supported an illegitimate system (Andolina 1999: 211; Collins 2001: 12; interview, Miguel Lluco, August 2, 1999). As indigenous leader Luis Macas said at the time, the electoral boycott was "a way of rejecting traditional elections, political mismanagement, and demogogic political parties" (quoted in *Diario Hoy*, September 9, 1991; cited in Lucero 2002: 87). Most honored the boycott (Andolina 1999: 219). This policy enabled CONAIE to avoid many of the problems that had plagued the campesino union CSUTCB in Bolivia, where parties fought for control of the highland indigenous movement.

National-level organizations claiming to represent the indigenous population existed prior to the formation of CONAIE. However, these have more patchy networks of base and second-tier organizations and a weaker national presence (Lucero 2002: 84; Sánchez López and Freidenberg 1998: 69). Two national-level organizations challenged CONAIE's dominance during the period under study.[4] The most serious challenge came from the Ecuadorian Federation of Evangelical Churches (FEINE), formed on November 26, 1980 (www.feine.nativeweb.org). The Missionary Evangelical Union began promoting Protestantism in the sierra province of Chimborazo in the 1960s. Its first generation of pastors became the founding leaders of provincial-level Asociaciones de Iglesias Evangélicos (Lucero 2002: 82). FEINE claims affiliated provincial-level Asociaciones de Iglesias Evangélicas or federations in seventeen sierra, Amazonian, and coastal provinces, although its greatest influence is in the central highland departments of Bolívar, Chimborazo, Cotopaxi, and Tungurahua. These associations link 600 churches (Andrade 2003: 127; PRODEPINE 1998: 16). The government estimates that FEINE represents approximately 17 percent of the indigenous population (Brysk 2000: 73n14). FEINE originally shunned politics, preferring to emphasize its confessional mission. Nevertheless, individual members and Protestant pastors participated in CONAIE-led mobilizations in the 1980s and 1990s. When FEINE became more involved in politics in the 1980s, it developed a conservative reputation, owing in part to its former president, Alonso Guacho, who headed the Office of Indigenous Affairs in the conservative Febres Cordero government. FEINE developed a more explicitly oppositional profile in the 1990s, partly in response to the loss of its members to CONAIE

---

[4] Other, smaller rivals include the old communist-party related FEI and the Ecuadorian National Indigenous Labor Movement (FENACLE), which is associated with the labor movement (Brysk 2000: 73).

(Andrade 2003: 119; Lucero 2002: 201). In the late 1990s, it grew in importance and eclipsed other movements, including ECUARUNARI, in parts of the sierra, particularly in Chimborazo, Ecuador's most indigenous province (interviews, María Fernanda Espinosa, July 19, 1999; Miguel Lluco, August 2, 1999).

Another CONAIE rival is the National Federation of Peasant, Indigenous, and Black Organizations (FENOCIN). Dating originally to the labor movements of the 1940s, the organization emerged as FENOC in 1968 to lead the independent peasant movement, working mainly on land and agrarian issues. In the 1970s, "militant Socialists" gained control of FENOC, radicalized it, and injected more of a class analysis that rejected many issues related to Indians' oppression as a subordinate ethnic group (Lucero 2002: 73). The words *Indígenas* and later *Negras* were added to the name in the 1990s to incorporate the ethnic dimensions of the struggle and to include Afro-Ecuadorians. FENOCIN defines itself as a "multiethnic campesino-indigenous organization" and claims to have more than 1,250 base community affiliates throughout the country (www.fenocin.nativeweb.org).

Although FEINE and FENOCIN traditionally have been moderate political movements focused mainly on sectoral demands, in an effort to compete with CONAIE, in the 1990s they increased their emphasis on ethnic rights and autonomy and took more radical and oppositional positions toward the government (Sarango Macas 1997: 313). Relations among the three largest national-level indigenous organizations can be tense, but at the local level affiliates work together and participate in periodic national-level mobilizations convoked by CONAIE, even if they are not CONAIE affiliates, provided that they support the purpose of the march. Relations became more tense in the late 1990s and early 2000s, as CONAIE fought to marginalize its two rivals. It pressured the government and international aid agencies to work only with CONAIE and to exclude representatives of non-CONAIE organizations from policy and development projects. In 1999, CONAIE was able to restructure the government's indigenous development agency, CODENPE, so that it recognized only "nationalities" and "peoples" in a bid to dismantle strong first- and second-tier FEINE and FENOCIN affiliates and their regional networks, which threaten CONAIE's hegemony. Although FEINE and FENOCIN were represented on CODENPE's superior council, the newly structured agency was viewed as an alliance between CONAIE and the government, until a rift emerged between the Gutiérrez government and the indigenous movement in 2003 (interviews, Pedro de la Cruz, July 21,

1999; Fernando García, July 21, 1999; Manuel Imbaquingo, July 20, 1999; Paulina Palacios, July 19, 1999).[5]

By the late 1980s, all provinces with indigenous population contained indigenous organizations at the local, microregional, and provincial levels. A 2000 World Bank study found the Ecuadorian indigenous population to be "extremely well organized" at the national, regional, and local level, with organizations that are "relatively strong" compared with neighboring countries (Van Nieuwkoop and Uquillas 2000: 6). The study reports approximately 2,300 grassroots indigenous organizations, consisting of comunas, cooperatives, and other units, which are organized into approximately 180 second-tier organizations (ibid.: 7).[6]

By the mid-1990s, CONAIE was articulating a coherent vision of a plurinational state, a project that calls for the radical transformation of all Ecuadorian political and economic institutions. Although it is a long way from achieving that goal, CONAIE can credibly claim responsibility for the most successful and dramatic social movement mobilizations in Ecuador since the democratic transition, including major demonstrations, marches, or roadblocks in 1990, 1992, 1994, 1997, 1999, 2000, and 2001, all of which included periods of extended civil disobedience. CONAIE's first major victory came in 1988 when, in response to the organization's demand, the government created the bilingual education agency National Director of Intercultural and Bilingual Education (DINEIB). Once DINEIB had been created, CONAIE used its control over the program to better coordinate and organize the heretofore dispersed and fractious set of organizations loosely allied to CONAIE (León 2001: 5). Thus, bilingual education was not just the movement's first great achievement; it became a powerful organizing tool. The Rodrigo Borja administration (1988–92) granted CONAIE the right to name the directors of the national bilingual education program and recognized CONAIE as the official negotiator for the indigenous population (Selverston 1994: 146).

Two years later the 1990 National Indigenous Uprising established CONAIE as a national political actor. The mobilization began June 4 when 200 Indians from Chimborazo occupied the Santo Domingo

---

[5] For an analysis of CONAIE's nationalities and peoples strategy, see Lucero (2002).

[6] These tiers refer to provincial and regional organizations that link the hundreds of first-tier, or base-level organizations (cooperatives, community centers) to the national organizations. According to the National Program for the Development of the Indigenous and Black Peoples (PRODEPINE) methodology, second-tier organizations unite at least four first-tier organizations and are usually called *unions*; third-tier organizations unite at least four second-tier organizations, and are often called *federations* (PRODEPINE 1998: 8).

Cathedral in Quito, undertook a ten-day hunger strike, and presented a list of demands to the government. Chief among these were the resolution of long-standing land conflicts, control over the bilingual education program, and protection from discrimination. Although the substantive demands were important, equally significant was the symbolic importance of embracing and expressing a collective indigenous identity in the face of persistent insults and humiliation. Local and regional indigenous organizations participating in the nationwide uprising added their own demands. The 1990 uprising served as a catalyst for CONAIE to mobilize its affiliates. Protests swept the sierra, particularly the provinces of Chimborazo, Cotopaxi, Bolívar, and Tunguruhua and the Amazonian province of Napo (Pallares 2002: 17). For nearly a week, coordinated roadblocks and market boycotts paralyzed transportation in the highlands and starved the cities of basic foodstuffs, while CONAIE affiliates occupied government buildings, participated in marches, and kidnapped military officials. In total, tens of thousands of Indians participated in land invasions, civil disobedience, and public protest. The uprising ended when President Borja agreed to sit down with CONAIE leaders and discuss their demands – an unprecedented event that ultimately led to the titling of 600,000 hectares of Amazon land for the 1,200 Huaorani and, following a subsequent April 1991 march, 1,115,475 hectares for the Quichua of Pastaza (Selverston 2002: ch. 4).

The significance of the 1990 uprising cannot be overstated. In the late 1980s, few rank-and-file members – or even leaders – of local movements nominally affiliated with CONAIE knew much about it (Sánchez López and Freidenberg 1998: 70n12). The uprising enabled CONAIE to link the diverse indigenous organizations in the country to the national organization and to inculcate a common identity as members of this organization and of a coordinated effort to pursue common goals as Indians. In addition, the uprising dramatically increased public awareness of Indians – their goals, needs, and circumstances – and CONAIE'S effective mobilization throughout much of the country stunned the political establishment. More mobilizations followed. In April 1991, OPIP militants marched from their Amazon home to Quito to demand titling of their collective land claims. On May 28–9, 1991, Indians participated in a symbolic takeover of congress and demanded amnesty for Indians imprisoned during earlier protests. In 1992, Ecuadorian Indians joined a hemisphere-wide mobilization to protest state-sponsored celebrations of the 500th anniversary of the European conquest of America's native peoples.

In June 1994, CONAIE defeated the right-wing Sixto Durán Ballén government's (1992–96) agrarian development law, which proposed the privatization of land and water rights and favored modern agribusiness, at the expense of smallholder indigenous farmers. During the "Mobilization for Life" – convened by CONAIE together with FENOC-I and FEINE – roadblocks obstructed commerce in fifteen of Ecuador's twenty-one provinces for two weeks, while indigenous leaders demanded a law more favorable to small farmers and collectively owned community lands. More than 3,500 indigenous communities and peasant organizations participated. Unlike the previous uprising, this one was met by government repression that left at least five indigenous participants dead. In the Amazon, participants occupied oil wells and halted oil production for several days. In urban areas, they mounted massive demonstrations and occupied public buildings. After weeks of tense negotiations and faxes from international organizations and observers denouncing the government's brutality, the agrarian law was changed to include many important indigenous demands, such as protection for their collective land-holding regimes, the continued public ownership of water, and the continuation of the agrarian reform process that Durán Ballén had sought to end (Andolina 1994: 19–20; 1999: 214). In addition to these substantive achievements, the negotiations changed the public image of CONAIE to that of a moderate, reasonable force, and made a public figure of CONAIE's main negotiator Nina Pacari, who earned the grudging respect of nonindigenous politicians for her moderate and conciliatory approach (interview, Jorge León, July 17, 1999). Moreover, the mobilization gained CONAIE numerous allies among popular movements and parties on the center-left and left opposing the government's neoliberal reforms and its exclusionary practices (Andolina 1999: 215). These achievements increased the confidence of CONAIE's leaders as they faced what would become perhaps the movement's most important decision: whether and how to participate in elections.

The numerous protests described in the preceding text may be viewed individually and appreciated for the variety of mobilization tactics, alliances, and achievements that resulted. It is more fruitful, however, to view the 1986–94 period as one sustained effort of a steadily growing and maturing social movement to pressure the Ecuadorian state and society to yield to its goal of establishing a plurinational state. Although the working class had been defeated by the economic transformations of the 1990s, the indigenous sector – no less affected – increased in organizational strength, public support, and the respect of the political elite, even as it struggled to maintain the unity of a fractious, diverse movement. The majority of its demands remained unfulfilled, but in 1995 the movement had a long list of substantive achievements: control over a state-supported bilingual education program, the collective titling of millions of hectares of land, and the repeal and rewriting of the agrarian reform law. But its most impressive achievements were yet to come. These would be achieved through a dual strategy of social movement and political party activity. They include the repeal or blockage of neoliberal reforms, the writing of a new constitution that codified a significant set of indigenous collective rights providing the basis for the establishment of political autonomy at the local and regional level, the creation of an agency dominated by CONAIE leaders within the executive for the design and implementation of indigenous policy, and the ouster of two governments.

UNDERSTANDING ETHNIC PARTY FORMATION

Because Ecuador already had a fairly decentralized political system at the beginning of the 1980s, individual indigenous leaders and local and provincial indigenous social movement organizations had an opportunity to participate in elections in alliance with parties, many of which actively courted the indigenous population after the abolition of literacy requirements for voting in 1979. Illiterates first voted in 1984. The enfranchisement of illiterates increased the indigenous rate of electoral participation from 19 to 45 percent between 1979 and 1986 (McDonald and Ruhl 1989: 314). Underregistration is less of a problem in Ecuador than in Bolivia: only approximately 10 percent of the indigenous are not registered to vote (Pacari Vega 2002: 2).

As in Bolivia, restrictive party registration requirements were the main impediment to the formation of ethnic parties. The 1977 Law of Parties required that parties present a membership list of 0.5 percent of registered voters for districts where the party wished to contest elections and to demonstrate a formal organization in 10 of the country's twenty-one provinces in order to compete in national elections, three of which must be the country's most populous provinces, and two of which are on the coast, where few Indians live. Provided they could surmount institutional barriers, throughout the period 1980–2002 Ecuador's party system was relatively open to new parties. The dominant four parties typically won less than 20 percent of the vote, presenting weak competition for popular new candidates. Only one party, the Social Christian Party (PSC) earned more than 20 percent of the vote in more than four elections since

TABLE 4.2. *Ecuador: Vote share for dominant and leftist parties*

Election	Combined Votes Dominant Parties	Combined Votes Leftist Parties	ENPS
1984(P)	55.9%	37.9%	
1984(L)	43.9%	33.4%	6.10
1986(L)	45.5%	32.3%	7.39
1988(P)	68.4%	29.5%	
1988(L)	62.2%	34.1%	4.63
1990(L)	62.3%	30.9%	6.29
1992(P)	57%	13.3%	
1992(L)	55.4%	19.8%	6.61
1994(L)	61.3%	23.3%	5.71
1996(P)	56.3%	19.3%	
1996(L)	68.1%	20.5%	4.80
1998(P)	78.1%	18.3%	
1998(L)	74.7%	18.9%	5

Notes: Dominant parties are Partido Social Cristiano, Democracia Popular, Izquierda Democrática, Partido Roldosista Ecuatoriano. Leftist parties are ID, Frente Amplia de la Izquierda, Partido Socialista Ecuatoriano, Liberación Nacional, Movimiento Popular Democrático, Nuevo Pais. (L) legislative elections; (P) presidential elections in all cases are first-round results.
Sources: Conaghan (1995: 441); Saltos and Vázquez (1998); www.georgetown.edu/pdba.

the return to democracy in 1978 (see Table 4.2). Voter loyalties shifted from election to election. Nevertheless, the four largest parties – all of which have competed since 1984 and continue to exist – have dominated the vote, collectively and individually. The combined share of votes for the four major parties has not fallen below 50 percent since 1986 and the general tendency has been toward greater electoral dominance between 1984 and 1998. Ecuador's party system is among the region's most fragmented, with an average effective number of parties for seats (ENPS) of 5.8 between 1978 and 1992. The high fragmentation of the legislature necessitates that the government form a coalition of several parties. This gives smaller parties the opportunity to become part of the government, as Pachakutik would do on several occasions.

As in Bolivia, the electoral strength of leftist parties declined in the late 1980s (see Table 4.2). This decline reflects the decline of the (ID) – one of the four dominant parties since the democratic transition – after its term in office under President Rodrigo Borja (1988–92). The weakness of parties on the left after 1992 opened space on this part of the political spectrum for the ethnic party that would form in 1996. Moreover, once the indigenous movement had established itself as the most dynamic oppositional movement and standard bearer of antineoliberalism, leftist intellectuals, party professionals, and popular movement activists were eager to hitch their wagons to CONAIE and its new party.

CONAIE was the first indigenous organization in Ecuador to form its own political party. This decision was made mainly at the instigation of its Amazonian leadership, which had far less experience with electoral politics than sierra leaders. The factor that finally tipped the balance in favor of the Amazonian position was a dramatic improvement in ballot access in 1994. This occurred, not coincidentally, at the same time that the indigenous movement had consolidated itself as Ecuador's most dynamic collective actor.

Strategic Decision-Making Scenario I

Pallares recounts the experience of one indigenous organization that formed a long-standing alliance with leftist parties between 1980 and 1996: the Union of Peasant and Indigenous Organizations of Cotacachi (UNORCAC). The organization's experience demonstrates the logic against forming new ethnic parties prior to 1996, as well as reasons for dissatisfaction with leftist party alliances. Through alliances with the left, UNORCAC won a seat on the Cotacachi, Imbabura, municipal council in 1980 and maintained it almost continuously to the present day. Thus, it is the longest-running example of indigenous municipal council representation (Pallares 2002: 73).

UNORCAC formed in 1977 and affiliated with FENOC. It made the decision to participate in local elections on the FADI ticket at a 1978 assembly. This was arranged with the national FADI leadership because that party had no organization in Cotacachi, a situation that made it easy for UNORCAC to monopolize the FADI ticket. UNORCAC's list finished third, earning a seat on the council for the first indigenous council member in Imbabura (Pallares 2002: 90–1). FADI's win attracted other leftist parties to the district and *mestizos* formed a local FADI organization. Thereafter UNORCAC had to negotiate with *mestizos* for places on the FADI list for its candidates. Some UNORCAC activists proposed at this time the creation of an indigenous party to build on the organization's electoral success and to eliminate the necessity of negotiating with *mestizos*. UNORCAC president and Cotacachi municipal councilor Alberto Andrango resisted. He argued against forming parties as follows:

As Indians we organize with peculiar interests, for our interests, such as the respect that we want them to give us. We want them [*mestizos*] to be conscious of our

situation, of our traditions, of our culture . . . but our UNORCAC also unites with
the Left to work together with the mestizo peasants, Indians, [and] the popular
sectors. . . . [T]o organize as an Indian party is not convenient because it means
only organizing as a race. We would be isolated in this way, and the struggle is
not only to obtain indigenous people's objectives.

    (Pallares 2002: 92, citing interview with Andrango in *Ecuador Debate* 12
    [1986], her translation)

In addition to the multiethnic nature of the district, and UNORCAC's
decision to work across races to build a broader support network, Pallares
observes that there were not enough able and willing indigenous candidates to form an autonomous indigenous party (2002: 93).

In 1986, UNORCAC left the FADI alliance and joined with the PSE, an
alliance that lasted until 1996. FADI had broken apart when one faction
left to join the ID, and the remainder joined the PSE or the newly formed
National Liberation (LN) (Pallares 2002: 94, 238n35). Although they consistently gained office with the PSE, UNORCAC leaders and municipal
councilors increasingly grew frustrated with the alliance. *Mestizo* PSE
leaders refused to allow UNORCAC a leadership position or a role in decision making in the local organization and resisted UNORCAC's demands
to place more of its candidates on the ballot and to run an indigenous candidate for municipal council president. Moreover, once in office *mestizo*
PSE councilors were more likely to work with *mestizos* from other parties and to ignore indigenous constituents and requests for public works
in indigenous-majority cantons. Indigenous council members also suffered mistreatment and disrespect from other council members and staff
(Pallares 2002: 96–7).

Open conflict broke out in 1992 over UNORCAC's insistence that an
indigenous candidate compete for municipal council president on the PSE
ballot. Local *mestizo* PSE militants also were dissatisfied with the relationship because they believed that an alliance with Indians cost the party
prestige in Cotacachi. This sentiment differed from that of the national
PSE leadership, which was cementing its relationship with FENOC and
actively courting the indigenous movement. Cotacachi Indians eventually
would prevail, but only after the formation of Pachakutik in 1996 (see
the following text).

Strategic Decision-Making Scenario II

The question of participating in electoral politics had long been debated
within the national indigenous movement. Andolina traces these discussions to the late 1980s, after the creation of CONAIE. According to

interviews conducted by Beck and Mijeski (2000), Amazonian indigenous leaders had been pushing for the creation of an indigenous political party since the successful 1990 National Indigenous Uprising had dramatically increased the visibility and mobilizational capacity of the indigenous movement. Unable to reach consensus, the organization lacked an official position, but prior to the 1988 national elections two distinct views were articulated: Amazonian leaders preferred to immediately compete in national elections through their own party; sierra leaders preferred to stay out of politics and to focus on the organization's institutional consolidation and movement identity. At a 1988 meeting, CONAIE's Political Committee resolved that indigenous militants should support the ID candidate, Rodrigo Borja, although the organization would not officially support him in order to maintain its autonomy (Andolina 1999: 217–18). In 1992, CONAIE boycotted the elections, demanding "actions not elections" (Sánchez López and Freidenberg 1998: 70).

Events in neighboring Colombia encouraged the faction pushing for an indigenous party. In 1990, three Colombian indigenous leaders participated in a national constituent assembly. The constitution that resulted created a district guaranteeing Indians two seats in the Senate and allowed social movements and independents to compete in elections. Newly formed indigenous parties were surprisingly successful in the 1990 constituent assembly elections and the local, regional, and national elections that followed (see Chapter 6). At its 1993 Congress, CONAIE resolved to participate in elections with its own party vehicle, following the successful example of Colombia's indigenous electoral circumscriptions, and to allow the movement to run independent candidates in local and provincial elections as soon as the law allowed. But sierra leaders continued to resist participation in national elections. They preferred to debate the issue further, while emphasizing participation in local elections in order to construct a new alternative model of government from the municipal level that would eventually be brought to higher levels of government. They also preferred to emphasize strengthening ties with other social sectors with a view toward forming a plurinational social movement organization that would not be a political party (Andolina 1999: 221–2; Cabascango 2002: 1; Collins 2001: 13; Sánchez López and Freidenberg 1998: 71–2).

Some indigenous leaders, particularly those from the sierra with a long experience of relations with parties, were concerned that participation in national elections might result in militants becoming co-opted by the parties, which would jeopardize the movement's autonomy (Collins 2001: 13; Sarango Macas 1997: 320). For that reason, in 1993 CONAIE only authorized local and provincial candidacies. In addition, the following principles were approved: (1) no alliances would be made with traditional political parties; (2) candidates must be different than traditional candidates, that is, not career politicians and professionals from the upper-middle class; (3) CONAIE should participate in alliance with other popular movements in order to broaden its electoral appeal and to construct a broad "common political project" (Andolina 1999: 222).

CONAIE's successful 1994 campaign against the Durán Ballén government's referendum transformed the political calculus. CONAIE, labor unions, and the left worked together to oppose the neoliberal economic reform package, but they supported measures that would improve access to the ballot for parties, movements, and independents. The new rules allowed political parties to form electoral alliances, which enabled parties to gain support in provinces where they lacked a base of supporters. A provision was eliminated that had required parties wishing to run in elections to register members in ten provinces, including coastal provinces. Parties wishing to run in national elections no longer had to present candidates in twelve of the country's then twenty-one provinces. There continued to be a relatively high (4–5 percent) threshold for parties to maintain registration following elections. The proscription on independent candidates also was repealed and individuals and organizations were allowed to run in any province where they could register 1.5 percent of voters (Birnir 2000: 10; Collins 2001: 8).[7]

The 1994 institutional changes enabled the indigenous movement to field candidates at the national level despite its geographic concentration in the sierra and Amazon and the scarcity of indigenous voters on the coast. According to interviews with and statements by CONAIE leaders, the changes in the electoral law generated by the 1994 referendum were crucial to the decision to compete in elections in 1996 with their own party (Cabascango 2002: 1; interview with Ampam Karakras in Montoya Rojas and Paredes 2001: 84; Pacari Vega 2002: 2). The campaign was crucial because its success convinced a significant cohort of CONAIE leaders that the public was sufficiently behind their neoliberal reform agenda that a national party uniting antineoliberal sectors would be successful. Moreover, the fact that seasoned political veterans of the leftist parties

---

[7] A 1979 political party law required that parties win 5 percent of the vote in two successive elections to maintain registration. This requirement had been eliminated in 1983, but it was reinstated after the 1992 elections at 4 percent. It was raised to 5 percent again in 1997 (Birnir unpublished manuscript: 19).

participated in the campaign convinced CONAIE leaders that it would be feasible and beneficial to include them in this project (Sánchez López and Freidenberg 1998: 72).

Collins observes that Ecuador's electoral organization always had favored the indigenous population because district magnitude (DM) is determined by the population of each province and tends to favor rural and more sparsely populated districts. Indigenous peoples are mainly concentrated in provinces where fewer votes are needed to win seats. In addition, the indigenous movement since the 1980s has been organized into territorially defined provincial-level federations that correspond to the country's provincial electoral districts. This organizational scheme favors the indigenous movement more than other social movements, which either are concentrated in urban areas, such as labor and feminist movements, or are not organized geographically (Collins 2001: 8, 9n13). Indigenous organizations were aware of these advantages and considered them in deciding to participate in elections. They considered themselves likely to win in the municipalities and provinces where they were well-organized and constituted a significant part of the population. Under such circumstances they could mobilize provincial- and municipal-level social movement organizations as electoral resources. All that was needed was a permissive institutional environment to ease access to the ballot (Andolina 1999; Collins 2001: 9; Sánchez López and Freidenberg 1998: 71).

Collins (2001) and Andolina (1999) argue that the most important feature of the 1994 reforms was the removal of the "psychological" or "ideological" barrier to participating in elections. Allowing groups to call themselves *independent candidates* or *political movements* enabled indigenous organizations to participate without having to call themselves a political party, a term that had negative connotations. This avoided the appearance of an abrupt change in CONAIE's antisystemic ideology. Even though the distinction between *parties* and *movements* is semantic, it gave the indigenous movement political cover.[8] I disagree. Although it is true that it was advantageous for the indigenous movement to call itself a movement rather than a party, this view underestimates the importance of real improvements in the law that made it easier to field candidates – such as the ability to form electoral alliances, which Pachakutik has done

[8] Pachakutik leaders argue that their "movement" lacks the internal hierarchy and rigid structure of a political party. Sánchez López and Freidenberg argue that these protestations are made for symbolic reasons: to enable Pachakutik to articulate a critique of the political system as illegitimate while operating within it as a party (1998: 76).

in each election, and the absence of the need to pull significant votes from coastal provinces.

The effectiveness and unity of the CONAIE-based antineoliberal movement again was tested in November 1995 in a second Durán Ballén referendum, which was necessitated by a persistent congressional impasse (Collins 2001: 14). The principal protagonists of this mobilization were the petroleum workers and other public sector unions, which attracted CONAIE's support and that of other progressive sectors. The main issue was privatization of social security – not a typical indigenous movement demand. This mobilization is interesting because the indigenous movement worked this time not just with other peasant and agrarian organizations, the poor, or the left. CONAIE joined with a broad spectrum of middle-class sectors opposing the privatization of social security and public enterprises, and other neoliberal reforms (Dávalos n.d.: 5–6; León 2001: 8). Once again the social movements prevailed, defeating every single proposal, despite a well-funded campaign by the government and business organizations. According to Andolina, this success, coming on the heels of two successful 1994 mobilizations, demonstrated to CONAIE leaders their electoral potential:

Unlike the 1994 mobilization, then, CONAIE immediately saw the NO campaign as a measuring stick for its electoral participation. Moreover, it *anticipated* it as a measuring stick. While the successful outcome did not determine CONAIE's decision to participate in elections in general, it convinced some remaining skeptics and compelled CONAIE to decide to participate at the *national* level. It raised expectations and the sense of possibility that they could win seats at the national level, and gave them the sense of obligation to civil society (who had rejected the *consulta* questions) to do so.

(Andolina 1999: 216, citing CONAIE documents from 1995; see also Collins 2001: 14)

Pressure increased within CONAIE for the transformation of "street" power into electoral power. In a May 8, 1995, interview with *Diario Hoy*, veteran sierra leader José María Cabascango explained the decision to form a party:

It is time that we indigenous think about power. We should infiltrate the powers that be at all levels in order to change things so that we don't have to continue putting up with the politicians' electoral maneuverings. When we have enough leaders we will found an authentically indigenous party.

(*Diario Hoy* [Quito] 1995: 2A, cited in Collins 2001: 13, her translation)

While some sierra leaders continued to resist the idea, Amazonian Indians would not be deterred from their goal of competing in the 1996 national elections with their own candidates in a movement they were calling the Movimiento Político Pachakutik (Cabascango 2002: 1). Meanwhile, a new coalition of social movement and labor leaders created the Movimiento de Ciudadanos por un Nuevo País (Nuevo País, NP) and decided to build on the success of the 1994–95 antineoliberal reform protests by presenting a consensus antineoliberal candidate for the 1996 presidential elections. They talked with former president Rodrigo Borja before settling on the popular television journalist Freddy Ehlers. Realizing that they would need the organizational and voting support of the indigenous movement, they approached some CONAIE leaders. In September 1995, CONAIE called a national assembly to discuss the discrepancies between the position of CONFENIAE, which already had announced that it would run candidates under the Movimiento Político Pachakutik banner, and CONAIE, which had only agreed to participate in local and regional elections (Lucero 2002: 89).

CONAIE leaders were faced with a fait accompli: CONFENIAE already had committed to the alliance with Nuevo País. CONAIE voted to join the alliance in order to not divide the movement (Andolina 1999: 222). Thus, at CONAIE's 13th Assembly (January 31–February 1, 1996) the Movimiento de Unidad Plurinacional Pachakutik was born. The name was a compromise between the CONAIE Political Council's choice of Movimiento Alternativo Plurinacional and CONFENIAE's Movimiento Político Pachakutik. At that meeting, they decided to ally with Nuevo País for the 1996 elections (Andolina 1999: 224–5).[9] Nuevo País contributed the experience and ideas of progressive intellectuals who could articulate broader demands beyond the indigenous agenda, as well as support in urban areas to complement Pachakutik's rural base (Sánchez López and Freidenberg 1998: 72). Both sectors – indigenous and nonindigenous – realized that without the other the political project would have a reduced chance of success.

Although it joined later than other sectors, CONAIE was a crucial partner of the coalition. Social movements had expected that CONAIE would take the leadership role, and this is reflected in the ordering of the alliance names – MUPP-NP (Andolina 1999: 225). Ehlers had refused to run without their explicit support, including former CONAIE president Luis Macas as the head of the alliance's legislative list (Collins 2001: 15).

---

[9] Another important decision was that CONAIE leaders would have to resign in order to run for elected office, a requirement intended to prevent electoral politics from contaminating the social movement organization.

By 1995, CONAIE was clearly the senior partner in an alliance with weaker labor and social organizations. Economic reforms had crippled the unions, leaving CONAIE as the strongest single social movement organization. CONAIE could have elected to go it alone in the electoral sphere. However, by 1995, CONAIE had decided to change its strategy, to broaden its programmatic agenda, and to work on issues of concern to the poor majority and the economically precarious middle class, on which it could build solidarity with other popular movements (Collins 2001: 14).

With few viable electoral options, much of the left joined the Pachakutik-NP alliance. The indigenous movement emerged as a national actor at the same time that the Berlin Wall fell and socialism was in crisis around the world. This crisis was manifested in Ecuador in the electoral decline of the left and the growing weakness of the labor movement. According to Jorge León, a longtime adviser to the movement, there is a strong correlation between the rise of the indigenous movement and the decline of a left that did not see the movement's political potential. Leftist party leaders not only rejected ethnicity as a political category and ethnic claims as irrelevant to their class agenda, they perpetuated a legacy of "colonial racism" that saw Indians as incapable of self-conscious political struggle. Once the indigenous movement had established itself as an important political force and the leftist parties had seen their own political effectiveness decline dramatically, leftist militants changed their views and joined the movement led by CONAIE (León interviewed in Montoya Rojas and Paredes 2001: 85–6.) With no social movements capable of challenging its dominance, including the declining labor movement, the indigenous movement became the core of the left-opposition, incorporating a number of leftist organizations seeking to transform their profile to take advantage of the popularity of CONAIE's discourse (Sánchez López and Freidenberg 1998: 71). In a similar way, and at about the same time, the Bolivian left threw its lot in with the dynamic coca growers movement.

Decision-Making Scenario III

The evangelical indigenous organization FEINE formed its own political party in 1998, the Movimiento Evangélico Indígena Amauta Jatari (Amauta Jatari). FEINE formed the party chiefly to counter the political influence of CONAIE and Pachakutik, which had been attracting many of FEINE's members, due to its greater political influence and the success it had achieved in 1996 as a political party. Until this time, FEINE had allied with political parties on the left. Amauta Jatari's director explained the decision:

We have seen the necessity of creating a political movement since we have lost various brothers who have gone to other parties, some have gone astray. We must recuperate those that want to participate in politics from a Christian point of view. They are going to return and they will get in line.

(my translation; M. Chucchilán, cited in Andrade 2003: 120)

FEINE leaders believed that forming their own party was the only way to compete against the dominance of the mostly Catholic CONAIE, which was now offering the opportunity to compete successfully in elections without the necessity of joining a *mestizo* political party (Andrade 2003: 120). The party was expected to return evangelicals to the church and to the evangelical political movement. Party leaders attempted to emphasize the distinct nature of their political program as a Christian organization and the greater moral and ethical quality of their political leaders. Within a political system known for its corruption, Amauta leaders emphasized the greater honesty of their candidates, given their avowed Christian faith. Whereas Pachakutik looked to traditional indigenous culture for new models of politics, Amauta looked to the Bible, while emphasizing indigenous values such as reciprocity and respect for nature (Andrade 2003: 125–6).

UNDERSTANDING ETHNIC PARTY PERFORMANCE

Pachakutik made dramatic gains in a short period of time, particularly in areas with large indigenous populations. The speed with which voters switched to Pachakutik indicates the weakness of loyalty to existing parties. In a decentralized political system, Pachakutik capitalized on its greatest strength: a dense network of affiliated grassroots organizations with almost a decade of experience in major regional and national mobilizations. Like all indigenous movement–based political parties discussed in this book, Pachakutik lacked the financial resources available to other aspiring national parties. It used its lack of resources as a campaign theme, hoping to appeal to the poor by demonstrating that the party was just like the majority of the people and, being so poor, would not be able to engage in the vote-buying and corruption of the traditional parties (Andolina 1999: 252).

The ability to form electoral alliances enabled Pachakutik to unite with leftist parties with strength in particular districts where the indigenous movement was weak. This enabled it to nearly double its congressional representation relative to seats it could have won on its own. The relative weakness of the tiny leftist parties enabled Pachakutik to act as the senior alliance partner and to absorb a good share of the left's human and financial resources. In the context of high party-system fragmentation Pachakutik quickly became a major player and the dominant leftist/antineoliberal electoral movement in congress.

For the May 19, 1996, elections, Pachakutik-NP presented candidates at all levels; in some districts the alliance united with ID and the leftist alliance Socialist Party-Broad Front (PS-FA) (Cabascango 2002: 1). Although with 20.60 percent of the vote its presidential candidate failed to make the run-off, the alliance captured 10 percent of the seats in the eighty-two-seat National Congress: a total of eight seats, consisting of one national deputy (former CONAIE president Luis Macas) and seven from the provinces [Azuay (two), Chimborazo, Cotopaxi, Napo, Pastaza, Pichincha]) which, in Ecuador's fragmented party system, made it the fourth-largest bloc in congress. Running in thirteen of the country's twenty-one provinces, Pachakutik picked up an additional sixty-eight seats in local elections, winning seven of every ten races it entered, eleven mayors in eight provinces, including the mayorship of Cuenca, Ecuador's third largest city; twelve provincial *consejeros* from eleven provinces; and forty-five municipal *concejales* from eleven provinces (Beck and Mijeski 2000: 17; Escobar 1996; Sarango Macas 1997: 318–19).

These results are astounding considering that it was Pachakutik's first election, the campaign period for the coalition was only three months long, and the indigenous movement could not afford to purchase media time. Pachakutik also elected the mayor of Cotacachi, Imbabura, running Quichua professional Auki Tituaña with strong support from both indigenous and *mestizo* cantons. He won a slim plurality of the vote (24.11 percent) but would be reelected in 2000 with more than 80 percent of the vote by running an administration that captured national and international attention for its emphasis on participation and interethnic negotiation. Although UNORCAC was pleased to help elect Cotacachi's first indigenous mayor, Tituaña was not an UNORCAC member and thereafter the organization would have to fight against *mestizo* and unaffiliated indigenous militants for spaces on the Pachakutik ballot (Pallares 2002 104–6).

In February 1997, CONAIE led a successful effort to oust President Abdalá Bucaram and to force the convocation of a constituent assembly to reform the political system – a CONAIE demand dating to 1990 that was a prerequisite for the fulfillment of its primary goal, the creation of a plurinational state (Collins 2001: 17). Although the indigenous movement originally had supported Bucaram, and some of its prominent leaders served in his government, his refusal to adopt the movement's economic and social programs, his institution of neoliberal economic reforms, the emergence of serious corruption scandals in his administration, and his increasingly erratic and embarrassing behavior lost the populist president his base among the urban and rural poor (Andolina 2003: 730–1). Nearly 15 percent of the country's population participated in the massive demonstrations that CONAIE organized. Following Bucaram's ouster, CONAIE, working with other social movements and the left, demanded the convocation of a constituent assembly within sixty days. Fabian Alarcon's interim government finally convoked the assembly after CONAIE convened a "Peoples Assembly," funded mainly by the petroleum workers, which forced the issue to the top of the political agenda.

Prior to the 1997 constituent assembly elections, a referendum was held on a number of political issues, including approval of the congress's quasi-legal ouster of Bucaram. Voters also approved a shift to open list panachage for congressional elections, which enables voters to vote for any candidate, notwithstanding their placement on the party's list, and to choose as many candidates as there are seats in their electoral district (Birnir 2000: 11). The change helps popular figures while also allowing voters to vote for multiple parties, which tends to help smaller ones on whom voters may not want to waste a single vote. In the constituent assembly elections, Pachakutik won seven of seventy representatives, in addition to three seats on allied lists, making it the third-largest force in that body.[10] The prior creation of Pachakutik enabled the indigenous movement to work formally from within the assembly through its delegates, informally as a social movement organization through a lobbying team composed of CONAIE's experienced leaders and advisors, and through its Pachakutik representatives in the congress, which remained in session during the assembly and passed, at a crucial moment late in the deliberations, International Labor Organization Convention 169 on the rights of indigenous peoples (Andolina 1999, 2003; Nielson and Zetterberg 1999; interviews in Quito with Miguel Lluco, August 2, 1999; Luis Macas, July 28, 1999; and Luis Verdesoto, August 3, 1999).

CONAIE's strategy during the constituent assembly was to distance itself somewhat from Pachakutik in order to negotiate directly with each representative. After the largest conservative party walked out over a

---

[10] Pachakutik ran alone, without the Nuevo Pais part of the original electoral alliance. See Andolina (1999: 234–5) for an explanation of this decision.

dispute concerning social security reform and the extension of the assembly's mandate, Pachakutik became the core of the now-dominant center-left bloc. The resulting 1998 Constitution was, at the time, the most progressive in the hemisphere with respect to indigenous rights. The charter established special electoral districts for indigenous and Afro-Ecuadorian communities corresponding to newly recognized, self-governing indigenous and Afro-Ecuadorian territories called "sectional autonomous governments" (Articles 224, 226, 228). Because much is left to implementing legislation that has yet to be passed, it is unclear what the scope and structure of the new autonomous governments will be. The new constitution also declared Ecuador a "pluricultural" state, recognition that fulfilled an important symbolic demand, made indigenous languages official in indigenous-populated areas, and recognized the right of indigenous peoples to practice customary law.

In 1998, not only did Ecuadorian Indians celebrate the realization of the hemisphere's most progressive regime of indigenous constitutional rights, the constitutional reform itself was widely viewed as a direct result of pressure from the country's indigenous movement. Moreover, the assembly demonstrated the effectiveness of the Pachakutik delegation, which achieved much of its agenda, despite its small size. In 1998's national elections, Pachakutik and Nuevo País resumed their alliance and backed Ehlers again for president, while Pachakutik forged an alliance with the PS-FA for other national races. Ehlers won only 14.75 percent of the vote and Pachakutik's representation declined to 6 percent, even though it earned eight seats again (two from the national list in alliance with the PS-FA and six provincial deputies), because the size of the legislature had increased. Pachakutik militants won only six of the seats, and four of these were indigenous (Beck and Mijeski 2000: 19). ENPS declined significantly in 1998, from 6.6 to 5, reflecting Pachakutik's absorption of smaller leftist parties. In 1998, Pachakutik also picked up twenty-seven mayors, five provincial prefects, fifty *concejales* and *consejeros*, and more than 100 members of village *juntas parroquiales* (Macas 2002: 6)[11] (see Table 4.3). That year, in its first electoral outing, Amauta Jatari ran for

---

[11] Pachakutik won three provincial *consejeros* in Cotopaxi, Morona-Santiago, and Napo, plus one in Azuay in alliance with ID-PS-FA. Pachakutik won twenty-three municipal councilors in Azuay (1), Bolívar (4), Cañar (1), Cotopaxi (2), Chimborazo (2), Imbabura (1), Morona-Santiago (8), Napo (4), plus an additional twelve in alliances: three with ID-PS-FA, one with ID-PS-FA-MICNP (New Country Independent Movement of Citizens), two with MICNP-PS-FA, one with ID, four with DP, and one with ID-DP (Collins 2001: 73).

TABLE 4.3. *Pachakutik electoral results*

	1996[a]	1997 ANC	1998[a]	2000	2002[b]	2004
Presidential 1st round	20.61%	—	14.74%	—	20.43% (1st)	—
Presidential 2nd round	—	—	—	—	54.79%	—
Constituent Assembly	—	7 of 70, 3 more in alliances	—	—	—	—
Congress Deputies	10.76% 8 (of 70)	—	8 (of 121)[c]	—	14 (of 100)[d]	—
Provincial prefects (21, until Orellana added in 2000)	0	—	5 (of 21)	5 (of 22)	—	6 (of 22)
Provincial *consejeros*	12 (of 79)	—	4	13	14 (of 67)[g]	?
Mayors	6 (of 215) or 11[e]	—	27 (of 215)	23 (of 215)	0 (of 2 elected)	16 (of 215)
President of Council	8 (of 173)	—	—	—	—	?
Municipal Councilors	39 (of 791), or 45[e]	—	35[f]	84 (of 880)	73 (of 677)[b]	?
Juntas parroquiales	—	—	100+	160 (of 788)	—	?

[a] MUPP-NP supported Freddy Ehlers.

[b] MUPP-NP allied with Partido Sociedad Patriotica for national and various subnational races.

[c] Two of these on lists with Partido Socialista-Frente Amplio.

[d] Five on its own, six in alliance with PSP, three more through other alliances.

[e] Sarango Macas (1997: 318–19) reports eleven mayors and forty-five municipal councilors. Both sources list each mayor and councilor by name and municipality. I believe the higher figure may reflect alliances that the TSE does not report as MUPP wins.

[f] Twenty-three on its own, twelve more in various alliance formations with ID, PS-FA, MICNP, and DP.

[g] Seven on its own, seven in coalition.

[h] Fifty-four on its own, nineteen in coalition.

Sources: Data for 1996 from Tribunal Supremo Electoral (1996). Data for 1998 from Macas (2002); Sánchez López and Freidenberg (1998: 73). ANC data from Andolina (1999: 235–6). 2000 data from Beck and Mijeski (2001); Cabascango (2002: 2); and Wray (n.d.: 34). 2002 data from Tribunal Supremo Electoral (2002). 2004 data from Cruz (2004).

TABLE 4.4. *Amauta Jatari/Amauta Yuyay electoral results*

	1998	2002	2004
President	–	39,171 votes, 0.85 percent	
Deputies	15,429 votes, 0 deputies 0.06% of total national valid vote	148,769 votes, 0 deputies	
Provincial *consejeros*	18,592 votes 0.18% of total national valid vote	91,071 votes, 0 provincial *consejeros*	
Mayors	–	–	3 mayors
Municipal councilors	16,316 votes 0.14% of total national valid vote	120,070 votes, 3 municipal councilors, including 1 in coalition with Socialist party	N/A

Sources: 1998 data from Raul Madrid, personal e-mail communication, July 1, 2003; 2002 data from Tribunal Supremo Electoral (2002); 2004 data from Tribunal Supremo Electoral www.tse.gov.ec/resultados2004.

local and national office in Imbabura and Cotopaxi. It fared poorly, winning less than 0.2 percent of the vote in contests for national deputy, provincial counselor, and municipal councilor (see Table 4.4).

The formation of a political party by no means ended CONAIE's career as a leader of massive protests against the political system. But the coexistence of a political party, controlling local and regional governments as well as a foothold in national government, and a social movement in constant opposition to the state required the construction of a complex and at times internally contradictory discourse. CONAIE rejects any association with the traditional political class and impugns the legitimacy of state institutions, while Pachakutik promotes the occupation of existing institutional spaces by indigenous movement representatives as a legitimate means of making public policy and working to change the system from within. The "dual strategy" proved to be a double-edged sword for the movement. On the one hand, indigenous organizations were able to work on two fronts – within the halls of congress in coalition with other progressive parties and in the streets with massive mobilizations in alliance with progressive social sectors. On the other, it led to confusion, tension, and even open conflict between the social movement organization CONAIE and the political party Pachakutik.

At times Pachakutik directly contradicts CONAIE's cherished principles; for example, by making alliances with traditional political parties – even those on the right – to achieve short-term goals. Pachakutik has allied with center-left parties in the congress as part of the governing coalition (e.g., 1998–99), a position that contradicts CONAIE's fervent oppositional stance. A severe division emerged in 1998 between CONAIE and Pachakutik deputy Nina Pacari surrounding her decision to ally with Popular Democracy (DP) to secure the second vice presidency of congress for herself, in exchange for Pachakutik's support for the DP's presidential choice. Moreover, she agreed to let a deputy from the conservative Partido Social Cristiano nominate her rather than a member of her own party. Many Pachakutik militants were furious that a representative of the indigenous movement would act in concert with a center-right party that was part of the neoliberal governing coalition and demanded that she resign (interview, Miguel Lluco, August 3, 1999). The dispute "detonated an internal decomposition" within Pachakutik (interview, Luis Macas, July 28, 1999). This incident compounded the disunity arising from internal disputes regarding Pachakutik's identity and mission, which make it difficult to articulate short- or long-term goals (Barrera and Unda 1999: 7; confidential interviews).

CONAIE leaders have criticized Pachakutik legislators for behaving like traditional politicians, for assimilating the corrupt, self-serving norms of Ecuadorian party politics, and for seeking political office as an end in itself, rather than a means to implement the indigenous movement's agenda (*Boletín ICCI* 2002b: 3; Sánchez G. 2002: 4; interview, Jorge León, July 17, 1999). They criticize Pachakutik mayors and legislators for not consistently supporting major indigenous movement mobilizations and, instead, calling for order and refusing to resign their seats (Lucas 2001: 3). Much of the criticism is based on the movement's ideological norms: that any Indian who obtains a position in government office is selling out and that indigenous officials should govern in accordance with the instructions of the indigenous organization that supported their candidacy, rather than the entire population of the district they represent (interview, Ampam Karakras, July 23, 1999).

Rather than creating a unified indigenous bloc in congress, Pachakutik deputies do not work together. One told Lucero in 1998, "there is no block, it is every deputy for him or herself" (Lucero 2002: 88). To the extent that Pachakutik deputies interviewed in 1999 were aware of what the others were doing, they openly expressed disdain for their efforts (interviews, Valerio Grefa, July 27, 1999; Bolívar Beltran, July 19, 1999).

The behavior of some members of Pachakutik's congressional leadership has caused the loss of parts of the original coalition. According to former Pachakutik deputy Luis Macas, they have alienated FENOCIN, Seguro Social Campesino, and other sectors originally within the party (interview, July 28, 1999). The peasant, black, and women's movements also have distanced themselves.

Whereas CONAIE's organizational strength and popular support were assets for the formation of a successful political party, once the party was formed the greater strength of the social movement organization inhibited somewhat the development of the party. For example, during CONAIE-led protests in 1999, Pachakutik and its congressional delegation kept a low profile. CONAIE leaders did not involve them in the protests or ask them to resolve the conflict with the government, having seen little evidence that their demands would be fulfilled without street protests (Dávalos n.d.: 8–9). Meanwhile Pachakutik legislators criticized CONAIE for excluding them from negotiations with the government (Lucas 2001: 3). CONAIE's increasing political prominence actually weakened Pachakutik. As it painted all parties and political institutions with the brush of illegitimacy, CONAIE rose in public esteem as a valid interlocutor for all excluded and disadvantaged sectors, as well as a broader sector of Ecuadorians disgusted with the corruption and self-interestedness of the political class. CONAIE's decision to marginalize its own legislators during the protests contrasts with the relations between movements and parties in Colombia and Bolivia. Colombian indigenous senators often participate in protests and negotiations alongside the National Indigenous Organization of Colombia and Bolivia's indigenous deputies Morales and Quispe lead street protests against the government. *Boletín ICCI*'s editors, themselves leaders of the indigenous movement, explain the problem this way:

In essence, this is a discussion of the role and the place of a social movement when it converts itself into a political movement. The conception of CONAIE as a social movement is that the political movement must be subordinated to the social movement. The problem with this conception is its corporatist origin. In effect, the moment in which a militant of CONAIE gains a mayor's office under the banner of the Pachakutik Movement, his/her actions must be accountable to the local sphere, which is by definition multicultural and diverse.

(my translation; *Boletín ICCI* 2002c: 3)

The open conflict between CONAIE and Pachakutik eroded public support and esteem for both. The fundamentally different dynamics and cultures of social movement organizations compared to political parties also generated tensions, although Pachakutik's connection to a parent social movement gives the party a culture that is more like a social movement than a party in terms of leadership recruitment and internal decision making. Although Pachakutik has become more institutionalized and hierarchical since its formation, like Bolivia's MAS it continues to be a loose association of various social movements with a great deal of decentralized decision making at the provincial level compared to other political parties (Collins 2001: 2–3; www.pachaktutik.org.ec). A key problem is that the lines of authority between Pachakutik and CONAIE have never been clear. Because the Amazonian organizations had already forged an electoral alliance with nonindigenous sectors prior to the formal creation of Pachakutik, CONAIE has no official relationship of parentage or superiority (Collins 2000a). The relationship is far more complex and contentious than, for example, the relationship between Colombia's Regional Indigenous Council of Cauca (CRIC) and the ASI, the party it spawned, or the relationship between Bolivia's coca growers' organizations and the MAS.

Further divisions were generated within the indigenous movement, and between the movement and its allies, as a result of dramatic protests in late 1999/January 2000 that culminated in the ouster of President Jamil Mahuad on January 21, 2000. CONAIE's economic grievances resonated with much of the population, including sectors of the military's junior officer corps. The military refused to dislodge hundreds of Indians from public buildings, including the National Congress. Instead, approximately 200 military officers arrived together and joined the protest, and more joined later (Collins 2000a: 40). After Indians marched to the presidential palace, President Mahuad fled and junior officers joined CONAIE president Antonio Vargas in a temporary overthrow of the government. The coup was reversed within hours owing to pressure from international actors and the decision of the military leaders to back out.

The coup's legacy was mixed. On the positive side, the indigenous movement cemented an alliance with midlevel military officers (Dávalos n.d.: 11). On the negative side, the coup attempt revealed the contradictions in the indigenous movement's dual strategy of attacking the system from outside while working within it. During the coup attempt CONAIE had called for all three branches of the government to be dissolved and for all legislators – including Pachakutik deputies – to resign. The latter refused to be categorized with the "corrupt" politicians of the country and remained in office. They also disagreed with CONAIE's demand for a plebiscite on the question of revoking the legislature's mandate. In addition, base-level indigenous leaders and militants, and many

Ecuadorians and international actors, criticized Vargas and the national leadership for acting without the knowledge or permission of the remainder of the movement (Collins 2000a). Subsequently CONAIE underwent an intense process of self-criticism and restructuring in order to reconnect the bases to the national leadership and to heal the wide rift between the Amazonian organizations, which had backed Vargas, and sierra organizations (Montoya Rojas and Paredes 2001: 84; *Boletín ICCI* 2002c: 2).

Despite internal conflict within the indigenous movement and the loss of key nonindigenous popular allies after 1998, in local and regional elections held on May 21, 2000, Pachakutik achieved its then-greatest electoral success. The party won five of the country's twenty-two prefectures, electing Cotopaxi's first indigenous provincial prefect; 27 mayors, of a national total of 215, the third-best showing of any party; thirteen provincial counselors; and 146 of 460 seats on parish advisory councils (*juntas parroquiales*), the highest number of any party (Cabascango 2002: 2). In those elections, rival Amauta Jatari elected a mayor, a handful of municipal councilors, and forty seats on parish councils (Andrade 2003: 125). A majority of Pachakutik's newly elected public officials were indigenous, particularly among the parish advisory councils (León 2001: 10). Pachakutik's 4.4 percent of the nationwide vote made it the sixth most successful party in 2000. It drew significant support from urban areas, and in some areas of the country became the dominant political force (Cabascango 2002: 2).[12] Despite these regional and local gains, its national electoral prospects remained limited by its failure to attract support in the coastal provinces, where the majority of the Ecuadorian population is concentrated, and where the party typically polls no more than 4 percent in any province.

Mobilizations in January and February 2001 demonstrated the increasing distance between the CONAIE leadership and its base organizations. Grassroots indigenous organizations, which rejected the national leadership and the choices it made in 2000 without consulting the bases, were the main protagonists. In these mobilizations, triggered again by economic policy issues, not only did the initiative shift from the national leadership to the bases, the agenda was scaled back to include a more modest set of explicitly indigenous demands (Dávalos n.d.: 15). Perhaps because of the bottom-up leadership of this mobilization, it was arguably the first in

---

[12] For example, in Bolívar, in 2000 Pachakutik won a representative to the National Congress, the prefecture, the mayor of the provincial capital, many *concejales* and *consejeros*, and "almost all" of the *juntas parroquiales* (Talahua 2000: 26).

which almost all of Ecuador's indigenous organizations participated in a united fashion (Dávalos 2001: 1–4).

Pachakutik and CONAIE faced another crisis when the movements could not agree on a presidential candidate for 2002, when many observers believed the indigenous movement would launch its first indigenous presidential candidate (*Latin American Weekly Report* 2002b: 21). In the spring of 2002, the main alternatives were Antonio Vargas, formerly CONAIE president and leader of the 2000 aborted coup, and Cotocachi mayor Auki Tituaña. Vargas had alienated other indigenous movement leaders and the movement's base with his actions during the coup. He had offended Pachakutik leaders by ignoring the party during the 1999–2000 demonstrations, never trying to create a united CONAIE-Pachakutik front and even demanding that the Pachakutik legislators resign. In early 2002, Vargas formed his own political movement called Frente Futuro Ecuador (Future Ecuador Front) to support his presidential candidacy, based mainly on his continued support within the Amazonian confederation CONFENIAE, as well as sectors of the evangelical indigenous organization FEINE (interview, Luis Macas, July 28, 1999).[13]

Vargas ultimately ran with Amauta Jatari, whose leaders were happy to take advantage of the indecision and disunity of their rival, despite the urging of many members not to exacerbate divisions within the indigenous movement (Andrade 2003: 128). However, without CONAIE's official endorsement, Vargas was unable to form any significant alliances with political parties or social movements. Vargas's campaign resources were minimal – he reportedly spent no money at all on media advertisements (*El Comercio* [Quito] 2002a), and he had trouble gathering the 81,219 signatures required to register for the presidential elections. On August 26, 2002, the Supreme Electoral Tribunal (TSE) disqualified his ticket based on a belief that many of its signatures had been falsified. Vargas claimed that he was being discriminated against because he is indigenous. The Constitutional Tribunal reinstated him on September 4, leading some to speculate that this was due to political pressure from elites wishing to split

---

[13] While most critics blamed Vargas for his opportunistic presidential run, others blamed FEINE for proposing Vargas's candidacy at the head of its political party in a bid to divide CONAIE by taking advantage of the split between CONFENIAE and ECUARUNARI – an accusation that FEINE leader Marco Murillo denied. Murillo noted that FEINE had decided to support an indigenous candidate for president in November 2001. "Confeniae invited us to their assemblies and verified that their bases support Vargas. . . . This announcement didn't divide [the indigenous movement]. What happened is that there are some who noticed our existence" (my translation; *El Comercio* [Quito] 2002b).

the indigenous vote, rather than to an error on the part of the TSE (Associated Press 2002a; personal communication, Scott Beck, September 19, 2002). A similar incident, discussed in Chapter 3, occurred in Bolivia earlier that year, when Felipe Quispe's MIP was disqualified, then reinstated, some say in order to drain votes away from the other, more formidable indigenous party.

At a March 2002 meeting, Pachakutik's National Political Council decided to propose Tituaña as its "precandidate" for president (Consejo Político Nacional 2002). Tituaña had developed a reputation as a moderate, pragmatic leader who could work across ethnic groups and social sectors. Ecuadorian government officials praised him for using moderation while other indigenous leaders were taking extreme positions to appeal to their base (*Latin American Andean Group Report* 2001: 2). Severe tensions between Vargas's and Tituaña's supporters emerged in the spring of 2002 and created confusion throughout the indigenous movement. Eventually, several organizations held assemblies to debate the issue and released explicit statements with respect to the movement's electoral participation. In an ECUARUNARI assembly held in Baños on December 13–14, 2001, the organization declared the indigenous movement to be in a "state of emergency" and resolved not to support any indigenous candidates for president or vice president in order not to exacerbate the crisis. They called for a total revision of the structure of the movement and its organizations in order to heal the breach between the communities and the leadership (*Boletín ICCI* 2002a: 1).

On March 8–9, 2002, CONAIE's National Political Council met to discuss the elections. It endorsed Pachakutik's proposal of Auki Tituaña as their presidential candidate and called on the party to undertake a massive voter registration campaign. It also urged Antonio Vargas and the Frente Futuro Ecuador to unite with Pachakutik and CONAIE in a single, unified front "to defeat the right and populism" (CONAIE 2002). ECUARUNARI met again in April 3–5, 2002, to discuss the election issue and affirmed the December 2001 decision not to support an indigenous candidate for president or vice president in 2002 (ECUARUNARI 2002: 1). Despite efforts to reach a consensus on the difficult issue, tensions persisted.

Leaders of CONAIE, the coastal organization National Coordinator of the Indigenous of the Ecuadorian Coast (CONAICE), CONFENIAE, and ECUARUNARI met in Quito on April 18–19, 2002. They resolved to "guarantee the unity of CONAIE" and to not support any indigenous candidate for president (Asamblea del Consejo de Nacionalidades y Pueblos

Indígenas, April 19, 2002; BBC Monitoring International Reports 2002). The leaders called on Pachakutik to respect this resolution and called on provincial-level Pachakutik coordinators to work with the organizations and communities in their provinces to consolidate and broaden the base for local indigenous government – essentially a return to the sierra leaders' position of the early 1990s. In July, while Pachakutik continued to champion Auki Tituaña as its presidential candidate, CONAIE attempted to hold the indigenous movement together by asking both candidates to withdraw (*Weekly News Update on the Americas* 2002b). Tituaña did so on July 7, while Vargas continued his campaign in defiance of the edict of the organization he formerly led.

Without a candidate of its own, the majority of the indigenous movement and Pachakutik threw its support behind retired Colonial Lucio Gutiérrez and allied with his new party, Patriotic Society Party (PSP) for the presidential elections and some other national races (Hidalgo Flor 2002). Gutiérrez had gained national prominence as part of the junta that ruled for a few hours during the January 21, 2000, ouster of President Jamil Mahuad. Gutiérrez served six months in jail for his participation. Although it had originally been part of the Frente Futuro Ecuador coalition, toward the end of the presidential campaign, FENOCIN, following extensive local assemblies in rural areas, also backed Gutiérrez and instructed its 1,250 base organizations to support him because he represented the majority of leftist voters (FENOCIN 2002; *El Comercio* [Quito] 2002b).

The PSP-Pachakutik alliance finished first in a field of thirteen candidates in the presidential race with 20.43 percent of the vote. In the congressional race, Pachakutik won five seats on its own, six in alliance with PSP, and three in alliance with other leftist parties: a total of 14 seats in the now 100-seat congress (*El Universo*, November 25, 2002). Gutiérrez won a decisive victory in the November second-round elections with 48 percent of the vote. Also up for grabs in this election were sixty-seven provincial council seats, two mayors, and 677 municipal council seats. Pachakutik-NP won seven of sixty-seven provincial council seats on its own, and an additional seven in coalitions; no mayors; and seventy-three municipal council seats, fifty-four on its own, and nineteen in coalition with the PSP and a variety of leftist parties. Pachakutik-NP won municipal councilors in eighteen of twenty-two provinces, indicating the wide geographical coverage of the movement. In six provinces, it won the largest number of council seats. In contrast, the alliance with Vargas did not help Amauta Jatari in its bid to compete with Pachakutik. The party finished last in the

2002 presidential race with 0.85 percent (39,171) of the vote, but elected two local officials in Chimborazo and another in coalition with the populist party Ecuadorian Roldosist Party (PRE) in neighboring Tungurahua. It elected no provincial *consejeros* or deputies to the national legislature. Although these results are poor, the party increased its vote share significantly and it competed in eleven of the country's twenty-two provinces (Tribunal Supremo Electoral 2002).[14]

After the 2002 national elections, the indigenous movement was poised to have a strong influence in the Gutiérrez administration. Although the president-elect assured foreign investors and elites that he would not let the Indians run the country, fifteen minutes after polls closed on November 24, it was Pachakutik that the president-elect thanked first. Hours later he boarded a plane back to Quito with family members and the president of Pachakutik, Miguel Lluco (Mendoza 2002). Following Gutiérrez's televised announcement that day regarding the nature of his cabinet, Lluco corrected reporters asking whether Pachakutik was "part of" the government. Rather, Lluco responded, "We are the government," indicating that Pachakutik intended to play a central role in public policy making (my translation, Ponce 2002). Indigenous leaders met with Gutiérrez at a forum in Quito immediately following the November runoff, at which CONAIE leaders asserted, and Gutiérrez acknowledged, that his win would have been "practically impossible" without CONAIE and the indigenous movement (*Diario Hoy* 2002). Gutiérrez named two prominent CONAIE and Pachakutik leaders to his cabinet: Nina Pacari, the first Indian and first woman named Minister of Foreign Relations; and Luis Macas, named Minister of Agriculture. Pachakutik also placed its militants at the head of the ministries of tourism, education, and the interior.

The honeymoon was short. Immediately following President Gutiérrez's announcement in February 2003, that austerity measures were imminent, the indigenous movement threatened to launch protests against his government, indigenous cabinet members notwithstanding (Associated Press 2003). In the first half of 2003, indigenous leaders in the government and the PSP-Pachakutik congressional delegation compromised on once-nonnegotiable demands – for example, they accepted most of the austerity package in exchange for the repeal of an increase in cooking gas. As Pachakutik Deputy Ricardo Ulcuango put it, "We are an alliance. Sometimes we'll agree and sometimes we'll disagree" (cited in Saavedra 2003: 1). However, the alliance ended on August 6, 2003, when

[14] I thank Raul Madrid and Roberta Rice for sharing electoral data from Ecuador.

President Gutiérrez expelled Pachakutik from the government because the Pachakutik congressional delegation refused to support his proposed civil service law. The Pachakutik Minister of Interior had resigned in July, and the party's Minister of Education was fired later that month (*Latin America Weekly Report* 2003d: 343). The move preempted an expected resignation by remaining Pachakutik ministers that the party was considering (Andrade 2003: 134). Lluco told the press: "in light of the serious mistakes of the President, we do not want to be accomplices or concealers . . . thus we are leaving the government" (*El Comercio* [Quito] 2003).

In the months that followed, CONAIE led demonstrations against the government and condemned it in the strongest language. The government response was repression at a level seldom seen in Ecuador against the indigenous movement. Gutiérrez also created a new indigenous, campesino, and black organization – Frente de Defensa de los Pueblos Indígenas Campesinos y Negros del Ecuador (FEDEPICNE) – allied with the President's party, which now controls the government's Indigenous Secretariat, formerly controlled by CONAIE (*Servindi* 2003b: 1). The rift between the president and Pachakutik generated open divisions between CONAIE and Pachakutik, and within CONAIE itself, with CONAIE and ECUARUNARI in opposition to the government and CONFENIAE and the coastal organization CONAICE declaring their support for Gutiérrez (*Latin America Weekly Report* 2003a: 10). ECUARUNARI president Humberto Cholango was detained in December 2003 after criticizing the president's policies on television. A wave of break-ins and robberies affecting the offices of the indigenous movement, which the movement attributes to the government, further intensified the sense of siege. On February 21, 2004, Pachakutik's national headquarters was attacked and its computers and other equipment stolen. Pachakutik leaders held the government responsible and alleged that the government was looking for information on their computers (ANPE 2004). The attack followed less than three weeks after an attempt on the life of CONAIE president Leonidas Iza, which left Iza unharmed but put three family members in the hospital. During a second day of CONAIE-sponsored demonstrations that began on February 16, battles between police and hundreds of indigenous protesters left at least seventeen people injured, including four gunshot victims (Associated Press 2004).

Preliminary results from the October 2004 regional election indicate a greater dispersion of the indigenous vote among several electoral options featuring indigenous candidates. After a tumultuous two years in and out of government, Pachakutik lost support as voters turned to leftist parties like the MPD, a former partner in the short-lived alliance with Gutiérrez, which did surprisingly well in indigenous provinces. In Chimborazo, FEINE's electoral vehicle, now competing under the name Amauta Yuyay, picked up three mayors, including the former Pachakutik stronghold of Guamote. Rather than supporting Pachakutik, the campesino organization FENOCIN allied with the PS-FA, winning four prefects and twenty-seven mayors. According to FEINE leader Marco Murillo, these two alternatives are attracting votes from voters dissatisfied with Pachakutik's "ethnocentrism" and its alliance with neoliberal parties (*El Universo* 2004). Pachakutik in 2004 increased its number of prefects to six, but its mayors declined from twenty-eight to sixteen (Cruz 2004; *Noticia Hoy* online 2004).

CONCLUSION

By the mid-1990s, the indigenous movement had become the most powerful Ecuadorian collective social actor and the object of increasingly favorable public opinion. Early in the decade, a sector of the indigenous movement wished to translate this political power into an electoral vehicle. A significant portion of the movement, however, was concerned that participating in elections would destroy the unity and autonomy of the movement and that, under the current electoral rules, it would be impossible to launch a national party. The first faction prevailed after two events occurred. First, popular efforts to defeat two neoliberal referendums in 1994 and 1995 demonstrated the indigenous movement's electoral potential and solidified alliances between the indigenous movement and other progressive, popular organizations. Second, one of those referendums approved changes in the electoral law that made it much easier for an indigenous electoral vehicle to register for national elections. This more favorable institutional environment was crucial to convincing skeptics in the indigenous movement that social movement strength could be translated into electoral strength. Similarly, in Bolivia in 1995, favorable institutional changes had convinced the coca growers that their social movement militancy could be converted into electoral strength. With Ecuador's lowland movement already in discussions to ally with nonindigenous social movements for the 1996 elections, the national organization CONAIE embraced the project in order to maintain the unity of the national movement.

Having already formed its own political vehicle, and having been the main societal force behind the convocation of a constituent assembly,

Ecuador's indigenous movement had the greatest impact on constitutional reform of any indigenous movement in Latin America. Thus, it was relatively more able to design the political institutions in which its new electoral vehicle would compete. As in Bolivia with the coca growers' party, once Pachakutik had been launched, with strong organizational support from a highly mobilized indigenous population, it competed well in its geographic base and filled the space left by a fractured, diminished left. The ability to form alliances enabled the party to expand into areas where the indigenous movement lacked a strong base.

As persistent economic crisis, corruption scandals, and incompetence drained support from traditional parties, Pachakutik consolidated itself as the premier anti-establishment option. Yet, the party has failed to obtain sufficient power within the political system to make radical changes or even to halt the inexorable pressure to liberalize the failing economy. Pachakutik's brief experience as part of a governing coalition demonstrates the difficulty of shifting from a social movement–oriented electoral vehicle that advances a specific identity and program to a national political institution, which must negotiate with opponents and seek national consensus.

5

"It Is Not a Priority"

The Failure to Form Viable Ethnic Parties in Peru

In many ways the Peruvian case resembles that of Ecuador or Bolivia. The three countries share the history and culture of the central Andes, a proportionally large indigenous population, a militant political left that declined in strength in the early 1990s, and a historically fragmented party system. However, no viable ethnic party emerged in Peru to represent the politically excluded indigenous population.

The main reason for this absence is that Peru's indigenous movement lacked the resources to take advantage of a relatively open institutional and political environment. A national organization that could plausibly claim to represent Peru's indigenous population did not form until 1998, and this has yet to consolidate itself as a permanent institution. Prior to that time, Peru's indigenous people were unable to form a single, unified organizational structure to represent its demands before the state. Not only has the movement been severely divided by region, with separate movements emerging in the Amazon and highlands, even within regions rival organizations struggle for dominance.

Although indigenous communities bear some of the responsibility for this failure, we can also blame the undemocratic context of the 1990s, when President Alberto Fujimori severely restricted the sphere of action for all social movements at a time when indigenous mobilizations had far greater political space in Ecuador and Bolivia. He was able to do so primarily because of the threat of terrorism from the Shining Path (Sendero Luminoso) guerrillas, which enabled Fujimori to label all oppositional activity as terrorism. The war against Shining Path, fought most brutally in the predominantly indigenous Amazon and highlands, further restricted the space for political organizing of any kind. Whereas in

Bolivia, Ecuador, Colombia, Venezuela, and Argentina indigenous peoples gained collective rights during constitutional reforms in the 1990s, in Peru indigenous people had restricted access to the process and the Fujimori-dominated Constituent Congress rolled back indigenous land and language rights and created no new political rights. Whereas in the other countries decentralization advanced in the 1990s, Fujimori recentralized the political system, which would not be decentralized until 2002. Ironically, the only institutional reform intended to improve the political representation of indigenous people – party list quotas requiring that 15 percent of candidates on party lists be indigenous, instituted for the 2002 regional elections – actually hurt fledgling indigenous parties, which now had to compete for candidates with other parties. Lacking resources to launch their own vehicles and to surmount burdensome registration requirements, indigenous organizations made temporary alliances with the largest parties, most of which did not share their agenda. The Peruvian left's stridently classist orientation, which denied the validity of ethnic claims, precluded alliances between indigenous organizations and leftist parties.

Despite these onerous obstacles to the formation of a political party, one Amazonian indigenous organization, the Interethnic Association for the Development of the Peruvian Jungle (AIDESEP), did launch its own electoral vehicle, MIAP. It had only limited, local success, because it was unable to amass the resources necessary for registration and campaigning, and because of persistent fraud by local election officials loyal to other parties. The great success of indigenous parties in neighboring Ecuador and Peru in 2002 has inspired some indigenous organizations to consider launching their own vehicles for the next national elections. Thus, although we have yet to see the fruits of political diffusion in Peru, the success of parties in Bolivia and Ecuador has put the issue of an indigenous party on the agenda for the main indigenous organizations.

INDIGENOUS SOCIAL MOVEMENTS IN PERU

Indigenous Peruvians comprise between one-third and 47 percent of the total population, depending on the source and how indigenous identity is measured.[1] They constitute a numerical majority in five of Peru's

---

[1] Peruvian anthropologist Rodrigo Montoya estimates one-third (Montoya Rojas 1993: 105); the Inter-American Indigenist Institute estimates 38.39 percent (Deruytterre 1997); Barie lists 47 percent (2003).

TABLE 5.1. *Peruvian indigenous population by department*

Department	Total Population	Total Indigenous Population over Age 5	Column 3/ Column 2
Amazonas	336,665	33,856	10.06
Ancash	955,023	303,249	31.75
Apurímac	381,997	247,130	64.69
Arequipa	916,806	157,779	17.21
Ayacucho	492,507	298,789	60.67
Cajamarca	1,259,808	3,769	1.09
Callao	639,729	38,637	6.04
Cuzco	1,028,763	570,194	55.43
Huancavelica	385,162	216,979	56.33
Huanuco	654,489	174,893	26.72
Ica	565,686	34,490	6.1
Junin	1,035,841	134,074	13.14
La Libertad	1,270,261	6,650	0.52
Lambayeque	920,795	24,042	2.61
Lima	6,386,308	578,521	9.06
Loreto	687,282	30,946	4.5
Madre de Dios	67,008	16,234	24.23
Moquegua	128,747	27,408	21.29
Pasco	226,295	27,420	12.12
Piura	1,388,264	4,705	0.34
Puno	1,079,849	712,763	66.01
San Martin	552,387	14,573	2.64
Tacna	218,353	47,454	21.73
Tumbes	155,521	760	0.49
Ucayali	314,810	33,177	10.54

Note: Ethnic identification is based on language being Aymara, Quechua, or another native language. Thus, this data misses those identifying themselves as "indigenous" but who do not speak an indigenous language.
Source: Instituto Nacional de Estadística e Informática, www.inei.gob.pe, based on 1993 census.

twenty-five departments: Apurímac, Ayacucho, Cuzco, Huancavelica, and Puno, collectively known as the Andean Trapezoid or, more pejoratively, as the Indian stain (see Table 5.1). If we compare the diversity and geographic dispersion of the Peruvian indigenous population with that of indigenous populations in Bolivia and Ecuador we find little difference. There are somewhat fewer subnational districts with an indigenous majority or significant minority, which means that political parties formed by indigenous movements would have a likelihood of success in a smaller proportion of the country. Yet attempts to form ethnic parties have been rare even in indigenous-majority departments. As in other Andean countries, Indians are divided between a numerous, densely concentrated sierra population and a smaller, more diverse and geographically dispersed Amazonian population. This division is particularly pronounced in Peru, where the two groups have received different legal treatment and organized themselves separately. There are seventy-two distinct ethnic groups and sixteen linguistic families in Peru. By far the most numerous highland group is the Quechua. Approximately 4,500,000 Peruvians speak Quechua, or 18 percent of the population. The Aymara population is concentrated in the department of Puno and comprises approximately half a million persons. The Amazonian population consists of approximately 350,000 individuals belonging to sixty-five distinct ethnic groups (Correo Indígena 2004: 1; Montoya Rojas 2002: 3, 8).

Compared to neighboring countries, Peru's indigenous movement has been less active, less institutionalized, and less successful. Nevertheless, it is an exaggeration to argue, as some analysts have, that Peru has no indigenous movement or "no significant indigenous organizations."[2] In this section, I examine reasons for the relative weakness and fragmentation of Peru's indigenous movement, as well as the implications of this weakness and disunity for the formation of ethnic parties. As with the other central Andean cases, indigenous organizations emerged separately in the highland and lowland regions.

What accounts for the relative weakness and greater fragmentation of the indigenous movement in Peru, compared to Ecuador and Bolivia? First, nonindigenous elites and provincial *mestizos* decided early in the twentieth century to promote indigenous culture and to appropriate historical Incan symbols for their own purposes. During the populist period of the 1930s–50s, when neighboring countries were promoting nation-building projects and imposing Spanish on indigenous populations, the Peruvian state and political elite did not impose Spanish or try to destroy indigenous culture. Instead they promoted indigenous culture and language through various folkloric festivals and organizations (De la Cadena 2000: 324; see also Degregori 1998b: 172–4). The Revolutionary Government of the Armed Forces (RGAF) (1968–79), which presided over a period of intense autonomous indigenous mobilization, incorporated indigenous symbols into its identity, recognized Quechua as an official language, promoted bilingual education, and issued legislation protecting

---

[2] For example, De la Cadena (2000: 323); Mayer (1996: 175) cited in Yashar (1998: 40); Yashar (1998: 24).

the rights of native and campesino communities. Thus, the educated, Spanish-speaking children of campesinos learned that non-Indians had appropriated the tools and symbols for constructing a distinct indigenous identity (Degregori 1998b: 173). In Bolivia, in contrast, neither *mestizo* elites nor the state had adopted such symbols, so they were available for indigenous movements seeking their own identity in the 1970s. Whereas the Peruvian state and *mestizo* political organizations frequently invoked the name of the indigenous rebel leader Tupac Amaru, their counterparts in Bolivia never invoked Tupaj Katari in a favorable way, leaving this symbol to the Katarists (Degregori 1998b: 194). This may partly explain why Peru's indigenous political activists choose not to prioritize ethnic symbols in their discourse and organizational methods and why highland indigenous organizations do not assert ethnocultural demands. Because the discourse of ethno-cultural revitalization traditionally has been the ambit of nonindigenous intellectuals and the state, rejecting this discourse was part of rejecting the domination of the political elite. As a result, sierra indigenous organizations do not explicitly defend cultural rights, as in neighboring countries, but participants speak Quechua and Aymara, retain cultural practices, and wear indigenous dress during important mobilizations. They mobilize as Indians, but not for indigenous cultural rights.

Another reason for the lesser propensity of Peru's indigenous to organize around indigenous identity is the pejorative meaning that the term *indio* has had in the sierra, where it is associated with servitude and poverty (Degregori 1998b: 168). Indigenous peoples may avoid self-identifying as such in order to avoid negative connotations. Although this sentiment prevails throughout Latin America, it is reinforced in Peru by Marxist and Maoist ideologues, who have attempted to de-Indianize the peasant population since the 1930s. More so than in other multiethnic Latin American countries, the Peruvian left rejects ethnic analysis and insists on more classist interpretations of oppression, often relying on a dogmatic form of Maoism or Trotskyism (interviews, Rodrigo Montoya Rojas, July 17, 2002; Richard Chase Smith, July 16, 2002; interview with Jaime Urrutia in Olivera and Paredes 2001: 78). In addition, massive urban migration, beginning in the 1950s and increasing in the 1980s as terrorist violence exploded, altered indigenous identities, authority, and organizational structures, and the nature of their claims before the state. Andean urban migrants hid cultural markers that might stigmatize them and, thus, reduce their economic and social opportunities in the city. Once settled in Lima, they spoke Spanish with their children in order to help them adapt (Marzal 1995: 77). Many ceased being *Indians* and became *cholos*, a new class of Peruvians created by the massive urban migration from the war-ravaged sierra that occurred during the 1980s.

Indigenous Movements in the Sierra

By the transition to democracy in 1979, two distinct networks of indigenous organizations had emerged in the sierra: one constructed by the Communist Party and the other by the RGAF. Both networks lacked the independence that highland indigenous movements in Ecuador and Bolivia enjoyed at this time. Moreover, whereas rival peasant networks also emerged in Bolivia and Ecuador, in Peru the two rival organizations were more roughly equal, which prevented the emergence of a single hegemonic regional campesino organization, such as Bolivia's CSUTCB or Ecuador's ECUARUNARI. Another distinction is the clear triumph of class analysis, particularly a radical Maoist line that crowded out most efforts to promote an ethno-national political ideology until quite recently. In Ecuador and Bolivia, a more ethno-nationalist tendency always has existed and it ultimately eclipsed the classist tendency. Finally, Peruvian sierra Indians endured harsher repression than did Indians in Ecuador or Bolivia. They had to contend not only with the landed oligarchy and the military, but also with one of the hemisphere's most violent guerrilla movements, Shining Path.

Until the 1970s, the history of indigenous movements in Peru bears many similarities to that of its central Andean neighbors. In the 1920s, President Augusto Leguía emitted a proindigenous discourse and tolerated independent campesino mobilization as part of a larger policy to modernize the state and to build a coherent Peruvian "nation" (Degregori 1998b: 170; Fernández Fontenoy 2000: 202). Beginning in 1920, legally recognized indigenous communities began to elect *juntas comunales*, continuing a centuries-old tradition of choosing rotating traditional authorities. Highland Indians struggled to remove themselves from harsh labor conditions and to regain agricultural land. Indigenous rebellion in the southern highlands intensified: a massive rebellion between 1920–23 encompassed five departments in the Andean trapezoid. After 1926, indigenous communities[3] presented thousands of lawsuits to claim lost lands (Remy 1994: 112).

---

[3] The number of legally recognized indigenous communities rose from fifty-nine in 1926, to 321 in 1930. By 1991, there were 4,315, now called campesino communities (Remy 1994: 112).

The indigenous rebellions of the 1920s convinced the radical left that Indians constituted a potential revolutionary class that it could lead (De la Cadena 2000: 128). These rebellions frightened the government and elites in light of the Bolshevik and Mexican revolutions that were occurring simultaneously and haunting memories of the great Tupac Amaru Indian rebellion of the 1780s (Fernandez Fontenoy 2000: 199; Rénique 1991: 70). After the formation of the Peruvian Communist Party and the American Popular Revolutionary Alliance (APRA) in the 1930s, both urban-based parties formed alliances with rural indigenous organizations (Fernández Fontenoy 2000: 201). For example, in the department of Cuzco, the Communist Party sought to create an urban-rural worker-peasant alliance and organized indigenous hacienda workers into *sindicatos* linked to the Cuzco Federation of Workers (FTC) (De la Cadena 2000: 187, 311). The expansion of rural education during the 1940s enabled a small number of campesinos to become literate and, thus, able to vote, which increased their political activity, even though the number of registered voters remained small (Rénique 1991: 196). The prevalence of the Communist Party in indigenous political struggles generated a fierce debate between those advocating a purely class-based struggle and those in the indigenista camp, who emphasized the cultural and racial basis of indigenous oppression. By the 1950s, the FTC and Communist Party had replaced the indigenistas as the main urban ally of the indigenous movements (De la Cadena 2000: 311).

President Luis Bustamante y Rivero (1945–48) tolerated campesino and other social movement activity. Many labor and campesino organizations formed during his administration, including the Communist Party-linked Campesino Confederation of Peru (CCP), formed in 1947, and the APRA-sponsored General Federation of Yanaconas and Campesinos of Peru (FENCAP) (Fernández Fontenoy 2000: 202). In the absence of progress on agrarian reform, massive land invasions commenced in the late 1950s (Handelman 1975: 62).[4] By 1960, the number of campesino organizations demanding access to land, the elimination of labor obligations to haciendas, the ability to market their products directly, and long-term leases on hacienda properties had increased. That year *mestizo* Hugo Blanco arrived to mobilize campesinos in Cuzco. The mass rallies that Blanco and others organized in Cuzco fostered a fundamental change in the collective self-perception of indigenous peoples. Once ashamed to

---

[4] Between 1956 and 1964, Fernández Fontenoy counts at least 413 separate campesino mobilizations, including seventy hacienda invasions in 1962 alone (2000: 202).

wear their ponchos and speak Quechua audibly in the city, thousands of campesinos filled the central plaza and Quechua was shouted from loudspeakers. Quechua had shifted from being a folkloric relic to being a language associated with radical political demands (De la Cadena 2000: 190). Access to primary education expanded in the indigenous highlands in the early 1960s. By 1963, enough Indians had become literate and gained the right to vote to constitute a distinct constituency worthy of presidential candidates' attention and appeals (Handelman 1975: 56, 84–5).

In the early 1960s, land invasions occurred throughout the country but most were in Cuzco, Pasco, and Junín. Handelman estimates that some 300,000 peasants participated in between 350–400 invasions during the 1960s (Handelman 1975: 121). These mobilizations encompassed *mestizo*-led movements in the central sierra, many of which were allied with APRA, as well as indigenous-led movements in the southern sierra, which received organizational support and advice from the urban left. Indigenous communities seeking access to land formed unions, chose a western-style board of directors, and affiliated with the departmental labor federation. Approximately 1,500 such unions received recognition between 1960 and 1964. But western forms of union organization coexisted with continuing forms of traditional ethnic authority. Indigenous communities formed unions in order to gain access to the resources and legal support of labor federations and to preclude the development of nonindigenous intermediaries. Once land was obtained, the unions were dissolved and prior forms of organization were used (Remy 1994: 114).

The indigenous rebellions of the 1960s differed from those of earlier eras. Whereas earlier indigenous rebellions promoted separatism and the return to precolonial modes of living without the domination of nonindigenous elites, in the 1960s indigenous movements fought for political incorporation and forged ties to urban groups – lawyers, students, unions, political parties – that helped them to articulate a broader political agenda and provided crucial financial and logistical support (Cotler 1970: 540–1; Handelman 1975: 115–27). The assumption by urban intellectuals and labor leaders that campesinos were the junior partner in the labor-peasant alliance, and needed the revolutionary urban vanguard to guide them, generated persistent tensions (De la Cadena 2000: 128).

Compared to Ecuador and Bolivia, in Peru the left was far more successful in dominating and manipulating indigenous political activity and the development of indigenous political ideologies. In the 1960s, Maoism gained dominance within the southern sierra radical left and in the campesino movements, which preferred Maoism because of its emphasis

on agrarian revolution (Fernández Fontenoy 2000: 207). Maoists rejected
the ethnic discourse of indigenista intellectuals and the Belaúnde government, emphasizing a more class-based line and the need for long-term
armed revolution (Rénique 1991: 231, 251). In 1964, the Maoist Partido
Comunista de Peru-Bandera Roja took over the CCP. Under its influence, in the 1960s and 1970s Peru developed one of the region's most
radical campesino movements (Roberts 1998: 211). After the 1962 military coup, hundreds of campesino activists were jailed. Repression was
intense and indigenous leaders lacked organizational skills and time to
devote to organizational duties. An additional problem was the lack of
unity among campesino communities, many of whom distrusted each
other and didn't believe they shared common interests. Thus, no interde-
partmental or national peasant organization formed to unite the highland
indigenous communities prior to the revolutionary military government.
Although the Maoist CCP and APRA's FENCAP were national organizations, they lacked roots in most of the sierra, where few campesinos
were aware of them. Most campesino organizations remained dependent
upon the leadership and resources of their political party sponsors (De la
Cadena 2000: 206; Handelman 1975: 147–50; Rénique 1991: 234).

On October 3, 1968, Juan Velasco Alvarado led a military coup and
established the RGAF. Velasco issued laws favoring the indigenous population of the sierra and Amazon: the 1970 Law of Campesino Communities and the Law of Native Communities, respectively. These laws
established distinct legal regimes and sociolegal categories for sierra
and Amazonian populations. Sierra indigenous communities were officially renamed *campesino communities* and allowed to name an official representative to the state (Remy 1994: 115). Velasco removed the
offensive word *indio* from government discourse and replaced it with
campesino, while promoting indigenous cultural rights (Degregori 1998b:
171; Fernández Fontenoy 2000: 199). In 1969, Velasco delivered the
agrarian reform that had been promised for more than a decade, one of the
most far-reaching in Latin America. By that year, about half the cultivable
land in Cuzco was in campesino hands, forced labor was virtually eliminated, and wages and prices for campesinos had improved. The reform
also shifted more political power to local levels, enabling state-sponsored
campesino organizations to replace the oligarchy as local authorities in
parts of the countryside. Although land redistribution was extensive, it
mainly targeted the approximately 10–15 percent of the peasantry located
on lands expropriated from haciendas. Temporary farm workers and
indigenous communities outside of traditional haciendas were ignored.

Moreover, agrarian reform created new conflicts, of which Maoist, Trotskyist, and New Left parties took advantage as they continued to promote peasant mobilization in the sierra (Fernández Fontenoy 2000: 203; Rénique 1991: 228; Roberts 1998: 211–12).

Rather than repress popular mobilization, as previous military governments had done, the Revolutionary Military Government encouraged popular groups to organize and to affiliate with its umbrella coordinating organization National System in Support of Social Mobilization (SINAMOS), established in 1971. While some groups complied, many resisted the government's effort to control their agenda, activities, and leadership. These formed alliances with leftist parties (Roberts 1998: 212–13). Independent of SINAMOS, diverse urban and rural organizations formed regional popular fronts that organized massive antigovernment strikes at the end of the military interregnum. Thus, between 1968 and 1980 there was a boom in the number, militancy, and links among popular organizations, which had cast off the vertical, clientelist relations of previous eras (Roberts 1998: 213). Yet indigenous organizations remained trapped in alliances in which they were the dependent, junior partner.

By the time of the 1968 military coup, the CCP had almost disappeared at the national level and departmental campesino federations were gravely weakened. After the coup, the CCP expanded in its base in the Andean Trapezoid (Degregori 1998b: 174). At its 1974 Fourth Congress, 144 base organizations from 13 departments were represented (Mallon 1998: 100). The CCP maintained its Maoist orientation and denounced efforts to form competing, especially ethnic, organizations (Degregori 1998b: 196). After 1973, the Maoist Revolutionary Vanguard (VR) displaced the PC-Bandera Roja as the dominant political party force in the CCP. VR had emerged in the mid-1960s after the Sino-Soviet conflict divided the Peruvian Communist Party, the majority of whose militants chose Maoism (Mallon 1998: 97–8). Under the influence of radical Marxists and Maoists, in the 1970s most peasants rejected an indigenous identity, which the left considered to be a "pathetic social condition" (De la Cadena 2000: 193). Throughout the 1970s and 1980s, as in Bolivia with the CSUTCB, political parties struggled to control leadership positions in the CCP and to dictate its mission and ideology. The methods used often were divisive and undemocratic, which impaired the effectiveness and strength of the movement (Rénique 1991: 286, 290–1).

To counter the influence of the CCP, in 1971 the military created its own peasant organization, the National Agrarian Confederation (CNA). It gained greater support than the CCP because it offered access to government resources and technical support (Rénique 1991: 248). By 1976, the CNA was opposing the military government, which was rolling back the agrarian reform. After General Francisco Morales-Bermúdez overthrew Velasco in 1975, he declared the CNA to be illegal (Fernández Fontenoy 2000: 204; Mallon 1998: 84). It reorganized as an autonomous organization in 1980 and quickly surpassed the CCP as Peru's most important campesino organization (Fernández Fontenoy 2000: 205). The CNA in 2002 had a presence in sixteen of the country's twenty-four departments. The CCP recovered somewhat in the 1990s. In 2002, it claimed to be the country's largest peasant federation, representing approximately 10,000 families organized into nineteen departmental federations that include campesino and native communities, small producers, co-ops, *rondas campesinas*, displaced peoples, and women's organizations (www.rcp.net.pe/ashaninka/coppip/ccp1.html).

Another important set of campesino organizations that emerged during the military government was *rondas campesinas*. Indigenous communities first formed these in 1976 in the northern department of Cajamarca in order to provide a means to prevent and sanction the increasingly rampant theft of livestock. In the three years that followed, hundreds of Cajamarca communities formed rondas, many of which affiliated with political parties. The rondas adapted their procedures and symbols from state institutions – the courts, police – for whose absence they compensated. That is, they were not based on traditional cultural authorities, as would be the rondas formed in the south in the 1980s to fight Shining Path. The northern rondas did, however, incorporate aspects of local, northern sierra culture and became a culture in themselves, inspiring festivals and songs (Starn 1992).

On balance, the period of the military government was one that enabled the campesino and indigenous movements to expand while creating a legal structure more amenable to indigenous cultural and ethnic rights claims. The government satisfied many campesino and indigenous demands, particularly for education and agricultural assistance, and for the recuperation of hacienda lands. Education levels increased dramatically between 1960 and 1980, when Peru rose from fourteenth to fourth compared to other Latin American countries (Cabrero 2002: 85–6). Illiteracy declined from 38.9 percent in 1961, to 27.2 percent in 1972, to 18 percent in 1981 (Remy 1994: 128n6). These gains resulted both from the progressive military's emphasis on national integration and pacification of the countryside, as well as persistent pressure applied by campesino and indigenous organizations.

After the return to democracy, indigenous peasants mainly allied with the VR, the Worker, Peasant, Student, and Popular Front (FOCEP), and the United Mariateguist Party (PUM) (Roberts 1998: 223). The PUM became the strongest leftist party, and the party of choice for sierra peasant organizations, by building a dense grassroots network. It dominated the CCP as well as the urban labor movement. In the late 1980s, PUM's support declined and APRA and the IU fought for control of the southern sierra vote (Rénique 1991: 357). Despite its achievements in literacy and land reform, the highland indigenous movement remained weak because of its internal fragmentation, caused in part by the penetration of political parties. For example, by the time of the transition to democracy, partisan conflict had "practically paralyzed" the Cuzco CCP affiliate (Rénique 1991: 344). The organization was unable to hold its fourth congress in 1980 because of partisan disputes; after the parties promised to stop trying to divide the organization, the congress was held in 1982. At the provincial level, rival federations cooperated with each other but departmental-level unity often could not be established (Rénique 1991: 347). Moreover, intense interethnic struggles between Aymaras and Quechuas over leadership weakened indigenous organizations (Rénique 1998: 313–17; interviews, Eduardo Cáceres, July 17, 2002; Víctor Torres, July 19, 2002).

By the late 1970s, the Marxist left had incorporated the ethnic and cultural claims of indigenous nationalities into its political discourse, drawing on the heritage of José Carlos Mariategui and the indigenists of the 1930s. The emergence in the early 1980s of two stridently classist armed movements terminated this tendency (Fernández Fontenoy 2000: 208). The Tupac Amaru Revolutionary Movement (MRTA) emerged in the Amazon in the early 1980s. Despite using the name of a famous eighteenth-century indigenous rebel leader, its base was the urban, *mestizo* left. The second movement, Sendero Luminoso, first gained attention in 1980 in its base in the impoverished, majority-indigenous department of Ayacucho. Because of its origins among the ethnically distinct dispossessed, many urban policymakers and intellectuals interpreted Sendero Luminoso's offensive as a "caste war," an indigenous millenarian movement seeking to reestablish the Incan empire (Remy 1994: 123–4). This was far from the case. Sendero made no mention of ethnicity in any of its documents, focusing instead on class struggle. Sendero attempted to exterminate indigenous identity as part of the process of "total war" (Mallon 1998: 116). It attacked indigenous and campesino organizations and massacred campesino leaders and indigenous authorities as rivals to its sole authority. It prohibited ethnic festivals and forced traditional indigenous leaders to resign (Degregori 1998a; McClintock 1998: 339n118; Roberts 1998: 261).

In 1982, the CNA held the first nationwide campesino strike in Peruvian history. However, by this time attacks by Sendero and the MRTA had caused the campesino movement to decline. Rural areas in the Andean Trapezoid became militarized and violence crowded out political activity (Fernández Fontenoy 2000: 205). The military was ordered to terrorize the peasantry, which the government believed to be the base of support for the insurgency (Manrique 1998: 193). In 2003, Peru's Truth and Reconciliation Commission determined that between 40,000 and 60,000 people died or disappeared in the fighting. Indigenous peoples suffered the most: three-quarters of the victims spoke Quechua (CNN 2003b). Another 600,000 mostly Quechua campesinos fled the violence for the cities (Starn 1998: 247). Thus, as sierra indigenous movements were becoming consolidated and helping to form nationwide, hegemonic organizations in neighboring Ecuador and Bolivia, in Peru, sierra Indians were being assassinated or recruited by the guerrillas or the army (Fernández Fontenoy 2000: 193).

Despite the violence, campesino and indigenous mobilization continued during the worst years of the war, particularly in areas where strong cultural traditions and authority structures provided an effective defense against the insurgency (Rénique 1998: 308). The first anti-Sendero rebellions occurred in response to attacks on indigenous community authorities. In the late 1980s, with the army's support, campesinos organized self-defense groups to fight the insurgency, also called *rondas campesinas* after the northern organizations (Degregori 1998a: 134–5; Remy 1994: 123–6). By the early 1990s, 3,400 rondas were operating in the northern sierra, organizing community public works processes and engaging in political protest (Starn 1992: 90). In 1986, President Alan García gave them legal standing to resist attacks from police and officials. Throughout this period, political parties, especially APRA, Patria Roja, and the PUM, tried to co-opt and control the rondas and to organize them into party-sponsored federations (Starn 1992: 103–5).

The presence of Sendero Luminoso, however, cannot fully explain the weakness of indigenous movements in the sierra. In Colombia, guerrilla organizations, paramilitaries, and the military have attacked indigenous organizations and leaders for at least four decades. Guerrillas operate in all Colombian departments where indigenous peoples are present and have assassinated numerous elected mayors and leaders of indigenous social movement organizations. Various armed actors have assassinated more than 500 indigenous leaders since the 1970s. Yet, in Colombia, the indigenous movement persists and even expands. The Guatemalan case also shows that indigenous identities and political organizations can survive intense violence (Warren 1998: 172). The Colombian and Guatemalan conflicts lasted far longer than the twelve-year period when Sendero Luminoso terrorized the Peruvian highlands, yet vibrant indigenous organizations survive in both countries.

In the early 1990s, after the Peruvian left had become significantly weaker, owing to the ravages of Sendero Luminoso and internal disputes, highland indigenous organizations became less dependent upon leftist parties. The weakness of all political parties since the collapse of the party system under Fujimori in the early 1990s left no strong party with which highland indigenous organizations could ally. On the other hand, this enabled them to assert greater political independence and to make multiple, temporary partisan alliances (interview, Eduardo Cáceres, July 17, 2002). Indigenous organizations and communities also have joined the numerous independent local, district, and regional fronts that emerged as the party system collapsed in the early 1990s. These fronts are fluid movements that work on a particular issue for a short period of time – such as the movement against privatization that emerged in Arequipa in the summer of 2002.

The Peruvian highland indigenous movements achieved an organizational milestone in October 1999 when communities in the highlands involved in mining conflicts formed the National Coordinator of Communities Affected by Mining (CONACAMI). In a few short years it became the most dynamic sierra indigenous organization. Organizer Miguel Palacín had been working with others since the mid-1990s to protest the increasingly harmful effects of unrestrained mining activities on campesino communities (García and Lucero 2002: 17). Of the 5,660 campesino communities recognized by the government, 3,200 of these have registered complaints regarding mining issues. Complaints escalated with the expansion of mining activities: from 4 million hectares mined in 1992 to more than 25 million in 2001. Complaints mainly concern environmental and health problems, as well as land conflicts and the social ills that accompany the bars and prostitution that follow mining camps (*Quehacer* 2001a). In 2002 CONACAMI had thirteen regional organization affiliates in sixteen departments, representing 1,135 communities, as well as ties to indigenous organizations in Bolivia and Ecuador (interview, Jorge Agurto, July 11, 2002; *Latinamerica Press* 2001: 1). The organization led a July 1–8, 2002, march (the National March for Life, Land, Water, and Agriculture) demanding that the government address the economic, social, and environmental harm caused by mining activities and that the government include indigenous rights (particularly territorial rights) in the new constitution (CONACAMI 2002).

CONACAMI, like other highland campesino organizations before it, does not present itself as an "indigenous" or "ethnic" organization and, thus, has been largely ignored by many of those studying such movements. Most of its member communities speak Quechua, but Quechua identity is not an explicit part of the movement's identity or rhetoric because Quechua Indians do not perceive the Quechua language and identity to be threatened. In recent years, however, CONACAMI has emphasized more the ethnic identity of its members and made claims based on international standards of indigenous and human rights (García and Lucero 2002: 18), perhaps in order to capitalize on the greater concern among international aid and development agencies for such struggles. For example, in February 2003 CONACAMI leaders traveled to Washington to file a petition against the Peruvian government in the Inter-American Commission on Human Rights, claiming that their rights under the American Convention on Human Rights and International Labour Organization Convention 169 on the rights of indigenous peoples had been violated (*Servindi* 2003a).

In the late 1990s, after the collapse of many Peruvian parties, highland indigenous organizations participated in elections through ephemeral alliances with political leaders. In 1998, through a variety of local alliances, the CCP elected ninety-six campesino mayors, all of whom were former campesino leaders (www.rcp.net.pe/ashaninka/coppip/ccp1.html). For the 1999 elections, the CCP made national-level alliances for the first time. CCP leaders negotiated with Alberto Andrade, (Somos Perú), Oscar Castañeda (Solidaridad Nacional) and Alejandro Toledo (Perú Posible). Only Toledo was willing to sign an accord with the organization. As the CCP organ *Voz Campesina* explained, this act convinced rural people, particularly campesinos, to vote for Toledo (Paredes Gonzales 2001: 8). For the 2001 elections, the CCP and its affiliates negotiated directly with Toledo on a second Act of Commitment, which this time had the support of many more organizations. Thus, their votes for Toledo were explicitly "conditioned" on his fulfillment of preelection promises (ibid.). In addition to this formal commitment, two CCP leaders – Paulina Arpasi of Puno and Lorenzo Ccapa of Cuzco – were postulated as congressional candidates on the Perú Posible list. These candidacies were negotiated individually with the candidates, since the CCP-Toledo alliance was not exclusive. Three prominent CCP leaders also ran on the Union for Peru (UPP) list in Piura and Moquegua (*Voz Campesina* 2001a).

Toledo's ethnic appeals were successful – he won an average of 50 percent of the vote in the southern Andean departments, pulling mainly from rural areas (*Voz Campesina* 2001b: 3). In fact, it was the rural areas that provided Toledo with sufficient votes to contest the second-round presidential elections in 2001 (Paredes Gonzales 2001: 8). Although Ccapa lost, Paulina Arpasi, a thirty-six-year-old Aymara woman from Puno, won a seat in congress. As the first female indigenous leader in congress, Arpasi attracted abundant media attention and was the focus of high expectations. Prior to her election, the few Indians who served in congress were not affiliated with indigenous organizations or organized constituencies and did not champion ethnic issues (Brysk 2000: 269).[5] Arpasi had been number five on Toledo's Perú Posible list. She won the highest preferential vote in the department of Puno (30,000+ votes), having earned public approval – even in urban and Quechua-dominated areas – for her high-profile leadership of the anti-Fujimori March of the Four Suyos (*Voz Campesina* 2001b: 7). Although the CCP initially was pleased with her success and expected her to channel CCP proposals to congress (*Voz Campesina*, 2001b: 3), they have been disappointed by what they consider to be her co-optation by Perú Posible and by her decision to emphasize her indigenous (rather than class) identity (interview, Wilder Sánchez, July 12, 2002). While being "too indigenous" for the CCP, Amazonian Indians and their advisors criticize Arpasi for not being "sufficiently indigenous," and for not championing the indigenous policy agenda (interview, Francisco Ballón, July 12, 2002).

The CNA also has participated in electoral politics in alliance with a variety of parties. Since the collapse of the party system these have most often been the new independent regional fronts. The CNA has placed greater importance on local and provincial political participation because their constituents are in rural areas and the problems they face are mainly local or provincial (interview, César Barría Marquillo, July 16, 2002). The organization is wary of national alliances with political parties, which have led to serious, even violent conflicts within the organization. For example, former president Julio Cantalicio Rivero allied with the right-wing Unión Nacional and allegedly used CNA resources for his campaign.

---

[5] Arpasi follows a handful of campesino leaders who have represented campesino interests in congress, beginning with Hugo Blanco and Andres Vargas, a CCP ex-president who represented the IU. Although they are not CCP leaders, two additional campesino leaders represented this sector in the Peru Posible delegation in 2001 (Walter Alejos, from Ayacucho, and Ernesto Herrera, from Moquegua) (interview, Wilder Sánchez, July 12, 2002; *Voz Campesina* 2001b: 7). In addition, two campesino leaders from organizational allies of the CCP won seats representing Apurímac and Arequipa (*Voz Campesina* 2001b: 7).

In May 2001, angry members occupied the headquarters for a week and destroyed computers. As a result, CNA avoided national alliances for the 2002 elections: "CNA leaders belong to a variety of political parties. It is better to maintain unity and to not ally with a single party" (my translation; interview, César Barría Marquillo, July 16, 2002).

The CCP and CNA participated in the 2002 regional elections through diverse alliances at the local and regional levels (interviews, Wilder Sánchez, July 12, 2002; César Barría Marquillo, July 16, 2002). Antolin Huascar explains the reason that the CNA Cuzco affiliate, Túpac Amaru Revolutionary Agrarian Federation (FARTAC), did not commit to a single electoral alliance:

> If we approached the elections in a joint strategy as FARTAC, we would fail, and this would be bad for all the campesinos. So in order not to fall in the trap of the creoles, we are taking another strategy, so that all the leaders that we have can take their own decision, in each zone, with a party or as a movement, to become *regidores* or mayors, municipal governments. Once they arrive there, we are going to convoke a meeting of all the *compañeros* that arrive, to raise a consciousness of what the objectives of the campesinos and FARTAC are. Once they arrive at the municipality, they have economic resources. We FARTAC leaders don't receive any salary, but once they are *regidores* or mayors they'll have some money to travel and talk to people. This is our strategy, to enter the local, provincial, and regional spaces, and to prepare for in the future that our people arrive in the congress.   (my translation; interview, Antolin Huascar, July 23, 2002)

In the late 1990s, Peruvian intellectuals of Quechua descent attempted to organize a national and international Quechua movement. They realized that a strong indigenous movement in Peru required the organization of a Quechua nationality. The Quechua do not constitute a cohesive ethnolinguistic group and lack a coherent intellectual movement, in contrast with the Quichua in Ecuador or the Aymara in Bolivia. There are eight distinct Quechua dialects and cultures, and Quechua speakers do not constitute a "nationality" in the sense that the less numerous Aymara or Amazonian groups do (interviews, Rodrigo Montoya Rojas, July 17, 2002; Richard Chase Smith, July 16, 2002). This situation is similar with respect to Quechua identity in Bolivia, but in that country the coca issue unites a sufficient number of Quechua to provide another basis for collective political action. Several conferences for Quechua intellectuals were held in 1999 and 2001, but they produced no substantive results. A main obstacle is the great internal social and economic diversity of the Quechua, which includes a significant sector of professionals, urban business people, and intellectuals. It is particularly difficult to bring these together with the more numerous, rural communities (interviews, Eliana Rivera Alarcon, July 22, 2002; David Ugarte, July 24, 2002). There is relatively less socioeconomic and geographic diversity among Quichua speakers in Ecuador and Quechua speakers in Bolivia.

In sum, the project to create a pan-indigenous identity in the sierra is still incipient. Until 1999, indigenous organizing in the sierra has focused on local economic issues and has lacked organizations that can link supporters based on ethnic identity. The most vibrant highland movement formed around social and economic problems derived from association with the mining industry, which lack cultural content. In contrast, the coca issue, which unites the Quechua population of Bolivia, evokes clear cultural associations with growing coca leaf, which has enabled the coca growers' movement to make cultural claims.

Indigenous Organizations in the Amazon

Political organization occurred more slowly in the lowlands. Between 1966–9 Peacecorp volunteer Richard Chase Smith helped to organize the approximately 4,000 Amuesha, who in 1969 founded their own federation, the Amuesha Congress. In 1979, a sector of the Amuesha formed Federation of Yanesha Communities (FECONAYA), which affiliated with the campesino division of the General Confederation of Workers of Peru (CGTP) (Smith 1996: 92). Their main issues were land claims and access to bilingual education (Brysk 2000: 64–5). Land conflicts surged in the 1960s and 1970s in response to the government's encouragement of colonization in Amazonian territories traditionally inhabited by Indians. In response, indigenous communities pressed legal claims in the courts (Urteaga Grovetto 2000: 282). The Asháninka, Shipibo-Conibo, and Aguaruna-Huambisa followed the Amuesha example and formed their own ethnic organizations (Smith 1996: 94). Among the largest and most active groups is the Asháninka, whose 50,790 members constitute approximately one-quarter of the Amazonian native population (Manrique 1998: 212, citing 1993 census).

The Velasco government's 1974 Law of Native Communities (revised in 1978) legally recognized native communities and conferred upon them some political and cultural autonomy (Brown and Fernández 1993: 206). The concept of the *native community* referred to indigenous groups with common ethnic origins living within a limited territory (Remy 1994: 118). However, this concept was not based on Amazonian forms of organization but, rather, on the Andean model, and its introduction tended to atomize the larger language-group-level identities that were also under construction at this time – a factor that retarded the development of ethnic federations similar to those that were coalescing at the same time in Bolivia and Ecuador. In 1975, approximately 250,000 Amazonian Indians lived in 1,035 legally recognized native communities (Urteaga Grovetto 2000: 280).

Amazonian federations group single ethnic communities in a given territory into a single, modern social movement organization (Remy 1994: 119). By the 1970s, educational advancements and previous experience in land conflicts had created a pool of leaders and some minor policy achievements followed. For example, the Aguaruna-Huambisa Congress, formed in 1976, forced the Ministry of Education to stop sending them teachers who couldn't speak their languages and to appoint members of their communities to these positions (Montoya Rojas 1993: 110). In 1979, Amazonian Indians began to form the first confederation of Amazonian peoples, AIDESEP, which united five smaller federations (Smith 1996: 96–7; *Perú Indígena* 1990b: 235). From the beginning there were tensions among the diverse groups, particularly between the Amuesha, who have a conciliatory culture, and the Asháninka who accrue status through successful confrontation (Smith 1996: 96). There also were rivalries between the Amuesha and the Aguaruna, who gained control of AIDESEP in 1980. The involvement of NGOs and political parties generated additional divisions. In 1987, the Amuesha Congress left to form Confederation of Amazonian Nationalities of Peru (CONAP), together with Shipibo and Yanesha organizations, and with the help of the urban intellectual indigenous organization Indian Council of South America (CISA), and the proindigenous NGOs Amazonian Center for Anthropology and Applied Practice (CAAAP) and Center for Amazon Research and Promotion (CIPA) (Smith 1996: 123n11).

During the 1980s, AIDESEP became the most active and internationally linked Peruvian indigenous organization. In 1982, it helped to form the international alliance that in 1984 became the Coordinator of the Indigenous Organizations of the Amazon Basin (COICA), which represents indigenous peoples of the eight Amazon Basin countries (AIDESEP 2000). AIDESEP grew rapidly in the 1980s and 1990s as a result of an influx of funding from domestic and international NGOs, as well as North American and European governments. By 1990, it united 222 regional and local organizations in the rainforest, with links to Andean organizations like the CCP. By 2000, it united forty-seven federations and six regional organizations throughout the Amazon, encompassing most of the sixty-four Amazonian peoples (AIDESEP 2000). As of July 2002, CONAP had thirty-five affiliated federations representing a population of approximately 150,000 Amazon Indians, in eleven departments. It is organized into five regional headquarters, twelve *directivos*, and a secretary of women's affairs (interview, César Sarasara, July 17, 2002; *Perú Indígena* 1990a: 251). CONAP remains the relatively weaker, less internationally connected organization.

External financial support for their projects and meetings, and the functioning of permanent offices and staff, transformed the Amazonian confederations. Whereas at the beginning of the decade they had little money for salaries or operating expenses, by the end of the 1980s funds received from a dozen foreign agencies enabled AIDESEP to afford a staff of approximately forty employees. This radically changed the meaning of political action and leadership in the Amazon because leadership now no longer required financial sacrifice and salaries facilitated the professionalization of leadership careers (Smith 1996: 91). It also injected fierce rivalries among indigenous organizations and NGOs working with them over access to the millions of dollars available. Member communities began to view AIDESEP as a source of funds and to judge its achievements based on the delivery of financial resources, rather than in terms of political effectiveness. Organization leaders became more focused on maintaining and improving relations with funders than with member organizations. Despite the poor political climate for indigenous rights in the 1980s and 1990s, thanks mainly to AIDESEP's efforts, the amount of land collectively titled to indigenous communities tripled. Moreover, the organization provided an opportunity to develop political skills and to act as a channel between indigenous peoples and the government (Smith 1996: 99–100).

The most severe challenge to the Amazonian indigenous movement came from the presence of guerrilla organizations. By the late 1980s, attracted by resources that could be extracted from the illegal coca trade, Sendero Luminoso and the MRTA were attacking Asháninka and Amuesha communities, selectively killing their leaders, forcibly recruiting others, and enslaving the population as producers of food and coca leaf, concubines, and low-ranking troops (Brown and Fernández 1993: 206; Manrique 1998: 212–13; Remy 1994: 127). Many Asháninka voluntarily joined Sendero. The Asháninka are internally diverse and prone to warfare and at the time of Sendero's arrival they were under pressure from invading colonists and their environmentally destructive activities. Thus, as in the sierra, Sendero initially appeared to offer an instrument for addressing serious security problems and only later alienated their hosts with their brutality. In response to the kidnapping of an important Asháninka leader in 1989, an Asháninka Army led an uprising against the MRTA that forced the guerrillas to retreat, relocate their forces, and abandon their strategy of intimidation. In 1991, the Asháninka led a second uprising, this time against Sendero. They had less success this time. Hundreds of Asháninka, without the army support and access to weapons that sierra indigenous communities enjoyed, chose to relocate rather than suffer further massacres (Manrique 1998: 213–17).

In the Amazon, relations with parties began later than in the sierra. Indigenous mayors and municipal councilors have been elected in many predominantly indigenous Amazonian districts since the institution of direct election of municipal governments in 1980, mainly through AIDESEP affiliates' local alliances with political parties. AIDESEP was founded at the moment of the transition to democracy, just as the leftist parties were resuming their electoral activities. Amazonian organizations experienced hostility from leftist parties, which considered all popular movements to be their political domain. The organization tried to avoid conflicts while maintaining its autonomy, but this was difficult because the various NGOs upon whom they were becoming financially dependent were allied with particular parties and tried to present themselves as the representatives of indigenous organizations (Smith 1996: 98).

In the late 1980s, AIDESEP decided to present candidates in local and regional elections and worked with the government to register thousands of undocumented Indians. They also held workshops for their affiliated federations on the electoral process and distributed information on political participation in indigenous languages (*Perú Indígena* 1990b: 240–1, 244). Between 1980 and 1993, through alliances between the indigenous organizations and locally strong parties, Amazonian Indians elected local and provincial mayors in seventy-eight Amazonian districts where they constitute a majority; AIDESEP held fourteen of these in 1993. Indigenous mayors gained representation in regional assemblies before Fujimori dismantled regional governments in 1993. Some Amazon Indians gained office by supporting his Cambio 90-Nueva Mayoría coalition in the 1990s. The Asháninka in particular approved of Fujimori's harsh policy against the guerrillas (interview, Adda Chuecas, July 15, 2002).

According to CONAP president César Sarasara, formal politics is a new experience for Amazonian Indians. In the past, mediators such as NGOs, anthropologists, and the clergy tried to isolate them from politics in order to shield them from political messes. "But with the passage of time, beginning in 1987 we began to participate. We began to elect indigenous mayors, but we also began to make alliances with popular organizations of the coast and sierra" (my translation; interview, July 17, 2002). It has been difficult to participate effectively, however, because of the lack of consensus among the communities, tribes, and organizations; the lack of financial resources; the great distances and geographic obstacles to travel for political activities in the Amazon; and a lack of political experience. That lack of experience and knowledge of norms for public spending caused several mayors to end up in jail for misusing funds.[6]

We, despite these difficulties, organize ourselves, and where there are more Indians we elect our mayor, and we try to link the organization with them. So there are many mayors elected and these also strengthen the organizations, but with many difficulties.   (my translation; interview, César Sarasara, July 17, 2002)

In the 1990s, CONAP pursued a strategy of local alliances and independent candidacies. In Aguaruna zones, candidates for provincial government mainly appeal to Indians, who outnumber non-Indians. In provinces where Indians are a minority, they seek alliances with other sectors and set their sights on lower levels of government. Candidates campaign by traveling the rivers and speaking at CONAP and other affiliate's meetings. Running as independents is difficult because it requires gathering many signatures and traveling to Lima to inscribe their candidacy. Nevertheless, independent candidacies are preferred because "our indigenous position always has been to not belong to political parties" (interview, César Sarasara, July 17, 2002). For the 2002 regional elections, they were able to register candidates for eight mayors and one provincial government. Candidates represent their local organizations, rather than CONAP, in order to keep the national organization free from involvement in electoral politics that might distract or divide it. Although in the past the national organization has chosen the candidates for these offices, more recently they are asking the local organizations to choose for themselves. CONAP does not aspire to seek national congressional offices until it has developed a strong regional electoral base.

---

[6] Anthropologist Adda Chuecas concurs that "criminal action" on the part of indigenous mayors is a result of lack of knowledge of the norms and pressure from indigenous constituents to address their needs. For example, an indigenous mayor might spend municipal resources on food for the poor or healthcare when that money was earmarked legally for other expenditures. The NGO CAAAP is working with indigenous officials to provide training in order to avoid these problems and to reduce the current high level of dependence on nonindigenous "advisors," who often manipulate indigenous mayors (interview, Adda Chuecas, July 15, 2002).

The Emergence of a National Indigenous Organization

In the late 1990s, a new effort was made to unite Peru's campesino and native populations into a single organization. Hundreds of delegates attended the founding Conference of the Permanent Conference of the Indigenous Peoples of Peru (COPPIP) in December 1997 in Cuzco. During 1998, the fledgling organization tried to influence a proposed law of indigenous rights that was before the Peruvian congress and defined its institutional apparatus and objectives. In 2000, a meeting was held to elaborate a five-year strategic plan and to address more immediate objectives. During a second national congress in 2001, some participants decided to create a more permanent leadership structure that encompassed Amazonian and Andean organizations. This group, led by AIDESEP and CONACAMI leaders, formed the Permanent Coordinator of the Indigenous Peoples of Peru (also COPPIP). In 2002, COPPIP held two additional congresses (August 8 and September 11) to consolidate itself institutionally and to define the indigenous movement's agenda (*Servindi* 2002d: 2). While COPPIP has maintained a more confrontational stance toward the government, some original members of the Conferencia Permanente, including the CNA, decided to work within government-created spaces.[7]

The driving organizational forces within this second COPPIP are AIDESEP, the most representative and effective Amazonian organization, which represented fifty-four federations in 2004, and the miners' organization CONACAMI, the most dynamic highland indigenous movement, which represented seventeen regional organizations the same year (*Correo Indígena* 2004). AIDESEP leaders served in the first phase of leadership; the role of National Directive Council was rotated to CONACAMI at the September 11, 2002, National Congress, while AIDESEP leader Gil Inoach Shawit assumed the vice presidency (*Servindi* 2002d: 1). The growing closeness between the main Amazonian and highland indigenous organizations was exemplified in July 2002, when AIDESEP and CONACAMI leaders both signed the accord with government ministers that ended CONACAMI's eight-day march (*Servindi* 2002c: 8). Sierra and Amazonian organizations also worked together to press for the inclusion of indigenous rights in the proposed constitutional reform: COPPIP, AIDESEP, CONAP, CONACAMI, CCP, Organization of Amazonian, Aymara, and Quechua Bases (OBAAQ), and diverse other organizations signed a petition demanding consideration of their claims in

---

[7] Telephone interview, Miguel Hilario, December 18, 2004.

February 2003 (*Servindi* 2003d: 2). Despite these achievements, COPPIP is not yet the coherent, institutionalized political actor that national organizations in neighboring countries have become. Its member organizations retain their autonomy while using COPPIP as a space to develop common strategies (García and Lucero 2002: 19).

UNDERSTANDING ETHNIC PARTY FORMATION

The Peruvian case shares some similarities with the other two central Andean cases. As in Ecuador, a literacy requirement for voting dampened political participation among the indigenous until it was lifted during the transition to democracy at the end of the 1970s. Suffrage was extended to illiterates in 1978 for the Constituent Congress elections and vastly expanded the political potential of the indigenous population.[8] In Cuzco, for example, the voting population increased 26 percent between 1980 and 1985; in heavily rural provinces, the increase was in the 30–45 percent range.

As in both Bolivia and Ecuador, gaining access to the ballot has been relatively difficult. A 1979 law required parties to present a list of 100,000 members (less than 1 percent of the national electorate) to register, which must include voters in at least half of the country's districts. These requirements have hindered party formation, particularly for regionally concentrated parties, which must demonstrate nationwide support (Birnir 2000: 15–16). Obstacles to ballot access increased in Peru in 1995 when signature requirements increased for registering national parties from 100,000 to 480,000 (Coppedge 1996: 18n29).

As in Ecuador, decentralization occurred at the time of the democratic transition. The 1979 constitution established directly elected municipal governments and created administrative regions, which were first established under the Alan García government (1985–90) (Ballon 1995: 266–7). But in Peru, President Fujimori (1990–2000) used the 1993 constitution to recentralize power and facilitate his reelection. Newly elected indigenous mayors had to fight Fujimori's centralization policy. Fujimori promulgated at least sixty norms – laws, decrees, ministerial resolutions – restricting the powers and resources of municipal governments and dismantled regional governments that had been created during the García regime (Pedraglio 1998). Thus, as indigenous mayors were taking office in Ecuador and Bolivia, and using this as a stepping stone to higher office,

---

[8] Suffrage had been denied to illiterates in 1896 (De la Cadena 2000: 90).

in Peru indigenous organizations were having a more difficult time consolidating electoral progress.

Of the countries studied in this book, Peruvian Indians were least able
to take advantage of the opportunity for constitutional reform in the
1990s. The Fujimori-dominated 1993 constitutional reform was a dis-
aster for indigenous peoples. Indigenous organizations and anthropologists mobilized unsuccessfully against Fujimori's changes and presented
a petition with 55,000 signatures to the Constituent Congress opposing
the elimination of land and language rights that had been recognized in
previous constitutions. But only two of its nineteen proposals ultimately
were included in the 1993 charter: rhetorical recognition of the ethnic
diversity of the Peruvian nation (art. 2[19]) and the right to practice customary law (art. 149), a right already protected by statutory law (Urteaga
Grovetto 2000: 287–8). The most devastating blow was the removal of
the inalienability and indivisibility of indigenous lands. Thus, Peruvian
indigenous organizations not only lacked the moral boost that successful
participation in constitutional reform gave to indigenous movements in
neighboring countries; they did not secure political rights or institutional
reforms that would have made it easier for them to gain a foothold in
the political system. They did not have an opportunity to forge strategic
ties to sympathetic social sectors. Moreover, without new constitutional
rights, they lacked an important incentive to form parties: that is, to ensure
their autonomous representation in the process of writing implementing
legislation.

A second opportunity to participate in constitutional reform occurred
at the beginning of the Alejandro Toledo administration. On December
6, 2001, Toledo announced the installation of a National Commission
of Andean, Amazonian, and Afro-Peruvian Peoples (CONAPAA), over
which the First Lady, Eliane Karp de Toledo, a Belgian anthropologist
and Quechua speaker, would preside. A key goal of the organization was
the preparation of a proposal for indigenous rights for the upcoming
constitutional reform. Indigenous organizations that were included were
optimistic that they would have a greater say in this process, in light of
the proindigenous rhetoric of Toledo and his wife, as well as the electoral
alliance between his party, Perú Posible, and campesino organizations,
which had brought three experienced campesino leaders to the national
congress (interview, Wrays Perez, July 11, 2002). However, indigenous
constitutional rights were discussed at only two of the twenty-seven
nationwide fora convened to discuss constitutional reform and the government failed to consult with indigenous organizations concerning these
rights, as required by ILO Convention 169 (*Servindi* 2003d: 1). By 2003,

relations between indigenous organizations and Karp's commission had become severely strained. Thereafter the national organization COPPIP promoted its own constitutional rights agenda. The organization was able to delay a congressional vote on the constitutional reform proposal until after the realization in April 2003 of a nationwide consultation among indigenous organizations, and the convocation of an Indigenous Forum in the Legislative Palace, during which the organization presented its proposal to congress (*Correo Indígena* 2004). Its proposals were ignored. The outcome of the constitutional reform process was still pending in 2005.

The main obstacle to ethnic party formation in Peru has been the lack of unity and organizational maturity of indigenous social movement organizations. The schism between the two national campesino confederations and the internal disunity that involvement in electoral politics generates are particularly challenging (interview, Nestor Guevara, July 23, 2002). Electoral activity mainly has been confined to temporary alliances with diverse parties at the local level. National political alliances have tended to lead to severe conflict within the organizations, as members have allegiances to different parties and competition for candidacies is often fierce. As CCP president Wilder Sánchez put it, "We are all in agreement on where we want to go, but once we get there each wants to be in charge. So at the time of naming candidates conflicts begin" (my translation; interview, July 12, 2002). The national schism is reflected at the departmental level. For example, within the indigenous movement in Cuzco there was an attempt between 1978–80 to create a party, the Revolutionary Agrarian Movement (Movimiento Agrario Revolucionario), which would have united the two rival departmental federations: the CNA affiliate FARTAC and the CCP affiliate Qosqo Departmental Peasant Federation (FDCQ). Tensions between the two organizations, as well as the prevailing sentiment that *gremio es gremio* – that is, that a campesino federation should not get involved in electoral politics – doomed the project. In addition, political parties with influence in the organizations prevented it (interview, Nestor Guevara, July 23, 2002). As a result, in Cuzco many campesinos hold public office at the local level, but there is no coherent political movement because they entered office on a variety of political tickets. Many originally entered with one of Fujimori's electoral vehicles. Because Fujimori's various personalist vehicles never developed permanent institutional structures or a cadre of leaders, there were openings for indigenous candidates throughout the country to fill out the list. Indigenous candidates compete against each other in many districts, particularly at the municipal level because mayors are the most important local authority and, thus, the target of most campesino demands (interview, Eliana Rivera, July 22, 2002). In 2002, President Alejandro Toledo enacted a decentralization law that reestablished regional government (the Law of Regional Elections No. 27683 [March 15, 2002]). A provision in the law required the reservation of 15 percent of the places on political party lists for municipal councils and regional assemblies for indigenous candidates (art. 12). Party list quotas mainly have been used to improve the representation of women, with excellent results in Europe and Latin America, provided that female candidates are placed in positions high enough on the list to win office (Htun and Jones 2002). The more common method of improving the representation of ethnic minorities is through the reservation of seats, as occurred in Colombia and Venezuela. And this is what indigenous organizations had wanted. Amazonian organizations had proposed creating a 10 percent indigenous quota in the national congress. This would consist of reserved seats for Indians elected without political party affiliation, which would have allowed indigenous candidates to gain office without having to work with traditional political parties, and without impairing the ability of the incipient indigenous party MIAP to compete (interview, Francisco Ballón, July 12, 2002).

While from a distance, the party list quota may offer a better way to achieve the representation of disadvantaged minorities in countries where that minority is a significant part of the population, this approach caused more problems than it solved. According to anthropologist Adda Chuecas, who worked with the National Electoral Juror (JNE) to write a law implementing the quota,[9] the result was disappointing. Indigenous participation was restricted to local governments at the district level, a space that indigenous organizations had been able to occupy without the quota (personal communication e-mail, October 24, 2002). The quota law applies to 101 districts in the Amazon basin (Morejon 2002).[10] In those departments or regions, the list of candidates for regional council must include at least two candidates who are members of native communities. For lists competing in the elections for provincial council, the 15 percent quota of native candidates is established according to the number of *regidores* (local officials) in the province (Nota de Prensa N. 087-2002-OCII/JNE, July 25, 2002).

---

[9] The JNE issued Resolución 277-2002-JNE on August 14, 2002. See www.jne.gob.pe.
[10] The departments are Amazonas, Ayacucho, Cajamarca, Cusco, Huánuco, Junín, Loreto, Madre de Dios, Pasco, San Martín, and Ucayali. Nota de Prensa No. 087-2002-OCII/JNE. A list of provinces can be found at www.jne.gob.pe, Nota de Prensa No. 103-2002-OCII/JNE.

The Peruvian experience indicates that the party list quota approach may be a poor method of improving the representation of indigenous peoples. Quotas hurt fledgling indigenous parties because the major parties have a better chance of winning and, thus, of recruiting the most qualified indigenous candidates. As Kanchan Chandra observes, voters and office seekers make choices with respect to party affiliation strategically and ethnic parties do not necessarily have a natural advantage in recruiting their own elites (2004: 14). In addition, according to AIDESEP leader Wrays Perez, the quota divides the indigenous movement by dispersing its leaders among parties: "This is a disadvantage for us, it will divide us up, and none of them are going to be elected" (interview, July 11, 2002). The danger also exists that nonindigenous parties will choose politically malleable Indians for their lists, rather than those affiliated with independent indigenous organizations (interview, Adda Chuecas, July 15, 2002). In fact, this is what happened in many areas. For example, of the thirty-two Indians presented on electoral lists in the Amazonian province of Tambopata in Madre de Dios, none of them had institutional support from an indigenous federation (Montoya Rojas 2003: 2). According to COPPIP leader Jorge Agurto, this is nothing new:

What has happened is that political parties have begun to include leaders for their lists for the assemblies, because they are required to. For the congressional elections, in departments with large indigenous populations, for those deputies elected by department they have chosen to include indigenous leaders so that they can compete for votes within the department. There are some departments where there are many Indians. So they are obliged to do so, including the traditional ones, such as Unidad Nacional, which is on the right, have had to include indigenous leaders on their lists, but only to gain the indigenous vote.

(my translation; interview, July 11, 2002)

During the summer of 2002, the Centro Bartolomé de las Casas and Casa Campesino in Cuzco held workshops with over 100 campesino leaders to teach them about the new electoral rules and to emphasize the importance of political participation.[11] Among the topics discussed was the new 15 percent quota. Most leaders were aware of the quotas and sought to take advantage of them. However, after the law was restricted to lowland "natives," Peru's highland indigenous population was not allowed to participate. Thus, in the Amazon, where an indigenous party is trying to compete, it must compete with other political parties for candidates, whereas in the highlands, where there is no indigenous

---

[11] The author attended a two-day workshop on July 25–6, 2002, for campesino leaders.

TABLE 5.2. *Peru: Vote share for dominant and leftist parties*

Election	Combined Votes Dominant Parties	Combined Votes Leftist Parties	ENPS
1980	87.3%	14.4%	2.46
1985	96%	24.7%	2.32
1990	69.5%	13%	5.84
1995	13%[a]	1.2%	2.89
2000	5.2%	–	4.15 (2001)

Notes: Dominant parties are Acción Popular, APRA, PPC, IU. Leftist Parties are in 1980 PRT, UNIR, UI, UDP, FOCEP; in 1985 IU and ASI; in 1990 IU and IS; in 1995 IU. All above votes are from national elections; for dominant parties, presidential and legislative results are averaged together. Leftist votes are presidential results only, the only figures I could obtain. All figures are percentages of all votes except for 1995, which is percentage of valid votes.
[a] In these elections, 41 percent of votes cast were null.
Sources: Dominant party data from Dietz and Myers (2001: 26). Leftist data from Tanaka (1998).

party, there is no quota law to promote greater indigenous representation through existing parties.

Given these formidable obstacles, even the collapse of Peru's party system in the early 1990s and the precipitous decline in support for leftist parties were not enough to secure the formation of an ethnic party. During the 1980s, Peru's political party system was relatively closed. Four parties – Acción Popular, APRA, PPC, and IU – shared on average 90 percent of the vote during the 1980s, with an effective number of parties for seats (ENPS) of 2.39. The system opened up considerably after the election of Alberto Fujimori in 1990. In 1995, the top four parties combined attracted only 10 percent of the vote (see Table 5.2). The collapse of the party system generated extreme fluctuations in ENPS, as numerous independent personalist vehicles absorbed much of the disaffected vote. The collapse of Peru's party system may be interpreted as a negative or positive condition for the formation of a regional- or national-level indigenous political party. On the one hand, the collapse of the four parties that had dominated 90 percent of the vote presents a clear playing field for a well-organized challenger. On the other, Peruvians' rejection of parties *per se*, and the now-common practice of forming "disposable," nonideological parties around particular candidates, may mean that no political parties are viable in the near term (Levitsky 1999: 86–7).

The Peruvian case is striking because of the vitality of the left throughout the 1980s and the subsequent near disappearance of the left in the

1990s. The enfranchisement of illiterates in 1978 increased the availability of campesino candidates and voters, which enabled the left to expand in the southern sierra (Rénique 1991: 331–5). Leftist parties allied within IU entered the democratic period with strong ties to the social movements that had confronted the military government and built on these relationships during the 1980s in order to institutionalize relatively new party organizations (Tanaka 1998: 131). The left was particularly strong in the 1980s in the Andean Trapezoid and in parts of Lima where Andean migrants had settled (Roberts 1998: 10). In the 1978 elections, five leftist organizations won a combined 29.5 percent of the vote – the best showing to date for the Marxist left in the region, with the exception of Chile, and nearly ten times the vote earned by the Peruvian Marxist left in 1963 (Roberts 1998: 222). In six elections between 1980–90, the left earned on average 21.2 percent of the vote. In contrast, between 1992 and 2000, the left only scored better than 2 percent of the vote in the 1992 Constituent Congress elections, when it earned 5.5 percent. After 1998, with the disappearance of the traditional left and the proliferation of new personalist parties, it is difficult to detect which parties might be leftist.

Yet, despite this decline in support for leftist parties, no indigenous party was able to take advantage of the wide open space on the left of the political spectrum. Neither did leftist political party professionals or intellectuals look to the indigenous movement as the basis of a dynamic antineoliberal opposition movement, as they did in Bolivia and Ecuador. There are two reasons for this. First, indigenous organizations gained few substantive achievements during the 1990s and could not be perceived as a dynamic or effective tool for political mobilization. They received little media or public attention and had virtually no ability to pressure the Fujimori government. Second, compared to other countries, the Peruvian left was more stridently classist in its orientation and did not consider ethnic issues or identities to be valid criteria for political organization. In sum, both the Peruvian left and the Peruvian indigenous movement were relatively weaker than their counterparts in the other central Andean countries, and neither was able to lead a coherent political project.

In the 1990s, a few smaller parties were formed in the highlands that attempted to project an identity as a party of the indigenous population. Renacimiento Andino, the party of Ciro Gálvez Herrera, a Quechua-speaker from Huancayo, was founded in April 1996 in that department (Gálvez Herrera 1996). Similarly, Maximo San Roman, a landowner and business owner of Quechua descent, who previously was president of the

Senate, formed the Force of Integration Together with Pride (FIJO). FIJO's platform included "the development of a pluricultural democracy and institutionality," the defense of Amazonian Indians' autonomy and terri-tory, and the economic demands of campesinos (FIJO 1999c: 2). Although San Roman claimed a Quechua identity and was invited to participate in indigenous conferences organized by intellectuals, campesinos did not consider him to be their representative. FIJO and Renacimiento Andino are the only two electoral movements that have had an ethnic discourse and identification with and closeness to sierra indigenous movements (interview, Jorge Agurto, July 11, 2002).[12] Their classification as ethnic parties is questionable, given the lack of identification between their urban professional leaders and the rural campesinos they purport to represent. This relationship is even more tenuous than that between urban-based indigenous intellectuals of Aymara descent in Bolivia in the early 1980s and the campesino communities and organizations with which they at least had more organic ties. It should be noted that Quechua is still spo-ken in many highland departments by nonindigenous intellectuals and professionals, a legacy of the days when regional elites sought to dif-ferentiate themselves from Lima by promoting cultural festivals. Thus, speaking Quechua does not necessarily imply indigenous identity.

Strategic Decision-Making Scenario I

Compared to the situation described in the highlands, efforts to form an ethnic political party are more advanced in the Amazon. At AIDESEP's 1996 National Congress, participants agreed to create a political pro-gram and to found Indigenous Movement of the Peruvian Amazon MIAP (MIAP 2001: 1). In June 1998, Asháninka Indians representing the Comu-nidad Nativa Asháninka Marankiari Bajo traveled to Lima to register a MIAP list for the October 1998 municipal elections to enable them to participate in the district of Perene (Comunidad Nativa Ashaninka Marankiari Bajo 1998). According to a press release,

We have decided to participate in the October 1998 local government elections in our young district with authentic Asháninka candidates in order to demonstrate

[12] Of lesser importance are efforts by individuals or small groups of intellectuals to form "indigenous" parties. For example, the tiny, Lima-based Movimiento Indio Tawantin-suyo was attempting to form a party in the summer of 2002. When asked what their base of support was, the representative interviewed said that their leadership in Lima meets with various delegations from different parts of the country. Interview, Jorge Perez, July 11, 2002.

our professional capacity to administer and implement in sustained practice integral, alternative, ethnodevelopment in accordance with our indigenous cosmovision and with respect, consultation, participation, and justice following historic delays.   (my translation; Comunidad Nativa Asháninka Marankiari Bajo 1998)

MIAP leaders recognized that, owing to their small numbers and lack of financial resources, it would be necessary to establish alliances with sympathetic social and political actors, while maintaining independence from political parties that had exploited and manipulated indigenous organizations in the past:

MIAP emerged as a political alternative for the indigenous citizens as well as non-indigenous that identify with our proposals, in order that they not be tricked or manipulated by parties and/or movements that lack a vision and a proposal of integral and sustainable development for the Amazon, and to fight in an organized manner for the application of their proposals.   (my translation; MIAP 2001: 3)

Anthropologists working with AIDESEP and CONAP claim that forming their own political party is a low priority for the organizations and that they prefer to participate in other ways, such as by forming their own indigenous parliaments, governed by indigenous cultural values (interview, Adda Chuecas, July 15, 2002). As advisor Francisco Ballón explains, "it's not that they don't want to form parties. It seems to me that as yet they have not arrived at having a level of consciousness sufficiently solid about the importance of parties" (interview, July 12, 2002). Indigenous organizations play the role of parties in the national arena, representing their interests as a lobby, rather than as elected officials. Amazon Indians also wish to avoid conflicts that have arisen as a result of competition for electoral office. For example, in the late 1990s, Aguaruna elders chose a candidate to run for municipal office. AIDESEP president Evaristo Nukguag didn't like it and presented his own candidacy and list for the same office. Both lost when they split the vote (interview, Francisco Ballón, July 12, 2002). The observations of anthropologists belie the enthusiasm for holding public office expressed by some of the organizations' leaders, and may reflect the preference of Peruvian anthropologists associated with NGOs to "protect" Amazonian peoples from electoral politics, which they fear may destroy their culture (interview, Rodrigo Montoya Rojas, July 17, 2002). Nevertheless, COPPIP coordinator Agurto concurs: "The theme of the political party is not on the agenda of discussion of the indigenous organizations. It is not a priority" (my translation; interview, July 11, 2002).

In addition to the problem of collecting signatures, there are many more obstacles to forming an ethnic party in the Amazon, compared to the highlands. Many NGOs will not fund organizations that participate in elections and this may dampen their leaders' enthusiasm for partisan politics. Leaders are more interested in maintaining good relations with donors, which provide more resources than access to public office. As in the sierra, disunity within the Amazonian indigenous movement, particularly between AIDESEP and CONAP, has kept the movement weak and divided, making political participation more difficult and delaying the formation of a single Amazonian party. The numerous advisors and financing organizations that permeate both organizations, which often try to manipulate their indigenous clients, exacerbate the disunity (interviews, Francisco Ballón, July 12, 2002; Adda Chuecas, July 15, 2002; Rodrigo Montoya Rojas, July 17, 2002).

Future Prospects

When interviewed in July 2002, highland indigenous leaders in Peru were energized by the success of indigenous candidates and parties in Bolivia the previous month. Leaders in Cuzco had had several contacts with Evo Morales and with Felipe Quispe. They also were aware of the success of Pachakutik in Ecuador. These examples inspired Peruvian indigenous organizations to think about forming parties (interviews, Nestor Guevara, July 23, 2002; Antolin Huascar, July 24, 2002). More generally, campesino leaders have been encouraged by the growing strength of leftist electoral and campesino movements in Bolivia, Brazil, Colombia, Ecuador, and Mexico. "If we look at Latin America, campesinos have begun to mobilize themselves. The rural population in Peru is scarcely 30 percent but the slums around the cities are all campesino migrants" (my translation; interview, Nestor Guevara, July 23, 2002). According to national CCP secretary-general Wilder Sánchez, his organization expects to create a political party in the future, with the goal of emulating the success of "our compañero Evo Morales" and the MAS in Bolivia, as well as the success of Pachakutik in Ecuador. The CCP organ *Voz Campesina* (2002: 11) devoted two articles to Morales's victory in Bolivia and its implications for Peruvian campesinos. The CCP is equally inspired by the success of Brazilian President "Lula" da Silva and his Workers Party. Sánchez seeks to emulate the MAS strategy of joining forces with other popular organizations, particularly in urban areas. He believes that the CCP can find support in the urban shantytowns around Lima and Andean cities where millions of campesino migrants from the countryside live. This strategy of base-level alliances with other popular organizations is to replace the past practice of urban intellectuals and notables in Lima forming parties and imposing them on the campesino communities. "We have constructed these alliances from the base, with these regional experiences, and seek to unite to create the national party, which would have organic support. This is perhaps a utopia, but we are in the process of constructing this because the political solution requires a political movement" (interview, Wilder Sánchez, July 12, 2002).

Thus, the diffusion effect observed in other countries may have begun to operate in Peru, although it has yet to spawn a viable party. Moreover, a serious barrier to ethnic party formation during the 1990s was only removed in 2001. Fujimori's policy of labeling all oppositional activity as terrorist and, thus, subject to persecution, seriously constrained efforts to form opposition parties. Since the ouster of Fujimori in 2001, there have been more opportunities for autonomous political action. As Huascar observed, "Now that he is gone we are trying anew to rise up to claim indigenous, originary, and Andean rights" (my translation; interview, July 23, 2002).

UNDERSTANDING ETHNIC PARTY PERFORMANCE[13]

Difficulty in registering the party for each election has inhibited the electoral performance of the Amazon indigenous party MIAP. Maintaining party registration also is a challenge because of a 1979 law requiring parties to win 5 percent of the national vote to retain registration. Although the country's most mature and consolidated indigenous organization sponsored the party, MIAP was unable to prevail against the lack of unity among Amazon organizations, the opposition of key funders and advisors

---

[13] Renacimiento Andino, the party of a Quechua-speaking intellectual, registered for the November 17, 2002, regional elections and won five provincial and twenty-seven district elections, including the provincial government of Tacna (*El Comercio* [Lima] 2002: A15; www.onpe.gob.pe). Its leader, Ciro Gálvez, was inscribed in the 2000 presidential elections and won 0.81 percent of the vote (interviews, Jorge Agurto, July 11, 2002; Nestor Guevara, July 23, 2002; www.georgetown.edu /pdba/Elecdata/Peru/pres2001.html). During his campaign Gálvez identified himself with the indigenous population, spoke Quechua and maintained a discourse of indigenous rights (interview, Jorge Agurto, July 11, 2002). But the party's rhetoric emphasized an Andean identity, rather than the demands of ethnically distinct Quechua or Aymara, and it had no ties with indigenous organizations (Gálvez Herrera 1996, 1997). The other personalist party led by a Quechua-speaking professional, Movimiento FIJO, won a few local elections in the late 1990s (interview, Eduardo Cáceres, July 17, 2002), but Máximo San Roman failed to collect sufficient signatures to get on the ballot in the 2000 presidential elections (interview, Nestor Guevara, July 23, 2002). Neither party was able to offer potential indigenous candidates the incentives offered by larger, more successful parties.

to its electoral project, and the greater interest among indigenous voters in pursuing other avenues to press their claims before the state. In addition, it was more difficult for MIAP leaders to reach out to sympathetic popular movements, given the sparse population of the Amazon, which indigenous communities share with armed guerrillas, drug traffickers, the military, and elites – none of whom are likely allies (Smith 1996: 91–8; interview, Francisco Ballón, July 12, 2002). Another severe obstacle was the need to compete for candidates with larger, better-funded, parties, especially after the institution of the indigenous quota in 2002.

Logistical obstacles also are immense. Signatures must be gathered across rugged rainforest terrain and transported to Lima. The lack of identity documents is a serious problem. In 2000, the Defensoría del Pueblo (human-rights ombudsperson) estimated that one third of adult Amazonian Indians lack documents (Defensoria del Pueblo 2000: 25). In addition, voting procedures can be complicated and electoral information is usually not available in indigenous languages. Indigenous votes often are nullified when ballots are filled out incorrectly (interview, Francisco Ballón, July 12, 2002). The great distances between indigenous communities and places of voter registration and voting may require expensive three to four day journeys each way. AIDESEP worked with the Defensoría, the Ministry of Defense, and the three electoral agencies between 1998 and 2002 to provide documents, but could not completely close the gap (interviews, Jorge Agurto, July 11, 2002; Ana Palomina, July 16, 2002; Wrays Pérez, July 11, 2002). Finally, fraud in the Amazon on the part of nonindigenous elites takes place far from the eyes of monitoring organizations and is, thus, difficult to rectify and punish (Defensoría del Pueblo 2000: 17–21; *Servindi* 2003c: 13).

For these reasons, success has been limited to the local level. MIAP and its affiliated lists won thirteen indigenous mayors in various Amazon provinces in the 1998 municipal elections.[14] Above this level, MIAP has had trouble registering because of the necessity of collecting 50,000 signatures. Party leaders are hoping to be able to do so by the 2006 elections,

[14] AIDESEP documents and interviews with militants indicate between twelve to fourteen indigenous mayors held office as of July 2002, but not all of these ran with MIAP. Apart from MIAP, local Amazonian indigenous political parties were formed for the 1998 municipal elections, such as the Movimiento Independiente Integracionista del Alto Amazonas (MIIAA), which represented the mostly Aguaruna indigenous communities of Manseriche (Alto Amazonas), and the Lista Independiente Indígena y Campesina de Yarinacocha, which represented indigenous communities in Yarinacocha (Ucayali) (Defensoria del Pueblo 2000: 11–13).

and to expand the party to include Afro-Peruvians and Andean Indians (interview, Wrays Perez, July 11, 2002). Unable to meet registration requirements to run on its own, during 1998–2001 MIAP formed alliances with registered parties. For example, MIAP signed an accord with the aforementioned FIJO to place three MIAP militants as candidates on FIJO's congressional list, but the list failed to garner sufficient signatures for valid registration (interview, Jorge Agurto, July 11, 2002). MIAP participated in the general elections for the first time in 2000 in alliance with Somos Peru, which gave them three candidates. They failed to win a seat. AIDESEP leader Wrays Perez attributes this to fraud perpetrated by President Fujimori, who persecuted Somos Peru. Avalo Huayio, the MIAP candidate in Amazonas, won the election but fraud prevented him from taking office (interviews, Jorge Agurto, Wrays Perez, July 11, 2002). For the 2001 elections, MIAP allied with Toledo's Peru Posible. Perez explains this decision:

We saw that some of their lines touched our vision with respect to indigenous rights. So we supported them and allied with them. We participated with one congressional candidate. This candidate lost by 250 votes because the elections use multiple seats. It was the department of Amazonas. And there the Peru Posible candidate won – we had various problems with him and we lost.

(my translation; interview, July 11, 2002)

According to Perez, "practically the entire Amazon voted for Toledo" (interview, July 11, 2002).

For the November 17, 2002, regional elections, MIAP was only able to inscribe the party in one province (Condorcanqui) in the department of Amazonas. Around 1,000 independent political organizations registered for the 2002 contests – approximately twenty-two for the regional governments, and another 947 for municipal offices (subject to verification of signatures) (*El Comercio* [Lima] 2002: A15). Outside of Condorcanqui, MIAP formed alliances with registered parties, particularly Peru Posible. In total, MIAP fielded twenty-four candidates for regional vice president, regional assemblies, and provincial and district offices. It won no offices on its own but, through a variety of alliances, a total of fourteen indigenous mayors took office in six Amazonian departments in 2002 (Participa Perú 2003: 9). Fraud may explain some of the losses (www.onpe.gob).

CONCLUSION

Although Peru presents a number of the conditions that promoted the successful formation of ethnic parties in Ecuador and Bolivia – a large indigenous population, an open party system, a defeated left, and the successful example of ethnic parties in neighboring countries – on their own these conditions were insufficient to promote the same result. Ballot access was persistently difficult, decentralization occurred only briefly, the Fujimori government effectively squashed oppositional movements of all kinds, and guerrilla movements persecuted independent indigenous political activity. In such a restrictive context Peru's weak and divided indigenous social movement has been unable to mount a successful political initiative.

There is reason to believe that with the transition toward greater democracy, the cessation of intense guerrilla violence in the highlands, and the creation of a national indigenous organization in 1999, Peru may yet produce an indigenous movement and corresponding political party similar to those of its central Andean neighbors. Interviews with leaders of the principal regional and national indigenous organizations evince a great interest in participating in formal politics. This interest is greatest in the Amazon, particularly within the Amazonian confederation AIDESEP, the country's most institutionalized and experienced indigenous organization. In the sierra, most leaders interviewed preferred to focus on accessing local and regional government and building a political base at lower levels before attempting to participate at the national level. Because most of the decisions affecting them are made at these subnational levels, they prefer to invest their scarce resources there. At the national level, where economic policy is made, they believe that their social movement organizations are better able than a handful of congressional representatives to pressure the executive for changes.

Perhaps by the 2006 national elections Peru's incipient national movement will become sufficiently consolidated to launch an ethnic party or to unify itself behind MIAP. This possibility would increase if the national organization COPPIP can generate a coherent political movement around the issue of indigenous constitutional rights or around economic issues, on which it may be able to forge common ground with other popular movements. In the context of a weak executive, a weaker party system, and ephemeral voter loyalty, an indigenous–popular alliance would face little competition, provided that it could manage its own internal conflicts.

6

Argentina, Colombia, and Venezuela

Unlikely Cases of Ethnic Party Formation and Success

In this chapter, three cases are treated collectively and systematically in order to emphasize similarities and contrasts among them. The most obvious similarity is the minuscule size of the indigenous population, which in each country lies somewhere between 1 and 3 percent of the total. These indigenous populations are internally heterogeneous and widely dispersed. Most Indians live in mono-ethnic indigenous communities located far from the capital city and many are pressed to the frontiers of national boundaries. Indigenous social movement organizations independent of state tutelage formed in all three countries in the early 1970s and linked themselves to the transnational indigenous rights network that emerged at the end of that decade. The political contexts also share similarities, most importantly a tendency toward decentralization in the 1990s. All three societies are primarily urban and industrialized, but are encircled by a more traditional, conservative landowning class.

It is the key contrasts between Colombia and Venezuela, on the one hand, and Argentina, on the other, that explain the variation in the propensity of successful ethnic parties to form in each country. In Colombia and Venezuela indigenous movements were relatively united and institutionalized prior to the opportunity for major constitutional reform. In both cases, indigenous peoples' organizations participated directly and successfully in those reforms, producing two of the most progressive régimes of ethnic constitutional rights in the region. In both countries, these rights included reserved seats for indigenous candidates. Moreover, the concentration of indigenous populations in both countries in specific subnational electoral districts provided relatively easy terrain for fledgling electoral vehicles. Finally, immediately prior to the formation of successful ethnic parties, traditional political parties experienced a marked decline in voter loyalty, opening space in the political system for challengers. In contrast, in Argentina the indigenous movement was extremely fragmented, did not participate directly in a constitutional reform, received no special political rights, and was more geographically dispersed, with no subnational indigenous-majority districts. In addition, traditional parties maintained their dominant position until the very end of the period under study.

The Colombian and Venezuelan cases are interesting because they explain the emergence of ethnic parties in unlikely settings, given the minuscule size of the ethnic minority that sponsored them. In Colombia and Venezuela, indigenous movements overcame the small size of their ethnic constituency by taking advantage of the opening presented by the convocation of a constituent assembly. Using skillful negotiation, persistent lobbying, and the support of sympathetic elites, indigenous movements in both countries achieved an extensive set of political reforms that created a permissive institutional environment for the political representation of small minorities. Both constitutional reforms not only recognized a broad set of indigenous peoples rights, they instituted reforms that significantly opened the political system to all new political parties and movements.

INDIGENOUS SOCIAL MOVEMENTS

Contemporary indigenous social movement organizations formed in the 1970s in all three countries. Until that time they experienced similar histories of confrontation with the state. Thereafter, their histories diverge and generate great variety in the key social movement variables of organizational maturity, unity, and affiliate network density. They also differ significantly with respect to relations between indigenous movements and political parties. In all three cases, political parties attempted to co-opt and manipulate the indigenous movement. They were relatively unsuccessful in Colombia, moderately successful in Venezuela until the emergence of independent indigenous organizations in the 1990s, and quite successful in Argentina. The greater dependence upon and penetration by political parties in Argentina may partially explain the decision not to form indigenous parties.

Colombia

Colombia is a crucial case for understanding the emergence of ethnic political parties in South America because Colombian Indians were the first to form viable parties. Taking advantage of symbolic and legal gains achieved during the 1990–1 constituent assembly, the results Colombian ethnic parties achieved dwarfed those of ethnic parties in Bolivia in the 1980s, despite their small numbers. The success of Colombia's ethnic parties inspired indigenous leaders in other countries to follow the same route. Similarly, the Colombian constitutional reform was the first in Latin America to significantly advance the protection of indigenous peoples' collective political rights and was a model for others in the region, particularly for Bolivia, Ecuador, and Venezuela (Van Cott 2000b).

Colombia's indigenous population is approximately 2.7 percent of the total, according to the 1993 census. Eighty-one distinct indigenous groups speaking sixty-four languages are scattered throughout the country, with concentrations in the southwestern departments of Cauca and Tolima and in lowland border areas. Indians are a numerical majority in the three sparsely populated Amazonian departments of Guainía, Vaupés, and Vichada (see Table 6.1). Despite its small size, the territorial presence of the indigenous population is extensive because 24.5 percent of the national territory is in protected indigenous *resguardos*. Approximately 81.7 percent of Indians live in these protected, self-governing areas (Roldán Ortega 2000: 49–50).

Colombia's contemporary indigenous organizations emerged from the peasant land movement of the 1960s and 1970s in the department of Cauca. Nasa (also called *Páez*), Guambiano, and Coconuco Indians formed the Regional Indigenous Council of Cauca (CRIC) in 1971 to further the struggle to recuperate traditional lands that had been taken by haciendas, as well as to strengthen indigenous cultures. The CRIC often worked with the campesino organization National Association of Campesino Users (ANUC) that the government formed in 1967 to control peasant land mobilizations. A rival, more traditional movement, also based in Cauca, now called the Indigenous Authorities of Colombia (AICO) (formerly Autoridades Indígenas del Suroeste, AISO) formed in 1977. While the Nasa and Coconuco dominate the CRIC, the Guambiano are the main force within AICO. In the 1970s, Indians in neighboring departments followed the CRIC model and formed departmental indigenous organizations.

By the 1980s, the indigenous movement had a substantial cadre of educated indigenous leaders, thanks to government spending on education in the 1960s and 1970s, as well as the institution of ethnoeducation programs targeted to indigenous communities, which began in 1978 (ww.onic.org.co). In 1980, CRIC led efforts by regional indigenous

TABLE 6.1. *Colombian indigenous population by department*

Department	Indigenous Population	% of Department
Amazonas	16,042	30.3
Antioquia	9,904	0.2
Arauca	2,657	2.7
Atlántico	0	0
Bolívar	0	0
Boyoca	3,050	0.2
Caldas	27,991	3.1
Caquetá	4,163	1.3
Casanare	4,358	2.5
Cauca	135,952	14.6
César	15,960	2
Chocó	24,860	7.1
Cordoba	23,271	2.1
Cundinamarca	1,859	0.1
Guainía	12,919	98.7
La Guajira	131,624	37.8
Guaviare	3,647	5.7
Huila	196	0
Magdalena	4,733	0.5
Meta	5,241	0.9
Nariño	49,487	4.3
Norte de Santander	2,226	0.2
Putumayo	17,321	7.8
Quindío	0	0
Risaralda	5,435	0.7
Santafé de Bogotá	0	0
Santander	0	0
Sucre	6,676	1.1
San Andrés y Provincia	0	0
Tolima	22,725	1.9
Valle del Cauca	6,812	0.2
Vaupés	17,833	51.7
Vichada	17,540	90.5

Source: Ruiz Salguero and Bodner (1995: 11), taken from 1990 municipal census.

organizations to convene a national meeting to organize opposition to
the government's proposed Indigenous Statute. That statute would have
dissolved the basic form of indigenous self-government, the *cabildo*, and
privatized collectively owned lands, known as *resguardos*.[1] The Turbay

[1] Indigenous *resguardos* have enjoyed legal protection since 1890 (Law 89). Based on the
Spanish colonial model, cabildos usually include a "governor, mayor, and five or six
members" (Ramírez de Jara 1997: 40).

government proposed to replace them with Communal Action Boards, which existed in nonindigenous communities. Opposition to this statute united diverse indigenous organizations and provided the main impetus for the formation of a national movement. At the 1980 First National Indigenous Encounter in Tolima, participants began preparations for a larger First National Indigenous Congress, held outside Bogotá in 1982. More than 2,000 indigenous representatives and a handful of indigenous university students created the National Indigenous Organization of Colombia (ONIC) (Ramírez de Jara 1997: 40). ONIC today represents approximately 90 percent of the country's organized indigenous population (Laurent 1997: 67; Wirpsa 1992: 49). It has a hierarchical leadership structure that presides over six operating areas (e.g., communications, projects, and finance) and eight program areas (e.g., education, human rights, women) (www.onic.org.co). The Cauca-based AICO gradually expanded its geographical base beyond Cauca (Laurent 1997: 67). It aspires to be a rival national movement, but lacks ONIC's geographical coverage. Whereas Amazonian regional organizations were formed prior to the creation of national organizations elsewhere in the Andes, in Colombia the Organization of Indigenous Peoples of the Colombian Amazon (OPIAC) did not form until 1995. OPIAC unites indigenous organizations in the six Amazonian states (www.opiac.org). It works within ONIC but also maintains its own activities.

In Colombia, prior to the late 1980s, two traditional political parties (Liberals and Conservatives) dominated national politics through the formal monopoly created by the National Front Pact (1957–74), and later through the clientelist ties established during this period. The Liberal and Conservative parties offered cash incentives and provided trucks to transport indigenous voters to the polls. Individual indigenous leaders participated with these parties in municipal, regional, and national elections in the 1970s and 1980s. But most indigenous organizations have avoided relations with these parties because they oppose their material interests (interview, Claudia Piñeros, March 9, 1997; interview, Antonio Jacanamijoy, in Ramírez de Jara 1997).

Whereas in neighboring countries leftist parties were popular among indigenous organizations in the 1970s and 1980s, in Colombia the left was too weak to present a viable alliance option.[2] The left was frustrated with the monopolization of power by the two main parties, but also severely divided by opposing positions on the option of armed struggle. This same

[2] The Communist Party had fluid relations with Nasa Indians in the 1930s and 1940s (Albó 1996: 786).

question divided the indigenous movement. A few leftist parties formed in
the late 1980s to participate in the municipal elections initiated in 1986.
Patriotic Union (UP), which was associated with the Communist Party
and the FARC guerrillas (Revolutionary Armed Forces of Colombia), was
the most important. However, right-wing paramilitaries assassinated and
intimidated its militants and drove the party nearly into extinction in
the mid-1990s. The M-19 Movement (M-19) guerrillas established warm
relations with the indigenous movement in southwestern Colombia in the
1980s and a number of its soldiers were indigenous. When the M-19
laid down its weapons and converted to a political party in 1990,
Democratic Action M-19 (ADM-19) it attracted support from indigenous communities and included some prominent indigenous leaders in its
list. Nevertheless, neither clientelist nor leftist parties succeeded in perme-
ating, controlling, and dividing indigenous organizations in Colombia as
they did elsewhere.

Venezuela

Almost a decade after the Colombian constitutional reform, Indians in
neighboring Venezuela secured the region's most extensive set of indigenous constitutional rights, including extensive political rights. It is the
only case in which ethnic parties formed in the context of a strong left,
demonstrating that successful ethnic parties can form even in the absence
of a vacuum on the left of the political spectrum, under certain conditions.

Venezuela's indigenous population is approximately 1.5 percent of
the total population and is comprised of thirty-eight distinct groups. By
far the largest group is the Wayuú (168,729 members). Indians mainly
are settled in ten states, principally in frontier zones (CONIVE 1999:
82; Sánchez 1996: 214). The largest number is in Zulia, home to the
Wayuú, and half of these live in the city of Maracaibo (interview, Dieter
Heinen, May 17, 2000). Although Indians are nationally a minuscule
minority, there are significant numbers in some states and municipalities. In Amazonas state, 49.71 percent of the population is indigenous
(see Table 6.2). According to the 1992 indigenous census, three of the
state's four municipalities had indigenous populations ranging between
88 and 97 percent, while the nonindigenous population was concentrated
in the urban municipality of Atures.[3] The next most indigenous state is
Delta Amacuro, with 19.8 percent, but two of its three municipalities

---

[3] The state has since been divided into seven municipalities but corresponding census data
for indigenous populations is not available.

TABLE 6.2. *Venezuelan indigenous population by state*

State	% of Population Indigenous (1992)
Amazonas	49.71
Anzoátegui	0.72
Apure	1.86
Aragua	0
Barinas	0
Bolívar	3.36
Carabobo	0
Caracas	0
Cojedes	0
Delta Amacuro	19.8
Falcon	0
Guarico	0
Lara	0
Merida	0.04
Miranda	0
Monagas	0.7
Nueva Esparta	0
Portuguesa	0
Sucre	0.09
Tachira	0
Trujillo	0.01
Yaracuy	0
Zulia	7.74

Source: Censo Indígena Venezuela 1992.

have significant indigenous populations: Antonio Diaz (82.9 percent) and Pedernales (40.58). In Bolívar, Indians are 3.36 percent of the population but constitute a majority in the municipality of Gran Sabana (60.83) and a significant minority in Sucre (29.14). In sum, even though the indigenous population in Venezuela is truly minuscule, concentrations of indigenous voters in particular state and municipal districts present opportunities for local and regional parties.

In Venezuela, until 1999 indigenous organizations were most active at the state level, particularly in the southeastern lowland states of Bolívar and Amazonas. Venezuela's oldest and most institutionalized regional indigenous federation is the Indigenous Federation of the State of Bolivar (FIB), founded in 1973. FIB was principally responsible for the creation of a national indigenous organization in 1989, the National Indian

Council of Venezuela (CONIVE). The national organization was relatively dormant until 1999, when it took advantage of the opportunity to participate in a national constituent assembly. That experience enabled CONIVE to consolidate itself institutionally, such that in 2000 CONIVE boasted sixty affiliates (CONIVE 2000).

Formerly a Federal Territory, in 1992 Amazonas became an independent state with a 49.7 percent indigenous population. The drafting of the state constitution and a law establishing its politicoterritorial division provoked indigenous organizations to launch a defensive movement to oppose proposed language that threatened indigenous territorial rights (Corao 1995: 409–11). In 1993, this movement became the Regional Organization of Indigenous Peoples of Amazonas (ORPIA). It receives institutional support from the human rights office of the Puerto Ayacucho Catholic Church, which has been working with indigenous organizations since 1991. ORPIA and its civil society allies successfully inserted unprecedented recognition and rights in the 1993 Amazonas Constitution, including recognition of the state as "multiethnic and pluricultural." They then won a series of Supreme Court decisions (December 5, 1996; March 4, 1997; December 10, 1997) striking down the governor's scheme of internal territorial division and requiring indigenous participation in the formulation of a new scheme (*La Iglesia en Amazonas* 1998: 22–3). Indigenous organizations are weaker outside of Bolívar and Amazonas. The Zulian indigenous movement is divided, due mainly to the intervention of political parties. In the other state with a large indigenous population, Delta Amacuro, no single federation had been formed as of May 2000, due to the lack of unity among groups in that state (interview, Dieter Heinen, May 17, 2000).

Compared to Colombia and the central Andes, Venezuela's regional and national organizations have had less institutional continuity. With the exception of the FIB in Bolívar, most are relatively new. Venezuelan organizations also have demonstrated relatively greater timidity with respect to alliances with nonindigenous actors. This is attributable to fears of co-optation or exploitation, as well as a belief that non-Indians are incapable of understanding indigenous aspirations and cultures. Although they often form short-term alliances to achieve immediate goals – such as the successful mobilization in Amazonas around the state constitution – indigenous organizations seldom invest in long-term strategic alliances (*Sendas* 1998c: 27, 29). Venezuelan indigenous organizations also suffer from internal divisions. Derived from differences surrounding ethnic identity and political party affiliation, factionalism impeded the consolidation of a national movement until 1999.

In Venezuela, political parties, which have monopolized channels to political power and resources for half a century, permeate indigenous politics. Clientelist relationships with the two dominant parties – Democratic Action (AD) and Independent Committee of Electoral Political Organization (COPEI) – generally have been unsatisfactory because the parties impose their own priorities and ignore or oppose indigenous organizations' policy agendas. Since indigenous organizations have no financial resources and will bring in few votes, parties place indigenous candidates toward the bottom of lists, where they are unlikely to win office. AD and COPEI have attempted to co-opt the indigenous and peasant populations through the establishment of dependent organizations. After the formation of the independent indigenous organization CONIVE, some indigenous organizations remained affiliated with AD or other political parties. Others support the leftist parties Radical Cause (LCR), MAS, or Fatherland for All (PPT) (Bello 1995: 12). Leftist parties have gained ground with indigenous voters by treating them with greater respect and having platforms that are closer to their programmatic goals (interviews, Luis Gómez Calcano, May 15, 2000; José Luis Gonzales, May 19, 2000). Relationships are particularly warm in remote rural areas where leftist parties have no organization and, thus, benefit from them most. For example, indigenous leader Liborio Guarulla Garrido, the current governor of Amazonas, was Radical Cause's coordinator in Amazonas prior to the creation of the ethnic party PUAMA.

Argentina

Argentina's indigenous population is far more urban than our other two cases, with perhaps half of the indigenous population living in cities. This urban–rural divide has led to the development of two distinct movements: local, rural movements with little articulation to one another, and urban intellectual movements with poor links to the countryside. Argentine Indians comprise twenty-four separate groups and constitute approximately 1.4 percent of the total population. Although no official census has been taken since the census of 1968, social scientists estimate that there are approximately 600,000 Indians living in rural, mainly mono-ethnic settlements, and another 500,000 Indians living in mixed neighborhoods in the slums of major cities. The latter represent a migration that began in the 1950s and 1960s, much earlier than in the other cases studied. The population of urban Indians is increasing rapidly (Balazote and Radovich 1999: 159; Crain 2000: 24; Tamagno 2001). This migration has given a sector of Argentina's indigenous movement an urban location and character that is not seen in our other cases, except perhaps among the Aymara of La Paz. Forced into the worst rural climates and urban slums, Indians are in the majority extremely poor and constitute perhaps the most miserable indigenous population in the region. These conditions prompted the Mayan Nobel Prize Laureate Rigoberta Menchú to declare during a 1995 visit: "in no place in the world have I seen the subhuman living conditions that exist here, and the lack of action to change this situation" (my translation, cited in Ortega 1996a: 12).

Outside the cities, Argentina's indigenous population is concentrated in the northwest, particularly in the provinces of Salta and Jujuy, the poorest and most indigenous state in Argentina (Andrew Crain, personal communication, February 7, 2001; Silvia Hirsch, personal communication, April 23, 2003). The largest group is the Kolla. Together with the Aymara and Quechua, to whom they are related, they comprise approximately 39.7 percent of the total indigenous population (Ortega 1996a: 21–2). Unfortunately, there is no data available on the proportional size of the indigenous population by province.[4] Instead, I present tables showing the distribution of indigenous groups by province and by people (Tables 6.3, 6.4). Table 6.3 also includes data from the 1991 census on the total population of each province. The best we can do to get an idea of the proportion of Indians in particular provinces is to compare the total population with estimates from the early 1990s of peoples living in that province. Using this method we can conclude that it is unlikely that there are any provinces with indigenous populations that exceed 25 percent. Thus, Argentine Indians face a relatively higher barrier to gaining office above the municipal level, in that they would have to do so through alliances with non-Indians.

The geographic dispersion and ethnic diversity of Argentina's indigenous population has contributed to a highly fractured indigenous movement with little national presence. Geographic and ethnic divisions are compounded by differences in lifestyle in different regions, variations in the level of acculturation, and the divergent demands of urban indigenous intellectuals and professionals and the rural communities. The most important indigenous organizations are local organizations representing specific ethnic groups. There are no geographically extensive regional or

---

4 The Argentine government was to have done a new indigenous census in 2001 but controversy regarding the timing and participation of indigenous organizations has delayed it. Personal communication, Elena Moras, Instituto Nacional de Estadísticas y Censos, April 8, 2003.

TABLE 6.3. *Argentine indigenous population: Distribution by state*

State	1991 Total Population	2001 Total Population	Peoples
Buenos Aires			Mapuche, Pampa, Ranquel
Catamarca	264,234	334,568	Diaguita-Calchaquí
Chaco	839,677	984,446	Toba, Wichi-Mataco, Mocoví
Chubut	357,189	413,237	Mapuche, Tehuelche
Entre Rios	1,020,257	1,158,147	Mocoretá, Timbú
Formosa	398,413	486,559	Toba, Wichi-Mataco, Pilagá
Jujuy	512,329	611,888	Kolaa, Chiriguano (Guaraní)
La Pampa	259,996	299,294	Mapuche, Ranquel
Mendoza	1,412,481	1,579,651	Huarpe
Misiones	788,915	965,522	M'byá-Guaraní
Neuquén	388,833	474,155	Mapuche
Rio Negro	n.d.	n.d.	Mapuche
Salta	866,153	1,079,051	Tupí-Guaraní, Chané, Chorote, Kolla, Chulupí, Wichi-Mataco, Toba, Tapiete, Pilaga
San Juan	n.d.	n.d.	Huarpe
Santa Cruz	159,839	196,958	Tehuelche
Santa Fe	n.d.	n.d.	Mocoví, Toba
Tierra del Fuego	69,369	101,079	Selk'nam (Ona), Hausch, Yagán-Yámana, Alacalufe
Tucuman	n.d.	n.d.	Quilmes, Diaguita-Calchaquí
Argentine cities	n.d.	n.d.	All groups

Source: Ortega (1996a: 22).

national confederations (Silvia Hirsch, personal communication, April 23, 2003).

Contemporary mobilization dates to the Peronist era. Although President Juan Perón did not fulfill his promise to return their land, he improved considerably the slave-like conditions and wages of rural indigenous workers and reduced the authoritarian control of hacienda owners. Years later many Indians maintain an allegiance to the Peronist party and avoid conservative parties, for whom landowners had forced them to vote (Crain 2000: 26; Schwittay 2000: 3–6). In addition, Perón politically incorporated a small class of urban indigenous intellectuals through patronage ties, establishing a strata of progovernment, co-opted indigenous bureaucrats, who promote a culturalist rights agenda (Serbín 1981: 411–12). During the 1950s, tensions emerged between the national and provincial levels of government over indigenous policy (Serbín 1981: 414–15).

TABLE 6.4. *Argentine indigenous population: Distribution by people*

People	Province	#	%
Wichí	Chaco, Formosa, Salta	24,000	7
Chorote	Salta, Formosa	1,200	0.3
Chulupí	Formosa	2,800	0.8
Toba	Chaco, Formosa, Salta, Santa Fe, Buenos Aires, Rosario	39,000	11.3
Mocoví	Santa Fe, Chaco	9,800	2.8
Pilagá	Formosa	27,700	8
Guaraní (Chané, Chiriguano)	Salta, Jujuy	2,600	0.8
Mb'ya-Guaraní	Misiones	1,500	0.4
Kolla	Jujuy, Salta, Buenos Aires (slums)	137,000	39.7
Calchaquí	Tucumán, Catamarca	62,000	18
Mapuche	Neuquén, Chubut, La Pampa, Buenos Aires	36,700	10.6
Tehuelche	La Pampa, Chubut, Santa Cruz	500	0.1
Yámana	Tierra del Fuego	50	0
TOTAL		344,850	100

Source: Servicio Nacional de Asuntos Indígenas, Ministerio de Salud y Acción Social, and Asociación Indígena de la República Argentina, 1977, cited in Pueblos Indígenas (2001).

Thereafter, indigenous policy mainly was made in the provinces, with brief periods of centralized authority, usually during military governments hostile to indigenous interests. In areas with substantial indigenous populations, provincial governments have used patronage and government jobs to co-opt indigenous leaders and to capture indigenous votes (Serbín 1981: 415–17).

Urban migrations created a university-trained class of middle class indigenous professionals and technicians (Bozzano 1996b: 62; Ortega 1996a: 12). Kolla and Mapuche intellectuals formed the Centro Indígena de Buenos Aires, which became the Coordinating Commission of Indigenous Institutions of Argentina (CCIIRA) in 1970. Parallel to this process, progressive Christian organizations began working with rural indigenous communities in the 1960s and helped to form modern social movement organizations. This resulted in a new class of more politically independent rural indigenous leaders, who clashed with the co-opted, urban, educated indigenous bureaucrats in the provincial and national governments. Landowners and the military created their own indigenous organizations to control the increasingly independent movement (Serbín 1981: 417–22).

The Indigenous Association of the Republic of Argentina (AIRA) formed in Buenos Aires in 1975 at the apex of the first wave of independent indigenous mobilization. Its leaders were acculturated indigenous university students and professionals in Buenos Aires without organic ties to provincial and local organizations and ethnic federations (Crain 2000: 26; Ortega 1996a: 12; Schwittay 2000: 11; personal communication, Silvia María Hirsch, April 7, 2003). The collapse of the Isabel Perón government in 1975 ended this era of indigenous activism. The independent indigenous movement was crushed, its leaders jailed, and its organizations dismantled (Serbín 1981: 425–30). In order to survive in this inhospitable context, AIRA emphasized cultural rights and forged ties to international organizations and the emerging transnational indigenous rights movement (Serbín 1981: 430).

After the return to democracy in 1983, a number of new organizations emerged and most received financial, technical, and political support from international sources and progressive religious organizations, which helped to train leaders, support economic development projects, and revitalize indigenous culture (Balazote and Radovich 1999: 160). Indigenous organizations mobilized jointly to secure the first law recognizing indigenous rights, Law 23.302 (1985) on "Indigenous Policy and Support of Aboriginal Communities." However, it took many years, and intense lobbying by legislators and the International Labour Organization, for implementation to occur, and the National Institute of Indigenous Affairs (INAI) envisioned in the law was not fully funded and operational until 1996 (Balazote and Radovich 1999: 159–60; Ortega 1996a: 13; Schwittay 2000: 11).

Argentine indigenous organizations have sought alliances with political parties and the state since the 1970s. These usually resulted in the co-optation of a handful of leaders and no advancement in the demands of grassroots indigenous organizations. This co-optation established a constant tension between progovernment and co-opted indigenous leaders and more independent, radical leaders and organizations. The primarily local or provincial emphasis of Argentine indigenous organizations is attributable to the fact that municipal and provincial governments are the political spaces that have the authority to resolve their most important problems. The response received varies depending on the configuration of provincial power, and the extent to which competitive parties perceive the indigenous vote to be important. For example, in Neuquén a provincial party, the National Popular Movement (MPN), has dominated politics since the province was recognized as such, and has targeted the Mapuche

as part of the large, poor population. Several Mapuche have been incorporated into the party and gained elected and appointive offices. A sector of
the party gained influence within the Confederación Mapuche Neuquina,
dividing that organization on the issue of involvement in formal politics
(Briones 1999: 48; Mombello 2002).

In Argentina, multiple *agrupaciones* or *sublemas* form within the major
national parties, particularly the Peronist Party. Indigenous organizations
have formed their own *agrupaciones* within the parties, such that in predominantly indigenous areas several lists will be composed of indigenous candidates (personal communication, Silvia Hirsch, February 22,
2001; Hirsch 2003: 96). Indians also have gained office with the Radical
Civic Union (UCR) and other parties at the provincial level in Chaco,
Neuquén, Salta, and Jujuy (Hirsch 2003: 94). At the national level, in
elections on May 14, 1995, an Ona indigenous leader from Tierra del
Fuego, Ermelinda Amalia Gudiño became the first Indian to serve in the
National Congress. She had been placed third on the departmental list for
the Peronist Party and took office after the first-listed candidate resigned
(Frites 1996: 49).

CONSTITUTIONAL REFORM CONJUNCTURE

Given the importance of participation in successful constitutional reforms
to the formation and performance of ethnic parties in countries with
minuscule indigenous populations, it is worth looking closely at and comparing these conjunctures in detail. The era of multicultural constitution-
alism in Latin America began in Colombia in 1990. That year the national
indigenous organization ONIC and the Cauca-based AISO ran candidates in the seventy-member national constituent assembly elections after
their demand for reserved seats was denied. Their expectations were low
because of the minuscule size of the indigenous population, its low level of
voter registration, and the lack of financial resources. Everyone was sur-
prised – including the indigenous movement – when they won two seats,
running as social movements. They were awarded an additional nonvoting seat to represent the indigenous guerrilla movement Quintín Lame.[5]

The indigenous constituent assembly delegates (representing ONIC,
AISO, and Quintín Lame) in alliance with the leftist ADM-19 – the
party of the demobilized M-19 guerrillas – successfully lobbied for the

---

[5] A Political Accord signed with the major parties prevented the government from awarding
a voting seat (Peñaranda 1999: 108).

constitutional recognition of a wide spectrum of indigenous rights. These included the creation of two reserved seats in the Colombian Senate for Indians, and one reserved indigenous seat in the lower chamber[6] – the first reserved seats for indigenous peoples in the Americas. In addition, the 1991 Constitution allows social movements to contest elections and provides state financing and free media time for political parties and movements with political representation. The reform process itself was enormously important for the evolution of indigenous politics in Colombia. Their unexpected win in the constituent assembly elections convinced Indians that they could be an electoral force by appealing to disaffected Colombians, since most of their votes came from non-Indians. During the constituent assembly, indigenous leaders developed lobbying and negotiating skills and forged ties to other social movements and leftist party leaders. The assembly made national figures of the indigenous delegates, who attracted abundant media attention (Van Cott 2000b).

Eight years later, Venezuela's indigenous population participated in a constituent assembly convoked by President Hugo Chávez. In addition to three seats reserved for Indians – the fulfillment of a Chávez campaign promise – in statewide elections indigenous organizations captured two seats representing the states of Amazonas and Zulia. The three reserved seats were held by CONIVE leaders elected in a nationwide process of consultations organized by the fledgling national organization. Regionally prominent indigenous activists won the other two seats: these were Atala Uriana Pocaterra, a Wayuú woman who briefly was Environment Minister under Chávez; and Amazonas indigenous activist Liborio Guarulla. The process of organizing to demand the establishment of the reserved seats, to defend CONIVE's three selected representatives, to educate its member organizations about the constituent assembly process, and to lobby for a strong commitment to indigenous rights in the constitution, enabled CONIVE to consolidate its presence as a national organization. With considerable institutional support and resources from the Chávez government, as well as NGOs and the Catholic Church, CONIVE emerged as the preeminent indigenous organization in the country. Its lobbying effort resulted in the most progressive indigenous constitutional rights regime in Latin America (Van Cott 2003a).

Among the most important rights achieved was the creation of three reserved seats in the 165-seat unicameral Venezuelan National Assembly,

---

[6] Instituted between 1994–8, and again in 2001 by Law 649, which also created two Afro-Colombian seats (Cunin 2003).

as well as reserved seats in state assemblies and local municipal councils where indigenous peoples are settled (art. 125, and Transitory Disposition 7). Unlike the Colombian reserved seats, which go to the two indigenous candidates winning the most votes in a nationwide indigenous district, in Venezuela the seats correspond to three circuits where the indigenous population is concentrated: a western region, encompassing Zulia, Merida, and Trujillo; a southern district, encompassing Amazonas and Apure; and an eastern district, encompassing Anzoátegui, Bolívar, Delta Amacuro, Monaga, and Sucre. This was the same system used to fill the reserved seats in the constituent assembly (interview, Luis Jesús Bello, May 23, 2000). In addition, in states with indigenous populations (those listed in the preceding text) one seat is reserved in the state legislative council, and each municipality with an indigenous population has one reserved municipal council seat. Transitory Disposition 7 allows indigenous peoples to create their own political party or to compete in reserved districts as a social movement organization (interviews, José Luis Gonzales, May 19, 2000; Guillermo Guevara, May 24, 2000).[7]

Compared to indigenous organizations in Colombia and Venezuela, Argentine indigenous organizations had far less impact on the 1994 constitutional reform, chiefly because they lacked representation within the congress that undertook the reform. Indigenous organizations, particularly the AIRA, lobbied vigorously for a strong indigenous rights regime, but they failed to expand the scope of indigenous rights beyond those already recognized in the 1985 indigenous law.[8] Although a great advance for Argentine Indians, the régime comes nowhere near the Colombian and Venezuelan constitutions, and includes no political rights, such as reserved seats. Moreover, few constitutional promises have been fulfilled, owing to bureaucratic resistance, as well as opposition from provincial elites (Ortega 1996b: 23). Having no direct representatives in the constitutional reform process Argentine Indians lacked the opportunity to forge ties with other popular movements and sympathetic elites or to experience the euphoria of successful, direct participation in formal politics.

---

[7] *Reglamento* 000302–119 of March 3, 2000, further regulates indigenous participation in elections: "All Indigenous Organizations and Communities may postulate candidates that are indigenous, provided only that they comply with requirements established in Transitory Disposition 7 of the Constitution of the Bolivarian Republic of Venezuela" (my translation).

[8] The Mapuche organization Coordinación de Organizaciones Mapuche did not participate because it questioned the legitimacy and rejected the domination of Argentine law (Briones 2000: 2).

UNDERSTANDING ETHNIC PARTY FORMATION

The main impetus for the formation of ethnic parties in the countries with small indigenous populations was institutional reform that instituted direct elections for local government. Indigenous organizations in all three countries struggled to compete for local offices as soon as they became available. In addition, the opportunity to participate in constitutional reforms was a particularly strong motivation for even weak indigenous organizations to take their chances in the electoral arena. Colombian indigenous organizations, not expecting to win office but hoping to put their demands on the agenda, did surprisingly well in constituent assembly elections in 1990. Similarly, in Venezuela, indigenous organizations formed electoral vehicles to enable them to influence constitutional reforms in the newly created state of Amazonas in 1997 and in the national constituent assembly in 1999. In both Colombia and Venezuela, their unexpected success in these initial elections as independent vehicles convinced indigenous organization leaders that a more durable electoral project would be viable, while reserved seats guaranteed a foothold in formal politics. In Argentina, in contrast, the dominance of the major parties precluded indigenous organizations' participation in national politics during the 1994 constitutional reform conjuncture. Indigenous organizations were too weak and fragmented to counter the hegemony of the larger national and provincial parties, and lacked reserved seats to guarantee national representation and the resources accruing to officeholders.

Colombia

Indigenous peoples' organizations participated in elections for the 1990 national constituent assembly after their demand for reserved seats was denied. It was not necessary to create a separate party vehicle because social movements were allowed to compete in the constituent assembly elections. Both organizations that had won seats in the constituent assembly decided to continue as electoral vehicles. Thus, the decision to participate in elections occurred after both organizations already had proved their ability to win, despite the small size of the indigenous population and its low level of registration. They had two strong incentives for doing so. First, they sought to ensure that the next congress would implement faithfully constitutional rights won in the assembly. Many of the rights won, particularly territorial rights, required implementing legislation. Second, indigenous organizations sought to gain access to *mestizo*-dominated local and regional governments in areas where Indians were numerous in order to steer public policy toward fulfilling material goals and to construct more culturally sensitive and responsive local governments.

The 1991 Colombian constitution dramatically opened the institutional environment for new parties. First, a single district for the National Senate was created in order to improve the representation of dispersed minorities of all kinds, since larger district magnitudes tend to provide more proportional representation. While DM declined in the lower chamber to an average of five seats, ethnic parties still have a fair chance of winning seats in a two-party-dominant system, and a law establishing up to five additional seats for ethnic and political minorities and Colombians living abroad offset the negative impact on small parties (Dugas 2001: 16). Second, the setting aside of two seats for indigenous peoples in the senate provided a base from which ethnic parties could build a movement outside the guaranteed indigenous district by marshaling resources accruing to incumbents. The 1991 Constitution and implementing legislation[9] provided financial support and free access to state-run media to legally recognized political parties and movements. Even though most of the funds go to the larger parties based on seats won, modest financial subsidies to parties with representation in congress and departmental assemblies have enabled new ethnic parties to construct party organizations. Third, official ballots are now supplied by the state, removing the logistical and financial burden of parties having to print and distribute their own ballots. Fourth, the constitution eliminated the requirement, in effect since the 1957 National Front pact, that an "adequate and equitable" proportion of administrative posts be given to the second largest party, a mandate that perpetuated the two-party system and limited the prospects for third parties (Dugas 2001: 16).

A final important institutional change was instituted prior to the constitutional reform in 1988: municipal decentralization with direct election of mayors. Direct election of departmental governors and assemblies followed three years later. Decentralization has enabled ethnic parties to compete in municipal and departmental races where indigenous peoples are concentrated and well-organized. The timing of departmental

---

[9] Law 134 of 1994 provides for legal parties to share a pool of state money based on their status as legally registered parties as well as on their voting strength in the previous elections. ASI has received a small amount of money from international NGOs for training and education programs, but is dependent upon the state for most of its funding, because members do not pay dues. Political parties also receive two minutes of radio and television time every forty-five days. Interview, Luis Carlos Osorio, February 26, 1997.

decentralization, which coincided with the creation of special reserved seats for Indians and the availability of party subventions, enabled ethnic parties to contest these newly created political spaces. Although a few indigenous candidates ran in the 1988 municipal elections, they ran as independents or as members of nonindigenous parties (Laurent 1997: 63). Only after 1991 did they run with ethnic parties.

Strategic Decision-Making Scenario I

In June 1991, as the constituent assembly was coming to a close in Bogotá, at an assembly in the department of Tolima, the demobilized Quintín Lame guerrillas and the CRIC, one of Colombia's strongest and most institutionalized departmental-level indigenous organizations, formed the ASI. The purpose, according to one of the organization's leaders, was to build on the achievements of the indigenous constituent assembly representatives and to gain a permanent political presence for the indigenous movement. They also sought to build on alliances with nonindigenous groups that were made prior to and during the constituent assembly (Peñaranda 1999).

The Quintín Lame was not an ordinary guerrilla movement. Cauca Indians formed the self-defense force in the early 1980s as attacks on indigenous communities from guerrilla organizations, paramilitaries, and drug traffickers increased in southwestern Colombia. During the 1980s, many indigenous communities were engaged in violent struggles with landowners to recuperate their traditional lands. Quintín Lame defended the communities from retaliation, helping them to recuperate more than 43,000 hectares. By 1987, the goal of land recuperation was largely fulfilled and the organization was financially exhausted. Its less than 200 members were unable to quell the onslaught of violence and were being assassinated at a high rate. Indigenous organizations and communities were demanding the demobilization of all guerrilla organizations and trying to forge more cooperative relations with the state. After 1989, Quintín Lame reached out to nonindigenous peasant and urban popular organizations and attempted to expand its geographic reach. On May 27, 1991, the Quintíns signed a peace accord with the government in exchange for a nonvoting seat in the constituent assembly, as well as considerable financial benefits (Peñaranda 1999: 76–93).[10]

---

[10] The organization managed 12 million pesos/month for six months, plus a lump sum grant of 9.5 million pesos, and 2 million pesos for each ex-combatant (Peñaranda 1999: 110–11).

The Quintín Lame followed the example of two other Colombian guerrilla organizations that had converted to political parties: the Popular Liberation Army (EPL) and the Movimiento M-19, which formed Hope, Peace, and Liberty (EPL) and ADM-19, respectively. Rather than convert the Quintín Lame into a political party identified with its parent guerrilla organization, as the others had done, its leaders sought to create a larger popular movement. Although ex-guerrillas play a large role in the party's leadership, they have not been among the party's most prominent candidates, which have been indigenous and popular leaders. Moreover, in contrast with those failed ex-guerrilla–based parties, ASI consciously avoided a hierarchical, military structure and promoted a decentralized leadership and the construction of pluralist arenas for the selection of leaders and agendas, while prioritizing the activities and autonomy of social movements within the ASI coalition (Peñaranda 1999: 125–6). ASI candidates are chosen democratically in regional and national assemblies held every two years (interview, Luis Carlos Osorio, February 26, 1997). According to Peñaranda, this strategy explains why the Quintín Lame, despite its small size and military failure, achieved a successful political transformation while the M-19 and EPL failed (1999).

Strategic Decision-Making Scenario II

Electoral competition created so much turmoil within the indigenous movement that ONIC retired from elections in 1993 in order to heal these conflicts and to focus on its social movement role (Antonio Jacanamijoy, interviewed in Ramírez de Jara 1997). ONIC's 1991–4 senate representative, Gabriel Mujuy Jacanamejoy, founded a new party in 1994 to secure his reelection. Mujuy's Colombian Indigenous Movement (MIC) attempted to build alliances with nonindigenous campesinos and poor urban workers, but its strength came mainly from Indians in the western lowland departments. Lacking a firm organizational base after ONIC pulled out of electoral politics, the party had limited success and disappeared after suffering electoral losses in 1998.

Venezuela

In Venezuela, electoral law changes in the late 1980 reduced opportunities for new parties. In 1989, in response to popular pressure to increase the accountability of politicians, uni-nominal elections were adopted for half of the Chamber of Deputies. In 1993, a mixed-member proportional representation system was implemented with SMDs contributing approximately half of the chamber. Lists remained closed and controlled by central party leaders (Coppedge 1997: 164; Levine and Crisp 1999: 391). Average DM decreased in 2000 from eight to six when a single-chamber National Assembly replaced the two-chamber legislature. Together with other institutional changes, this resulted in a less proportional vote-to-seat ratio that helped the larger parties and reduced the effective number of parties in the legislature (Molina 2002). However, the retention of SMD for part of the Assembly was an advantage for concentrated ethnic minorities. In fact, an indigenous party won a nominal seat in Amazonas in 2000.

Decentralization has offset the restrictive impact of the electoral system. A 1988 electoral law provided for direct election of state governors and created the position of directly elected mayor. The first elections for both positions were held in 1989. Separation of local and regional from national elections in the late 1980s helped smaller parties at the expense of the two dominant parties (Levine and Crisp 1999: 386). The uncoupling of local and state from national elections explains the surge in the 1990s of new regionally based parties, such as LCR and MAS (Levine and Crisp 1999: 405). As noted in the preceding text, institutional changes specifically helping indigenous peoples were incorporated into the 1999 Constitution.

Strategic Decision-Making Scenario I

Indigenous organizations, led by university-educated Indians, began to form their own parties in the 1990s to take advantage of the 1989 decentralizing reforms. The PUAMA is the most successful of these indigenous organization–based parties. PUAMA formed in November 1997 during the battle over the territorial division of the new state of Amazonas. The CONIVE affiliate in Amazonas, ORPIA, particularly its affiliates in the municipality of Manapiare, created the party so that indigenous peoples could participate in elections while allowing ORPIA to maintain its role as a social movement organization (interview, Guillermo Guevara, May 24, 2000). Because most mayors and governors in Amazonas opposed indigenous demands for protection of their territories from colonists, extractive activities, and the construction of power lines, elections were viewed as a way to defend their territorial rights, at least in areas with a significant indigenous population (interview, Luis Gómez Calvano, May 15, 2000). One of the party's founders, Benjamin Pérez, explains this decision:

The motivation emerged from the necessity to present a political response to our struggles and to defend our participation rights within the democratic structures of our country. In addition, because we have 40 years experience voting and have served merely as a staircase for the traditional political parties. We met in families, communities, ethnic groups, and organizations, and then we organized a Multiethnic Assembly in November 1997, in the community of Marieta, where we decided to create our political movement with an indigenous ideology.

(my translation; Pérez 1999: 8)

In addition to a lack of economic resources, PUAMA surmounted numerous obstacles. Political parties and the state governor opposed the party's registration and delayed its publication in the state's *Gazeta Oficial*. Critics ridiculed the party, while traditional politicians called indigenous politicians "subversives and revolutionary guerrillas" that were being manipulated by the Catholic Church (Pérez 1999: 9).

Indigenous organizations that had not done so prior to the 1999 constituent assembly formed political parties for the 2000 nationwide elections in Amazonas, Bolívar, Delta Amacuro, and Zulia in order to compete for seats within and outside of reserved seats created by the constitutional reform. Some of these new parties – including all of the ones formed in Zulia – are affiliated with nonindigenous parties (interview, José Poyo, May 22, 2000). Because anyone can vote in the indigenous districts, parties can and do create their own indigenous vehicles, using candidates that are not affiliated with the independent indigenous organizations. This is a difficult challenge because the indigenous population is small in most of these districts and the candidates of independent indigenous organizations may be out-voted by a better-funded challenger sponsored by AD or COPEI. Indigenous organizations also tried to form alliances with existing parties. However, without financial resources or many votes to offer them, these alliances were not of great importance (interview, José Luis Gonzales, May 19, 2000).

Argentina

Argentina's political institutions exhibit two features that should encourage the formation of ethnic parties: a decentralized federal system and a long tradition of strong provincial parties. Argentine federalism was strengthened by the 1994 constitutional reform and Argentina is the most decentralized country in our sample. Whereas decentralization helps indigenous peoples in subnational districts where they constitute a majority or significant minority, where they lack the numbers to capture regional governments they are worse off because local and regional interests are more likely than the national government to oppose indigenous peoples' most pressing interests: access to territory and the use of natural resources (e-mail communication, Claudia Briones, June 13, 2003). Because indigenous voters do not comprise a significant portion of the population of any province, they are relatively less able to take advantage of decentralization.

Argentine Indians' experience with parties reflects the lack of consensus within the indigenous movement – even within particular organizations, provinces, and ethnic groups – on an appropriate political strategy. Some groups, like the Coordinación de Organizaciones Mapuche, eschew party politics altogether, while others believe that participation in parties with access to power is the only way for indigenous representatives to gain a voice in policy decisions affecting their communities (Briones 2002: 105; Hirsch 2003: 96). Many indigenous voters fear that breaking from clientelist bonds will cost them access to state resources and vital social service programs (personal communication, Carlos Salamanca, June 14, 2003). As a result, local and language-group-level indigenous organizations often are permeated by political parties, which discourage independent electoral vehicles.

Despite these barriers, Argentine Indians have made some attempts to form their own local parties. According to anthropologist Silvia Hirsch, the Kollas in Jujuy and the Wichi are among those doing so (personal communication). In Formosa, the Toba living in a peri-urban neighborhood of the city of Nam-Qom have formed a party called *Fraternidad Popular*, which reaches out to nonindigenous popular organizations (personal e-mail communication, Carlos Salamanca, June 14, 2003).

UNDERSTANDING ETHNIC PARTY PERFORMANCE

Four conditions largely explain the superior electoral performance of ethnic parties in Colombia and Venezuela, compared to Argentina. First, indigenous organizations sponsoring ethnic parties need not extend throughout the national territory to achieve national representation if they have a strong base in a particular electoral district with a significant indigenous population. Fledgling ethnic parties in both countries used a strong organizational base in one or two departments to project themselves to the national level. Electoral laws overrepresenting sparsely populated Amazonian departments enabled ethnic parties to elect national representatives with very few votes. When these districts constituted brand new territorial entities, results were particularly good. In Colombia, for example, ethnic parties formed just prior to the creation of six new departments, three of which were majority indigenous (Guainía, Vaupés, and Vichada) and one of which had a significant indigenous minority (Amazonas). In Venezuela, Indians constituted almost half the population of the new state of Amazonas. Indigenous parties competing in these districts not only had a large natural constituency, they didn't have to compete against entrenched incumbent parties.

Second, a relatively united, organizationally mature indigenous social movement organization, with a dense network of affiliates in the area targeted for electoral competition, can compete against better-financed parties at the local and subnational levels. At this level, indigenous voters have strong ties to their own social movement organizations and these ties may be sufficient to attract votes away from traditional parties.

Third, a permissive institutional environment that reserves space for indigenous candidates in the formal political system is particularly helpful. Reserved seats – in the Colombian Senate, the Venezuelan National Assembly, and local and state governments in Venezuela where indigenous populations are present – energized indigenous voters and provided an institutional base from which indigenous organizations could build an electoral vehicle. Reserved seats provide a foothold in the political system as well as symbolic, institutional, and material resources for fledgling ethnic parties. In both cases, these reserved seats immediately inspired the creation of parties that ran outside of the reserved districts in order to maximize indigenous representation. Thus, ironically, having successfully argued that indigenous peoples would be unable to obtain equitable representation without reserved seats, indigenous organizations immediately proved themselves wrong.

Finally, a moderately open party system – where loyalty to existing parties is weak and fragmentation lowers the number of votes necessary to gain seats – enables new parties to obtain the access to influence and resources necessary to maintain registration and grow in strength. In contrast, ethnic parties could not take hold in Argentina's relatively closed system, where two or three parties have dominated since the return to democracy in 1983 (see Table 6.5). One of those parties, the Justicialist Party (PJ), has dominated posttransition politics through its deep roots in popular organizations. The considerable autonomy enjoyed by local *agrupaciones* allows for diverse forms of activism to thrive within the patronage networks of the PJ, reducing incentives for extra-PJ competition (Levitsky 2001: 29–30, 46). In fact, Argentine Indians have been most

TABLE 6.5. *Argentina: Vote share for dominant and leftist parties*

Election	PJ + UCR	Add FREPASO	Combined Votes Leftist Parties	ENPS
1983(P)	92.1%			
1983(L-D)	86%		1.87	2.94
1985(L-D)	77.5%		0.35	2.37
1987(L-D)	81%		3.14	2.58
1989(P)	79.7%			
1989(L-D)	76%		4.11	2.68
1993(L-D)	72.7%		2.4	2.82
1995(P)	66.9%	96.1%		
1997(L)	82%[a]			2.74
1999(P)	86.6%[a]			
2001(L-D)	60.5%[a]		9.5	2.84

Notes: Dominant parties are PJ, UCR, Front for a Country in Solidarity (FREPASO). (P) presidential; (L) legislature; (L-S) senate; (L-D) chamber of deputies.
[a] FREPASO in alliance with UCR.
Sources: Camara Nacional Electoral (www.pjn.gov.ar/cne); www.georgetown. edu/pdba, McGuire (1995: 200–48); Levitsky (2000: 56–69); figures for 1993 from Steven Levitsky, personal communication.

successful working within *agrupaciones* of the PJ. The traditional weakness of left-wing parties in Argentina, attributable to the dominance of the labor-movement-based PJ (Burgess and Levitsky 2001: 14), deprived the indigenous movement of potential allies.

These four conditions enabled indigenous organizations in Colombia and Venezuela to overcome significant obstacles, such as the lack of sufficient resources for traveling to remote rural areas to campaign, and difficulty registering indigenous voters (interview, Jesús Avirama, March 10, 1997; interview with Gabriel Muyuy Jacanamejoy, in Wirpsa, 1992: 50).

Colombia

The auspicious conditions enumerated in the preceding text were present in abundance in the 1990s in Colombia. During the previous decade, Colombia's Liberal and Conservative parties had shared more than 90 percent of the votes in every national election. After 1991, owing to the greater permissiveness of the institutional environment and a brief surge for leftist parties, the Liberal and Conservative parties shared between 70.2 and 76.2 percent of the vote in legislative elections. Thus, we see a

TABLE 6.6. *Colombia: Vote share for dominant and leftist parties*

Election	Combined Votes Dominant Parties	Combined Votes Leftist Parties	ENPS
1982(P)	98.4%		
1982(L-D)	96.6%		1.98
1986(P)	94.1%	4.5%	
1986(L-D)	91.4%	4.4%	2.45
1990(P)	83.7%	12.5%	
1990(L)	92.2%	[a]	2.18
1990(ANC)	62.4%	29.7%	4.40
1991(L-D)	76.2%	10%	2.98
1994(P-1)	89.8%	3.8%	
1994(L)	67.7%	3.2%	2.53
1998(P)	68.4%		
1998(L-D)	72.9%	[b]	2.74
2002(P)	31.7%		
2002(L)	40%	[b]	7.01

Notes: Dominant parties are: Partido Liberal (PL), Social Conservative Party (PSC), Movimiento de Salvación Nacional (MSN). Leftist parties are UP; ADM-19. (P) presidential; (P-1) first-round presidential; (L) legislature; (L-D) chamber of deputies; (ANC) National Constituent Assembly.
[a] No data available.
[b] No seats obtained.
Sources: Boudon (2000); Dugas (1993); García Sánchez (2001); Hartlyn and Dugas (1999); Pizarro Leongómez (1997); www.georgetown.edu/pdba and www.registraduria.gov.co.

moderate decline in the combined vote share of the dominant parties (see Table 6.6). Severe party-system fragmentation accompanied the dealignment, as hundreds of new vehicles formed. In 2002, forty-two parties gained seats in the Colombian Senate, thirty of which gained a single seat. ENPS increased significantly in 2002: in the Senate to 9.39, in the Chamber of Deputies to 7.01.

The opening on the left was especially important. Leftist parties gained significance following peace negotiations during the Betancur administration in 1984. UP, formed as an umbrella coalition for parties and movements on the left, first competed in 1986, when its presidential candidate won 4.5 percent of the vote, tripling the left's traditional vote share. In 1990, the M-19 formed the political party ADM-19. Its greatest triumph was the National Constituent Assembly election of 1990, when it captured 27 percent of the vote, second only to the Liberal Party. These two parties never matched the success of their initial outings and they had all but disappeared by the late 1990s.[11] Thus, leftist parties succeeded only briefly, between 1986–91, never to recover their former support in the wake of systematic antileft violence and the strategic mistakes of its leaders. Some leftist militants joined the ASI in the 1990s, particularly in southwestern Colombia, continuing a tradition of warm relations between the left and the indigenous movement in that part of the country. In fact, indigenous leader Jesús Piñacué ran as vice presidential candidate on the ADM-19 presidential ticket in 1994. Thus, ethnic parties expanded in the space created by a discouraged and demoralized left.

In 1991, both AICO and ONIC, the movements with elected representation in the Constituent Assembly, won a seat in the reserved indigenous senatorial district. In 1994, AICO again won a seat in the reserved senate district and elected one departmental deputy and six municipal councilors in Cauca. In 1997, it elected five mayors. In 1998, it won an indigenous senate seat. By 2000, AICO had expanded beyond its base in the Guambiano ethnic group and the southwestern departments of Cauca and Nariño. That year AICO won four mayors, distributed among the departments of Antioquia, Cauca, and Nariño; seventy-four municipal councilors in eleven departments (Caldas, Cauca, Córdoba, Huila, Nariño, Sucre, Guajira, Guainía, Meta, Putumayo, Vichada); and three deputies in departmental assemblies (Antioquia, Cauca, Vichada). In 2002, for the fourth consecutive time, AICO claimed one of the two reserved indigenous seats and also picked up one of the Chamber of Deputies seats reserved for Indians, Afro-Colombians, and Colombians living abroad (www.eltiempo.com, March 11, 2002) (see Table 6.7).

The MIC in 1994 re-elected Mujuy, ONIC's indigenous senator, and secured four departmental deputies and twenty-three municipal council seats, mainly in the lowland departments with proportionally large indigenous populations. In 1997, the party won one mayor. In 1998, the MIC failed to recapture a seat in the indigenous senatorial district; no results for this party could be found after that loss, which cost the party crucial funding and its legal registration.

ASI far outpaced its rivals. It won a "third" (that is, unreserved) senate seat in 1991, 1998, and 2002. In 1992, the party won representation in thirty-eight municipalities in ten departments, far beyond its base in Cauca. These victories included a seat on the Bogotá city council

---

[11] The UP failed to earn more than 2 percent of the votes in national elections after 1991 and its lingering presence in some municipalities has declined since 1994 (García Sánchez 2001: 9–10). After 1994, ADM-19 fails to appear in electoral statistics.

TABLE 6.7. *Electoral Results for AICO and ASI*

Election	AICO	ASI
1990 Constituent Assembly	1 delegate	–
1991 National	1 indigenous senator	1 senator
1992 Regional and Local		1 legislative assembly seat 38 municipal councilors
1994 National	1 indigenous senator	1 national deputy
1994 Regional	1 legislative assembly seat 6 municipal councilors	6 legislative assembly seats 8 mayors 127 municipal councilors
1997 Regional and Local	5 mayors	1 governor 6 legislative assembly seats 6 mayors 200 municipal councilors (approx.)
1998 National	1 indigenous senator	1 senator 1 indigenous senator 2 national deputies
2000 Regional and Local	1 governor (with ASI) 3 legislative assembly seats 4 mayors 74 municipal councilors	1 governor (with AICO) 8 legislative assembly seats 11 mayors 146 municipal councilors
2002 National	1 indigenous senator 1 national deputy	1 senator
2003 Regional and Local	1 governor 3 mayors 2 legislative assembly seats 69 municipal councilors	1 legislative assembly seat 6 mayors 146 municipal councilors

Source: www.registraduria.gov.co.

and a seat in Antioquia's departmental Legislative Assembly, despite the small indigenous population in both districts (interview, Luis Carlos Osorio, February 26, 1997). The negative impact of electoral success was increased division within the organization generated by competition for candidacies. As ASI leader Luis Carlos Osorio, explains, ASI developed the same personalist rivalries that plague the traditional parties. For example, in 1994 two prominent leaders, ANC delegate Francisco Rojas Birry and CRIC leader Jesús Piñacué, insisted on heading their own lists for the Senate. Splitting the vote, they both lost (interview, Luis Carlos Osorio,

February 26, 1997). Competition for candidacies for the 1994 national elections generated eight distinct party lists: three registered for the special indigenous district and five registered to compete in the national electoral district. This dispersed the indigenous vote and also caused serious conflicts within indigenous organizations. In 1994's local and regional elections the party elected eight mayors (seven in Cauca), 127 municipal councilors (eighty-two in Cauca), and six departmental assembly deputies (two in Cauca) (Laurent 1997: 74; Peñaranda 1999: 128). In coalition with another party, ASI elected Afro-Colombian leader Zulia Mena to the lower chamber of Congress in the reserved Afro-Colombian district. Mena's presence in the House of Deputies enabled ASI to maintain its registration as a political movement and, thus, access to state media and financial resources (interview, Luis Carlos Osorio, February 26, 1997).

In 1997, ASI won the first governorship for an ethnic party (Vichada)[12] and finished second in gubernatorial contests in Cauca and Vaupés. That year the ASI assembly deputy in the department of Antioquia, Eulalia Yagary, earned re-election with more votes than any other candidate and twice as many as her closest competitor. ASI also elected six mayors, six departmental assembly deputies, and close to 200 municipal councilors (Peñaranda 1999: 128). In 1998, former CRIC president Jesús Piñacué, representing the ASI in alliance with a progressive opposition coalition, finished fifteenth in a field of more than 300 national senatorial candidates. In addition, ASI won a senate seat in the indigenous district and two national deputy seats in two majority-indigenous, sparsely populated Amazonian departments (Guainía and Vaupés).

In 2000, ASI joined with AICO to elect the first indigenous governor of Cauca, ex-indigenous senator Floro Tunubulá. That year ASI elected eleven mayors in four departments (Cauca, Cundinamarca, Chocó, Risaralda); 146 municipal councilors in twenty departments (Antioquia, Caldas, Cauca, Córdoba, Cundinamarca, Chocó, Huila, Nariño, Risaralda, Norte de Santander, Santander, Sucre, Tolima, Valle de Cauca, La Guajira, Guainía, Amazonas, Putumayo, Vaupés, Vichada); and eight departmental deputies in five departments (Antioquia, Cauca, Guainía, Vaupés, Vichada). In 2002, Senator Piñacué won re-election in the non-indigenous national district, this time finishing twelfth in the nationwide district. Senator Rojas Birry, who had won election in the indigenous district in 1998 as an ASI candidate, broke with ASI prior to the elections; he was re-elected to his seat representing the Valle del Cauca-based

[12] According to Peñaranda. Other sources say the first governorship was in Guainía.

regional party Movimiento Huella Ciudadana (www.eltiempo.com, March 11, 2002).

Given the small size of the indigenous population, the performance of ASI and AICO is truly astounding. In a study of the performance of nontraditional parties following the 1991 constitutional reform, García Sánchez found that only five of forty-eight such parties had gained power in more than 2 percent of the country's 1,100 municipalities between 1988 and 2000. ASI was among this elite group. AICO was among the twelve that had won more than 1 percent. ASI and AICO were among only eight parties that had been re-elected (2001: 7). ASI also is among the most enduring nontraditional parties: of the five parties that won in more than 2 percent of the country's municipalities, only ASI and the Movimiento Cívico Independiente (MCI) were formed prior to 1997 (García Sánchez 2001: 13).

Like Ecuador's Pachakutik and Bolivia's MAS, ASI incorporates non-indigenous popular organizations and their leaders. As a result, the party experiences the same internal tension between those who think the party should emphasize its indigenous identity and agenda, and those who prefer to emphasize its status as a multiethnic alliance of popular organizations. Although most of its candidates are indigenous – particularly for the most visible offices – some are not, and there have been problems with sectors of the Cauca ASI organization not wishing to support *mestizo* candidates. Another tension concerns the relationship between indigenous social movement organizations and the party. In Antioquia, there is no problem – ASI and the Organización Indígena de Antioquia are essentially the same organization there. In the party's home state of Cauca, things are more complicated. Although CRIC formally takes the position that it is not involved in elections, many ASI candidates come from the ranks of CRIC's leadership (interview, Claudia Piñeros, March 9, 1997). The CRIC executive committee includes a delegate from ASI, and they tend to work together on political mobilizations in the department. For example, ASI deputies, councilors, and mayors participated in a 1996 demonstration in which CRIC blocked the Panamerican Highway. Some ASI militants, however, saw this as a problem that may distance the party from nonindigenous sectors whose support they would like to attract. During Floro Tunubulá's term as governor of Cauca, indigenous activists were perturbed when the governor refused to remove a *mestizo* mayor from office. Tunubulá countered that this was not legally within his power and that as governor he also represented the *mestizo* citizens of the town, most of whom supported the mayor (Rappaport, n.d.: 360).

The principal obstacle to the advancement of ethnic political parties in Colombia is violence against indigenous movement leaders, party militants, and public officials. Virtually all Latin American indigenous movements experience some type of violence, usually on the part of rural elites, often with the passive approval of local officials. The situation in Colombia is far more complicated and serious. Colombian Indians must battle guerrillas and paramilitaries, both of which are present in the majority of the municipalities governed by ASI and AICO, as well as drug traffickers and the state (García Sánchez 2001: 2, 14). Hundreds of indigenous leaders were murdered with impunity in the 1990s, including the president of the CRIC and several indigenous mayors. Others have been intimidated and have left politics or moved to other countries to escape death threats, including an ASI leader interviewed for this book.[13] Assassinations and threats against local elected officials have become commonplace. Entire indigenous communities have had to relocate to escape the violence (CNN 2003c; www.etniasdecolombia.org; García Sánchez 2001: 2).

Venezuela

Although Venezuela shares some auspicious conditions with Colombia, its indigenous movement is younger and less experienced and there is only one state (Amazonas) in which demographic conditions give an ethnic party an edge. In contrast to Colombia, where indigenous parties often receive more votes from non-Indians than Indians, in Venezuela indigenous parties mainly attract indigenous voters, partly because they make no attempt to attract non-Indians, partly because at the local and state levels non-Indians mostly oppose their interests (interview, Dieter Heinen, May 17, 2000). Thus, it is unlikely that ethnic parties would have been able to expand outside of reserved indigenous districts had it not been for the collapse of the political party system and the resurgence of a left whose leaders were disposed toward allying with tiny ethnic parties.

Venezuela is the only case in our sample in which leftist parties increased in strength after the fall of the Berlin Wall in 1989, even prior to the additional surge from the Chávez movement. Beginning in 1998, leftist

---

[13] Indigenous mayors are not the only ones targeted. Between 1995 and 1997, 22 of the country's 1,062 mayors were assassinated; three resigned after receiving death threats. In 1996 alone, sixty-seven were attacked or kidnapped by guerrillas or paramilitaries. In the 1997 municipal elections, 800 candidates withdrew following threats. Van Cott (2000b: 253–4).

TABLE 6.8. *Venezuela: Vote share for dominant and leftist parties*

Election	Combined Votes Dominant Parties AD + COPEI	+ LCR + MAS	Combined Votes Leftist Parties	ENPS
1983(P)	91.5%		3.5%	
1983(L)	78.5%		5.8%	2.42
1988(P)	92.9%		2.7%	
1988(L)	78.4%		10.2%	2.83
1993(P)	46.2%	68.2%	21.9%	
1993(L)	46.7%	67.8%	31.9%	4.50
1998(P)	11%	40.1%[a]	56.3%	
1998(L-S)	36.3%	48.1%	35.1%	
1998(L-D)	36.8%	48.9%	35.1%	6.31
2000(P)	0%	27.65[b]	79.3%	
2000(L)	21.2%	30.73[b]	56.1%	3.77

Notes: Dominant parties are AD, COPEI, LCR, MAS. Leftist parties are MAS, LCR, MVR, Polo Patriótico, PPT. (P) presidential; (L) unicameral legislature; (L-S) senate; (L-D) chamber of deputies.

[a] MAS ran in coalition with MVR.

[b] In 2000, LCR ran in a coalition that backed Arias and gained 37.5 percent of the vote. MAS ran in the coalition that backed President Chávez and won 59.8 percent. LCRs share of the former was 18.95 percent; MAS's share of latter was 8.70 percent.

Sources: Crisp and Levine (1998); Dietz and Myers (2001); Kornblith and Levine (1995); Molina V. (2002); Penfold Becerra (2000); www.georgetown.edu/pdba, www.cne.gov.ve.

parties most often ran in coalition with Chávez's electoral coalition, Polo Patriótico, which includes the party he founded to compete in the 1998 elections, Fifth Republic Movement (MVR), as well as smaller center-left and left parties such as the Communist Party (personal communication, David Myers, February 13, 2002). Polo Patriótico has dominated elections since 1998, far outdistancing more established parties of the left and center. The combined vote share of Chávez's party plus the three other leftist parties averaged 52.9 percent. Both main presidential candidates in 2000 positioned themselves on the left (Molina V. 2002: 17) (see Table 6.8).

Rather than growing in the space vacated by a declining left, as occurred in Bolivia, Colombia, and Ecuador, the ethnic party PUAMA grew as part of an alliance with a leftist party within the national context of a dominant left. PUAMA and the national indigenous organization CONIVE enjoy close relations with President Chávez and PUAMA ran in alliance with the leftist Patria Para Todos in some state-level contests in 2000. PUAMA offered to PPT an organization in rural areas that it lacked in Amazonas. Despite the obstacles faced to its registration, PUAMA won a seat in the Amazonas Legislative Council in the November 1998 regional elections and, in alliance with the PPT, became the third-largest party in the state (Pérez 1999: 9). In the 1999 constituent assembly elections, the party gained a seat for Liborio Guarulla, PUAMA's Legislative Council representative and a former state organizer for the leftist LCR.

In January 2000, following approval of new political rights for Indians, the human rights office of the Amazonas Catholic Church, working mainly with ORPIA and PUAMA, organized four municipal workshops on political participation in order to educate Indians about their new political rights and to enable them to formulate strategies and discuss alliances for the upcoming elections. More than 1,000 Indians participated in these assemblies, which culminated in the First State Assembly of Indigenous Political Participation. The nineteen peoples represented agreed to unite around PUAMA for the 2000 elections (*Sendas* 2000: 6–7). In those contests, again in alliance with the PPT, PUAMA retained its status as the third-strongest party in the state and the strongest party in the municipality of Manapiare (Pérez 1999: 8–9). The PUAMA-PPT alliance won the governorship for Liborio Guarulla in a close election that required a manual recount and revoting in several districts. PUAMA won a seat for indigenous leader Guillermo Guevara in the National Assembly by winning 11.65 percent of the vote in Amazonas' nominal district (0.04% of national vote).[14] PUAMA-PPT elected an indigenous representative to the Amazonas legislative council (there are six total seats on the council, including one indigenous reserved seat). ORPIA won the indigenous seat. The PUAMA-PPT alliance also elected mayors in three of the state's seven municipalities: Autana, Manapiare, and Rio Negro (www.cne.cantv.net).

Elsewhere, indigenous parties performed poorly. In Bolívar state, the FIB created a new party – MOPEINDIGENA – to compete in the 2000 elections. According to results obtained from the National Electoral Court, none of their candidates won. In Anzoátegui, indigenous organizations competed for a National Assembly seat through an alliance between the national organization CONIVE and the leftist MAS. Other indigenous activists ran as candidates for the National Assembly on the AD and MVR lists; a third represented the Unión de Técnicos Medios Agropecuarios Indígenas. The same parties also ran indigenous candidates

---

[14] José E. Molina V. calculated this based on official data. PUAMA won a nominal seat in the second circumscription with 1,837 of 15,765; 41.5 percent of the votes in Amazonas were invalidated. There were very few voters in that district. Personal communication, September 20, 2002.

for state and municipal office (*Observador Indígena* 2000: 8). None were successful.

On July 30, 2000, thirty-four indigenous candidates competed for three reserved indigenous National Assembly seats, all of which CONIVE's constituent assembly delegates easily won. CONIVE and its affiliates sponsored 130 candidates for reserved indigenous seats throughout the country. Apart from the three national offices, this consisted of eight representatives in state Legislative Councils and forty-five indigenous municipal councilors (CONIVE 2000). Mostly leaders of local and regional indigenous organizations, the candidates had been chosen through a customary process of consensus-building in local and regional assemblies, similar to the process leading up to the constituent assembly (interview, Dieter Heinen, May 17, 2000; CONIVE 2000). In 2000, CONIVE was considering the idea of forming a national party (interview, José Poyo, May 22, 2000).

CONCLUSION

Indigenous movements in Colombia and Venezuela, although weaker than movements in the central Andean countries with larger indigenous populations, enjoyed a high level of unity and autonomy. They took advantage of a more permissive institutional environment and the extraordinary opportunity presented by constitutional reform to mobilize dense networks of affiliates behind new political projects. Although decentralization was a great boon in Colombia and Venezuela, the case of Argentina demonstrates that in countries with small indigenous populations the degree of decentralization – in terms of the relative powers of the national and regional governments – is crucial to the ability of indigenous peoples to form cohesive, geographically extensive social movement organizations. Whereas Colombian and Venezuelan indigenous movements enlisted the aid of national elites in securing a progressive regime of indigenous constitutional rights, in Argentina provincial elites used their relatively greater autonomy to resist interference by the national government on indigenous rights issues (personal e-mail communication, Claudia Briones, June 13, 2003). Many of the barriers that Argentine Indians face in constructing modern social movement organizations – geographic dispersion, proportionally small size within the national population, distance from the capital city, lack of financial resources, internal diversity – are not appreciably greater than those faced by Colombian or Venezuelan Indians. But variations in the distribution of power within the political system led Argentine indigenous organizations to focus on local and provincial politics, while Colombian and Venezuelan Indians in the 1980s chose to project their activities to the national level. Ethnic parties' success at the national level – through participation in constitutional reforms and national elections – enabled them to take over local and regional governments. Thus, they demonstrate an internal "boomerang effect" (Keck and Sikkink 1998). By successfully pressuring the national political community, indigenous organizations and their parties achieve greater autonomy at the subnational level.

A final important distinction is that both Colombia and Venezuela had nominally democratic governments in the 1960s and 1970s. Argentina, in contrast, was under military rule for much of the 1970s that did not end until 1983. While indigenous movements in Colombia and Venezuela were forming dynamic organizations, in Argentina the Dirty War silenced opposition political activity. This comparison resonates with that made between Bolivia and Ecuador, on one hand, and Peru on the other. While indigenous movements were consolidating themselves in the first two countries, Peruvian indigenous communities were struggling to survive against the dual onslaught of Sendero Luminoso and the Peruvian military. Clearly, a democratic political system provides more fertile terrain for the construction of successful social movements and challenger political parties.

7

Conclusions and Implications

Ethnic parties formed and became viable or successful in South America under diverse circumstances. After reviewing the case studies presented in Chapters 3 through 6, some clear patterns emerge. These patterns are illuminated in the following text. This chapter concludes with a discussion of the implications of the emergence of viable ethnic parties for democracy in Latin America and for the political future of indigenous peoples in the region.

EXPLAINING ETHNIC PARTY FORMATION

In every country studied at least one indigenous peoples' organization tried to launch an ethnic party. They did so even when their organizations were relatively weak and there were significant institutional obstacles or an unfavorable configuration of power in the party system. The reason that came up consistently across the case studies was that nonindigenous parties repeatedly had manipulated, betrayed, and exploited indigenous peoples. When indigenous peoples' organizations formed alliances with leftist parties, their class allies, they lacked decision-making power and were unable to place indigenous militants in a satisfactory number of candidate positions high enough on the list to gain office. The parties abandoned indigenous issues following elections and required that indigenous elected officials maintain their primary loyalty to the party rather than to indigenous organizations.

Thus, if indigenous leaders believe that they have no other avenue to winning elected office, and access to elected office is considered vital to achieving collective goals, indigenous organizations may decide to form parties even under adverse conditions. And it is important to emphasize that achieving those goals is the paramount motivation for most of the ethnic parties studied here, rather than access to avenues for professional advancement. Indigenous politicians who became involved in corruption or who appeared to be seeking personal advancement above movement goals were quickly disowned by the party and the movement.[1] In no case were ethnic parties perceived as an *alternative* to indigenous social movements and extra–systemic mobilizations. Rather, they are repeatedly referred to as an additional tool or a new arena for the pursuit of movement goals, and are consistently given a lower priority than social movement cohesion and effective action. In fact, in Colombia an indigenous organization that had competed successfully in elections decided to deregister as a political party in order to salvage the organization and its social movement role, after competition had caused deep personal and factional rifts and a diffusion of movement energy and resources. Preserving the movement *qua* movement is more important to indigenous movements than launching a successful party. Preserving the movement is vital to maintaining and strengthening indigenous cultures, collective identity, and group cohesion, the most valuable political resources indigenous peoples possess.

Indigenous Social Movements: Resources, Opportunities, and Organization

The decision to form an ethnic party and the ability to obtain sufficient resources to register it depends upon several factors related to the strength of and resources available to indigenous social movements. First, indigenous organizations were more likely to launch electoral vehicles in districts where they constitute a significant proportion of the population and where organizations have strong ties of loyalty throughout the district's indigenous population. A large number of affiliated voters improves the chances that a sufficient number of signatures can be collected for registration. Second, indigenous organizations were more likely to extend their activities into the electoral arena after they had secured significant substantive policy achievements as social movements. The confidence and encouragement generated by such achievements inspires indigenous leaders to

---

[1] See, e.g., the fate of Ecuadorian indigenous leaders Rafael Pandam and several Pachakutik Amazonian congressional deputies, described in Chapter 4, and the drop in support for the lowland organization CIDOB when its leaders took jobs in the Bolivian government, described in Chapter 3.

seek challenges in different terrain. Indigenous movements that failed to secure such policy achievements found themselves too dependent upon the state, political parties, and other external actors (e.g., NGOs, international donors) to risk electoral independence.

One type of policy success particularly likely to lead quickly to the formation of an ethnic party was successful participation in a constitutional reform that resulted in the codification of new ethnic rights. Effective participation in constitutional reform processes through direct, successful engagement with the state and political elite enabled indigenous organizations to gauge the level of their political strength and public support. This impact was most powerful in Colombia, Ecuador, and Venezuela, where indigenous movement representatives were elected to constituent assemblies. In those assemblies, indigenous representatives forged alliances with a broad spectrum of sympathetic allies while the intense and disproportionate media attention they received made them national figures (Van Cott 2000b, 2002, 2003a). In Bolivia, indigenous organizations had direct contact with the team of government officials writing the constitutional reform and had just elected an Aymara vice president. In addition, they participated in a massive mobilization concerning the issue of greatest interest to them – the 1996 agrarian reform law. Sustained pressure from lowland and highland groups resulted in a substantially altered law, although it was less than highland groups had hoped for. In all four cases, indigenous movements formed ethnic parties immediately following constitutional reforms. Successful participation in these processes – especially where indigenous representatives had won election to constituent assemblies – and the higher public esteem this engendered, combined with more favorable institutional environments resulting directly from the reforms, convinced movement leaders that their electoral chances were reasonably good and that launching an electoral project was worth the trouble. Moreover, indigenous leaders saw congressional representation as necessary to ensure the implementation of their new constitutional rights, most of which required implementing legislation to be written by the next congress.

Permissiveness of the Institutional Environment

The most important institutional variables affecting ethnic party formation are improved ballot access, decentralization, and the reservation of seats for indigenous representatives. Where high signature requirements or financial penalties for poor electoral performance exist, new, small parties are less likely to achieve registration. In three of the four cases where ethnic parties formed (Colombia, Ecuador, Venezuela), ballot access improved immediately prior to the formation of ethnic parties. Improved ballot access enabled social movements not willing to or able to construct formal political party organizations to compete in elections. This was crucial to the decision-making process of indigenous organizations in Ecuador, Colombia, and Venezuela that wished to preserve an "antisystemic" stance, that lacked the resources to form separate party structures, or that wished to protect their status as social movements. In the only positive case where ballot access did not improve, Bolivia, indigenous organizations repeatedly saw the National Electoral Court reject their registration or revoke it when their electoral vehicles could not attract enough votes. The ASP had to borrow the registration of three different nearly defunct leftist parties in order to secure registration; the registration of Bolivia's second-most successful party, the MIP, probably would have been rejected if not for pressure from traditional party leaders on the Court to accept its questionable registration materials in order to split the indigenous vote.

Decentralization encouraged indigenous peoples to form political parties to compete in elections because it improved the chance that such vehicles could win by creating districts where indigenous peoples are a majority or significant minority, and where the cost of competition is low, compared to national contests. Provided that a sufficient number of Indians are registered to vote, there is organizational unity within the district (that is, no rival indigenous organizations to split the indigenous vote), and elections are relatively free of fraud, local elections appear to be a "sure thing." Where indigenous populations were present but not a majority, reserved seats made elections another type of "sure thing" for prospective ethnic parties. The reservation of seats for Indians provided a foothold in the formal political system that aspiring parties could use to pursue electoral politics outside of the reserved seat district. In both cases where these were instituted (Colombia, Venezuela), indigenous parties immediately formed to maximize indigenous representation by contesting elections outside the indigenous district.

Openness of the Party System

The most important party system variable with respect to ethnic party formation is the political strength of the left relative to indigenous movements. In Bolivia, Ecuador, Colombia, and Peru, the electoral left experienced a marked decline in the 1990s. Class cleavages had begun eroding in the 1970s and the organizations that channeled them – unions and peasant organizations – were on the decline by the end of the 1980s, following years of structural transformation and economic austerity, and the defection of most indigenous communities toward ethnic rather than class-based associations (Roberts 2002: 4). In a context of weak leftist parties and lower-class organizations, it was indigenous movements that most effectively raised the banner of anti-neoliberalism. The decline of leftist parties opened space on the left of the political spectrum at a time when indigenous organizations had achieved a high level of organizational maturity, as well as real substantive and symbolic results, and were seeking to expand their terrain of action. The availability of a pool of politically experienced leftist party professionals and intellectuals seeking to join a dynamic political project, who provided resources, candidates, and expertise for some of the fledgling ethnic parties, offset the indigenous organizations' own lack of formal political experience. This leftist flotsam also helped indigenous leaders to develop "master frames" that combine particularistic cultural demands and autonomy claims with an anti-neoliberal discourse appealing to a broad sector of lower-class voters and to unattached voters disaffected with corrupt and unresponsive traditional parties.[2]

Relatively strong indigenous movements forged alliances with relatively weak and fragmented electoral lefts in Bolivia, Colombia, and Ecuador. In Bolivia, the ASP, and its splinter IPSP, would not have been able to compete in any election if not for the willingness of leaders of a succession of nearly defunct but legally registered leftist parties to loan it their registration. In Ecuador, alliances with leftist parties enabled the indigenous movement–based party Pachakutik to compete in cities and coastal districts where it lacked a base of support. The Venezuelan case demonstrates that the left need not be weak for ethnic parties to form, provided that electoral alliances are allowed by law, and the left is willing to make alliances that respect the autonomy and authority of indigenous movements. In Venezuela, where the left surged rather than declined after 1990, the leftist party PPT saw an advantage in an alliance with the ethnic party PUAMA because the urban-centered PPT lacked a base in the predominantly indigenous and rural state of Amazonas.[3] In fact, the left was

---

[2] On social movements and framing processes, see McAdam, McCarthy, and Zald (1996b: 5–7). On "master frames" see Snow and Benford (1992).

[3] In November 2003, the Mexican indigenous organization Movimiento Unificador de Lucha Triqui (Unifying Movement of the Triqui Struggle), which represents the Triqui Indians, joined with the Nueva Izquierda de Oaxaca (New Left of Oaxaca) to form a new party, Unidad Popular, to compete in elections in the indigenous-majority state of Oaxaca.

TABLE 7.1. *Ethnic party performance*

Low Viability

Movimiento Indio Tupaj Katari (MITKA) and its offspring (Bolivia)
Movimiento Indígena de la Amazonía Peruana (MIAP) (Peru)
Movimiento Revolucionario Tupaj Katari (MRTK), MRTKL and its offspring
  (Bolivia)
Eje Pachakuti (Bolivia)
Movimiento Indígena Amauta Jatari (Ecuador)

Moderate Viability

Movimiento Indígena Pachakuti (MIP) (Bolivia)
Autoridades Indígenas de Colombia (AICO) (Colombia)
Partido Unido Multiétnico de Amazonas (PUAMA) (Venezuela)

Success

Movimiento Unido Plurinacional Pachakutik (MUPP) (Ecuador)
Asamblea de la Soberanía de los Pueblos/Izquierda Unida (ASP/IU) (Bolivia)
Instrumento Político de la Soberanía de los Pueblos/Movimiento al Socialismo
  (IPSP/MAS) (Bolivia)
Alianza Social Indígena (ASI) (Colombia)

so weak that a prominent indigenous leader had been state coordinator for the leftist party LCR before he helped to create a new regional ethnic party, PUAMA. Both the left and the indigenous movement had much to gain from an alliance.

UNDERSTANDING ETHNIC PARTY PERFORMANCE

Table 7.1 lists all ethnic parties that won at least one election. Parties that only participated in one or a few elections and won only a handful of seats, had trouble expanding beyond a small base, and/or had difficulty maintaining legal registration, are classified as having "low viability." Those that have participated in numerous elections and consistently have won seats at the local or regional level exhibit "moderate viability." Also in this category are relatively new parties that, although they have only participated in the most recent national elections, performed so successfully that they are likely to do well in subsequent elections. Finally, "successful parties" are those that contest power at the national level or

The UP represents the Triqui and fifteen other indigenous groups in the state, as well as *mestizo* communities, and claims to be the first "Indigenous Party" in the country (*Latin American Weekly Report* 2003c: 11).

that have a broad geographical coverage of much of the national territory and representation at the national level. These categories and cutoffs are somewhat arbitrary, but they enable us to sort and rank the ethnic parties studied in terms of their performance.

Indigenous Social Movements: Resources and Opportunities

Social movement organizations that formed viable ethnic parties had an average of fourteen years of political experience and a prior history of successful political mobilization. Individuals or small groups of elites who formed parties without the backing of an established indigenous organization were unlikely to win sufficient votes to maintain registration and win elections. Viable parties also were affiliated with dense networks of indigenous organizations that extended throughout the target geographic area. Successful candidates could depend on the free labor and loyalty of members of these affiliated organizations to serve as a counterweight to their competitors' greater access to financial resources for campaigning, advertising, and patronage.

The sponsoring indigenous organizations of the most viable and successful parties enjoyed relatively high organizational unity. This was particularly true in Colombia, Ecuador, and Venezuela, where a single indigenous confederation unites the majority of the indigenous population. In Bolivia, although the indigenous movement lacks an overarching national confederation that unites lowland and highland organizations, and within both regions dominance is contested by several organizations, the group that launched the most successful party – the coca growers of Cochabamba – was united behind the leadership of Evo Morales and the goal of stopping the eradication of coca leaf. The coca growers are part of the national peasant organization CSUTCB which, while weaker in the lowlands, does have a presence in all nine departments. Organizational unity enables the indigenous movement to survive the inevitable fractionalization and personal rifts that occur when militants compete against each other for candidate slots. It also reduces the likelihood that ethnic parties will proliferate and divide the indigenous vote as each organization seeks representation. Although all of the indigenous organizations that sponsored political parties experienced considerable internal disunity, those that were successful managed to contain disputes within a single organizational structure.

Ethnic parties were more successful in countries where there were relatively more subnational electoral districts that had indigenous majorities or significant minorities (more than 25 percent indigenous). With respect to the three cases with large indigenous populations, ethnic parties became viable in Bolivia and Ecuador, where 78.7 and 42.9 percent of subnational districts, respectively, are at least 25 percent indigenous, whereas in Peru, where only 28 percent of subnational districts were at least 25 percent indigenous, ethnic parties performed poorly. Although the size of Peru's indigenous population is roughly comparable to Ecuador's, it is concentrated in five of twenty-five departments, whereas in Ecuador, it is more evenly distributed, so as to comprise a majority in three, and a significant minority in six provinces. In the three countries with minuscule indigenous populations, ethnic parties became viable in Colombia and Venezuela, with 15.1 and 0.04 percent of their subnational districts being at least 25 percent indigenous, but in Argentina, where no province is at least 25 percent indigenous, ethnic parties failed to take hold. The impact of population size is mediated by the number of seats available in the district, the formula for turning votes into seats, and the number of parties competing effectively in the district. The more seats available, the more favorable the electoral formula is toward small parties, and the larger the number of parties competing effectively in the district, the more likely it is that indigenous organizations with a significant minority can win elections.

Ethnic parties demonstrated three successful strategies for winning elections in districts where they constituted a minority: (1) they attracted unattached, disaffected voters by offering an appealing alternative to the dominant parties; (2) they incorporated nonindigenous popular organizations, leftist cadres, and intellectuals into the party and projected a platform that appeals to a wide spectrum of voters, particularly the lower and struggling middle classes; and (3) they formed electoral alliances with nonindigenous political parties. Alliances with nonindigenous organizations and social sectors enabled ethnic parties to compete successfully even when the number of indigenous voters dropped well below 25 percent. The case of Cauca, Colombia, where Indians make up less than 15 percent of the population, but a coalition of ethnic parties elected an indigenous governor in 2000, is a good example.

Permissiveness of the Institutional Environment

Decentralization opened up space for weak, underfinanced indigenous peoples' organizations to participate independently in formal politics at a relatively low cost. Even where indigenous populations have little prior electoral experience, ethnic parties can win elections where they have the numbers. Decentralization has such a profound impact on ethnic minorities that the face of politics changed overnight when Bolivia instituted direct municipal elections in 1995. But decentralization alone was not sufficient to enable Argentine Indians to form viable ethnic parties. In fact, too much decentralization may actually impede the electoral efforts of subordinate minorities when it occurs in countries where the group is too dispersed and minuscule to constitute a majority or significant minority in subnational units, and where provincial elites have relatively more power than the national government. Argentine provincial elites blocked efforts by national politicians and NGOs to codify new or implement existing indigenous rights. Because the most important level of politics is local and provincial, Argentine Indians have lacked an incentive to create a strong national organization that would enable them to pool resources and to become an effective collective political actor, as Indians with the same minuscule numbers did in Colombia and Venezuela. Thus, we must unpack the term "decentralization" in order to identify the real benefit to subordinate ethnic groups: the ability to directly elect local and/or subnational levels of government. The other principal attribute of decentralization – the shifting of autonomous powers and resources to local government – may actually increase the leverage of local and regional elites over subordinate ethnic groups, particularly where ethnic minorities lack the numbers or ability to forge alliances that would enable them to gain control over those governments.

The formation of new electoral districts in areas of high indigenous population also improved electoral performance for new ethnic parties. Fledgling ethnic parties did not have to compete with incumbents or established party organizations in these newly created districts. Such was the case in the mid-1990s in the new state of Amazonas, Venezuela, and several new departments in Colombia.

The other helpful institutional change is reserved seats for indigenous candidates. In both countries where reserved seats were instituted, indigenous peoples' organizations immediately formed political parties that competed successfully outside of reserved districts using resources accruing to parties in office.[4] The steady supply of resources gives fledgling ethnic parties an advantage. In contrast, promoting indigenous representation through party-list quotas, as done in Peru during regional

---

[4] Indigenous electoral circuits exist in Panamá to guarantee participation of Kuna Indians. These are unlikely to promote the formation of ethnic parties because Article 133 of the Constitution prohibits the formation of political parties based on race, sex, or religion.

elections in 2002, tends to impair ethnic party performance by increasing competition for popular indigenous candidates and fragmenting the indigenous vote among nonethnic and ethnic parties. Successful indigenous movement–based parties already have to compete for strong indigenous candidates once they achieve success and traditional parties seek to lure them away. The requirement that all parties include the indigenous intensifies this competition.

Openness of Party System

All six national party systems, with the exception of Argentina, experienced either persistent fragmentation or a moderate increase in fragmentation between 1980 and 2002. In Colombia, Peru, and Venezuela, party-system dealignment further opened the system. As the near-monopoly of the two dominant, elite-based parties eroded in Colombia and Venezuela, numerous new independent personalist and civil-society-based parties formed. They took advantage of significant institutional openings to compete in local, regional, and to a lesser extent, national elections. In Peru, however, despite the collapse of the party system and high fragmentation, ethnic parties performed poorly. Thus, opening space in the party system is necessary, but not sufficient for the success of new ethnic parties.

Leftist electoral decline also contributed to successful ethnic party performance Although ethnic parties achieved electoral viability without incorporating the left, the level of electoral success was far higher among those that did. The examples of Pachakutik in Ecuador, the ASP/IPSP/MAS in Bolivia, and ASI in Colombia attest to the electoral potential of indigenous movement/leftist party/popular movement coalitions. But leftist decline is not necessary for ethnic party success, provided that leftist parties and indigenous organizations are able to form mutually beneficial alliances, as the case of PUAMA-PPT in Venezuela demonstrates. In the context of an electorally dominant left, PUAMA gained the governorship and representation in the National Assembly through an alliance with the PPT.

Electoral results after 2000 show a dramatic increase in party system dealignment in our six cases. Traditional parties in Argentina, Bolivia, and Colombia experienced their worst performance in decades: In Bolivia and Colombia, dominant parties earned less than half the vote, while in Argentina, they barely earned 60 percent. Thus, the opportunities for new parties and cleavages to emerge and endure may be greater in the next decade than they were in the 1990s. However, to the extent that dominant

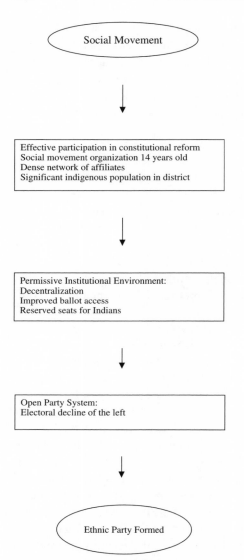

FIGURE 7.1. Model of Ethnic Party Formation.

parties lose ground to leftist challengers – as they have in Bolivia, Brazil, Ecuador, Uruguay, and Venezuela – the probability that more viable ethnic parties will form actually may decline if leftist militants feel they don't need the indigenous movement in order to gain power. Resurgent leftist parties may decide to go it alone or to seek to dominate indigenous

movements with whom they are allied. Indigenous politicians may prefer to join surging leftist parties – as occurred in Ecuador in the 2004
regional elections (*Noticia Hoy Online* 2004). According to some analysts, the "new left" is less ideological and Marxist and is actively courting
excluded groups – including indigenous people – with a message that combines democratic incorporation with opposition to neoliberalism (FOCAL
2003: 10–11). Thus, it may be more willing to share control with indigenous organizations than were leftist parties in the past. This raises another
challenge: If leftist parties effectively incorporate indigenous peoples and
their demands, will independent ethnic parties be able to compete without the resources that leftist militants provide, and in competition with
parties offering a similar anti-neoliberal, antisystem message?

LOOKING AHEAD

We can predict that ethnic parties are more likely to form where an indigenous social movement organization is fourteen years old, has achieved
some success in the social movement sphere, and has a dense network
of affiliates extended throughout the target area; where the organization
participated effectively in a constitutional reform; where obstacles to ballot access are relatively low; where decentralization opens the possibility
for competition in districts where indigenous peoples are concentrated;
where the left is relatively weak; and where seats have been reserved for
indigenous candidates. Such parties will perform best when these additional conditions are present: persistently high or moderately increased
party-system fragmentation; leaders of a declining electoral left seek to
join a more dynamic electoral project; a relatively high level of organizational unity exists within an ethnic movement that has a dense network of
organizational affiliates; and the existence of at least one subnational district (preferably, newly formed districts) where Indians are a majority or
near majority. These predictive models are depicted in Figures 7.1 and 7.2.

But such conditions rarely occur together. Instead, it is more useful to identify four "ideal types" of successful ethnic party formation
in Latin America (see Table 7.2). In Model 1, exemplified by Bolivia's
ASP/IPSP/MAS, a majority ethnic population develops regionally strong
organizations with dense networks of affiliates. The movement secures
new constitutional rights that require implementing legislation. Once
municipal decentralization occurs and the left experiences a steep electoral
decline, ethnic parties form and quickly achieve success, which increases
in subsequent elections.

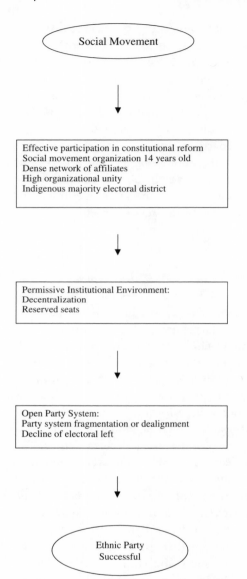

FIGURE 7.2. Model of Ethnic Party Performance.

In Model 2, exemplified by Ecuador's Pachakutik, a significant ethnic minority with a unified and institutionalized national organization
boasting a dense network of affiliates successfully participates in a constitutional reform. The reform process energizes the ethnic population,

TABLE 7.2. *Four models of successful ethnic parties*

Model 1 Bolivia's ASP/IPSP/MAS	Model 2 Ecuador's Pachakutik	Model 3 Colombia's ASI	Model 4 Venezuela's PUAMA
Majority ethnic population	Large ethnic minority	Minuscule indigenous population with regional concentrations in rural districts	Minuscule indigenous population with regional concentrations in rural districts
Regional ethnic social movement organizations with dense networks of affiliates	National ethnic social movement organization with dense network of affiliates	National ethnic social movement organization with dense network of affiliates including strong regional organizations	National ethnic social movement organization with strong regional affiliates
New constitutional rights requiring implementing legislation	Successful participation in constitutional reform	Successful participation in constitutional reform	Successful participation in constitutional reform
	Eased ballot access	Eased ballot access	Eased ballot access
Municipal decentralization	Decentralized electoral system	Reserved seats for ethnic minority	Reserved seats for ethnic minority
Electoral decline of left	Electoral decline of left	Regional and municipal decentralization	Decentralized electoral system
	Example of successful ethnic parties in neighboring countries	Weak electoral left	Strong electoral left and party alliances are legal
			Example of successful ethnic parties in neighboring countries

demonstrates the electoral potential of the ethnic minority, and results in eased access to the ballot for regionally concentrated groups. The success of ethnic parties in a neighboring country inspires ethnic elites to consider forming a party. In the context of a weak electoral left and long-standing decentralization, the ethnic party, once formed, quickly dominates elections in areas where the ethnic minority is concentrated and well-organized.

In Model 3, exemplified by Colombia's ASI, a small, widely dispersed ethnic population, with majority concentrations within sparsely populated rural districts, and with a national ethnic social movement organization with strong regional affiliated organizations, successfully participates in a constitutional reform. The reform process energizes the ethnic population and demonstrates the electoral potential of the ethnic minority. Constitutional reforms requiring implementing legislation improve access to the ballot for social movements, further incipient decentralization efforts, and establish reserved seats for the ethnic minority. In the context of a weak electoral left, the ethnic minority builds a regionally strong movement with a national presence in cooperation with other popular movements.

In Model 4, exemplified by Venezuela's PUAMA, a small, dispersed ethnic population, with majority concentrations within sparsely populated rural districts, and with a national organization with strong regional affiliates, successfully participates in a constitutional reform. The reform process energizes the ethnic population and demonstrates the electoral potential of the ethnic minority. Constitutional reforms requiring implementing legislation improve access to the ballot for social movements and establish reserved seats for the ethnic minority. Successful ethnic parties exist in three neighboring countries. In the context of a strong and resurgent left, the ethnic minority builds a regionally strong movement with a national presence in cooperation with an urban-based leftist party.

Although the first successful Latin American ethnic parties required the convergence of a high number of the conditions enumerated in the preceding text, it may be easier for similar parties to form in neighboring countries under less auspicious conditions. The rapid success of ethnic parties in Colombia, Ecuador, and Bolivia in the 1990s has inspired indigenous organizations in neighboring countries, just as the success of ecology parties in the early 1980s in a small set of countries with favorable conditions inspired ecological movements elsewhere in Europe where conditions were less favorable and, indeed, social movements around the world (Kitschelt 1989: 38; Mayer and Ely 1998: 3). This diffusion effect emerged in author interviews in Peru immediately following national elections in neighboring Bolivia, where two indigenous parties combined for 27 percent of the vote. Indigenous leaders interviewed that had not previously given serious thought to forming ethnic parties expressed an interest in doing so for the next national elections because of the success of ethnic parties in Bolivia and Ecuador.

In fact, even where conditions are manifestly unfavorable, indigenous peoples' organizations have formed viable parties. Beyond our case sample, in Guyana, where Amerindians are 7 percent of the population, indigenous communities launched their first political party, the Guyana Action Party (GAP), and competed in the March 19, 2001, elections. The GAP had to overcome legislation passed by the dominant parties that disqualified the party's leader and presidential candidate, and that reduced from two to one the number of seats available in each of the two electoral districts where indigenous people comprise a majority of the population. Guyana's party system is markedly different from others in the region because it historically has been organized around an ethnic cleavage that pits the Indo-Guyanese 48 percent of the population against the 38 percent of the population identifying itself as Afro-Guyanese (Joseph 2001a: 4–5). In its manifesto, GAP decries the domination of Guyanese politics by the two dominant race-based parties and offers the GAP as an alternative to this "ethnic trap" (Joseph 2001a: 4). The traditional parties responded after huge crowds turned out for GAP leaders in indigenous-dominated regions and political analysts speculated that the GAP could prevent either party from dominating the next government by drawing significant support from disaffected voters. The party finished third in the March 2001 elections, capturing two seats in the sixty-five-seat parliament – one in each of the indigenous-majority districts. It also swept local elections in the majority-indigenous Rupununi district, which will give it considerable influence over land, natural resource, and environmental issues (Joseph 2001b: 3). These preliminary results from Guyana show that even with small numbers and under adverse conditions, ethnic parties may form and become electorally viable.

IMPLICATIONS FOR THE FUTURE OF DEMOCRACY AND INDIGENOUS PEOPLES

What are the implications of the emergence and success of ethnic parties for democracy in the region, and for the indigenous peoples they represent? Will the new ethnic parties weaken democracy by increasing conflict among ethnic groups? Will participation in the formal political system impair the integrity and autonomy of indigenous cultures and forms of organization?

The preponderant view within the literature on political parties in divided societies is that ethnic parties tend to exacerbate ethnic conflict by strengthening the more extreme members of each group, while making it more difficult to convert narrow group claims into the public interest (Horowitz 1985: 291, 298). But in South America, although some new ethnic parties wield stridently ethnonationalist discourses (e.g., Bolivia's MIP), most recognize that their electoral viability depends on attracting support from nonindigenous voters. In addition, after decades of mobilization as movements, they understand that separatist appeals tend to backfire and lead to increased repression and the general public's rejection of their more moderate rights claims. During the 1980s and 1990s, the discourse of most indigenous peoples' organizations was one of inclusion and equitable participation in the larger state and society, while protecting a zone of autonomy for the development of indigenous culture. Channeling ethnic conflicts through the formal political system may encourage greater cooperation and moderation by providing incentives for multiethnic alliances. In fact, the best-performing ethnic parties are based on a strong indigenous movement organization that incorporates sympathetic nonindigenous sectors.

The new ethnic parties have had a number of positive effects on democratic institutions. First, they have improved the level of representation for a once-excluded group, an outcome that is particularly significant in countries with large indigenous populations. When marginalized groups find representation in democratic institutions, the legitimacy of those institutions increases for the group, and for other groups aspiring to find adequate representation. Incorporating excluded groups deepens democracy by decentering the universalizing assumptions upon which most modern democracies were founded (Laclau 1996: 33). Second, these ethnic parties offer a model of healthy party–society relations for other parties to emulate. One of the greatest weaknesses of contemporary Latin American parties is their distance from social groups and lack of responsiveness to voters. Roberts attributes this to the degeneration of "encapsulating" and "programmatic" linkages between society and parties (2002a: 21). "Encapsulating linkages" are derived from organic relationships with organized groups and opportunities for participation beyond voting (Roberts 2002a: 16). "Programmatic linkages" are derived from consistent ideologies and policy commitments (Roberts 2002a: 18). The new ethnic parties offer a healthy model of party–voter linkage because they are more effectively connected to civil society through organic ties to social movements and the associative networks in which they operate, and because they offer a coherent ideology and programmatic goals. They employ what Kitschelt calls a "logic of constituency representation" rather than a "logic of party competition" (1989: 5). This mode of linkage is more likely to ensure stability in voter loyalties, which should promote lower electoral volatility.

Third, the new ethnic parties have put themes on the agenda that had not previously found a place in mainstream political discourse: the value of recognizing and respecting cultural diversity; the problem of racial discrimination and oppression; and the need of civil society groups for autonomy from political parties and the state. Similarly, the Green Party transformed German politics by introducing into mainstream politics issues that had previously been considered "unconventional, marginal, and utopian" (Mayer and Ely 1998: 18). The popularity of new themes forces other parties to incorporate them into their own agendas. Thus, even when parties are small, they can have an important policy impact. National representation provides a platform to challenge the political status quo and the ideologies, symbols, and values on which it is based (Herzog 1987: 326). Ethnic parties are serving as voices for all of the disenfranchised and disaffected, offering a critique of the state and regime that otherwise might not be represented in national politics.

Fourth, the new ethnic parties have introduced more transparent and democratic models of doing politics. Several ethnic parties have been crusaders against corruption and patronage. In the Ecuadorian congress, for example, although some indigenous legislators have been caught in the web of corruption and clientelism that pervades Ecuadorian politics, others have been among the most important crusaders against corruption and have denounced and expelled party members linked to it. A Pachakutik deputy was head of the Commission on Corruption (Fiscalización) during the Alarcon government (interview, Luis Macas, July 28, 1999). As former Pachakutik deputy Luis Macas recalls:

All of the deputies in our delegation worked on this. This definitely facilitated that our movement achieved an important place in the Congress. We refused to agree with any other party or the government on the distribution of patronage, for example, which we oppose. Unfortunately, this is a practice here in Ecuador. There are many negotiations under the table in which money plays an important role. We have always tried to avoid these activities and to denounce them when they occur.   (my translation, interview, July 28, 1999)

In Bolivia, following the 2002 elections, both ethnic party leaders refused to participate in the postelectoral pact making on which Bolivian governments have been erected since 1982. Evo Morales passed up the possibility of gaining the presidency because it would have required an alliance with a neoliberal party opposed to his constituency's interests, and because it would have betrayed the promise of honest, accountable politics on which he had campaigned. Morales's party, MAS, has distinguished itself by its ethical behavior. In August 2002, it championed a failed proposal to lower congressional salaries; in November of that year, it returned Bs 4.4 million (approximately U.S.$580,000) to the National Electoral Court, 54 percent of the public funds it had received (Orduna 2002b). In June 2003, representatives from the two ethnic parties were among fifty opposition legislators that went on hunger strike to demand that the government end congressional holidays a month early so that the congress can address serious social issues, and that the government stop dragging its feet on legislation affecting land rights and help for farmers. After forty-two of the legislators gave up the strike, seven mostly indigenous legislators con-tinued, demanding that a poor community be allowed to establish a uni-versity (CNN 2003a).

Indigenous politicians, however, are not immune from the temptations of office.[5] In Ecuador, two Amazonian Pachakutik deputies defected to join the Bucaram government's alliance and were later expelled from Congress and jailed on corruption charges (Andolina 1999: 230; Collins 2001: 15n26; Sarango Macas 1997: 320). Many new indigenous officials are new to politics and do not understand their responsibilities and the laws regulating the handling of public funds or how to protect themselves from manipulation and corruption (Sarango Macas 1997: 320). This has been a problem for indigenous congressional representatives in Colombia and Bolivia as well: indigenous constituents expect indigenous represen-tatives to be honest and to resist corruption and the traditional games of politics; yet they also expect them to deliver public works to their com-munities, and when they don't they are criticized harshly.[6]

The new ethnic parties are more likely to be internally democratic, in contrast with many traditional Latin American parties, because they often incorporate indigenous cultural norms of consensus building and

[5] Pachakutik expelled two of its Amazonian deputies after the two voted with the governing bloc in order to gain committee seats. Both later were expelled from Congress and jailed on corruption charges (Andolina 1999: 230; Collins 2001: 15n26; Sarango Macas 1997: 320). In Nicaragua, several autonomous region governors elected by indigenous parties have been charged with corruption and embezzlement. Two successive indigenous governments were accused of fraud in the 1990s, leading to the defeat of indigenous parties in the 1998 elections (Ruiz Hernández and Burguete Cal y Mayor 2001: 45).

[6] Andolina argues that some of the Amazonian deputies' constituents continued to support them because they expected their politicians to deliver these resources (Andolina 1999: 230).

participatory decision making. Although there are cases of a single figure dominating an ethnic party, there are more cases where leadership and candidate renewal is the norm. For example, in 1997 the ASP held primaries to allow members to select the party's candidate – an unusual practice for a Bolivian party. Participatory norms may extend to public policy making and affect nonethnic parties. After Pachakutik began a practice of discussing proposed laws with the people affected, some Ecuadorian legislators from other parties began to incorporate more popular participation into the design of laws (interview, Luis Macas, July 28, 1999).

The impact of the ethnic parties on democratic participation is particularly evident at the local level. In Ecuador, where Pachakutik dominates local government it has introduced more participatory models of democratic governance, which have improved the accountability and public approval of government. For example, in Cotacachi, Pachakutik mayor Auki Tituaña won reelection in 2000 with 80 percent of the vote on the strength of his participatory, honest, and inclusive mode of governing, which won praise from nonindigenous residents (*Boletín ICCI* 2000b: 23; *Latin American Andean Group Report* 2001: 2). In 2004, he was reelected again with 55 percent of the vote in a crowded field (www.tse.gov.ec/resultados2004). In Cotacachi and other Pachakutik municipalities, leaders are incorporating the indigenous cultural practice of making decisions by consensus in large, participatory assemblies where anyone can speak. They are forming committees that unite government officials and civil society organizations to work on particular policy and planning issues (Flor 2001; MUPP 1999a; Radcliffe 2001; Rodriguez n.d.). In Colombia, during the administration of Floro Tunubulá, the indigenous ASI-AICO governor of the department of Cauca, numerous public assemblies and smaller meetings with civil society gave individuals and social organizations a role in decision making. Tunubulá also inaugurated a departmental Web site (www.gobcauca.gov.co) listing expenditures, contract offerings, bids, and award processes, to create greater transparency in an area prone to cronyism and corruption (oral presentation, Floro Tunubulá, Washington, DC, March 29, 2004; personal communication, Joanne Rappaport, March 29, 2004; Gobernación de Cauca 2003). Outside our case sample, similar practices are underway in majority-indigenous Guatemala, which has Latin America's largest number of municipalities governed by indigenous officials (León 2002: 26). Guatemalan indigenous authorities formed the Guatemalan Association of Indigenous Mayors and Authorities (AGAAI) in 1996 in order to develop a common approach to maximizing their autonomy and infusing municipal government with Mayan values (Ruiz Hernández and Burguete Cal y Mayor 2001: 40).[7]

Finally, the success of ethnic parties has increased the propensity of traditional parties to reach out to indigenous voters and to incorporate their demands and their most popular leaders into these parties. With the specter of two insurgent indigenous parties looming, Bolivian parties in 2002 recruited indigenous candidates more aggressively than ever before. Of the approximately fifty ethnically indigenous legislators elected in 2002, seventeen entered with nonindigenous traditional parties. The NFR was so eager to recruit Alejo Véliz, a prominent Quechua peasant leader, that it offered him his choice of a uni-nominal deputy or senatorial candidacy, or the leadership of its pluri-nominal list. In the past, indigenous leaders that ran with nonindigenous parties usually ran in districts where the party had poor prospects, or as alternates for nonindigenous candidates.

Increased representation at multiple levels of government has raised the collective self-esteem of indigenous peoples and provided substantive policy benefits. At the national level, indigenous representatives participate in the writing of legislation that affects indigenous peoples' most important issues. Although they seldom get exactly what they want, they often are able to affect the shape of legislation, to block or alter particularly odious laws and policies, and to force the government to pay attention to issues of interest to their constituents. For example, in Bolivia in April 2003, Chiquitano deputy José Bailaba worked with indigenous organizations and NGOs to force the government to conduct an environmental audit of the Cuiaba gas pipeline, which runs through Chiquitano and Ayoreo territories, and to investigate indigenous claims that the project is not in compliance with a variety of government mandates (Hindery 2003). The same month, in Ecuador, Shuar deputy Felipe Tsenkush registered objections to a new mining law, pointing out the potential harm to the environment and noting that the law violates articles 84 and 88 of the Constitution, which require such laws to be formulated in consultation with indigenous peoples. He also convinced a congressional human rights commission to travel to Pastaza to investigate the indigenous leaders' claim that a foreign petroleum company had violated their human rights (Centro de Derechos

---

[7] Since 1987, Guatemalan civic committees may run candidates for municipal presidents without registering as political parties, which has increased the participation of indigenous community organizations in local government (Ruiz Hernández and Burguete Cal y Mayor 2001: 39).

Económicos y Sociales 2003a, 2003b). As former national deputy Luis Macas argues,

For the first time in the National Congress, we have made a presence for indigenous peoples' voice to be heard clearly and directly. Previously there always had been mediators – unions, political parties spoke for the indigenous movement. Often they spoke on our behalf without our permission or knowledge. We now have a political presence in Congress as well as a political space in the national context. It's not just the physical presence of the indigenous in Congress; more important is the ability of the indigenous movement to present its proposals.

(my translation; interview, July 28, 1999)

However, negative impacts accompany these benefits. Participation in party politics causes disunity and factionalism within indigenous communities and organizations (Carling 2001: 279). Factionalism is a problem that numerous interview subjects mentioned. Kitschelt notes that factionalism is common to parties based on diverse social movements, which primarily are formed by nonprofessional politicians lacking professional incentives or skills. The emphasis of such parties on promoting democratic participation within the party tends to lead to intense internal political and personal conflicts (Kitschelt 1989: 143).

A second danger is the "contamination" of indigenous cultures by their participation in political parties, which are Western institutions based on liberal values endorsing competition and individual achievement. In indigenous cultures, harmony and consensus are valued over competition, and the advancement of the community is valued over the success of individuals. State decision-making systems are alien to indigenous cultures, in which collective decisions typically are based on the consensus achieved after long discussions, with the opinion of the eldest members of the community given particular respect (Wessendorf 2001: 13). Despite their efforts to be inclusive, government officials often must make decisions quickly in order to take advantage of opportunities or to adhere to mandatory administrative norms, and they may be forced by a variety of constraints to impose unpopular decisions. Party politics disrupts the balance of authority within indigenous communities by favoring younger, more educated, and acculturated members to the detriment of traditional elders. Mexican indigenous movement activists Margarito Ruiz Hernández and Aracely Burguete Cal y Mayor comment on these challenges:

The caciques or traditional authorities were substituted by the municipal councils. Similarly, in many places, electoral processes substituted the community assemblies as the mechanism of appointment of officials. Likewise, many of the best leaders of the communities were elected as local or federal deputies. Thus the

local indigenous communities were significantly 'adjusted', and had to give up
their own political culture, in order to be integrated into the state institutions.

Some leaders consider that such changes constitute an opportunity that can be
exploited in order to gain self-government. But others, on the contrary, consider
that they form new integrationist mechanisms that increase the breakdown of
regional organisation and of traditional indigenous governments. Some believe
that, either way, the indigenous challenge is to find the necessary balance that
enables indigenous peoples to accede to local government within the new legal
framework, whilst at the same time strengthening the leadership of their peoples.
However, many believe that such a balance is not possible.

(Ruiz Hernández and Burguete Cal y Mayor 2001: 36)

Laclau states the problem succinctly: "any victory against the system also
destabilizes the identity of the victorious force" (Laclau 1996: 27).

Third, successful new parties may reduce the effectiveness of indigenous social movements by distracting them from past priorities, such as
the defense of territorial autonomy and the construction of new political
institutions rooted in indigenous values and modes of self-government
and participation. The problem is even more serious when ethnic parties consist of coalitions among indigenous social movement partners and
diverse nonindigenous allies. When an ethnic movement participates in
broader struggles and makes appeals outside of its base constituency it
risks losing its original identity, as well as the organizational dynamism
and unity based therein. The result is often the weakening and disori-
entation of the ethnic organization serving as the coalition leader and
its distancing from the party it sponsored (Laclau 1996: 45; Rappaport
n.d.: 360–1). Ethnic parties also may reduce the leverage of indigenous
social movement organizations if government officials prefer to negotiate
with indigenous elected representatives rather than movement leaders,
who may be more radical. This problem occurred in Colombia under the
Samper government (Van Cott 2000b: ch. 4).

Fourth, indigenous peoples' organizations may risk the loss of crucial external funding if they participate in elections, particularly funding
from government sources. Indigenous Peoples Fund Director, Diego Iturralde, observes that indigenous organizations that have participated in
elections have lost funding because leaders that were once considered to be
"wise, pure, transparent and clean," are now considered to be "contam-
inated" by politics (Iturralde 1997: 359). In Peru, some anthropologists
and other professionals working with Amazonian indigenous organizations have strongly discouraged them from becoming involved in electoral
politics, which they worry will contaminate indigenous cultures (interview, Rodrigo Montoya Rojas, July 17, 2002).

Finally, indigenous elected officials' lack of political experience and technical capacity has caused severe problems. Indigenous access to municipal government power has brought greater pressure for indigenous politicians to have advanced educational qualifications and knowledge of bureaucratic rules and processes and, in their absence, to depend upon nonindigenous advisers, who tend to interfere in decision making. Indigenous leaders' failure to be effective or to resist efforts to dislodge them are great disappointments to indigenous movements, which can dampen enthusiasm in future elections (Ruiz Hernández and Burguete Cal y Mayor 2001: 35–6). Indigenous leaders elected to public office must constantly balance the need to represent their indigenous organization and to advance the indigenous rights agenda with the responsibility of representing the entire district, much of which may be nonindigenous.

On balance, the emergence of ethnic parties in South America has been positive for democratic institutions in the region, while having mixed results for indigenous peoples and their cultures. Because most only have been active since 1995, it is too early to assess the enduring positive and negative results. In the near term, however, indigenous peoples throughout the region are excited about the possibility of achieving autonomous self-representation at last, and about contributing to the construction of a new, more participatory, and tolerant model of democracy.

References

Agurto A., Jorge. 2001. "La Mesa de Diálogo Permanente para las Comunidades Nativas." *Ideele* 139 (July): 61–3, 80.

AIDESEP. 2000. "Primer boletín de la Asociación Interétnica de Desarrollo de la Selva Peruana." August. amazon@amazonalliance.org.

Albó, Xavier. 1994a. "And from Kataristas to MNRistas? The Surprising and Bold Alliance between Aymaras and Neoliberals in Bolivia." In Donna Lee Van Cott, ed. *Indigenous Peoples and Democracy in Latin America*. New York: St. Martin's Press, pp. 55–82.

————. 1994b. "El retorno del indio." *Revista Andina* 9, 2 (December): 299–331.

————. 1996. "Andean People in the Twentieth Century." In Frank Salomon and Stuart B. Schwartz, eds. *The Cambridge History of the Native Peoples of the Americas*. Vol. III, South America, Part 2. Cambridge: Cambridge University Press, pp. 765–871.

————. 1997. "Alcaldes y concejales campesinos/indígenas: La lógica tras las cifras." In Various Authors. *Indígenas en el Poder Local*. La Paz: Ministerio de Desarrollo Humano.

————. 1999a. "Diversidad Etnica, Cultural y Linguistica." In Fernando Campero Prudencio, ed. *Bolivia en el Siglo XX: La Formación de la Bolivia Contemporanea*. La Paz: Harvard Club de Bolivia, pp. 451–82.

————. 1999b. *Ojotas en el poder local. Cuatro años despues.* Cuadernos de Investigación 53. La Paz: hisbol, PADER, CIPCA.

————. 2001. "Estructuremos una Bolivia basada en el respeto a sus Naciones." In *"Ocaso o rebelión del indio?" Temas en la Crisis*, no. 58, V/VI: 11–13.

Alcántara Sáez, Manuel and Flavia Freidenberg. 2001. "Los partidos políticos en América Latina. *América Latina Hoy* 27 (April): 17–35.

Alvarez, Sonia E., Evelina Dagnino, and Arturo Escobar. 1998. "Introduction: The Cultural and the Political in Latin American Social Movements." In Sonia E. Alvarez, Evelina Dagnino, and Arturo Escobar, eds. *Cultures of Politics, Politics of Cultures: Re-visioning Latin American Socia Movements*. Boulder, CO: Westview Press, pp. 1–29.

Amnesty International. 2001. "Bolivia: Chapare-Human Rights cannot be eradicated along with the coca leaf." Amnesty International Press Release, October 25. http//:web.amnesty.org/library/print/engamr180102001.

Andolina, Robert. 1994. "Ecuador: Second Indigenous Uprising Secures Concessions on Agrarian Reform." *Abya Yala News* 8, 3: 19–20.

———. 1998. "CONAIE (and others) in the Ambiguous Spaces of Democracy: Positioning for the 1997–8 *Asamblea Nacional Constituyente* in Ecuador." Paper prepared for delivery at the 1998 meeting of the Latin American Studies Association. Chicago, Illinois. September 24–6.

———. 1999. "Colonial Legacies and Plurinational Imaginaries: Indigenous Movement Politics in Ecuador and Bolivia." Ph.D. Diss. Department of Political Science, University of Minnesota.

———. 2000. "El movimiento indígena en los espacios ambiguos del poder. Lecciones de la Asamblea Constituyente y el 21 de Enero." *Boletín ICCI-Ary Rimay*, vol. 2, no. 14 (May). http://icci.nativeweb.org.

———. 2001. "Between Local Authenticity and Global Accountability: The Ayllu Movement in Contemporary Bolivia." Paper prepared for the workshop "Beyond the Lost Decade: Indigenous Movements and the Transformation of Development and Democracy in Latin America." Princeton University, March 2–3.

———. 2003. "The Sovereign and Its Shadow: Constituent Assembly and Indigenous Movement in Ecuador." *Journal of Latin American Studies* 35, 4 (November): 721–50.

Andrade, Pablo. 2000. "Teoría democrática, democracia política y movimientos sociales: Elementos para una revisión crítica del cambio político en las sociedades andinas." In Julie Massal and Marcelo Bonilla, eds. *Los movimientos sociales en las democracias andinas*. Quito: FLACSO, IFEA, pp. 41–53.

Andrade, Susana. 2003. "Gobiernos locales indígenas en el Ecuador." *Revista Andina* 37, 2: 115–36.

A.N.P.E. 2004. "En Ecuador, Nuevo ataque al Movimiento Indígena: Allanamiento/robo en las oficinas de Pachakutik." Agencia de Noticias Plurinacional del Ecuador. February 21.

Arana, Cecilia. 2002. "Entrevista a Evo Morales Ayma: 'Queremos llevar el poder del pueblo para que el pueblo tenga poder.'" *Así es* (May–June): 6.

Arauco, Isabel and Ana María Belmont. 1997. "El Movimiento Bolivia Libre. La gobernabilidad y la democracia en Bolivia." In Various Authors. *Gobernabilidad y Partidos Políticos*. La Paz: CIDES–PNUD, pp. 121–38.

Archondo, Rafael. 1997. "De cómo los indígenas orientales decidieron apostor por la política." *La Razón*, Recta Final, elecciones 1997, March 22, p. 1.

Arnson, Cynthia, ed. 2001. *The Crisis of Democratic Governance in the Andes.* Washington, DC: Woodrow Wilson International Center for Scholars.

Arocha, Jaime. 1998. "Inclusion of Afro-Colombians: Unreachable National Goal?" *Latin American Perspectives* 25, 3 (May): 7–89.

Aruquipa Z., José Antonio. 2001. "Bolivia: Indigenous Groups Enter Politics." *Latinamerica Press*, received April 25 by e-mail.

Asamblea del Consejo de Nacionalidades y Pueblos Indígenas del Ecuador (ACNPIE). 2002. Statement dated April 19, La Merced. Received April 22 by e-mail from info@conaie.ecuanex.net.ec.

Assies, Willem, Gemma van der Haar, and André Hoekema, eds. 2001. *The Challenge of Diversity: Indigenous Peoples and Reform of the State in Latin America.* Amsterdam: Thela Thesis.

Associated Press. 2002a. "Ecuador: Panel Reinstates Candidate." Associated Press online, September 4, 2002. Load date: September 5, 2002.

———. 2002b. "Presidential Candidate Says He Was Disqualified for Being an Indian." AP Worldstream. August 27. Load date: August 28.

———. 2003. "Ecuador's Indian Leaders Threaten to Protest Economic Austerity Measures." AP World–General News. February 19. Received February 20 by e-mail from Amazon Alliance.

———. 2004. "17 Injured in Demonstrations in Ecuador." Associated Press. February 17. Received February 25, 2004 by e-mail from Amazon Alliance.

Avirama, Jesús and Rayda Márquez. 1994. "The Indigenous Movement in Colombia." In Donna Lee Van Cott, ed. *Indigenous Peoples and Democracy in Latin America.* New York: St. Martin's Press, pp. 83–106.

Balazote, Alejandro O. and Juan C. Radovich . 1999. "Present Situation of Indigenous Populations in Argentina." *CultureLink* (August): 157–63.

Ballón, Eduardo. 1995. "La democracia en los tiempos del colera: Peru 1970–1990." In Pablo González Casanova y Marcos Roitman Rosenmann, eds. *La democracia en América Latina. Actualidad y perspectivas.* Mexico: La Jornada ediciones, pp. 261–84.

Barié, Cletus Gregor. 2003. *Pueblos indígenas y derechos constitucionales en America Latina: un panorama.* 2nd ed. Mexico: Gobierno de la Republica.

Barrera, Augusto and Mario Unda. 1999. "Elementos para discutir la situación actual del MUPP-NP." *Pachakutik: Revista de debate político* 1 (July): 3–7.

BBC Monitoring International Reports. 2002. "Indian Group Will Not Have Own Candidate in Presidential Election." BBC Monitoring International Reports. April 23. Load date: April 24.

Beck, Scott H. and Kenneth J. Mijeski. 2000. "The Electoral Performance of Ecuador's Pachakutik Political Movement, 1996–1998."

———. 2001. "Barricades and Ballots: Ecuador's Indians and the Pachakutik Political Movement." *Ecuadorian Studies* 1 (September). http://www.yachana.org/ecuatorianistas/journal/journal.html.

Becker, Marc. 1999. "Comunas and Indigenous Protest in Cayambe, Ecuador." *The Americas* 55, 4: 531–59.

Bello, Luis Jesús. 1995. "Propuesta para el proyecto de la Organización Regional de Pueblos Indígenas de Amazonas." *La Iglesia en Amazonas* (Puerto Ayacucho) 71 (December): 12–16.

Bengoa, José. 2000. *La emergencia indígena en América Latina.* Santiago: Fondo de Cultura Económica.

Birnir, Jóhanna Kristín. 2000. "The Effect of Institutional Exclusion on Stabilization of Party Systems in Bolivia, Ecuador and Peru." Paper presented at the XXII International Congress of the Latin American Studies Association. Miami, Florida, March 16–18.

———. n.d. "Party Formation and Survival in New Democracies: The Andes."

Blanco, Hugo. 1972. *Land or Death The Peasant Struggle in Peru.* New York: Pathfinder Press.

Boletín Boliviapress. 2002a. "Destituyen a viceministra de educación Esther Balboa." *Boletín Boliviapress* 18, November 28, e-mail received November 29, 2002.

———. 2002b. "Las reformas a la constitución se encuentran estancadas." *Boletín Boliviapress* 15, September 23, e-mail received September 25, 2002.

Boletín ICCI. 2000a. "El XV Congreso de la ECUARUNARI y la definición del proyecto estratégico de los pueblos indígenas." *Boletín ICCI-Ary Rimay,* vol. 2, no. 14 (May). http://icci.nativeweb.org.

———. 2000b. "Foro Debate: Diez Años de Levantamiento Indígena del Inti Raymi de 1990. La Construcción de un País Plurinacional." *Boletín ICCI–Rimay,* vol. 2, no. 20 (November): 1–18. http://icci.nativeweb.org.

———. 2002a. "Ausencia de liderazgo indígena?" *Boletín ICCI-Ary Rimay,* vol. 4, no. 36 (March). http://icci.nativeweb.org.

———. 2002b. "El proceso electoral ecuatoriano." *Boletín ICCI-Ary Rimay,* vol. 4, no. 38 (May). http://icci.nativeweb.org.

———. 2002c. "Evaluación política del movimiento indígena ecuatoriano." *Boletín ICCI-Ary Rimay,* vol. 4, no. 34 (January). http://icci.nativeweb.org.

———. 2002d. "Significaciones del levantamiento de febrero del 2001." *Boletín ICCI-Ary Rimay,* vol. 3, no. 24 (March). http://icci.nativeweb.org.

———. 2003. "Pachakutik no ha desaparecido del registro electoral del T.S.E." *Boletín ICCI-Ary Rimay,* vol. 5, no. 55 (October). http://icci.nativeweb.org.

Boletín Indígena. 2003. "Pueblos Indígenas de Argentina consolidan su proyecto histórico." *Boletín Indígena* (La Paz) 11, 2 (March): 8–9. http://www.fondoindigena.org.

Bonfil Batalla, Guillermo, comp. 1981. *Utopía y Revolución. El pensamiento político de los indios en América Latina.* Mexico: Editorial Nuevo Imagen.

Boudon, Lawrence. 2000. "Party System Deinstitutionalization: The 1997–1998 Colombian Elections in Historical Perspective." *Journal of Interamerican Studies and World Affairs* 42, 3 (fall): 33–58.

Bozzano, Roberto L. 1996a. "19 de Abril día de Indio Americano." In Eulogio Frites, Hugo O. Ortega, and Roberto L. Bozzano, eds. *Abya-Yala. La tierra de los pueblos indios.* Buenos Aires: Asamblea Permanente por los Derechos Humanos, Comisión de Pueblos Indígenas, pp. 61–3.

———. 1996b. "Los indios aún subsisten y reclaman lo que es suyo." In Eulogio Frites, Hugo O. Ortega, and Roberto L. Bozzano, eds. *Abya-Yala. La tierra de los pueblos indios.* Buenos Aires: Asamblea Permanente por los Derechos Humanos, Comisión de Pueblos Indígenas, pp. 58–60.

Briones, Claudia. 1999. "'Weaving the Mapuche People': The Cultural Politics of Organizations with Indigenous Philosophy and Leadership." Ph.D. Diss. Department of Anthropology, University of Texas, Austin.

———. 2000. "The Politics of Indigenous Re-Presentation. Mapuche Views on State Law and Juridical Pluralism." Paper presented at the American Anthropological Association Meeting. San Francisco, California, November.

————. 2001. "Lo local y lo nacional: Explorando tendencias actuales en los reclamos indígenas en Argentina." Cuarto Congreso Chileno Antropología. Universidad de Chile, November 19–23. http://rehue.csociales.uchile.cl/ antropologia/congreso/s1612.html.

————. 2002. "'We are Neither an Ethnic Group nor a Minority, but a Pueblo–Nación Originario.' The Cultural Politics of Organizations with Mapuche Philosophy and Leadership." In Claudio Briones and José Luis Lanata, eds. *Contemporary Perspectives on the Native Peoples of Pampa, Patagonia, and Tierra del Fuego. Living on the Edge.* Westport, CT: Greenwood, pp. 101–20.

Brown, Michael E. and Eduardo Fernández. 1993. *War of Shadows: The Struggle for Utopia in the Peruvian Amazon.* Berkeley: University of California Press.

Bruhn, Kathleen. 1997. *Taking on Goliath. The Emergence of a New Left Party and the Struggle for Democracy in Mexico.* University Park: Penn State University Press.

Brysk, Alison. 2000. *From Tribal Village to Global Village. Indian Rights and International Relations in Latin America.* Stanford: Stanford University Press.

Brysk, Alison and Carol Wise. 1997. "Liberalization and Ethnic Conflict in Latin America." *Studies in Comparative International Development* (Fall): 76–104.

Buliubasich, Catalina and Héctor E. Rodríguez. 2001. "Organizaciones Wichi y Guaraní de la Provincia de Salta: Formas de Interpelación al Estado." Cuarto Congreso Chileno Antropología. Universidad de Chile. November 19–23. http://rehue.csociales/uchile.cl/antropologia/congreso/s1622.html.

Burgess, Katrina and Steven Levitsky. 2001. "Explaining Mass Populist Party Adaptation: Environmental and Organizational Determinants of Party Change in Argentina, Mexico, Peru and Venezuela." Paper prepared for the XXIII Meetings of the Latin American Studies Association. Washington, DC, September 6–8.

Bushnell, David. 1993. *The Making of Modern Colombia. A Nation in Spite of Itself.* Berkeley: University of California Press.

Cabascango, José María. 2002. "Participación indígena en procesos electorales." *Boletín ICCI-Ary Rimay*, vol. 4, no. 38 (May). http://icci.nativeweb.org.

Cabezas Castillo, Tito. 1995. "Partidos y organismos electorales. Una relación que debe mejorarse. El Caso de Ecuador." In Carina Perelli, Sonia Picado S., and Daniel Zovatto, comp. *Partidos y clase política en América Latina en los 90.* San José, Costa Rica: Instituto Interamericano de Derechos Humanos.

Cabrero, Ferran. 2002. *La Revolución Pactada. Globalización y transformación de la guerrilla en América Latina.* Barcelona: Flor del Viento Editores.

Cáceres C., Sergio. 2001. "Felipe Quispe: 'Al 21060 hay que enterrarlo junto con Víctor Paz.'" *el juguete rabioso* 2, 36 (July 15–28): 8–9.

Calla, Ricardo. 1993. "Hallu hayllisa huto. Identificación étnica y procesos políticos en Bolivia." In Carlos Iván Degregori, ed. *Democracia, etnicidad y violencia política en los países andinos.* Lima: IFEA, IEP, pp. 57–81.

Canessa, Andrew. 2000. "Contesting Hybridity: Evangelistas and Kataristas in Highland Bolivia." *Journal of Latin American Studies* 32, 1 (February): 115–44.

Canton, Santiago. 1995. *"Partidos Políticos en las Américas: Desafíos y Estrategias."* Washington, DC: National Democratic Institute.

Cárdenas, Víctor Hugo. 2002. "La participación campesino–indígena." *La Razón* (La Paz), July 1, p. A28.

Carling, Joan. 2001. "Summary/Strategies/Recommendations." In Kathrin Wessendorf, ed. *Challenging Politics: Indigenous Peoples' Experiences with Political Parties and Elections*. Copenhagen: IWGIA, pp. 278–82.

Carrasco, Morita. 2002. "El movimiento indígena anterior a la reforma constitucional y su organización en el Programa de Participación de Pueblos Indígenas." University of Texas, Working paper. http://www.utexas.edu/cola/llilas/centers.

Casen, Cécile. 2002. "Evo Morales puede cambiar la lógica del poder en Bolivia." *el juguete rabioso* (La Paz) (June 9): 11.

Castro, Sonia. 1992. *Censo Indígena Venezolana de 1992*. Tomo 2. Presidencia de la República, Oficina Central de Estadística e Informática.

———. 1993. *Censo Peruviano*. Instituto Nacional de Estadistica e Informática. http://www.inei.gob.pe.

———. 2001. *Censo Nacional de Población y Vivienda*. Bolivia.

———. 2002. "Mucha Esther para tan poco Mallku." *Los Tiempos* (Cochabamba), online, May 27. http://www.lostiempos.com.

CEDIB. 2001. "Definido binomio Mallku–Evo las elecciones de 2002." *"30 días" de noticias*, October, p. 90.

Centro de Derechos Económicos y Sociales. 2003a. "Codificación Mineria atenta contra los Derechos Ambientales y Colectivos." Boletín de Prensa. Received April 21 by e-mail.

———. 2003b. "Comisión del Congreso del Ecuador Visitará Sarayacu." Boletín de Prensa. Received April 21 by e-mail.

Cesar, Mike. 2001. "Bolivia: Expression of the Indigenous Majority." *Latinamerica Press*, received April 25 by e-mail.

Chandra, Kanchan. 2004. *Why Ethnic Parties Succeed: Patronage and Ethnic Head Counts in India*. New York: Cambridge University Press.

Chhibber, Pradeep K. 1999. *Democracy without Association: Transformation of the Party System and Social Cleavages in India*. Ann Arbor: University of Michigan Press.

Chiriboga, Manuel and Fredy Rivera. 1989. "Elecciones de enero 1988 y participación indígena." *Ecuador Debate* 17 (March): 181–221.

Chirinos Segura, Luis. 1998. "Marco legal de la participación ciudadana en gobiernos locales." *ideele* 111 (September).

Choque, María Eugenia and Carlos Mamani. 2001. "Reconstitución del ayllu y derechos de los pueblos indígenas: el movimiento indio en los Andes de Bolivia." *Journal of Latin American Anthropology* 6, 1: 202–24.

CIDOB. 1995. "Análisis Estratégico CIDOB. Informe redactado por la comisión mixta en base de informes elaborados por consultores." Santa Cruz: CIDOB.

———. 1996. "Movimiento Político. Comisión Técnica Política." June, mimeo.

———. 1997. *"A la sociedad boliviana, a los pueblos indígenas y a los partidos políticos. Carta abierta."* Santa Cruz: CIDOB.

———. 2000. *Oyendu. Voz de la CIDOB*. Vol. 2, no. 9 (December).

CNN. 2003a. "Bolivia Calls Emergency Session of Congress Amid Hunger Strike." June 2. http://www.cnn.com.

———. 2003b. "Peru: 60,000 People Died or Disappeared." June 18. http://www.cnn.com.

———. 2003c. "UN Concerned for Indians in Colombia's Civil War." May 23. http://www.cnn.com.

Collins, Jennifer N. 2000a. "A Sense of Possibility: Ecuador's Indigenous Movement Takes Center Stage." *NACLA Report on the Americas* 33 (March–April): 40–9.

———. 2000b. "Una transición desde las elites hacia una democracia participativa: apuntes sobre el papel emergente de los movimientos sociales en Ecuador. In Julie Massal and Marcelo Bonilla, eds. *Los movimientos sociales en las democracias andinas*. Quito: FLACSO, IFEA, pp. 55–71.

———. 2001. "Opening Up Electoral Politics: Political Crisis and the Rise of Pachakutik." Prepared for delivery at the 2001 meeting of the Latin American Studies Association. Washington, DC, September 6–8, 2001.

Comisión Nacional Interétnica del Peru. 2001. "Declaración de Pachacamac." Lima, August. http://www.fondoindigena.org/noticias/noto06.htm.

Comunidad Nativa Asháninka Marankiari Bajo. 1998. "Indígenas Asháninka organizados Participarán en las elecciones municipales de su Distrito." Press release.

CONACAMI. 2002. "Por la vida, la tierra, el agua y el agro!!!" Comunicado de CONACAMI, Lima, July.

Conaghan, Catherine. 1995. "Politicians against Parties: Discord and Disconnection in Ecuador's Party System." In Scott Mainwaring and Timothy R. Scully, eds. *Building Democratic Institutions. Party Systems in Latin America*. Stanford: Stanford University Press, pp. 434–58.

CONAIE. 2001. "Resoluciones. Asamblea Extraordinaria de la CONAIE." January 8.

———. 2002. "Resoluciones del Consejo Político Nacional." March 8–9. Received March 13 by e-mail from info@conaie.ecuanex.net.ec.

CONAPAA. 2002. *Reforma Constitucional: Bases de una propuesta de los pueblos Andinos y Amazónicos*. Comisión Nacional de los Pueblos Andinos y Amazónicos. Lima, March 13.

Condo, Freddy. 1998. *La Marcha del siglo. Marcha de las naciones originarias. El tiempo del instrumento político. Testimonios de: Roman Loayza y Modesto Condori*. La Paz: Ediciones Alkamiri.

CONIVE. 1999. "Presentación del CONIVE." *La Iglesia en Amazonas* (Puerto Ayacucho) 83–4 (January–June): 82–94.

———. 2000. "La Participación Política es un Derecho de los Pueblos Indígenas de Venezuela." Consejo Nacional Indio de Venezuela. Pamphlet.

Consejo Político Nacional. 2002. "Resoluciones del consejo político nacional." Movimiento de Unidad Plurinacional Pachakutik. Quito, March 8–9.

Coppedge, Michael. 1996. "Latin American Parties: Political Darwinism in the Lost Decade." Paper prepared for National Endowment for Democracy conference on "Political Parties and Democracy," November 18–19.

———. 1997. "District Magnitude, Economic Performance, and Party-system Fragmentation in Five Latin American Countries." *Comparative Political Studies* 30, 2 (April): 156–85.

_____. 1998. "The Evolution of Latin American Party Systems." In Scott Mainwaring and Arturo Valenzuela, eds. *Politics, Society and Democracy: Latin America*. Boulder, CO: Westview Press, pp. 171–206.

COPPIP. 2001. "Declaración de San Marcos." Conferencia Permanente de los Pueblos Indígenas del Peru. August 25.

Corao, Carlos M. Ayala. 1995. "El Estado constitucional y autonomía de pueblos indígenas." In Antonio A. Cancado Trindade and Lorena González Volio, comps. *Estudios Básicos de Derechos Humanos* II. San José, Costa Rica: Instituto Interamericano de Derechos Humanos, pp. 397–423.

Cordero, Carlos. 2002. "El país está dividido entre dos fuerzas políticas." *El Deber*, sección "Usted Elige." July 6, p. A13.

Correo Indígena. 2004. "Indígenas del Perú inaugurarán sede institucional." *Correo Indígena* 3, 16. Received February 26 by e-mail from coppip@amauta. rcp.net.pe.

Corte Nacional Electoral. 2002. "Elecciones Generales de Bolivia 2002: Documentos Básicos para Observadores Internacionales." La Paz, Bolivia.

Cotlear, Daniel. 1989. *Desarrollo campesino en los Andes*. Lima: IEP.

Cotler, Julio. 1970. "Traditional Haciendas and Communities in a Context of Political Mobilization in Peru." In Rodolfo Stavenhagen, ed. *Agrarian Problems and Peasant Movements in Latin America*. Garden City, NY: Anchor Books, pp. 533–58.

Crain, Andrew. 2000. "Indigenous Land Regularization in Latin America." University of Colorado School of Law.

CRIC. 1981. *Diez años de lucha. Historia y documentos*. Bogotá: CINEP, Consejo.

_____. 1990. *Historia del CRIC*. Popayán, Colombia: Consejo Regional Indígena del Cauca.

Crisp, Brian F. and Daniel H. Levine. 1998. "Democratizing the Democracy? Crisis and Reform in Venezuela." *Journal of Interamerican Studies and World Affairs* 40, 2: 27–61.

Cruz, Alberto. 2004. "Las elecciones de Ecuador y la unidad de la izquierda." *Rebelión*, October 31. http://www.rebelion.org_noticia.php_id/-6950.

CSUTCB. 1996. *VII Congreso CSUTCB. Documentos y Resoluciones*. La Paz: CSUTCB.

_____. n.d. "Historia de los Movimientos Indígenas en Bolivia." Downloaded May 15, 2002, from CSUTCB Web site: http://www.pueblosindio. org/csutcb3.html.

Cunin, Elisabeth. 2003. "La política étnica entre alteridad y estereotipo. Reflexiones sobre las elecciones de marzo de 2002 en Colombia." *Análisis Político* (Bogotá) 48 (January–April): 77–93.

Dalton, Russell L., Scott C. Flanagan, and Paul Allen Beck, eds. 1984. *Electoral Change in Advanced Industrial Democracies: Realignment or Dealignment?* Princeton: Princeton University Press.

Dandler, Jorge. 1999. "Indigenous Peoples and the Rule of Law in Latin America: Do They Have a Chance?" In Juan E. Méndez et al., eds. *The (Un)Rule of Law and the Underprivileged in Latin America*. Notre Dame: University of Notre Dame Press, pp. 116–51.

Dávalos, Pablo. 1999. "Declaración del primer encuentro de los pueblos quechuas de America." Pissaq, Qosqo, November 7.

———. 2000. "La CONAIE: Actor social? Sujeto político?" *Boletín ICCI-Ary Rimay*, vol. 2, no. 18 (September). http:// icci.nativeweb.org.

———. 2001. "Coyuntura política y movimiento indígena: Elementos para el análisis." *Boletín ICCI "RIMAY."* Vol. 3, no. 24 (March): 1–7.

———. n.d. "Movimiento indígena ecuatoriano: La constitución de un actor político." Downloaded February 2003 from ICCI Web site, http://icci.nativeweb.org. (16pp.)

Defensoría del Pueblo (Peru). 2000. *Situaciones de Afectación a los Derechos Políticos de los Pobladores de las Comunidades Nativas.* Serie Informes Defensoriales no. 34. Lima, March.

Degregori, Carlos Iván. 1993. "Identidad étnica, movimientos sociales y participación política en el Perú." In Carlos Iván Degregori, ed. *Democracia, etnicidad y violencia política en los países andinos.* Lima: IFEA, IEP, pp. 113–33.

———. 1998a. "Harvesting Storms: Peasant Rondas and the Defeat of Sendero Luminoso in Ayacucho." In Steve J. Stern, ed. *Shining and Other Paths. War and Society in Peru, 1980–1995.* Durham, NC: Duke University Press, pp. 128–57.

———. 1998b. "Movimientos étnicos, democracia y nación en Perú y Bolivia." In Claudia Dary, comp. *La construcción de la nación y la representación ciudadana en México, Guatemala, Péru, Ecuador y Bolivia.* Guatemala: FLACSO, pp. 159–225.

De la Cadena, Marisol. 2000. *Indigenous Mestizos: The Politics of Race and Culture in Cuzco, Peru, 1919–1991.* Durham, NC: Duke University.

Del Granado, Juan. 2002. "Los indígenas en el parlamento son una poderosa señal para el modelo." *La Razón* (La Paz) (online), July 7. http://www.la-razon.com.

Deruyttere, Anne. 1997. *Indigenous Peoples and Sustainable Development. The Role of the Inter-American Development Bank.* Forum of the Americas, April 8. Washington, DC: Inter-American Development Bank.

Diario Hoy. 1995. "Indígenas: Un proyecto político más agresivo." *Diario Hoy* (Quito), May 8, p. 2A.

———. 2002. "Análisis de Hoy: La CONAIE y Gutiérrez." *Diario Hoy* (online), December 2.

Dietz, Henry and David Myers. 2001. "The Process of Party System Collapse: Peru and Venezuela Compared." Paper prepared for presentation at the 2001 Congress of the Latin American Studies Association. Washington, DC, September 6–8.

Domingo, Pilar. 2001. "Party Politics, Intermediation and Representation." In John Crabtree and Laurence Whitehead, eds. *Towards Democratic Viability.* London: Palgrave Press.

Domínguez, Jorge I. 1995. "Los Desafíos de los Partidos Políticos en América Latina y el Caribe." Prepared for the conference on political parties in Latin America and the Caribbean under the auspices of the UNDP and the Fundacaión F. Ebert, Cartagena, Colombia.

Dugas, John, comp. 1993. *La Constitución de 1991: Un pacto político viable?* Bogotá: Universidad de los Andes.

Dugas, John. 2001. "Sisyphus in the Andes? The Pursuit of Political Party Reform in Colombia." Paper prepared for delivery at the 2001 Meeting of the Latin American Studies Association. Washington, September 6–8.

The Economist. 2004. "Bolivia's troubles: From here to 2007, without falling?" *The Economist* (January 24): 33–4.

ECUARUNARI. 2002. "Acuerdos y resoluciones de la Asamblea-Taller." Otavalo, Imbabura, April 3–5. Downloaded April 10, 2002 from ECUARUNARI Web site: http://ecuarunari.nativeweb.org/acuerdo3abrilo2. html.

El Comercio (Quito). 2002a. "Albaro Noboa gastó más en cuñas de TV." *El Comercio* (online), October 16.

———. (Quito). 2002b. "La Feine busca arranzarse a traves de Vargas." *El Comercio* (online), March 14.

———. (Quito). 2002c. "Perfil de Lucio Gutiérrez." *El Comercio* (online), September 8.

———. (Lima). 2002d. Suplemento. "Acuerdo Nacional." *El Comercio* (Lima). July 21.

———. (Quito). 2003. "Pachakutik se quedo fuera del poder." *El Comercio*, August 7 by e-mail.

El Diario. 2002a. "Después de 20 años de democracia, Bolivia tiene un Parlamento multiétnico." *El Diario* (La Paz) (online). August 3.

———. 2002b. "Discursos encendidos de congresistas del MAS subieron temperatura." *El Diario* (La Paz) (online). August 4.

———. 2002c. "Oficialismo acaparó comisiones y comités en Cámara de Senado." *El Diario* (La Paz) (online). August 27.

———. 2002d. "Pueblos indígenas se posicionaron ideológicamente en el Congreso." *El Diario* (La Paz) (online). August 4.

Ellner, Steve. 1988. *Venezuela's Movimiento al Socialismo. From Guerrilla Defeat to Innovative Politics*. Durham: Duke University Press.

el juguete rabioso. 2002. "Evo Morales y la teoría del 'CERCO INTERIOR.'" *el juguete rabioso* (June 23): 9.

El Peruano. 2001. "Plan de Acción para los Asuntos Prioritarios." Comisión Especial Multisectorial para las Comunidades Nativas, Mesa de Diálogo y Cooperación para las Comunidades Nativas. *El Peruano* (Lima), Separata Especial, July 24.

El Universo. 2002. "Perfiles," *El Universo* (Quito) (online), December 31. http://www.eluniverso.com.

———. 2004. "Feine y Fenocin plantearon crear grupo de alcaldes." *El Universo* (Quito) (online), October 31. http://www.eluniverso.com.

Escobar, Gabriel. 1996. "Indians of Ecuador Coalescing in Quest for Political Power." *Washington Post* July 23, p. A12.

Espinoza, Claudia. 2002. "Evo y Felipe, las diferencias." *Pulso Semanario* (La Paz), June 28–July 4, p. 21.

Eyzaguirre, Gloria. 1997. "No debió 'prestarse' al MBL. Fabricano fabricó su propia derrota." *La Razón* (La Paz), June 11, p. A14.

FENOCIN. 2002. "Unidad en la Diversidad." Boletín de Prensa. Quito, October 17.

Fernández Fontenoy, Carlos. 2000. "Sistema político, indigenismo y movimiento campesino en el Perú." In Julie Massal and Marcelo Bonilla, eds. *Los movimientos sociales en las democracias andinas*. Quito: FLACSO, IFEA, pp. 193–211.

FIJO. 1999a. *Boletín Informativo del Movimiento Independiente Fuerza de Integración Juntos con Orgullo-FIJO*. no. 13, October 16. Lima.

———. 1999b. *Boletín Informativo del Movimiento Independiente Fuerza de Integración Juntos con Orgullo-FIJO*. no. 14, October 23. Lima.

———. 1999c. "Preguntas y respuestas acerca de FIJO Fuerza de Integración. Fundamentos Políticos de Presentación." Mimeo. Lima, April.

Findji, Maria Teresa. 1992. "From Resistance to Social Movement: The Indigenous Authorities Movement in Colombia. In Arturo Escobar and Sonia E. Alvarez, eds. *The Making of Social Movements in Latin America: Identity, Strategy, and Democracy*. Boulder, CO: Westview Press, pp. 112–33.

Flor R., Eulalia. 2001. "Interculturalidad al fronterizar poder, política y representación en Ecuador: Experiencias en algunos municipalidades." Prepared for presentation at the Latin American Studies Association Congress. Washington, DC, September 6–8.

Flores Galindo, Alberto. 1988. *Buscando un Inca*. Lima: Editorial Horizonte.

FOCAL. 2003. "What's New, What's Left in Latin America?" *Editorial. FOCAL POINT. Spotlight on the Americas* 2, 2 (February): 10–11.

———. 2004. Andean Forum 2004. "Broadening Citizenship: Political Parties and New Trends in Participation. Conference Report." Quito, Ecuador, February 19–20.

Foweraker, Joe. 1995. *Theorizing Social Movements*. London: Pluto Press.

Foweraker, Joe and Todd Landman. 1997. *Citizen Rights and Social Movements. Comparative Statistical Analysis*. London: Oxford University Press.

Frites, Eulogio. 1996. "Panorama histórico y actual de los pueblos indígenas de Argentina." In Eulogio Frites, Hugo O. Ortega, and Roberto L. Bozzano, eds. *Abya-Yala. La tierra de los pueblos indios*. Buenos Aires: Asamblea Permanente por los Derechos Humanos, Comisión de Pueblos Indígenas, pp. 27–54.

Gálvez Herrera, Ciro. 1996. *Renacimiento Andino. Discurso de fundación*. Huancayo. Pamphlet.

———. 1997. *Discurso del Dr. Ciro Galvez en el primer encuentro regional centro peruano del Renacimiento Andino*. Huancavelica, August 16. Pamphlet.

Gamarra, Eduardo A. and James M. Malloy. 1995. "The Patrimonial Dynamics of Party Politics in Bolivia." In Scott Mainwaring and Timothy R. Scully, eds. *Building Democratic Institutions: Party Systems in Latin America*. Stanford: Stanford University Press, pp. 399–433.

García, María Elena. 2003. "The Politics of Community: Education, Indigenous Rights, and Ethnic Mobilization in Peru." *Latin American Perspectives* 30, 1 (January): 70–95.

García, María Elena and José Antonio Lucero. 2002. "Absence and Movement: Re-thinking Indigenous Politics in Peru." Revised draft September 2002.

García Sánchez, Miguel. 2001. "La Democracia Colombiana: Entre las reformas institucionales y la guerra. Una aproximación al desempeño de las terceras fuerzas en las alcaldías municipales. 1988–2000." Paper prepared for

248 *References*

presentation at the 2001 Congress of the Latin American Studies Association. Washington, DC, September 6–8.
George, Alexander. 1979. "Case Studies and Theory: The Method of Structured, Focused Comparison." In Paul Larson, ed. *Diplomacy: New Approaches to History, Theory and Policy.* New York: Free Press, pp. 43–68.
George, Alexander L. and Timothy J. McKeown. 1985. "Case Studies and Theories of Organizational Decision Making." *Advances in Information Processing in Organizations* 2: 21–58.
Glenn, John K. 2003. "Parties Out of Movements: Party Emergence in Post Communist Eastern Europe." In Jack A. Goldstone, ed. *States, Parties, and Social Movements.* New York: Cambridge University Press, pp. 147–69.
Goldstone, Jack A., ed. 2003. *States, Parties, and Social Movements.* New York: Cambridge University Press.
González Casanova, Pablo and Marcos Roitman Rosenmann, coord. 1995. *La democracia en América Latina. Actualidad y perspectivas.* Mexico: La Jornada ediciones.
Gray Molina, George. 2002. "The Offspring of 1952: Poverty, Exclusion and the Promise of Popular Participation." Paper presented at the conference "The Bolivian Revolution at 50: Comparative Views on Social, Economic, and Political Change." Harvard University, Cambridge, Massachusetts, May 2–3.
Grijalva Jiménez, Agustín, ed. 1998. *Datos Básicos de la Realidad Nacional.* Quito: Corporación Editora Nacional. Cited in Birnir 2000.
Grofman, Bernard and Arend Lijphart, ed. 1986. *Electoral Laws and Their Political Consequences.* New York: Agathon Press.
Gros, Christian. 1988. "Una organización indígena en lucha por la tierra: El Consejo Regional Indígena del Cauca." In Francoise Morin, ed. *Indianidad, Etnocidio, Indigenismo en América Latina.* Mexico: Instituto Indigenista Interamericano, Centre D'etudes Mexicaines et Centramericaines.
———. 1993. "Derechos indígenas y nueva constitución en Colombia." *Análisis Político* 19 (May–August): 8–23.
———. 1997. "Indigenismo y etnicidad: el desafiío neoliberal." In María Victoria Uribe and Eduardo Restrepo, eds. *Antropología en la modernidad.* Bogotá: Instituto Colombiano de Antropología, pp. 15–58.
Grueso, Libia, Carlos Rosero, and Arturo Escobar. 1998. "The Process of Community Organizing in the Southern Pacific Coast Region of Colombia." In Sonia E. Alvarez et al., eds. *Cultures of Politics/Politics of Cultures: Revisioning Latin American Social Movements.* Boulder, CO: Westview Press, pp. 196–219.
Guarachi, Paulino. 1994. "Relación Estado-Pueblos Indígenas." In *Buen Gobierno para el Desarrollo.* La Paz: Fundación Milenio, PNUD, ILDIS, pp. 227–231.
Gunther, Richard and José Ramón-Montero. 2002. "Introduction: Reviewing and Reassessing Parties." In Richard Gunther, José Ramón-Montero, and Juan J. Linz, eds. *Political Parties: Old Concepts and New Challenges.* Oxford: Oxford University Press, pp. 1–38.
Gustafson, Bret. 2002. "Indigenous Movements and State Processes in Bolivia: Racism, Regional Politics, and the Paradoxes of Intercultural Reform." In David

Maybury-Lewis, ed. *Identities in Conflict: Indigenous Peoples and the State in Latin America*. Cambridge: Harvard University Press, pp. 267–306.

———. 2003. "Political Defense in the Chapare. Voices from Bolivia." *Cultural Survival Quarterly* 26, 4 (Winter): 49.

Guzmán, Gustavo and Victor Ordina. 2002. "El 'Factor indígena' no televisado: Evo Morales y Felipe Qusipe: los votos inesperados." *Pulso Semanario* June 7–13, pp. 12–13.

Guzmán, Mauricio León. 2003. *Etnicidad y exclusión en el Ecuador: una Mirada a partir del Censo de Población de 2001*. Draft. Sistema Integrado de Indicadores Sociales del Ecuador-SIISE.

Hall, Peter A. 2003. "Aligning Ontology and Methodology in Comparative Politics." In James Mahoney and Dietrich Rueschemeyer, eds. *Comparative Historical Analysis in the Social Sciences*. New York: Cambridge University Press, pp. 373–406.

Halpern, Adam and France Winddance Twine. 2000. "Antiracist Activism in Ecuador: Black-Indian Community Alliances." *Race and Class* 42, 2 (October–December): 19–31.

Handelman, Howard. 1975. *Struggle in the Andes. Peasant Political Mobilization in Peru*. Austin: University of Texas Press.

Harmel, Robert and John D. Robertson. 1985. "Formation and Success of New Parties: A Cross-National Analysis." *International Political Science Review* 6, 4 (October): 501–23.

Hartlyn, Jonathan and John Dugas. 1999. "Colombia: The Politics of Violence and Democratic Transformation." In Larry Diamond et al., eds. *Democracy in Developing Countries: Latin America*. 2nd ed. Boulder: Lynne Rienner Publishers, pp. 249–307.

Hauss, C. and D. Rayside. 1978. "The Development of New Parties in Western Democracies since 1945." In L. Maisel and J. Cooper, eds. *Political Parties: Development and Decay*. Beverly Hills: Sage, pp. 31–57.

Healy, Kevin. 1988. "Coca, the State and the Peasantry in Bolivia, 1982–1988." *Journal of Interamerican Studies and World Affairs* 30, 2 and 3 (Summer/Fall): 105–26.

———. 1991. "Political Ascent of Bolivia's Peasant Coca Leaf Producers." *Journal of Interamerican Studies and World Affairs* 33, 1 (Spring): 87–120.

———. n.d. *"The Political Activism of the Bolivian Peasant Sindicatos in the New Democratic Order of the 1980s."* Occasional paper no. 6. Columbia–New York University consortium.

Herzog, Hanna. 1987. "Minor Parties: The Relevancy Perspective." *Comparative Politics* 19 (April): 317–29.

Hidalgo Flor, Francisco 2002. "Elecciones en Ecuador: Organicidad e inorganicidad en la votación de Lucio Gutiérrez." Received by e-mail from espaciosec@yahoo.es.

———. 2003. "El movimiento indígena ecuatoriano en los laberintos del poder." Received by e-mail from espaciosec@yahoo.es.

Hindery, Derrick. 2003. "Government of Bolivia Initiates Inspection Phase in Environmental Audit of Cuiaba Gas Pipeline." Amazon Watch. April 22.

Hirsch, Silvia María. 1999. "De la comunidad a la nación: Participación cívica y política entre los guaraníes del noroeste argentino." Seminario 2, Instituto de Desarrollo Económico y Social, Buenos Aires.

———. 2000. "Inventing the Generic Guaraní: Pan–Indianism and Politics among the Guaraní Indians of Northwest Argentina." Paper presented at the American Anthropological Association Meeting. San Francisco, California, November.

———. 2003. "The Emergence of Political Organizations among the Guaraní Indians of Bolivia and Argentina: A Comparative Perspective." In Erick D. Langer, ed. *Contemporary Indigenous Movements in Latin America.* Wilmington: Scholarly Resources, pp. 81–101.

Horowitz, Donald L. 1985. *Ethnic Groups in Conflict.* Berkeley: University of California Press.

Htun, Mala. 2004a. "From 'Racial Democracy' To Affirmative Action: Changing State Policy on Race in Brazil." *Latin American Research Review* 39, 1: 60–89.

———. 2004b. "Is Gender like Ethnicity? The Political Representation of Identity Groups." *Perspectives on Politics* 2, 3: 439–58.

Htun, Mala and Mark Jones. 2002. "Engendering the Right to Participate in Decisionmaking: Electoral Quotas and Women's Leadership in Latin America." In Nikki Craske and Maxine Molyneux, eds. *Gender and the Politics of Rights and Democracy in Latin America.* London: Palgrave, pp. 32–56.

Huanca Ayaviri, Félix. 2001. "Gestión autónoma de los territorios indígenas." In *"Ocaso o rebelión del indio?" Temas en la Crisis,* vol. V/VI, no. 58, 31–3.

Hug, Simon. 2001. *Altering Party Systems. Strategic Behavior and the Emergence of New Political Parties in Western Democracies.* Ann Arbor: University of Michigan Press.

Ignazi, Piero. 1996. "The Crisis of Parties and the Rise of New Political Parties." *Party Politics* 2, 4: 549–66.

Inter-American Commission on Human Rights. 2000. "Second Report on the Situation of Human Rights in Peru. Chapter X. The Rights of Indigenous Communities." Organization of American States. OEA/Ser.L/V/II.106, Doc. 59 rev. June 2.

Iturralde, Diego. 1997. "Comentario de Diego Iturralde." In Magdalena Gómez, coord. *Derecho Indígena.* Mexico City: Instituto Nacional Indigenista, pp. 356–60.

Iturri S., Jaime. 2002. "Todos trabajaron para Evo." *La Razón* (La Paz), July 1, p. A26.

Jackson, Jean E. 1991. "Being and Becoming an Indian in the Vaupés." In Greg Urban and Joel Sherzer, eds. *Nation-States and Indians in Latin America.* Austin: University of Texas Press, pp. 131–55.

———. 1996. "The Impact of Recent National Legislation in the Vaupés Region of Colombia." *Journal of Latin American Anthropology* 1, 2 (Spring): 120–51.

———. 1999. "The Politics of Ethnographic Practice in the Colombian Vaupés." *Identities: Global Studies in Culture and Power* 6, 2–3 (July): 281–317.

———. 2002a. "Caught in the Crossfire: Colombia's Indigenous Peoples during the 1990s." In David Maybury-Lewis, ed. *The Politics of Ethnicity: Indigenous Peoples in Latin American States.* Cambridge: Harvard University Press, pp. 107–33.

———. 2002b. "Contested Discourses of Authority in Colombian National Indigenous Politics: The 1996 Summer Takeovers." In Jean E. Jackson and Kay B. Warren, eds. *Indigenous Movements, Self-Representation and the State in Latin America.* Austin: University of Texas Press, pp. 81–122.

Jackson, Jean E. and Kay V. Warren, eds. 2002. *Indigenous Movements, Self-Representation and the State in Latin America.* Austin: University of Texas Press.

Jenkins, J. Craig and Bert Klandermans, eds. 1995. *The Politics of Social Protest. Comparative Perspectives on States and Social Movements.* Minneapolis: University of Minnesota.

Jimeno, Myriam. 1996. "Juan Gregorio Palechor: tierra, identidad y recreación étnica." *Journal of Latin American Anthropology* 1, 2 (Spring): 46–77.

Jones, Mark P. 1995. "A Guide to the Electoral Systems of the Americas." *Electoral Studies* 14, 1: 5–21.

———. 1997. "A Guide to the Electoral Systems of the Americas: An Update." *Electoral Studies* 16, 1: 13–15.

———. 2000. "Explaining the High Level of Party Discipline in the Argentine Congress."

Joseph, Adrian. 2001a. "Indigenous Party Meets Opposition." *Latinamerica Press* 33, 5 (February 19): 4–5.

———. 2001b. "Racial divisions mar elections." *Latinamerica Press* 33, 11 (April 2): 3.

Journal of Democracy. 2001. Special Issue on Politics in the Andes. *Journal of Democracy* 12, 2.

Journal of Theoretical Politics. 1989. *Journal of Theoretical Politics* 1, 3. Special Issue on Party System Change.

Jurado Nacional de Elecciones. 2002a. *Elecciones Regionales y Municipales 2002. Legislación Electoral.* Lima: Jurado Nacional Electoral.

———. 2002b. Ley de Elecciones Regionales No. 27683. March 15.

Karakras, Ampam. 2001. "Planteamientos de los pueblos 'indígenas' al estado ecuatoriano." Paper prepared for the workshop "Beyond the Lost Decade: Indigenous Movements and the Transformation of Development and Democracy in Latin America." Princeton University, March 2–3.

Keck, Margaret E. 1992. *The Workers' Party and Democratization in Brazil.* New Haven: Yale University Press.

Keck, Margaret E. and Kathryn Sikkink, eds. 1998. *Activists beyond Borders: Transnational Advocacy Networks in International Politics.* Ithaca: Cornell University Press.

King, Gary, Robert O. Keohane, and Sidney Verba. 1994. *Designing Social Inquiry: Scientific Inference in Qualitative Research.* Princeton: Princeton University Press.

Kitschelt, Herbert. 1989. *The Logics of Party Formation: Ecological Politics in Belgium and West Germany.* Ithaca: Cornell University Press.

Klein, Herbert S. 1992. *Bolivia. The Evolution of a Multi-Ethnic Society.* 2nd ed. New York: Oxford University Press.

Kornblith, Miriam. 1998. *Venezuela en los noventa: Las crisis de la democracia.* Caracas: IESA.

Kornblith, Miriam and Daniel H. Levine. (1995). "Venezuela: The Life and Times of the Party System." In Scott Mainwaring and Timothy R. Scully, eds. *Building Democratic Institutions: Party Systems in Latin America*. Stanford: Stanford University Press, pp. 37–71.

Kriesi, Hanspeter. 1995. "The Political Opportunity Structure of New Social Movements: Its Impact on Their Mobilization." In Craig J. Jenkins and Bert Klandermans, eds. *The Politics of Social Protest. Comparative Perspectives on States and Social Movements*. Minneapolis: University of Minnesota, pp. 167–98.

Laakso, Murkuu and Rein Taagepera. 1979. "Effective Number of Parties. A Measure with Application to Western Europe." *Comparative Political Studies* 12: 3–27.

Laclau, Ernesto. 1996. *Emancipation(s)*. London: Verso.

La Iglesia en Amazonas. 1998. "Nueva decisión de la Corte Suprema de Justicia sobre la División Político Territorial del Estado Amazonas." *La Iglesia en Amazonas* (Puerto Ayacucho) 80 (March).

La Prensa. 2002a. "Bloqueo: el 'duchazo' crea dudas." *La Prensa* (La Paz), January 29. Reprinted in *"30 días,"* January, p. 18.

———. 2002b. "El gobierno desactiva conflictos a 9 días del 30." *La Prensa* (La Paz), Ud. Elige, June 21, p. 9.

———. 2002c. "La campaña por el voto nulo se centra en la "U." *La Prensa* (La Paz), June 25. p. 4.

———. 2002d. "La muerte de 57 cocaleros sigue en la impunidad." *La Prensa* (La Paz), January 22. Reprinted in *"30 días,"* January, p. 15.

———. 2002e. "Los indígenas del oriente y occidente marchan en La Paz." *La Prensa* (La Paz), June 21.

———. 2002f. "'Mallku' infraganti: ducha y nexos sospechosos." *La Prensa* (La Paz), February 3. Reprinted in *"30 días,"* February, p. 21.

———. 2002g. "Mallku: Nuestros ministros serán los Mamani y Yujra." *La Prensa* (La Paz), Ud. Elige, June 28, p. 8.

———. 2002h. "Movimientos sociales externos apoyan al MAS." *La Prensa* (La Paz), Ud. Elige, June 25, p. 6.

———. 2002i. "Quieren separar a Evo de Diputados." *La Prensa*, January 22. Reprinted in *"30 días,"* January, p. 15.

———. 2002j. "Sin estrategia de campaña." *La Prensa*, June 22, 2002, p. 9.

———. 2002k. "Una declaración atentatoria." *La Prensa* (La Paz), Ud. Elige, June 28, p. 3.

———. n.d. "Guerra sucia, al estilo andino." *La Prensa*, p. 12.

La Razón. 2001. "El Mallku advierte que no permitirá ninguna división." *La Razón* online.

———. 2002a. "Algunas caracteristicas del próximo parlamento." *La Razón* (La Paz)(online), June 7.

———. 2002b. "Desde camiones hasta helicópteros en campaña." *La Razón*, June 25, p. B5.

———. 2002c. "Evo peleará en el parlamento primero y luego en las calles." *La Razón*, July 1, p. A26.

————. 2002d. "Falta de voluntad para abrir el candado de la Constitución." *La Razón*, June 4, p. A11.

————. 2002e. "Las encuestas electorales perdieron en las ánforas." *La Razón*, July 1, p. A33.

————. 2002f. "Los partidos gastaron $us 20 millones sólo en Tv." *La Razón*. July 29, pp. B6–7.

————. 2002g. "Los partidos pierden su tiempo buscándonos." *La Razón*, July 4, p. A10.

————. 2002h. "Los pasillos del parlamento se llenaron de diversidad, se llenaron de Bolivia." *La Razón* (La Paz)(online), August 3.

————. 2002i. "Morales no es más diputado y el Gobierno ya piensa en detenerlo." *La Razón*, January 24. Reprinted in *"30 días,"* January, p. 17.

————. 2002j. "8 tendencias pueden poner en jacque a Evo y al MAS." *La Razón* (online), September 8.

————. 2002k. "Resultados oficiales de las elecciones 2002." *La Razón* (online), July 9.

————. 2002l. "Rocha previene alianzas con Evo." *La Razón*, June 28, p. B5.

————. 2002m. "Víctor Hugo Cárdenas dice que el MIP y el MAS no sólo deben oponerse." *La Razón*, July 2, p. A10.

Laserna, Roberto. 2002. "Evo se fortalecerá y habrá reacciones de rebelión." *La Razón* (La Paz), June 27, p. B5.

Latin American Andean Group Report. 2001. "The Rise of Auki Tituaña." *Latin American Andean Group Report* RA-01-03, April 3, p. 2.

————. 2002. "Goni Urges Banzer to Step Down." *Latin American Andean Group Report* RA-01-04, May 15, p. 6.

————. 2002a. "Coca Conflict Escalates into 'Nightmare.'" *Latin American Weekly Report* WR-02-05, January 20, p. 53.

————. 2002b. "Electoral Year with Big Questions." *Latin American Weekly Report* WR-02-02, January 8, p. 21.

————. 2003a. "Conaie Regroups as Opposition Force." *Latin American Weekly Report* WR-03-32, August 19, p. 10.

————. 2003b. "Is 'Indigenous Fundamentalism' the New Hemispheric Threat?" *Latin American Weekly Report* WR-03-45, November 18, p. 1.

————. 2003c. "Oaxaca Gets 'First Indigenous Party'" *Latin American Weekly Report* WR-03-45, November 18, p. 11.

————. 2003d. "President Defies PK by Sacking Minister." *Latin American Weekly Report* WR-03-29, July 29, p. 34.

————. 2004a. "Quispe Quits Seat to 'Liberate' the Aymara." *Latin American Weekly Report* WR-04-22, June 8, p. 5.

————. 2004b. "Reforms Enable New Electoral Calendar." *Latin American Weekly Report* WR-04-08, February 24, p. 6.

Latinamerica Press. 2001. "Sustainable for Whom?" *Latinamerica Press* 33, 45–6 (December 17): 1, 12.

Laurent, Virginie. 1997. "Población indígena y participación política en Colombia." *Análisis Político* 31 (May–August): 63–81.

Lazarte, Jorge R. 1991. "Partidos, Democracia, Problemas de Representación e Informalización de la Política (El caso de Bolivia)." *Revista de Estudios Políticos* 74 (October–December): 574–614.

Ledebur, Kathryn. 2002. "Bolivia: Coca and Conflict in the Chapare." Washington Office on Latin America Briefing Series (July). http://www.wola.org/publications.

León T., Jorge. 2001. "El contexto y el sistema político en el movimiento indígena ecuatoriano." Paper prepared for the workshop "Beyond the Lost Decade: Indigenous Movements and the Transformation of Development and Democracy in Latin America." Princeton University, March 2–3.

———. 2002. "La política y los indígenas en América Latina: La redefinición de las relaciones entre el Estado y los pueblos indígenas." Prepared for Oxfam America and Ford Foundation project "Avizorando los retos para los pueblos indígenas de América Latina en el nuevo milenio: territorio, economía, política e identidad y cultura." CD-ROM.

Levine, Daniel H. and Brian F. Crisp. 1999. "Venezuela: The Character, Crisis, and Possible Future of Democracy." In Larry Diamond, Jonathan Hartlyn, Juan J. Linz, and Seymour Martin Lipset, eds. *Democracy in Developing Countries. Latin America*, 2nd ed. Boulder, CO: Lynne Rienner, pp. 367–428.

Levitsky, Steven. 1999. "Fujimori and Post-Party Politics in Peru." *Journal of Democracy* 10, 3: 78–92.

———. 2000. "The 'Normalization' of Argentine Politics." *Journal of Democracy* 11, 2: 56–69.

———. 2001. "Inside the Black Box: Recent Studies of Latin American Party Organizations." *Studies in Comparative International Development* 36, 2 (Summer): 92–110.

Levitsky, Steven and Maxwell A. Cameron. 2001. "Democracy without Parties? Political Parties and Regime Collapse in Fujimori's Peru." Paper prepared for presentation at the Congress of the Latin American Studies Association, Washington, DC, September 6–8.

Lieberman, Evan S. 2001. "Causal Inference in Historical Institutional Analysis." *Comparative Political Studies* 34, 9 (November): 1011–35.

Lijphart, Arend. 1986a. "Degrees of Proportionality of Proportional Representation Formulas." In Bernard Grofman and Arend Lijphart, eds. *Electoral Laws and Their Political Consequences*. New York: Agathon Press, pp. 170–9.

———. 1986b. "Proportionality by Non-PR Methods: Ethnic Representation in Belgium, Cyprus, Lebanon, New Zealand, West Germany, and Zimbabwe." In Bernard Grofman and Arend Lijphart, eds. *Electoral Laws and Their Political Consequences*. New York: Agathon Press, pp. 113–23.

Lima, Constantino. 1996. "Respuesta al blasfemante texto de Luciano Tapia." La Paz.

Lipset, Seymour Martin and Stein Rokkan, eds., 1967. *Party Systems and Voter Alignments. Cross-National Perspectives*. New York: The Free Press.

Los Tiempos. 2002a. "Campesinos las nuevas 'vedetes' electorales." *Los Tiempos* (Cochabamba)(online), April 4.

———. 2002b. "Colorido Congreso inició sus labores." *Los Tiempos*, August 3.

———. 2002c. "Congreso se estrena con color y tropiezos." *Los Tiempos* (online), August 3.

———. 2002d. "El MAS plantea dejar sin efecto la erradicación de coca en el país." *Los Tiempos* (online), July 7.

———. 2002e. "MIR se viste de poncho o pollera en cargos públicos." *Los Tiempos* (online), August 17.

———. 2002f. "Movimiento campesino tiene 2 brazos: democrático y social." *Los Tiempos* (online), August 3.

———. 2002g. "NFR, Alejo firman un pacto electoral." *Los Tiempos* (online), March 20.

———. 2002h. "7 partidos se repartirán Bs 73 millones de recursos fiscales." *Los Tiempos* (online), April 20.

Lucas, Kintto. 2001. "A propósito del ultimo levantamiento indígena: Divorcio entre movimiento político y movimiento social." *Boletín ICCI-Ary Rimay*, vol. 3, no. 23 (February). http://icci.nativeweb.org.

Lucero, José Antonio. 2002. "Arts of Unification: Political Representation and Indigenous Movements in Bolivia and Ecuador." Ph.D. Diss., Department of Politics, Princeton University.

Luciano, José Carlos. 1995. "Lo negro en el Perú." *Ideele* 81 (November): 50–7.

Lynch, Nicolás. 1999. *Una Tragedia sin Héroes: La derrota de los partidos y el origen de los independientes. Peru, 1980–1992.* Lima: Fondo Editorial Universidad Nacional Mayor de San Marcos.

Macas, Luis. 2002. "La lucha del movimiento indígena en el Ecuador." *Boletín ICCI-Rimay*, vol. 4, no. 37 (April): 1–8. http://icci.nativeweb.org.

MACPIO. 2001. *Pueblos indígenas y originarios de Bolivia. Diagnóstico nacional.* La Paz: Ministro de Asuntos Campesinos, Pueblos Indígenas y Originarios.

Maguire, Diarmuid. 1995. "Opposition Movements and Opposition Parties: Equal Partners or Dependent Relations in the Struggle for Power and Reform?" In Craig J. Jenkins and Bert Klandermans, eds. *The Politics of Social Protest. Comparative Perspectives on States and Social Movements.* Minneapolis: University of Minnesota, pp. 199–228.

Mainwaring, Scott. 1999. *Rethinking Party Systems in the Third Wave of Democratization: The Case of Brazil.* Stanford: Stanford University Press.

Mainwaring, Scott and Timothy Scully, eds. 1995. *Building Democratic Institutions: Party Systems in Latin America.* Stanford: Stanford University Press.

Mair, Peter. 1997. *Party System Change. Approaches and Interpretations.* Oxford: Clarendon Press.

Máiz, Ramón. n.d. "Nation and Politics: The Political Mobilization of Ethnic Difference by Nationalism."

Mallon, Florencia E. 1998. "Chronicle of a Path Foretold? Velasco's Revolution, Vanguardia Revolucionaria, and' Shining Omens' in the Indigenous Communities of Andahuaylas." In Steve J. Stern, ed. *Shining and Other Paths. War and Society in Peru, 1980–1995.* Durham, NC: Duke University Press, pp. 84–117.

Mamani R., Pablo. 2003. "El rugir de la multitud: Levantamiento de la ciudad aymara de El Alto y caida del gobierno de Sánchez de Lozada." http://www.alertanet.org/pmamani.htm.

Manifesto of Tiahuanacu. 1980. In Yves Materne, ed. *The Indian Awakening in Latin America*. New York: Friendship Press.

Manrique, Nelson. 1998. "The War for the Central Sierra." In Steve J., Stern, ed. *Shining and Other Paths. War and Society in Peru, 1980–1995*. Durham, NC: Duke University Press, pp. 193–223.

Mantilla Cuellar, Julio, Edith Gutierrez Rojas, and Julio Rosendo Mantilla Gutierrez. 2000. *"La Champa Guerra". Del TINKU de la Guerra al TINKU del Amor. Abril Rojo, Septiembre Negro*. La Paz: Centro Multidisciplinario en Ciencias Sociales.

Marzal, Manuel M. 1995. "Perception of the State among Peruvian Indians." In Lourdes Giordani and Marjorie M. Snipes, eds. *Indigenous Perceptions of the Nation-State in Latin America. Studies in Third World Societies* 56 (August), pp. 61–81.

Massal, Julie and Marcelo Bonilla. 2000. "Introducción: Movimientos sociales, democracia y cambio socio-político en el área andina." In Julie Massal and Marcelo Bonilla, eds. *Los movimientos sociales en las democracias andinas*. Quito: FLACSO, IFEA, pp. 7–38.

Mauceri, Philip and Jo-Marie Burt, eds. 2004. *Politics in the Andes: Identity, Conflict, Reform*. Pittsburgh: University of Pittsburgh Press.

Mayer, Lawrence C. 1972. *Comparative Political Inquiry. A Methodological Survey*. Homewood, Ill: The Dorsey Press.

Mayer, Margit and John Ely. 1998. "Success and Dilemmas of Green Party Politics." In Margit Mayer and John Ely, eds. *The German Greens: Paradox between Movement and Party*. Philadelphia: Temple University Press, pp. 3–26.

Mayorga, René Antonio. 1995. *Antipolítica y Neopopulismo*. La Paz: CEBEM.

McAdam, Doug. 1996. "Conceptual Origins, Current Problems, Future Directions." In Doug McAdam, John D. McCarthy, and Mayer N. Zald, eds. 1996. *Comparative Perspectives on Social Movements*. Cambridge: Cambridge University Press, pp. 23–40.

McAdam, Doug, John D. McCarthy, and Mayer N. Zald, eds. 1996a. *Comparative Perspectives on Social Movements*. Cambridge: Cambridge University Press.

———. 1996b. "Introduction: Opportunities, Mobilizing Structures, and Framing Processes – Toward a Synthetic, Comparative Perspective on Social Movements." In Doug McAdam, John D. McCarthy, and Mayer N. Zald, eds. *Comparative Perspectives on Social Movements*. Cambridge: Cambridge University Press, pp. 1–20.

McClintock, Cynthia. 1998. *Revolutionary Movements in Latin America. El Salvador's FMLN and Peru's Shining Path*. Washington, DC: U.S. Institute of Peace.

———. 1999. "Peru: Precarious Regimes, Authoritarian and Democratic." In Larry Diamond, Jonathan Hartlyn, Juan J. Linz, and Seymour Martin Lipset, eds. *Democracy in Developing Countries. Latin America*, 2nd ed. Boulder, CO: Lynne Rienner, pp. 309–65.

McCoy, Jennifer, et al. 1994. *Venezuelan Democracy under Stress*. New Brunswick, NJ: Transaction Publishers.

McDonald, Ronald H. and J. Mark Ruhl. 1989. *Party Politics and Elections in Latin America*. Boulder, CO: Westview Press.

McGuire, James W. 1995. "Political Parties and Democracy in Argentina." In Scott Mainwaring and Timothy R. Scully, eds. *Building Democratic Institutions: Party Systems in Latin America*. Stanford: Stanford University Press, pp. 200–48.

Mendoza, Mónica. 2002. "El triunfo en la segundo vuelta electoral." *El Universo* (online), November 25.

Mesa Nacional de Pluralismo Jurídico. 2002. *Propuesta de Reforma Constitucional en Materia de Pueblos Indígenas y Comunidades*. Lima: Mayo.

MIAP. 2001. "El MIAP y su aporte a la construcción de un nuevo Perú." Mimeo. Satipo, January.

Ministerio de Desarrollo Sostenible y Planificación. 2000. *Elecciones Municipales 1999, alcaldes y concejales del 2000*. Serie de Cuadernillos de Investigación Numero II. La Paz: Ministerio de Desarrollo Sostenible y Planificación.

Molina V., José E. 2001. "El sistema de partidos venezolano: De la partidocracia al personalismo y la inestabilidad. La des-institucionalización y sus consecuencias." Prepared for presentation at the 2001 Congress of the Latin American Studies Association. Washington, DC, September 6–8.

———. 2002. "The Presidential and Parliamentary Elections of the Bolivarian Revolution in Venezuela: Change and Continuity (1998–2000)." *Bulletin of Latin American Research* 21, 2 (April).

Mombello, Laura. 2002. "Aboriginalidad, provincias y nación: Construcciones de alteridad de contextos provincials. UBACYT 2001–2002." University of Texas, Working paper. http://www.utexas.edu/cola/llilas/centers/claspo.

Monge, Carlos. 1998. "La Comunidad: Tierra, institucionalidad y identidad en el Perú Rural." In Carlos Iván Degregori, ed. *Comunidades: Tierra, instituciones, identidad*. Lima: Diakonía, CEPES–Arariwa.

Montoya Rojas, Rodrigo. 1993. "Libertad, Democracia y Problema Etnico en el Perú." In Carlos Iván Degregori, ed. *Democracia, etnicidad y violencia política en los países andinos*. Lima: IFEA, IEP, pp. 103–12.

———. 2002. "Cultura y Poder."

———. 2003. "Petardo contra el movimiento indígena." *Servindi – Servicio de Información Indígena* 16 (November): 2.

Montoya Rojas, Rodrigo and Martín Paredes. 2001. "El regreso de Pachakutic. Una entrevista con Ampam Karakras y Jorge León." *Quehacer* 128 (January–February): 84–7.

Morejon, Gillian. 2002. "For Peru's Indigenous People, Participating in Politics Is Both an Individual and a Collective Right." October 10, mimeo.

Moreno, Erika. 2000. "An Empirical Analysis of Gubernatorial Elections in Colombia and Venezuela." Prepared for presentation at the Latin American Studies Association meeting. Miami, Florida, March 16–18.

Morin, Francoise. 1983. "La indianidad como nación contra el Estado." In Various Authors. *L'indianité au Pérou, mythe ou réalité*. Paris: CNRS.

Movimiento al Socialismo. 2002. "Territorio, soberanía y vida." In *Opiniones y Análisis. Elecciones Generales 2002–2007. Propuestas electores*. La Paz: Fundación Hans-Seidel, FUNDEMOS, pp. 59–88.

Movimiento Indígena Pachakuti. 2002. "Poder, Tierra y Territorio!!! Tupak Katari Vuelve." In *Opiniones y Análisis. Elecciones Generales 2002–2007. Propuestas electores*. La Paz: Fundación Hans-Seidel, FUNDEMOS, pp. 121–34.

Mozaffar, Shaheen. 1997. "Electoral Systems and their Political Effects in Africa: A Preliminary Analysis." *Representation* 34, 3 and 4: 148–56.

———. 2000. "Institutions, Context and Political Representation: Africa in Comparative Perspective." Prepared for presentation at the 96th Annual Meeting of the American Political Science Association. Washington, DC, August 31–September 3.

Mozaffar, Shaheen, James R. Scarritt, and Glen Galaich. 2003. "Electoral Institutions, Ethnopolitical Cleavages and Party Systems in Africa's Emerging Democracies." *American Political Science Review* 97, 3 (August): 379–90.

Mudde, Cas. 1996. "The Paradox of the Anti-Party Party: Insights from the Extreme Right." *Party Politics* 2, 2: 265–76.

MUPP. 1999a. "Desafíos de los municipios innovadores." *Pachakutik. Revista de debate político* 1 (July): 66–7.

———. 1999b. "Documentos. Congreso del Movimiento de Unidad Plurinacional Pachakutik-Nuevo Pais."

Murillo, Marco A. 1999. "Indigenous communities caught in the crossfire." *NACLA Report on the Americas* 33, 1 (July/August): 10–11.

Murillo Ilbay, Marco. 2001. "Proyecto político y de desarrollo de la FEINE: objectivos y propuestas." Paper prepared for the workshop "Beyond the Lost Decade: Indigenous Movements and the Transformation of Development and Democracy in Latin America." Princeton University, March 2–3.

Muyuy Jacanamejoy, Gabriel. 1998. "Indígenas colombianos y su relación con el Estado." In Ilena Almeida y Nidia Arrobo Rodas, comps. *En defensa del pluralismo y la igualdad. Los derechos de los pueblos indios y el Estado.* Quito: lioteca Abya-Yala.

Myers, David. 1998. "Venezuela's Political Party System: Defining Events, Reactions and the Diluting of Structural Cleaveages." *Party Politics* 4, 4: 495–521.

NACLA. 2001. "Indigenous Leaders under Attack in Colombia." *NACLA Report on the Americas* 35, 1 (July): 4.

National Endowment for Democracy. 1996. "Political Parties and Democracy." Report of proceedings of conference held in Washington DC, November 18–19.

New York Times. 1997. "Indians in Argentina Regain Ancestral Land." *New York Times*, March 20, p. 9.

Nielsen, Anna and Par Zetterberg. 1999. "The Significance of Political Parties for Civil Society. How the Creation of Pachakutik Has Influenced CONAIE's Struggle in Ecuadorian National Politics." Uppsala, Sweden: Uppsala University.

Noticia Hoy Online. 2004. "La dispersión política de los gobiernos locales empieza a contraerse." *Noticia Hoy Online.* October 20, p. 5.

Núñez, Jorge. 1999. "La democracia en Ecuador: actualidad y perspectivas." In Pablo González Casanova y Marcos Roitman Rosenmann, eds. *La democracia en América Latina. Actualidad y perspectivas.* Mexico: La Jornada ediciones, pp. 282–323.

Observador Indígena. 2000. "Indígenas compiten en Mega-Elecciones." *Observador Indígena* (Anzoátegui) 14, 11 (May): 8.

O'Donnell, Guillermo. 1994. "The State, Democratization, and Some Conceptual Problems (A Latin American View with Glances at Some Post-Communist Countries)." In William C. Smith, Carlos H. Acuña, and Eduardo A. Gamarra, eds. *Latin American Political Economy in the Age of Neoliberal Reform*. Miami: North-South Center, pp. 157–79.

Olivera, Luis and Martín Paredes. 2001. "Indios o ciudadanos. Una entrevista con Jaime Urrutia." *Quehacer* 128 (January–February): 69–78.

Ordeshook, Peter C. and Olga V. Shvetsova. 1994. "Ethnic Heterogeneity, District Magnitude, and the Number of Parties." *American Journal of Political Science* 38, 1 (February): 100–23.

Orduna, Víctor. 2002a. "Después de domingo, vuelve la realidad." *Pulso Semanario* (La Paz), June 28–July 4, p. 6.

———. 2002b. "El parlamentario convencido. Los tres meses y un día de Evo Morales." *Pulso Semanario*. November. Received April 8, 2003 by e-mail.

Orduna, Víctor and Gustavo Guzmán. 2002. "El día después de la IV Marcha Indígena." *Pulso Semanario*, June 21–27, pp. 16–17.

Ortega, Hugo O. 1996a. "A 500 Años, Los pueblos indios en la Argentina." In Eulogio Frites, Hugo O. Ortega, and Roberto L. Bozzano, eds. *Abya-Yala. La tierra de los pueblos indios*. Buenos Aires: Asamblea Permanente por los Derechos Humanos, Comisión de Pueblos Indígenas, pp. 11–22.

———. 1996b. "Derechos de los Pueblos Indios. La Cuestión es la Tierra." In Eulogio Frites, Hugo O. Ortega, and Roberto L. Bozzano, eds. *Abya-Yala. La tierra de los pueblos indios*. Buenos Aires: Asamblea Permanente por los Derechos Humanos, pp. 23–6.

Pacari Vega, Nina 2002. "The Democratically Underprivileged in Ecuador." Newsletter, Unit for the Promotion of Democracy, Organization of American States. http://www.upd.oas.org/newsletter/democracy99.pdf.

Pacheco, Diego. 1992. *El indianismo y los indios contemporaneas en Bolivia*. La Paz: hisbol.

Padilla, Guillermo. 1996. "La ley y los pueblos indígenas en Colombia." *Journal of Latin American Anthropology* 1, 2 (Spring): 46–77.

Pallares, Amalia. 2002. *From Peasant Struggles to Indian Resistance. The Ecuadorian Andes in the Late Twentieth Century*. Norman: University of Oklahoma Press.

Palma Capera, Alfonso and Oskar Benjamin Gutiérrez. 1994. "Special Indian Districting: Unresolved Political Problems in Colombia." *Abya Yala News* 8, 3 (Fall): 14–15.

Paredes Gonzales, Carlos. 2001. "Valioso instrumento democratizador." *Voz Campesina* 1, 2 (April): 8–10.

Paredes, Martín. 2001. "Hay una fuerte agresión a los pueblos amazónicos. Entrevista con Guillermo Naco." *Quehacer* 132 (September–October): 90–5.

Participa Perú. 2003. "Los indígenas en el gobierno local: Interculturalidad y desarrollo local en el Río Tambo." *Participa Perú* 7 (September): 9–10.

Patzi Paco, Félix. 1999. *Insurgencia y sumisión: Movimientos indígeno-campesinos (1983–1998)*. La Paz: Muela del Diablo.

Pedraglio, Santiago. 1998. "Contrarreforma en los municipios." *ideele* 111 (September).

Peñaranda, Ricardo. 1999. "De rebeldes a ciudadanos: El caso del movimiento armado Quintín Lame." In Ricardo Peñaranda and Javier Guerrero, comps. *De las armas a la política*. Bogotá: Tercer Mundo, pp. 75–131.

Penfold Becerra, Michael. 2000. "El Colapso del sistema de partidos en Venezuela: Explicación de una Muerte Anunciada." Prepared for delivery at the 2000 meeting of the Latin American Studies Association. Miami, Florida, March 16–18.

Perelli, Carina, Sonia Picado S., and Daniel Zovatto, comp. 1995. *Partidos y clase política en América Latina en los 90*. San José, Costa Rica: Instituto Interamericano de Derechos Humanos.

Pérez, Benjamin. 1999. "Participación en el Movimiento Político Indígena' Pueblo Unido Multiétnico de Amazonas' (PUAMA)." *La Iglesia en Amazonas* 85 (September): 8–9.

Perú Indígena. 1990a. "Entrevista con el secretario de la Confederación de Nacionalidades Amazónicas del Peru (CONAP): Sr. Anibal Francisco Coñibo." *Peru Indígena* 12 (28): 251–9.

_____. 1990b. "Entrevista con el señor Miqueas Mishari Mofat, Presidente de la Asociación Interétnica de Desarrollo de la Selva Peruana (AIDESEP)." *Peru Indígena* 12 (28): 235–50.

_____. 1990c. "Entrevista con el Sr. Juan Rojas Vargas, Secretario General de la Confederación Campesina del Perú (CCP)." *Peru Indígena* 12 (28): 261–4.

Pessoa, Vicente. 1998. "Procesos Indígenas de participación política y ciudadana en los espacios de gobierno y desarrollo municipal." In V. Alta, et al. comps. *Pueblos Indígenas y Estado en América Latina*. Quito: Universidad Andina Simon Bolivar, pp. 169–203.

Phillips, Alan. 1995. "Preface and acknowledgments." In Minority Rights Group, ed. *No Longer Invisible. Afro-Latin Americans Today*. London: Minority Rights Publications, pp. vii–x.

Pina, Juan. 2001. "Paulina Arpasi, la voz de los indígenas." *Revista Perfiles del Siglo XXI*, no. 101, December. http://www.revistaperfiles.com.

Pizarro Leongómez, Eduardo. 1997. "Hacia un sistema multipartidista? Las terceras fuerzas en Colombia hoy." *Análisis Político* 31: 82–104.

_____. 1999. "Las terceras fuerzas en Colombia hoy: Entre la fragmentación y la impotencia." In Ricardo Peñaranda and Javier Guerrero, comps. *De las armas a la política*. Bogotá: Tercer Mundo, pp. 297–333.

Población Indígena. n.d. "Población Indígena." http://www.eurosur.org/FLACSO/mujeres/argentina/demo-5.htm.

Ponce, Javier. 2002. "Es posible la conformación de un gobierno de consenso nacional?" *El Universo* (online), December 1.

Portugal Mollinedo, Pedro. 1989. "Una experiencia de organización política india." *Textos Antropólogos* 1, 1: 103–15.

Prada Alcoreza, Raúl. 2002. *Análisis sociodemográfico. Poblaciones Nativas*. La Paz: Fondo de Población de las Nacionales Unidas, Instituto Nacional de Estadística.

Premdas, Ralph. 1995. *Ethnic Conflict and Development: The Case of Guyana*. Aldershot: Avebury.

Presencia. 1997a. "Indígenas piensan en organizar un partido." *Presencia*, June 13, p. 6.

_____. 1997b. "La miseria obligó a los indígenas a vender su voto." *Presencia*, June 23, p. 4.

————. 1997c. "Ni los indígenas votaron por candidatos del Cidob." *Presencia,* June 4, p. 7.

PRODEPINE. 1998. *Censo nacional de organizaciones indígenas y negras e indice de fortelecimiento institucional.* Quito: PRODEPINE.

Psacharopoulos, George and Harry Anthony Patrinos, eds. 1994. *Indigenous People and Poverty in Latin America. An Empirical Analysis.* Washington, DC: The World Bank.

Pueblos Indígenas. 2001. "Acta de Compromiso después de la toma del INA." October 29. Received October 29 by e-mail from pueblosindigenas@sinectis.com.ar.

Pulso Semanario. 2002a. "Cómo marcharon las campañas?: sus autores las evalúan." *Pulso Semanario* (La Paz), June 21–27, p. 12.

————. 2002b. "La clase política le dio la sigla a Felipe para evitar que se una a Evo." *Pulso Semanario* (La Paz), June 21–27, p. 13.

Quehacer. 2001a. "El problema de la tierra otra vez. Entrevista con Miquel Palacín, CONACAMI." *Quehacer* 130 (May–June): 110–11.

————. 2001b. "Esta mesa nadie la instala. Entrevista con Margarita Benavides." *Quehacer* 132 (September–October): 102–6.

Quispe Huanca, Felipe. 1999. *El indio en escena.* La Paz: Editores Pachakuti.

Radcliffe, Sarah. 2001. "Indigenous Municipalities in Ecuador and Bolivia: Transnational Connections and Exclusionary Political Cultures." Paper prepared for the workshop "Beyond the Lost Decade: Indigenous Movements and the Transformation of Development and Democracy in Latin America." Princeton University, March 2–3.

Rae, Douglas W. and Michael Taylor. 1970. *The Analysis of Political Cleavages.* New Haven: Yale University.

Rappaport, Joanne., ed. 1996. "Ethnicity Reconfigured: Indigenous Legislators and the Colombian Constitution of 1991." Special Issue. *Journal of Latin American Anthropology* 1, 2 (Spring).

————. n.d. "Intercultural Utopias: Public Intellectuals, Cultural Experimentation, and Ethnic Dialogue in Colombia."

Rappaport, Joanne and Robert V. H. Dover. 1996. "The Construction of Difference by Native Legislators." *Journal of Latin American Anthropology* 1, 2 (Spring): 22–45.

Ramírez de Jara and María Clemencia. 1997. "Indigenous Peoples Six Years after the New Colombian Constitution." *Cultural Survival Quarterly* 21, 2 (Summer).

Remy, María Isabel. 1994. "The Indigenous Population and the Construction of Democracy in Peru." In Donna Lee Van Cott, ed. *Indigenous Peoples and Democracy in Latin America.* New York: St. Martin's Press, pp. 107–30.

————. 1991. *Los sueños de la sierra. Cusco en el siglo XX.* Lima: CEPES.

Rénique, José Luis. 1998. "Apogee and Crisis of a 'Third Path': Mariateguismo, 'People's War,' and Counterinsurgency in Puno, 1987–1994." In Steve J. Stern, ed. *Shining and Other Paths. War and Society in Peru, 1980–1995.* Durham, NC: Duke University Press, pp. 307–38.

Reuters. 1999. "Unos 80.000 indígenas piden participar desarrollo Perú–Ecuador." Received May 15 by e-mail from amazoncoal@igc.org.

————. 2000. "Bolivian Indians Form Their Own Political Party." Received November 15 by e-mail from amazon@amazonalliance.org.

Riester, Jurgen. 1985. "CIDOB's Role in the Self-Determination of the Eastern Bolivian Indians." In Theodore Macdonald, ed. *Native Peoples and Economic Development: Six Cases from Latin America*. Cambridge: Cultural Survival, pp. 55–74.

Riker, William H. 1986. "Duverger's Law Revisited." In Bernard Grofman and Arend Lijphart, eds. *Electoral Laws and Their Political Consequences*. New York: Agathon Press, pp. 19–42.

Rivera Cusicanqui, Silvia. 1987. "Luchas campesinas contemporáneas en Bolivia: El movimiento katarista (1970–1980)." In René Zavaleta Mercado, comp. *Bolivia Hoy*. 2nd ed. México: Siglo 21 Editores, pp. 129–68.

————. 1991. "Aymara Past, Aymara Future." *NACLA Report on the Americas* XXV, 3 (December): 18–23.

————. 1993. "La Raiz: Colonizadores y Colonizados." In Xavier Albó and Raúl Barrios, coords. *Violencias Encubiertas en Bolivia*. La Paz: CIPCA-Aruwiyiri, pp. 27–54.

Rivero Pinto, Wigberto. 2003. "Indígenas y Campesinos en las elecciones: El poder de la Bolivia Emergente." http://www.developmentgateway.org.

Roberts, Kenneth M. 1998. *Deepening Democracy? The Modern Left and Social Movements in Chile and Peru*. Stanford: Stanford University Press.

————. 2001. "Political Cleavages, Party–Society Linkages, and the Transformation of Political Representation in Latin America." Paper prepared for delivery at the 2001 Meeting of the Latin American Studies Association. Washington, DC, September 6–8.

————. 2002a. "Party–Society Linkages and Democratic Representation in Latin America." *Canadian Journal of Latin American and Caribbean Studies* 27, 53: 9–34.

————. 2002b. "Social Inequalities without Class Cleavages in Latin America's Neoliberal Era." *Studies in Comparative International Development* 36, 4 (Winter): 3–33.

Roberts, Kenneth M. and Erik Wibbels. 1999. "Party Systems and Electoral Volatility in Latin America: A Test of Economic, Institutional, and Structural Explanations." *American Political Science Review* 93, 3 (September): 575–90.

Rocha, José Antonio. 1992. "Apuntes entorno al planteamiento político aymara." *La Cosmovisión Aymara*. La Paz: Hisbol.

Rodríguez P., Alfredo. 2002. "Se profundiza división entre indígenas." *El Deber* (Santa Cruz) (online). October 29.

————. n.d. "Tesis sobre la construcción de poder local, democracia local y gobiernos locales alternativos." Downloaded May 13, 2003 from http://www.pachakutik.org.ec/archivos/congreso3.htm.

Rohter, Larry. 1999. "Colombia: Indian Tribe Seeks Asylum." *New York Times*, May 1, p. A5.

Roldán Ortega, Roque. 2000. *Indigenous Peoples of Colombia and the Law. A Critical Approach to the Study of Past and Present Situations*. Bogotá: Gaia, COAMA, ILO.

Rolon Anaya, Mario. 1999. *Política y Partidos en Bolivia.* 3rd ed. La Paz: Libreria Editorial "Juventud."

Romero, Anibal. 1994. *Decadencia y crisis de la democracia.* Caracas: Editorial Panapo.

———. 1996. Comments at NED forum on "Political Parties and Democracy." Washington, DC, November 18–19.

Romero Ballivian, Salvador. 1998. *Geografía Electoral de Bolivia.* 2nd ed. La Paz: FUNDEMOS.

Romero Bolaños, Fernando. 1998. "La participación en la gestión municipal." *ideele* 111 (September).

Rospigliosi, Fernando. 1995. "La amenaza de la 'Fujimorización' gobernabilidad y democracia en condiciones adversas: Perú y los países andinos." In Carina Perelli, Sonia Picado S., and Daniel Zovatto, comps. *Partidos y clase política en América Latina en los 90.* San José, Costa Rica: IIDH, pp. 311–33.

Ruiz Hernández, Margarito and Aracely Burguete Cal y Mayor. 2001. "Indigenous Peoples without Political Parties: The Dilemmas of Indigenous Representation in Latin America." In Kathrin Wessendorf, ed. *Challenging Politics: Indigenous Peoples' Experiences with Political Parties and Elections.* Copenhagen: IWGIA, pp. 20–63.

Ruiz Salguero, Magda Teresa, and Yolanda Bodner. 1995. *El Caracter multiétnico de Colombia y sus implicaciones censales.* Bogotá: Departamento Administrativo Nacional de Estadística.

Saavedia, Luis Angel. 2003. "Indigenous Politicians Face Dilemma." *Latinamerica Press.* 35, 3 (Feb. 12): 1–2.

Saltos, Napoleon y Lola Vásquez. 1998. *Ecuador: Su realidad.* Quito: Fundación José Peralta.

Sánchez, Enrique, comp. 1996. *Derechos de los pueblos indígenas en las constituciones de América Latina.* Bogotá: Disloque Editores.

Sánchez, G., Ménthor 2002. "Existe un nivel de coherencia política?" *Boletín ICCI-Ary Rimay,* vol. 4, no. 43 (October). http://icci.nativeweb.org.

Sánchez León, Abelardo. 2001. "Todos tenemos derecho a ser peruanos. Una entrevista con Rodrigo Montoya Rojas." *Quehacer* 132 (September–October): 80–9.

Sánchez López, Francisco and Flavia Freidenberg. 1998. "El proceso de incorporación política de los sectores indígenas en el Ecuador: Pachakutik, un caso de estudio." *América Latina Hoy* 19: 65–79.

Sanjinés C., Javier. 2001. "'Mestizaje cabeza abajo': la pedagogía al revés de Felipe Quispe, 'el Mallku.'" Prepared for presentation at the Congress of the Latin American Studies Association. Washington, DC, September 6–8.

Sarango Macas, Luis Fernando. 1997. "El Movimiento indígena frente a los Estados nacionales. El Caso de Ecuador." In Magdalena Gómez, coord. *Derecho Indígena.* México City: Instituto Nacional Indigenista, pp. 311–26.

Sartori, Giovanni. 1986. "The Influence of Electoral Systems: Faulty Laws or Faulty Method?" In Bermard Grofman and Arend Lijphart, eds. *Electoral Laws and Their Political Consequences.* New York: Agathon Press, pp. 43–68.

Schedler, Andreas. 1996. "Anti-political-establishment Parties." *Party Politics* 2, 3: 291–312.

Schultz, G. M. 2003. "A New Day for Bolivia." *NACLA Report on the Americas* 37, 3: 8–10.

Schwittay, Anke Fleur. 2000. "From Rural Workers to Indigenous Citizens: The Articulation of an Indigenous Identity and Land Struggle in Northwestern Argentina." Paper presented at the American Anthropological Association meeting. San Francisco, California, November.

Scrutton, Alistair. 2002. "Bolivia's Angry Indians Find Political Voice." *Cuzco Weekly*, July 5, p. 28.

Seleme Antelo, Susana. 2002. "Elecciones 2002: se impuso la diversidad." *El Deber* (Santa Cruz), July 5, p. A18.

Selverston, Melina. 1994. "The Politics of Culture: Indigenous Peoples and the State in Ecuador." In Donna Lee Van Cott, ed. *Indigenous Peoples and Democracy in Latin America*. New York: St. Martin's Press, pp. 131–52.

Selverston-Scher, Melina. 2001. *Ethnopolitics in Ecuador: Indigenous Rights and the Strengthening of Democracy*. Miami: North-South Center Press.

Sendas. 1998a. "El aliado: su relación coyuntural y no estratégica." *Sendas* 6, 19, (April–September): 29.

———. 1998b. "La Comisión Interamericana de Derechos Humanos Sesionó en Caracas." *Sendas* 6, 19 (April–September): 41.

———. 1998c. "Las organizaciones indígenas y los aliados. Una relación en Construcción." *Sendas* 6, 19 (April–September): 27–9.

———. 2000. "Asambleas Indígenas para la Participación Política." *Sendas* (Puerto Ayacucho) 8, 24 (January–March): 6–7.

Serbín, Andrés. 1981. "Las organizaciones indígenas en la Argentina." *América Indígena XLI* 3 (July–September): 407–33.

Servindi. 2002a. "Aprueban ley de conocimientos colectivos sin adecuada consulta a indígenas." *Servindi-Servicio de Información Indígena* 11 (July): 5–6.

———. 2002b. "Comisión de diálogo Sobre Industrias Extractivas avanza con muletas." *Servindi-Servicio de Información Indígena* 15 (October): 5–6.

———. 2002c. "Comunidades esperan que gobierno oficialice diálogo tripartito." *Servindi-Servicio de Información Indígena* 11 (July): 7–8.

———. 2002d. "COPPIP elige Consejo Directivo y afianza unidad indígena nacional." *Servindi-Servicio de Información Indígena* 15 (October): 1–4.

———. 2002e. "Informe Anual del Mundo Indígena 2001–2002." *Servindi-Servicio de Información Indígena* 15 (October): 8–12

———. 2002f. "La Setai: de mal a peor?" *Servindi-Servicio de Información Indígena* 15 (October): 7–8.

———. 2002g. "Movimiento indígena evalúa críticamente relación con gobierno." *Servindi-Servicio de Información Indígena* 11 (July): 1–4.

———. 2002h. "Movimiento indígena peruano se unifica y fortalece en la COPPIP." *Servindi-Servicio de Información Indígena* 13 (August): 5–6.

———. 2003a. "Comunidades afectadas por la minería denuncian al estado ante la CIDH." *Servindi-Servicio de Información Indígena* 20 (February): 5–6.

———. 2003b. "Crónica de una ruptura anunciada." *Servindi-Servicio de Información Indígena* 27 (August): 1–3.

———. 2003c. "Fraude oficialista en Tahuanía." *Servindi-Servicio de Información Indígena* 20 (February): 13.

————. 2003d. "Inician campaña para incluir derechos indígenas en Constitución Política." *Servindi-Servicio de Información Indígena* 20 (February): 1–2.

Sieder, Rachel, ed. 2002. *Multiculturalism in Latin America: Indigenous Rights, Diversity and Democracy*. London: Palgrave/MacMillan.

Signi, Alejandro. 1993. "Primer Congreso de los Pueblos Indígenas del Edo. Amazonas." *La Iglesia en Amazonas* 62–63 (December): 26–9.

Smith, Richard Chase. 1985. "A Search for Unity within Diversity. Peasant Unions, Ethnic Federations, and Indianist Movements in the Andean Republics." In Theodore Macdonald, Jr., ed. *Native Peoples and Economic Development: Six Cases from Latin America*. Cambridge: Cultural Survival, pp. 5–38.

————. 1996. "Las políticas de la diversidad. Coica y las Federaciones Etnicas de la Amazonia." In Stefano Varese, coord. *Pueblos indios, soberanía y globalismo*. Quito: Biblioteca Abya Yala, pp. 81–125.

————. 2002. *A Tapestry Woven from the Vicissitudes of History, Place and Daily Life: Envisioning the Challenges for Indigenous Peoples of Latin America in the New Millenium*. Lima: Ford Foundation, Oxfam America.

Snow, David A. and Robert D. Benford. 1992. "Master Frames and Cycles of Protest." In Aldon D. Morris and Carol McClurg Mueller, eds. *Frontiers in Social Movement Theory*. New Haven: Yale University Press.

Starn, Orin. 1992. "I Dreamed of Foxes and Hawks: Reflections on Peasant Protest, New Social Movements, and the Rondas Campesinas of Northern Peru." In Arturo Escobar and Sonia E. Alvarez, eds. *The Making of Social Movements in Latin America. Identity, Strategy and Democracy*. Boulder, CO: Westview Press, pp. 89–111.

————. 1998. "Villagers at Arms: War and Counterrevolution in the Central-South Andes." In Steve J. Stern, ed. *Shining and Other Paths. War and Society in Peru, 1980–1995*. Durham, NC: Duke University Press, pp. 224–57.

Stavenhagen, Rodolfo. 1992. Challenging the Nation-State in Latin America." *Journal of International Affairs* 34, 2 (Winter): 421–40.

————. 1996. "Indigenous Rights: Some Conceptual Problems." In Elizabeth Jelin and Eric Hershberg, eds. *Constructing Democracy: Human Rights, Citizenship, and Society in Latin America*. Boulder, CO: Westview Press, pp. 141–60.

Taagepera, Rein and Matthew Soberg Shugart. 1989. *Seats and Votes: The Effects and Determinants of Electoral Systems*. New Haven: Yale University Press.

Talahua, Gilberto. 2000. "Hay que integrar todos nuestros espacios políticos en un solo proyecto." *Boletín ICCI "Rimay."* 2, 20 (November): 25–6.

Tamagno, Liliana. 2001. "Y no han perdido su identidad...Indígenas toba en la ciudad, organización civil y organización religiosa." Cuarto Congreso Chilenode Antropología November 19–23, Universidad de Chile. http://rehue.csociales.uchile.cl/antropologia/congreso/s1615.html.

Tanaka, Martin. 1998. *Los espejismos de la democracia: El colapso del sistema de partidos en el Perú, 1980–1995, en perspectiva comparada*. Lima: Instituto de Estudios Peruanos.

Tapia, Luciano. 1995. *Ukhamawa Jakawisaxa (Asi es nuestra vida). Autobiografía de un aymara*. La Paz: Hisbol.

Tarrow, Sidney. 1996. "States and Opportunities: The Political Structuring of Social Movements." In Doug McAdam, John D. McCarthy, and Mayer N. Zald, eds. *Comparative Perspectives on Social Movements.* Cambridge: Cambridge University Press, pp. 41–61.

———. 1998. *Power in Movement: Social Movements and Contentious Politics.* 2nd ed. Cambridge: Cambridge University Press.

Thomas, Clive S., ed. 2001a. *Political Parties and Interest Groups: Shaping Democratic Governance.* Boulder, CO: Lynne Rienner Publishers.

———. 2001b. "Studying the Political Party–Interest Group Relationship." In Clive S. Thomas, ed. *Political Parties and Interest Groups: Shaping Democratic Governance.* Boulder, CO: Lynne Rienner Publishers, pp. 1–23.

———. 2001c. "Toward a Systematic Understanding of Party–Group Relations in Liberal Democracies." In Clive S. Thomas, ed. *Political Parties and Interest Groups: Shaping Democratic Governance.* Boulder, CO: Lynne Rienner Publishers, pp. 269–91.

Ticona Alejo, Esteban. 2000. *Organización y liderazgo aymara. 1979–1996.* La Paz: Universidad de la Cordillera.

Ticona, Esteban, Gonzalo Rojas, and Xavier Albó. 1995. *Votos y Wiphalas: Campesinos y Pueblos Originarios en Democracia.* La Paz: CIPCA.

Tiempo de Opinión. 2002. "Se lo imagina?" *Tiempo de Opinión* (La Paz), June 28, pp. 8–9.

Tilly, Charles. 2003. "Afterword: Agendas for Students of Social Movements." In Jack A. Goldstone, ed. *States, Parties, and Social Movements.* New York: Cambridge University Press, pp. 246–56.

Tribunal Supremo Electoral. 1996. *Resultados electorales 1996.* Quito: República de Ecuador.

———. 2002. *Resultados electorales 2002.* Quito: República de Ecuador. CD-ROM.

United Nations. 1986. "Study of the Problem of Discrimination against Indigenous Populations." New York: UN Sub-Commission on the Prevention of Discrimination and Protection of Minorities. UN doc. E/Cn.4/Sub.2/1986/7Add.4.

Urteaga Crovetto, Patricia. 2000. "Territorial Rights and Indigenous Law: An Alternative Approach." In Willem Assies et al., eds. *The Challenge of Diversity. Indigenous Peoples and Reform of the State in Latin America.* Amsterdam: Thela Thesis, pp. 275–94.

VAIPO. 1998. *Desarrollo Con Identidad: Política Nacional Indígena y Originaria.* Viceministerio de Asuntos Indígenas y Pueblos Originarios, República de Bolivia.

Van Cott, Donna Lee. 1994. "Indigenous Peoples and Democracy: Issues for Policymakers." In Donna Lee Van Cott, ed. *Indigenous Peoples and Democracy in Latin America.* New York: St. Martin's Press, pp. 1–27.

———. 2000a. "Party System Development and Indigenous Populations in Latin America: The Bolivian Case." *Party Politics* 6, 2 (April): 155–74.

———. 2000b. *The Friendly Liquidation of the Past: The Politics of Diversity in Latin America.* Pittsburgh: University of Pittsburgh Press.

———. 2002. "Constitutional Reform in the Andes: Redefining Indigenous-State Relations." In Rachel Sieder, ed. *Multiculturalism in Latin America: Indigenous Rights, Diversity and Democracy.* London: Palgrave Press, pp. 45–73.

————. 2003a. "Andean Indigenous Movements and Constitutional Transformation: Venezuela in Comparative Perspective." *Latin American Perspectives* 30, 1 (January): 49–70.

————. 2003b. "From Exclusion to Inclusion: Bolivia's 2002 Elections." *Journal of Latin American Studies* 35, 4 (November): 751–76.

————. 2003c. "Institutional Change and Ethnic Parties in South America." *Latin American Politics and Society* 45, 2 (Summer): 1–39.

Van Nieuwkoop, Martien and Jorge E. Uquillas. 2000. *Defining Ethnodevelopment in Operational Terms: Lessons from the Ecuador Indigenous and Afro-Ecuadorian Peoples Project*. LCR Sustainable Development Working Paper No. 6. Washington, DC: World Bank.

Various Authors. 1997. *Indígenas en el poder local*. La Paz: Ministerio de Desarrollo Humano, Secretaría Nacional de Participación Popular.

————. 2000. "Foro Debate: Diez Años del Levantamiento Indígena del Inti Raymi de 1990. La Construcción de un País Plurinacional." *Boletín ICCI-Ary Rimay*, vol. 2, no. 20 (November). http://icci.nativeweb.org (28 pp).

Vega Díaz, Ismael and Carlos Mora Bernasconi. 2001. "Pueblos indígenas, medio ambiente y desarrollo." *Quehacer* 132 (September–October): 96–101.

Vegas R., Leopoldo. 2002. "Es el reflejo de la realidad." *El Deber* (Santa Cruz), sección "Ud. Elige." July 6, p. A13.

Velásquez Sagua, Héctor. 1996. "Autodesarrollo, democracia y participación: una experiencia de la Unión Nacional de Comunidades Aymaras." In Diego Iturralde and Esteban Krotz, eds. *Desarrollo Indígena: Pobreza, Democracia y Sustentabilidad*. La Paz: Fondo Indígena, pp. 58–62.

Voz Campesina. 2001a. *Voz Campesina* 1, 1 (March).

————. 2001b. *Voz Campesina* 1, 2 (April).

————. 2002. *Voz Campesina* 2, 13 (June).

Wade, Peter. 1993. *Blackness and Race Mixture: The Dynamics of Racial Identity in Colombia*. Baltimore: Johns Hopkins University Press.

———— 1997. *Race and Ethnicity in Latin America*. London: Pluto Press.

Waisman, Carlos H. 1999. "Argentina: Capitalism and Democracy." In Larry Diamond, Jonathan Hartlyn, Juan J. Linz, and Seymour Martin Lipset, eds. *Democracy in Developing Countries. Latin America*, 2nd ed. Boulder, CO: Lynne Rienner, pp. 71–129.

Warren, Kay. 1998. "Indigenous Movements as a Challenge to the Unified Social Movement Paradigm for Guatemala." In Sonia Alvarez, et al., eds. *Cultures of Politics, Politics of Cultures: Re-visioning Latin American Social Movements*. Boulder, CO: Westview Press, pp. 165–95.

Weekly News Update on the Americas. 2002a. "Ecuador: Indigenous Ministers Named." *Weekly News Update on the Americas, Issue #675*. Received January 5, 2003 by e-mail.

————. 2002b. "Indigenous Candidacy Upheld." *Weekly News Update on the Americas*. Posted September 8. http://www.americas.org/news/nir/20020908_indigenous_candidacy_upheld.asp.

Wessendorf, Kathrin. 2001. "Introduction." In Kathrin Wessendorf, ed. *Challenging Politics: Indigenous Peoples' Experiences with Political Parties and Elections*. IWGIA Document No. 104. Copenhagen: IWGIA, pp. 10–19.

Whitehead, Laurence. 2001. "High Anxiety in the Andes. Bolivia and the Viability of Democracy." *Journal of Democracy* 12, 2: 6–16.

Wirpsa, Leslie. 1992. "Interview with Gabriel Muyuy Jacanamejoy. Taking Responsibility: In Colombia, Electoral Politics and Grassroots Activism Complement One Another." *Cultural Survival Quarterly* (Fall): 49–52.

———. 1994. "140 Indigenous Leaders Killed since 1990: Landowners Fight Indian Legal Claims to Land." *National Catholic Reporter* 31, 3 (November 4): 14–16.

World Bank. 1979. *World Development Report 1979*. Washington, DC: Oxford University Press.

———. 1987. *World Development Report 1987*. Washington, DC: Oxford University Press.

———. 1991. *World Development Report 1991*. Washington, DC: Oxford University Press.

———. 1998/99. *World Development Report 1998/99. Knowledge for Development*. Washington, DC: Oxford University Press.

Wray, Natalia. n.d. "Los cambios en las relaciones políticas entre pueblos indígenas, los estados y las sociedades nacionales en la región amazónica de Bolivia, Ecuador y Perú durante la última década." *Pueblos Indígenas de América Latina: Retos para el nuevo milenio*. Ford Foundation, Oxfam America, multimedia CD–ROM.

Yaksic Feraudy, F. and Luis Tapia Mealla. 1997. *Bolivia: Modernizaciones empobrecedoras, desde su fundación a la desrevolución*. La Paz: Muela del Diablo.

Yampara, Simon. 1995. *Pachakuti-Kandiri en el Paytiti*. La Paz: SIYAH.

Yashar, Deborah J. 1998. "Contesting Citizenship: Indigenous Movements and Democracy in Latin America." *Comparative Politics* 31, 1 (October): 23–42.

———. 1999. "Democracy, Indigenous Movements, and the Postliberal Challenge in Latin America." *World Politics* 52 (October): 76–104.

———. 2005. *Contesting Citizenship in Latin America: Indigenous Movements and the Postliberal Challenge*. New York: Cambridge University Press.

Yishai, Yael. 1994. "Interest Parties: The Thin Line between Groups and Parties in the Israeli Electoral Process." In Kay Lawson, ed. *How Political Parties Work. Perspectives from Within*. Westport, CT: Praeger, pp. 197–225.

Zamosc, Leon. 1995. *Estadística de las áreas de predominio étnico de la sierra ecuatoriana*. Quito: Ediciones Abya-Yala.

Zurita Vargas, Leónida. 2003. "The Bolivian Coca-Growers Movement." *Cultural Survival Quarterly* 26, 4 (Winter): 40–51.

Interviews

Interviews in Bolivia

Bertha Beatriz Acarapi, MIR municipal councillor (El Alto), June 19, 2002, El Alto.

Jaime Apaza, Consejo Nacional de Ayllus y Markas de Qullasullo, July 17, 2001, La Paz.

Elena Argirakis, MIR advisor, June 19, 2002, La Paz.

Iván Arias, advisor to Tomasa Yarhui, (MACPIO), June 19, 2002, La Paz.

Víctor Hugo Cárdenas, Vice President of Bolivia (1993-7), July 14, 2001, La Paz.
José María Centellas, MNR, June 25, 2002, La Paz.
María Eugenia Choque, Taller de Historia Oral Andina (THOA), June 20, 2002, La Paz.
Guido Chumiray, Vice Minister of Indigenous Affairs, Quiroga government, June 25, 2002, La Paz.
Marcial Fabricano, CIDOB, July 8, 1997.
George Gray Molina, director Maestrías en Desarrollo, Catholic University, July 12, 2001, La Paz.
Marcial Humerez Yapachuia, MAR, June 25, 2002, La Paz.
Jorge Lazarte, Corte Nacional Electoral, July 12, 2001, La Paz.
Jorge Lema, president, Comisión de Política Agraria, MNR, June 20, 2002, La Paz.
Román Loayza, ASP deputy, June 21, 1997, La Paz.
Carlos Mamani, THOA, July 16, 2001, La Paz.
Daniel Mamani, advisor, Quiroga government, June 25, 2002, La Paz.
René Antonio Mayorga, CEBEM, July 18, 2001, June 25, 2002, La Paz.
Carlos Romero, CEJIS, June 23, 2002, La Paz.
Hugo Salvatierra, legal advisor to CPESC and CIDOB, July 3, 2002, Santa Cruz.
Esteban Ticona, Universidad de la Cordillera, July 18, 2001, La Paz.
Leonardo Tumburini, CEJIS, July 3, 2002, Santa Cruz.
Miguel Urioste, Fundación Tierra, July 18, 2001, La Paz.
Alejo Véliz, Asamblea de la Soberanía de los Pueblos, July 17, 2001, La Paz.

Interviews in Colombia

Jesús Avirama, ASI, March 10, 1997, Popayán.
Virginie Laurent, doctoral candidate, University of Paris, March 11, 1997, Popayán.
Lorenzo Muelas, Indigenous Senator, March 4, 1997, Bogotá.
Antonio Navarro Wolff, mayor of Pasto, February 13, 1997, Pasto.
Luis Carlos Osorio, ASI, February 26, 1997, Bogotá.
Claudia Piñeros, ASI deputy to Assembly of Cauca, March 9, 1997, Popayán.
Francisco Rojas Birry, secretary-general, ASI, February 24, 1997, Bogotá.

Interviews in Ecuador (All Conducted in Quito)

Bolívar Beltran, office of Nina Pacari, Congress, July 19, 1999.
Pedro de la Cruz, FENOCIN, alternative deputy, Partido Socialista, July 21, 1999.
María Fernanda Espinosa, FLACSO, July 19, 1999.
Fernando García, FLACSO, July 21, 1999.
Valerio Grefa, National Deputy, representing Napo, MUPP-NP, July 27, 1999.
Osvaldo Hurtado, CORDES, August 2, 1999.
Manuel Imbaquingo, CODENPE, July 20, 1999.
Ampam Karakras, CONAIE, July 23, 1999.
Jorge León, CEDIME, July 17, 1999.
Miguel Lluco, Pachakutik, August 2, 1999.
Luis Macas, ICCI, July 28, 1999.
Paulina Palacios, legal advisor, ECUARUNARI, July 19, 1999
Luis Verdesoto, August 3, 1999.

Interviews in Peru

Jorge Agurto, COPPIP, July 11, 2002, Lima.
Francisco Ballón, CIPA, July 12, 2002, Lima.
César Barría Marquillo, executive director, Confederación Nacional Agraria, July 16, 2002, Lima.
Eduardo Cáceres, APRODEH, formerly secretary-general, PUM, July 17, 2002, Lima.
Adda Chuecas, CAAAP, July 15, 2002, Lima.
David Flores, Casa Campesina, July 24, 2002, Cuzco.
Nestor Guevara, FARTAC, July 23, 2002, Cuzco.
Antolin Huascar, FARTAC, July 23, 2002, Cuzco.
Rodrigo Montoya Rojas, anthropologist, July 17, 2002, Lima.
Ana Palomina, Defensoría del Pueblo, Native Communities, July 16, 2002, Lima.
Jorge Perez, Movimiento Indio Tawantinsuyo, July 11, 2002, Lima.
Wrays Pérez, AIDESEP, July 11, 2002, Lima.
Eliana Rivera Alarcón, Colegio Andino, July 22, 2002, Cuzco.
Wilder Sánchez, secretary-general, CCP, July 12, 2002, Lima.
César Sarasara, president, CONAP, July 17, 2002, Lima.
Richard Chase Smith, Instituto de Buen Común, July 16, 2002, Lima.
Victor Torres, advisor to CCP, July 19, 2002, Lima.
David Ugarte, Universidad Nacional de San Antonio Abad del Cuzco, July 24, 2002, Cuzco.

Interviews in Venezuela

Luis Jesús Bello, Human Rights Ombudsman, Amazonas, May 23, 2000, Puerto Ayacucho.
Beatriz Bermúdez, director, Office of Indigenous Affairs, May 18, 2000, Caracas.
María Pilar García-Guadilla, professor, Universidad Simon Bolívar, May 16, 2000, Caracas.
Luis Gómez Calcano, Universidad Central, May 15, 2000, Caracas.
José Luis Gonzales, FIB, May 19, 2000, Ciudad Bolívar.
Guillermo Guevara, President, ORPIA, May 24, 2000, Puerto Ayacucho.
Dieter Heinen, Instituto Venezolano de Investigación Científica, May 17, 2000, outside Caracas.
Janet Kelly, professor, IESA, May 15, 2000, Caracas.
José Poyo, CONIVE, May 22, 2000, Caracas.

Telephone Interviews

Miguel Hilario, Commission for the Autonomy of the Shipibo-Conibo Peoples, May 26, 2002; December 18, 2004.
Martin Scurrah, Oxfam America, May 14, 2003.

Index

64–5, 69–71, 85–6, 96, 220; in
Colombia 194–5; in Ecuador 26,
100, 113; in Peru 26–7, 141, 163,
166, 176; in Venezuela 197
De la Cruz, Pedro 105
De la Cruz Villca, Juan 67, 94
Democracia Popular (Ecuador) 104,
126, 129
Diffusion effect 42–3, 172–3, 226
District magnitude 24, 30–1, 119, 194,
197, 219
Durán Ballén, Sixto 112, 118, 120

Ecology parties (Green parties) 13–14,
23, 25, 226, 229
Ecuadorian Constitution (1998) 29,
124–6
Ecuador Runacunapac Riccharimui
(ECUARUNARI) 44, 104–7, 109,
134, 137
Ehlers, Freddy 121, 126
Eje Comunero 66
Eje de Convergencia Patriótica 66–7
Eje Pachakuti (*see also* Movimiento
Pachakuti) 17, 66–7, 76, 82, 94,
217
Ejército Guerrillero Tupak Katari
(EGTK) 81, 92
Ejército Popular de Liberación/
Esperanza, Paz y Libertad (EPL)
196
Escóbar, Filemón 80, 90

Fabricano, Marcial 61–2, 75–6, 92–3
Federación Agraria Revolucionaria
Tupac Amaru de Cuzco (FARTAC)
156, 165
Federación Ecuatoriana de Indígenas
Evangélicas (FEINE) 44, 108–9,
112, 122–3, 133, 138
Federación Ecuatoriana de Indios
(FEI) 44, 103, 108
Federación Indígena del Estado de
Bolívar (FIB) 45, 183–4, 209
Federación Nacional de
Organizaciones Campesinas
(FENOC) 104, 115–16

Federación Nacional de
Organizaciones Campesinas e
Indígenas (FENOC-I) 112
Federación Nacional de
Organizaciones Campesinas,
Indígenas, y Negras (FENOCIN)
44, 109, 30, 135, 138
Fernández, Max 84
Flores, Genaro 54, 65, 81–4
Fraternidad Popular 199
Frente Amplio de la Izquierda (FADI)
104–5, 115–16
Frente Futuro Ecuador 133–5
Frente Obrero, Campesino,
Estudiantil y Popular (FOCEP)
151
Frente de Unidad de Liberación
Katarista (FULKA) 79, 81–2, 84
Fuerza de Integración Juntos con
Orgullo (FIJO) 170, 175
Fuerzas Armadas Revolucionarias de
Colombia (FARC) 182, 196
Fujimori, Alberto 140–1, 153, 155,
163–4, 168–9, 173, 175–6; alliances
with indigenous peoples 160, 165

Gálvez Herrera, Ciro 169, 173
García, Alan 152, 163
Green parties (*see* Ecology parties)
Guarachi, Paulino 57, 67
Guarulla Garrido, Liboria 185, 191,
209
Gudiño, Emerlinda Amalia 190
Guevara, Elsa 94
Guevara, Guillermo 209
Gutiérrez, Lucio 99, 109, 135–8
Guyana Action Party (GAP) 227

Huascar, Antolin 156, 173

Instrumento Político de la Soberanía
de los Pueblos (IPSP) (*see also*
Movimiento al Socialismo) 17, 78,
86–7, 216–17, 221, 223, 225
International Labor Organization
Convention No. 169 125, 154, 164
Iza, Leonidas 137